The handicapped student in
the regular classroom

The handicapped student in the regular classroom

BILL R. GEARHEART

Professor of Special Education, University of Northern Colorado,
Greeley, Colorado

MEL W. WEISHAHN

Professor of Special Education, University of Northern Colorado,
Greeley, Colorado

SECOND EDITION

Illustrated

The C. V. Mosby Company

ST. LOUIS • TORONTO • LONDON   1980

SECOND EDITION

Previous edition copyrighted 1976

Printed in the United States of America

The C. V. Mosby Company
11830 Westline Industrial Drive, St. Louis, Missouri 63141

Library of Congress Cataloging in Publication Data

Gearheart, B   R
    The handicapped student in the regular classroom.

    Bibliography: p.
    Includes index.
    1. Handicapped children— Education.
I. Weishahn, Mel W., 1940-   joint author.
II. Title.
LC4015.G38   1980   371.9   79-23706
ISBN 0-8016-1760-X

GW/VH/VH 9 8 7 6 5 4 3 2 1   02/C/223

PREFACE

The first edition of this text was written before the passage of Public Law 94-142 and was published less than two months after its passage. We were interested in assisting the regular classroom teacher to be better prepared to teach the mildly handicapped student, whom we believe should be in the regular class for the greatest possible part of the day, consistent with his individual needs. We are delighted that the law and the regulations that were finally made official in 1977 were consistent with our earlier projections. It is now a pleasure to be able to reflect on the provisions of PL 94-142, The Education for All Handicapped Children Act, as they are presently being implemented.

This second edition is similar to the first, but has been expanded in a number of ways. We have tried to provide more information regarding the education of secondary school students, for we found that this was a shortcoming of our first edition. We have also separated the chapters on mental retardation and learning disabilities. Although there are similarities in some of the educational provisions that are commonly used with mild levels of mental retardation and learning disabilities, the differences outweigh the similarities.

This text remains dedicated to the proposition that there is no single method of educating handicapped children that can be accepted as the "right" method, *except as that method is planned individually for a particular student.* The requirement for an individualized educational program (IEP), a significant part of PL 94-142, dictates this type of thinking. Unlike some who write about education of the handicapped student in the regular class, we do *not* believe that all handicapped students belong in the regular classroom. The requirements of the law, which direct the provision of a wide continuum of services, including residential programs where needed, indicate that the lawmakers would agree with this position.

We do believe that during the 1940s and 1950s special education classes were over-promoted and misused in many parts of the nation. The system of declaring a student "mentally retarded" and placing him in a special class became an accepted method of taking care of problem students. In some instances these students were mentally handicapped, but others were primarily behavior problems or students whose ethnic or cultural background was the basic reason for low scores on academic and intelligence tests. During the 1960s a number of events occurred that led to the present practice of maximization of regular classroom experience for all handicapped students. In a number of differing settings, it was verified beyond doubt that a number of students who had been earlier diagnosed as educable mentally retarded had potentially greater ability than had earlier been believed. This related particularly to bilingual and bicultural children and those who lived in extreme poverty. Court decisions throughout the land accelerated what might have otherwise been a very slow evolutionary movement. These children were returned to regular classrooms in large numbers. In a somewhat different type of movement, children who had experienced serious educational problems but had been denied any type of special educational help because they were not visually impaired, hard of hearing, or mentally handicapped were recognized as learning disability children and became eligible for special educational assistance. But they remained in the regular classroom for most of the day, and the teacher now felt the need to provide some sort of special assistance for this newly recognized group.

Fortunately, programs that called for the joint efforts of special educators and regular classroom teachers had been in effect for many years, as applied to the needs of the hearing impaired and visually impaired. The resource-room and the itinerant-teacher concepts for these children with sensory losses became accepted, with the nonspecial education teacher providing the majority of the child's instructional program. The special education teacher assisted the regular classroom teacher in planning, obtained specialized instructional materials, and provided needed specialized educational programming (such as braille and language development), which the nonspecial education teacher could not be expected to provide. This concept has now been applied to programs for the mildly mentally retarded and the learning disabled with considerable success, but such success requires some special understandings and training for the regular classroom teacher.

This text was designed to provide basic information about the various types of handicapping conditions and to focus on the "what to do" and "how to do it," as these questions relate to the regular classroom teacher. Since 1970, some states have added require-ments to teacher training and certification programs, either through direct legislative enactment or through regulation, so that all teachers must receive some formal training in this important area. The question is no longer one of "Should all teachers learn how to deal with handicapped children?" but rather "What should they learn?" This text has been prepared to answer this question and is designed for both in-service and preservice programs.

This book was originally developed as the result of a strong expression of need on the part of regular educators who require assistance in their efforts to educate mildly handicapped students but are "turned off" by the jargon that makes up so much of the basic professional language in special education. We have attempted to provide a text that cuts through most of this professional gobbledy-gook and provides both an introduction to this field and some basic teaching ideas that should be of significant value.

We were pleased at the positive response to our first edition and were happy to receive hundreds of unsolicited communications in which we found some kind words along with criticisms and suggestions for revisions and additions. We want to publicly thank those contributors, most of whom we will never know, for their interest and contributions.

We want to thank Clifford Baker for a great deal of general assistance and Carol Gearheart for critiquing the entire manuscript, providing both general editorial help and specific professional suggestions regarding content. We also recognize and value the contents of the chapter provided by Barbara Coloroso and greatly appreciate her contributions. We again must thank Ronald Stewart, who took the majority of the photographs used as illustrations in this text. We believe that his personal interest in special education led to more meaningful photographic efforts. To all of these individuals, and to students and friends who continue to assist us in our daily efforts, we express our heartfelt gratitude.

Bill R. Gearheart
Mel W. Weishahn

A NOTE ON TERMINOLOGY

We have attempted to use a minimum of special terminology, and when such is used, we have tried to define or explain it in simple terms. Nevertheless, the use of certain words in this text may deserve special comment.

Mainstreaming is discussed and defined, but throughout the text it is used interchangeably with the word *integration*. Mainstreaming is the more popular word, perhaps the more commercial word, but we have some concern that children may be placed in the mainstream and never really become a part of it. Integration (to us) means becoming a part of the mainstream and implies joint efforts on behalf of special and general educators to assist in meaningful integration. However, because of the frequent use of the word mainstreaming and the necessity of its use when quoting others who use it repetitively, these two terms are used interchangeably and should be construed to mean the same process.

The terms *regular classroom teacher, general educator,* and *nonspecial educator* are meant to indicate the same group of beautiful people to whom we have attempted to relate in this text. What we really mean are *educators who are not specially trained special educators*. Readers are asked to understand that we do not intend to imply ordinariness or to indicate that regular classroom teachers are "just" regular classroom teachers. The regular classroom teacher is—in our eyes—the most important person in the integration process.

Handicapped and *handicapping conditions* are terms used regularly in every chapter. Our special education colleagues sometimes engage in long debates as to whether and when the words *handicapped, disabled, deficient,* or some other choice adjective should be used. We would be delighted to find a more satisfactory descriptive adjective, but until then, we hope that the reader will understand that we have used handicapped and handicapping conditions because we felt they would be generally understood.

Finally, we had to relate to the current concern with the use of pronouns. In a recent professional text we found an instance in which the woman who wrote the text used the masculine pronoun and indicated at the start that "he" refers equally to "she" in all cases. Thus, logically, we might use the feminine pronoun and indicate that "she" refers equally to "he" in all cases. However, after considerable soul-searching and long and intensive consideration, we have elected to use "he" and "she" in whatever manner it first occurred to us to use them in each instance (undoubtedly this related in many cases to a real individual—an actual "he" or "she") and hope that the reader might understand.

CONTENTS

1 THE HISTORICAL AND PHILOSOPHICAL BASE FOR EDUCATION OF THE HANDICAPPED

As we enter the 1980s, the concept of education of the handicapped within the regular classroom environment is commonly recognized by most educators, although not fully accepted by all nonspecial educators (hereinafter called regular educators or regular classroom teachers). In 1970 such an idea would have been foreign to many, if not most, regular educators, and many special educators would have tended to raise their eyebrows, too. What has happened is a minor revolution, all within ten short years. The requirement to educate the handicapped in the regular classroom setting whenever possible is now a matter of federal mandate. Most state education agencies have at least tacitly accepted this concept, but it is the regular classroom teacher who must accept and embrace it if it is to work.

This emphasis on education of the handicapped in the regular classroom and the resulting need to further explore questions relating to interpretation and implementation of this concept were the motivations for this text. The various states have, in one way or another, recognized the need for the regular classroom teacher to become better informed about the handicapped. A number of states now require as a part of basic teacher certification that all teachers have some type of training for teaching the handicapped. The manner in which they have supported this idea varies, but the fact that they have supported it, or at least recognized it, is undeniable. We hope that the ideas and insights provided in this volume will assist the regular classroom teacher to more successfully fulfill his or her role in this overall project. We believe the goal of education of the handicapped in the least restrictive environment is an important one, and when this least restrictive environment is the regular class, all the better.

In the course of the attempt to accomplish this goal, there have been some misunderstandings and confusion. Our hope in preparing the second edition of this text is that we can promote understanding, reduce confusion, and thus assist in the orderly development of this interesting and important area.

In the early 1970s, the term "mainstreaming" came into common use with relation to this principle. Mainstreaming has a number of definitional variations and has engendered a number of misconceptions. To some, it apparently means the return of all handicapped students (including those now served through other types of educational efforts) to the regular classroom. It may also indicate to some that *no* student should be served in a totally segregated setting. The reasons for the mainstreaming emphasis are many, ranging from evidence of lack of effectiveness of various special educational efforts or indications that members of various ethnic groups have been improperly placed in special education programs, a form of racial segregation, to the fact that special education has sometimes been used as a place for any student who does not "fit" existing programs or who cannot adjust to a particular teacher, regardless of whether the available special education program is appropriate for the student's special needs. It was also recognized that many handicapped students, namely the visually impaired, crippled, and other health impaired, had been successfully integrated for many years. This success led to the increased realization that other handicapped students could be successfully educated in regular classrooms.

We believe that all the preceding factors are real and provide justification for much greater emphasis on retention in regular classrooms rather than special education placement for students who seem to have different educational needs than the others with whom school authorities have grouped them. We further believe that many students formerly placed in special classes can function as well, or better, in regular classrooms if the teacher is provided with meaningful information, materials, and assistance. *However, our concept of mainstreaming is that of maximum integration in the regular class, combined with concrete assistance for the nonspecial education teacher.* The role of many special educators may be that of a helping or assisting teacher—one who works cooperatively by sharing unique skills and competencies with general educators who also have a great deal to contribute to the education of handicapped students.

The remainder of this chapter is devoted to a statement of our philosophy of education for the handicapped, plus a historical account of the development of special education. The statement of philosophy is the basic point of view from which this text has been developed. The historical account is provided (1) so that the reader may better understand the basis for present programs and practices and (2) to attempt to "tie together" the total fields of general and special education and the major forces that have shaped their development. We believe this will promote better understanding of various handicapping conditions and the manner in which we should modify or adapt educational materials, methods, and (in some cases) goals, due to the nature of the handicap.

Although it is recognized that there are serious limitations imposed by classifying or labeling students on the basis of medically derived systems, it is also recognized that state legislatures, state departments of education, and many colleges, universities, and local school districts are still providing for these students on a categorical basis. It is not our intent to promote the use of labels or categories; however, from a practical point of view, teachers and administrators are currently identifying and serving students on the basis of the most identifiable behavior, for example, a vision problem, a behavior disor-

der, or a hearing difficulty. When considering the practices in the field today, we believe that a common entry must be established that will most closely approximate the student's behavior. As a result, this text is organized on the basis of categorical entry. Regular classroom teachers will, in all likelihood, continue to initially identify students on the basis of observable behavior.

In this text we will call hearing impaired students *deaf, hard of hearing, hearing handicapped,* or *hearing impaired* even though we are fully aware that some members of the special education fraternity might view these as old-fashioned terms. We understand that there is other available terminology, but have lived long enough to see that new terms just become new labels. We believe that although the public has some misunderstandings about deafness or hearing problems even after decades of efforts to promote better understanding, the introduction of a new term for these problems serves no useful purpose. We will also persist with the idea that there is such a thing as mental retardation (mental handicap or limited intellectual ability) even though errors have been made in assessments of mental ability, particularly with children who are culturally different from the majority middle-class population. *Our major effort has just one central goal—to assist teachers to more effectively work with handicapped students in their classrooms. We will attempt to attain this goal in the most simple, straightforward manner possible.*

PHILOSOPHY OF EDUCATION FOR THE HANDICAPPED

We believe that all individuals in American society have the right to receive an adequate education, one that will permit them to develop their abilities to the fullest possible extent. We believe that if they have unique needs that relate to their ethnic background, earlier lack of opportunity, or other similar factors, educational programs should be modified and specialized to meet these needs. We believe that the handicapped individuals of this nation have a similar right and that the public, tax-supported educational systems of the nation must adjust and adapt existing educational programs and offerings to make this possible. Educational planning should emphasize the learning strengths and abilities of the handicapped, and labeling according to handicap should be avoided whenever possible. On the other hand, students who have hearing or visual impairments must have certain specific assistance that relates directly to their sensory loss; thus it will often be advantageous to the student and to his educational programming to think of him as and at times call him visually impaired (handicapped or disabled) or hearing impaired. Too often in the past we have not recognized moderate hearing losses or visual impairments to the serious detriment of the individual. We believe it would be a professionally unforgivable error to be so concerned about labeling that we permit or encourage teachers to overlook hearing losses or other disabilities because we are afraid to use the term *"hearing impaired."* We believe this principle applies to all handicapping conditions.

Handicapped children and youth should be served in the regular classroom whenever possible, and additional efforts should be directed toward increasing the effectiveness of such programming. (This is the major purpose of this text.) If a student must receive specialized assistance in a small, separate grouping of others with special needs, we should provide such help but keep him in the normal classroom setting as much as possible. If the student has been removed for all or part of the school day, careful attention should be given to ensure that he is returned to the regular classroom at the earliest pos-

sible time, consistent with his social and educational well-being.

Special educators are needed because (1) the student's needs may be so unusual that the regular classroom teacher cannot adequately meet them, and thus they must be met through direct special educational service; (2) the student and the regular classroom teacher may require the support provided through specialized or adapted materials and equipment; and (3) assistance in assessment or direct consultive efforts may spell the difference between success and failure.

Certain principles closely related to the preceding philosophy are of prime importance. These include the following:

1. Early intervention is highly desirable in all cases where the handicap is readily identifiable.
2. Minority or low socioeconomic status may present unusual problems in assessment, and special care must be taken where this may be a factor.
3. Some disabilities may be more appropriately viewed as symptoms rather than as specific physical disorders and may exist at one time in life and not exist at another.
4. Even in the case of a specific, irreversible disability, the need for special educational services may vary from full-time, special class service at one time in the student's life to little or no service at another time.
5. A wide variety of services and the total spectrum of service delivery capabilities is essential.
6. Services for a broad age range, preschool through high school, are essential.
7. A broad, flexible assessment program including provision for initial and ongoing assessment and formal and informal evaluation is required.

8. Parents must be involved in both assessment and program planning. A certain amount of involvement is now required by law and regulation; in many instances, even more involvement than is legally required will be of great benefit.
9. The concept of the least restrictive environment, when properly applied, will effectively unite the skills of the regular educator and the special educator, thus providing maximum assistance to the handicapped student.

DEVELOPMENT OF PROGRAMS FOR THE HANDICAPPED—HISTORICAL ORIGINS

In almost any arena of human behavior, the present state of evolution can be better understood if we are aware of those historical events which, in effect, spawned the present. Education of the handicapped is no exception. Although the history of early efforts to assist (or to eradicate) the handicapped can be documented in great detail, we will examine only the skeletal outline, hoping that this may promote some understanding of the present form and structure of educational provisions for the handicapped. In the interest of brevity, we will consider all events prior to 1800 as early history and review the total historical development as follows:

Early history	Origin of man to 1800
Era of institutions	1800 to 1900
Era of public school—special classes	1900 to 1960/70
Era of accelerated growth	1960 to present

It must be noted that these eras overlap to a considerable extent; no fine line of demarcation exists. Quite often we find that although a new "era" may have begun in some parts of the nation, the older era is far from over in others. With this limitation in mind, we will proceed with our historical outline.

Early history—origin of man to 1800

The early history of societal involvement with the handicapped is primarily one of misunderstanding and superstition. It would seem likely that blindness, deafness, and mental retardation have existed since the beginning of the human race, and early references clearly document such practices as abandonment of handicapped infants in an attempt to become free of the burden of their care. Roman history repeatedly refers to "fools" kept by the wealthy for entertainment, and the belief that individuals who were considerably "different" from normal in appearance or behavior were possessed by demons or evil spirits was almost universal.

Historical writers such as Zilboorg and Henry (1941), Pritchard (1963), and Kanner (1964) have provided comprehensive accounts of the manner in which we have related to the handicapped, mainly accounts of inhumanity that developed as a result of fear and ignorance.

The early historical origins of present-day programs for the handicapped will be reviewed without the cumbersomeness of repeated references to specific source data. The majority of documentation of the following information may be found in the preceding three references or in Gearheart and Litton (1979).

Most early records refer to handicapped or defective individuals in such a manner as to make it quite difficult to determine whether those referred to were mentally retarded, mentally ill, or perhaps deaf and unable to communicate. In many societies a father could determine whether he wanted a newborn infant; if he indicated he did not, it might be thrown off a cliff, left in the wilderness, or perhaps simply left by the roadside. Such infanticide was supported by the common belief that individuals who were un-usually different were possessed by demons or evil spirits and that the actions taken were not directed against the human infant but against the demon. At one time the Romans even extended this absolute rule of the father over infants to include the possibility that any female infant might be so disposed of, with general public acceptance.

There were, of course, short periods of time during which specific rulers imposed more humane practices, but the foregoing, repugnant as it may seem today, was the general practice in much of the "civilized" Western world for centuries.

The Middle Ages and the rise and further development of Christianity brought about varied effects, depending on the type of handicap, the geographic location, and the specific era. Although the idea of love and concern for others gained some headway, the handicapped were variously viewed as fools, nonhuman, or perhaps witches, witches being an obvious throwback to earlier demon-ology. The belief that the mentally ill or retarded were possessed by demons or evil spirits at times led to the offering of prayers or in some instances the practice of exorcism. On many occasions this exorcism was somewhat rigorous, but not nearly so final as the later treatment of witches, such as burning at the stake.

Although there were some bright spots, all the more bright for their infrequent appearance, until the sixteenth century the general picture was very bleak. The handicapped were not accepted as totally human and were misunderstood, mistreated, and in many cases put to death. Leading philosophers, national governments, and the organized church all shared responsibility for this attitude.

Then, slowly and with frequent backsliding, the picture began to change. During the latter part of the sixteenth century a Spanish monk, Pedro Ponce de León, was successful in teaching a small group of deaf pupils to speak, read, and write. This was a major breakthrough and led to a reversal of the official position of the church that the deaf could not speak and were uneducable, a position based on the writings of Aristotle. In the following century an early version of finger spelling for the deaf was developed by Juan Bonet, and in 1760, the Abbé de l'Eppe opened a school for the deaf in Paris. Organized education for the deaf became a reality.

An associate of the Abbé de l'Epee became interested in the blind and by 1784 had established a school for the blind, also in Paris. This man, Valentin Huay, had also associated with such intellectuals as Voltaire and Rousseau, and after a traumatic personal experience, in which he witnessed ten blind men being exploited for public entertainment, he vowed to improve the lot of the blind. The National Institution for Young Blind People was the result of this resolve.

Only a few years later, in 1798, an event took place near Aveyron, France, that was to lead to educational programs for the retarded. A boy of 11 or 12 years of age was found roaming "wild" in the woods. Discovered by hunters, this boy was unable to speak, bore the scars of years of encounters with wild animals, and was most animal-like in appearance. He bit and scratched all who approached, chose his food by smell, and was in nearly all respects more animal than human. This boy (eventually named Victor) was taken to Paris to be observed by students who were studying the development of primitive faculties. There, Phillipe Pinel, a renowned scientist, declared him to be an incurable idiot, but Jean Marc Gaspard Itard, who also saw him there, thought otherwise. He obtained custody of Victor and launched an involved program to civilize and educate him, hoping to make him normal. The record of Itard's work, *The Wild Boy of Aveyron* (Itard, 1962), is an important classic in the education of the retarded. Although Itard despaired of efforts he saw as fruitless (his expectations were far too high), one of Itard's students, Edouard Seguin, became a major force in the development of educational programs for the retarded.

Thus we see that educational programs for the deaf, blind, and retarded had their beginnings within less than half a century, all in or near Paris, France. Perhaps the most fitting comment on the long era brought to a close by these new efforts is that the change, the opening of a new chapter in the history of treatment of the handicapped, was long overdue. May we never again see these "good old days."

Era of institutions — 1800 to 1900

Historical documentation of the nineteenth century as the era of institutions is conclusive; the consistency of this trend is in marked contrast to the variability of treatment and care of the handicapped in all of the preceding centuries. The beginnings of this movement were outlined previously, but the total effort and the manner in which it swept Europe and the United States is a reflection of the combination of a critical need on the part of the population of handicapped persons, an awareness of this need on the part of professionals (both physicians and educators), and changing attitudes among the general population permitting its popular acceptance.

Some of the motivations of the general public may seem less than desirable in light of accepted philosophy today. Considerable support for institutionalization seems to have come from the fact that such a practice kept these undesirable and physically unattractive persons out of the public eye and thus off the public conscience. This, of course, is unacceptable today, but was a vast improvement over deliberate infanticide or the use of prisons as holding centers for the handicapped.

Institutions for the handicapped were initially developed for the blind, the deaf, and the mentally retarded, with those for the blind and deaf initiated at about the same time and those for the retarded coming some fifty to sixty years later.

The first institutional programs for the handicapped were initiated in Europe, with France, Germany, Scotland, and England leading the way. By 1800, recognized programs for the blind existed in France, England, and Scotland; for the deaf, in France, Germany, Scotland, and England. Institutions specifically for the mentally retarded were not begun until 1831, when the first such program was initiated in France, but multipurpose institutions such as the Bicetre and Salpetriere, in Paris, had housed a variety of societal outcasts—the blind, senile, mentally ill, prostitutes, and mentally retarded—since the seventeenth century. Perhaps one reason for the later start of institutional programs for the retarded was the fact that until the early nineteenth century there was little differentiation made between the mentally ill and the mentally retarded, and until the work of Itard and Seguin, there was little hope for these people.

A great deal might be said about the multiplicity of factors that encouraged the development of publicly supported institutions for the blind, deaf, and retarded during the nineteenth century. Sociopolitical changes throughout the world, expansion of the concept of individual worth, and a general increase in the level of education, led by the ideal of free public education, all contributed significantly. The development of psychiatry as a distinct subdiscipline of medicine and the differentiation between the mentally ill and mentally retarded also played major roles in developing programs for the mentally retarded. The effectiveness of braille in teaching the blind and the success of both oral and manual methods with the deaf were major factors in these two areas of development. Better communication systems, particularly between Europe and the United States, and the formation of national and international interest groups, formal and informal, led to a rapid exchange of new ideas and success stories that, although sometimes slightly exaggerated, were nevertheless quite effective in the promotion of new programs.

Although there was a definite trend toward institutional programs for the handicapped, several leaders of the time advocated that wherever possible, handicapped students should attend educational programs along with their nonhandicapped peers in the public schools. In 1810, Johann Wilhelm Klein began to promote the principle of education of blind children in local schools for nonhandicapped children, and in 1819, Klein prepared a guide to assist regular classroom teachers who had blind children enrolled in their classes. In 1842, the government of Lower Austria took an official stand on this matter and issued the following formal statement, a decree (undoubtedly written by Klein [1845]), cited in Lowenfeld (1973):

According to experiences the existing institutions for the blind are insufficient to accept all the blind who are in need of education. Those who are accepted must as a rule be removed from their home conditions and be transferred into an environment strange to them until then. There they become acquainted with desires and habits of a kind which they cannot satisfy in their future lives. Therefore, the need is obvious that education of blind children according to their needs be provided in their parental home and in the school of their community, and that education of the blind be whenever possible incorporated into the regular institutions for the people's education, the public schools [translation by Lowenfeld, p. 14].*

---

*From Lowenfeld, B. *The Visually Handicapped Child in School*, copyright © John Day Publishers.

Other leaders in the field of education of the blind voiced similar views, but for the most part, except for Klein's efforts, institutions for the handicapped were the accepted means of providing educational service during the 1800s.

The principle of institutions for the blind, the deaf, the retarded, and the mentally ill was now well established. In institutions for the blind and deaf (these included a limited number of partially seeing, who were not totally blind, and hard of hearing, who were not profoundly deaf) the emphasis was on the teaching of skills that would permit adjustment to the sensory loss and return to the world of the nonhandicapped. In institutions for the mentally retarded and the mentally ill the hope was for a "cure" for the condition, and the success rate here was much less than in programs for the deaf and blind. Particularly in the case of the mentally retarded (this usually meant the more severely retarded), the rate of return to society was so low that it soon became a basic assumption that few would return; the institution became a place of residence until death.

A new trend was just beginning at the end of the century, a trend toward public school classes for students with various handicapping conditions. Alexander Graham Bell, in an address to the National Education Association in 1898, suggested that an "annex" to the public school should be formed to provide special classes for the deaf, the blind, and the mentally deficient. Then, in 1902, he further urged that this "special education" should be provided so that these children would not have to leave their homes (to attend institutions) and that the National Education Association should actively pursue such educational provisions. As a result, the N.E.A. officially formed a Department of Special Education, thus originating a name that remains to this day (Gearheart, 1974). These efforts by Bell and the actions of the public schools, which soon followed, ushered in a new era.

Era of public school—special classes— 1900 to 1960/70

Educational efforts designed specifically for handicapped students had their origin before the turn of the century (1900), but such efforts were sporadic and met limited acceptance and success. The order of introduction of special programs in the public school was reversed as compared to that of institutional programs, with public school classes for the retarded coming before those for deaf or blind. Such classes had been attempted in New York, Cleveland, and Providence (Rhode Island) before 1900, but they tended to be classes provided for "problem children" and probably included more acting-out nonretarded than retarded students. Then, early in the twentieth century, several cities tried gathering groups of students who had been previously unschooled and who, for the most part, were definitely mentally retarded. Like the institutions, the schools were interested in a return to normalcy, including normal learning ability, and were for the most part unsuccessful. Thus these early classes for the mentally retarded were often unsatisfactory, and many were dropped soon after initiation. Later in the century, particularly after the appearance of a more adequate way to determine degree of mental retardation (Lewis Terman's revision of the Binet test of intelligence—the Stanford-Binet), classes for the more mildly retarded were started and were successful enough to warrant continuation.

Day-school classes for the visually impaired and hearing impaired were slower in starting but did not tend quite so much to the start-and-stop pattern that characterized early classes for the retarded. With institutions for the deaf and blind, the institutional setting was more truly a school, and parents were more likely to accept and support this residential school setting. Thus there was not the kind of urgency that was felt regarding the mentally retarded.

With the enactment of compulsory school attendance laws in the early part of the century came the problems involved in providing for *all* minors, including the handicapped. It should be noted that since most states provided residential schools for the blind and deaf and the more severely mentally retarded were often institutionalized at an early age, the real problem for school officials was that of provision for the more mildly retarded.

It is fairly safe to assume that most school districts first attempted to educate the mildly retarded within the regular class setting. Because many educators visualized these students as learning almost exactly the same way as all other students, the practice of "failing" students, holding them in a given grade until they could do most of the work of that grade, was first attempted. This was common practice, so it was reasoned that it should work with these students whose main difference was that they were *much* slower than normal rather than just a little slower than normal. The only problem was that it did not work; there were often related behavior problems, and so the special class evolved and flourished. Although there were some special classes for students with visual and hearing handicaps and special programs for those with speech defects or unusual physical or orthopedic problems, the major early thrust in the public schools was for special classes for the mildly retarded, with a few students whose major problem was behavioral (resulting in low academic performance) included in classes for the retarded for good measure.

Although there were a few who may have felt that these mildly retarded should stay in the regular class, their dismal academic record soon led to popular acceptance of the special class model for the low-or border-line-IQ student who experienced failure in the regular classroom. Few regular classroom teachers complained when they lost (to the special class) those students who were experiencing serious academic problems. In fact, they were often tempted to send along another student or two, those without the prerequisite low IQ but with academic problems similar to those with lower intelligence. In some cases, for a variety of reasons, these students (who actually were not eligible for such placement) were placed in the special class, perhaps on a so-called trial placement, which sometimes lasted for years.

After about 1920, as special classes for the mentally retarded (these soon became more popularly named classes for the *educable mentally handicapped* to differentiate from the few programs existing for the trainable mentally retarded) continued to grow in popularity, there was also a slower but measurable growth in special programs for students with less than normal visual acuity (called classes for the blind, visually handicapped, visually impaired, or partially seeing) and classes for those with less than normal hearing (called classes for the deaf, hearing handicapped, aurally handicapped, or acoustically handicapped). In addition, there were special programs for students with speech problems, and often a special room for students with heart problems, orthopedic handicaps, or crippling conditions. Some classes for students whose major problems related to unacceptable or antisocial behavior were also initiated, but as often as not, if the problem was not too severe these students were placed in the class for the retarded, and those who could not get along in this obviously special setting were expelled from school on the basis of their bad effect on others.

Commencing during the 1920s, an inaccurate but nevertheless widely accepted practice led to the use of the terms *special education classes* and *special education teacher* to refer to classes and teachers of the educable mentally handicapped, with any other type of special education program or service named in relation to the specific handicap involved, that is, for example, class for hard of hearing, crippled, and speech therapy program. This practice continues in some locations and is important to note because the term *"special education"* is meant to include all handicapping conditions and in many states also includes programs and services for talented, gifted, or creative students. The teacher of nonhandicapped, the so-called regular classroom teacher, should remember that providing for handicapped students in the regular class, with or without specialized assistance, means providing for *all* handicapped students, not just the educable mentally handicapped.

We should indicate at this point just how and why the definition of special education differs in various areas of the United States. For all practical purposes, special education is defined on a state-by-state basis in relation to two factors: (1) specific legislation defining special education for purposes of special state reimbursement to those districts providing such programs or services and (2) legislation relating to mandatory education of the handicapped.

In many states both of the preceding types of legislation have been enacted, but the first type exists in only some states.

There is some acceptance of a national definition of special education, but due to the fact that education is primarily a state function, a degree of variation continues. Two national groups have, in effect, defined special education, and it seems predictable that with one exception (that exception is gifted, talented, or creative students), there will be much more agreement between the states in the near future. The two national definitions are primarily operational in nature and are provided by the Council for Exceptional Children, an organization of professionals who work with exceptional children, and the Bureau of Education for the Handicapped, a major component of the United States Office of Education. These two national entities have provided definitions through the scope of their efforts, definitions actually more meaningful than theoretically oriented verbalizations, which find limited application in practice.

The Council for Exceptional Children has twelve divisions, seven of which relate to recognized categories of exceptionality. These seven are (1) the Association for the Gifted, (2) the Council for Children with Behavioral Disorders, (3) the Division for Children with Communication Disorders, (4) the Division for Children with Learning Disabilities, (5) the Division on Mental Retardation, (6) the Division on the Physically Handicapped, Homebound, and Hospitalized, and (7) the Division for the Visually Handicapped, Partially Seeing, and Blind. Thus we see that in addition to the three areas of handicap having a well-established historical base, special education now includes the gifted, those with behavioral disorders and learning disabilities, and the physically handicapped.

The Bureau of Education for the Handicapped was established in 1966 after an unusually comprehensive round of hearings conducted by congressional committees into the effectiveness of then existing federal programs for the handicapped. A variety of internationally recognized special educators, plus representatives from the Council for Exceptional Children, the National Association for Retarded Citizens, the United Cerebral Palsy Associations, Inc., and others gave consistent testimony to the effect that an earlier reorganization within the Office of Education had seriously limited the effectiveness of federal dollars spent on behalf of the handicapped. Their recommendation was the establishment of a bureau within the Office of Education to coordinate all educational activities established to directly benefit the handicapped. The Bureau of Education for the Handicapped was established through legislative enactment and became the focal point of the efforts of special educators throughout the nation and, to some extent, spokesmen for the field.

The Bureau of Education for the Handicapped fulfills a variety of responsibilities as dictated through federal legislation, which brought it into being and continues to provide funding for specific congressional concerns. Because it is responsible for keeping the Congress informed as to needs of the handicapped, the bureau must periodically make estimates as to numbers of school-age children in the various categories of handicap, which in turn provides another type of definition of scope of special education as it relates to the handicapped. Although some members of the bureau might like to avoid talking about categories of handicap, their estimates of needs have been traditionally made in the following categories: (1) visually disabled, (2) deaf, (3) hard of hearing, (4) speech handicapped, (5) crippled and other health impaired, (6) emotional disturbed, (7) mentally retarded, and (8) learning disabled. Thus we see the same handicapping conditions as those recognized by the Council of Exceptional Children, except that for purposes of estimating needed personnel for the nation, the bureau has often used two subcategories, deaf and hard of hearing, rather than a single category.

We view special education as a subsystem of the total educational system, responsible for the provision of specialized or adapted programs and services (or for assisting others to provide such services) for exceptional children and youth. We must remember that exceptional students may be defined in a variety of ways, depending on the state in which one is involved in special educational programming. We should also note that the emphasis of this text is on the handicapped, not the gifted, but the classroom teacher would be well advised to plan for those gifted or creative students who will sooner or later make their presence known.

This section of the historical review has been called the era of special classes and indicated as spanning the time interval from 1900 to 1960/70. The dual dating of the close of this era is due to the fact that although there was a considerable increase in the utilization of service delivery plans other than the special class during the 1960s, many special classes remained in 1970. By calling this the era of special classes, we do not mean that other means of serving the handicapped were not in use during this time. Many students with physical disabilities and those with visual or hearing impairments were integrated with excellent success.

It must also be recognized that "special class" may mean either full-time or part-time special class. For example, speech therapy has been conducted for years in small groups of two to four students, in a totally segregated special setting, usually for time periods of only thirty to forty minutes per day, two or three days per week. Programs for the visually impaired have sometimes consisted of segregated special classes at the preschool level and while learning special skills such as braille, but these same students may be almost totally integrated in the regular classroom from second grade on through school.

This first sixty to seventy years of the twentieth century is properly called the special class era because this was the *major* means whereby handicapped students were served and it represented definite evolution beyond the institutional era. It was characterized by general educators happily sending problem students to the special class for the mentally handicapped and by special educators accepting a number of students who should not have been so placed. Toward the end of the era it became a time of contradictory and inconclusive efficacy studies, and claims—verified in court—that special classes were sometimes "dumping grounds," other times a vehicle of segregation, and in certain geographical areas a convenient way to do something about culturally different, bilingual children without actually initiating a bilingual program.

As the era came to a close a generally negative feeling was left in the minds of many whenever the words "special class" were uttered, particularly when the reference was to a self-contained special class. The misuse

of the special class is not questioned by most special educators, but the assumption that the special class is *never* the right program is just as wrong as the earlier assumption that it was always the right one. Our concern must become that of evaluation of individual needs, and programming must be designed to meet those needs. Any other procedure may lead to additional negative results.

Era of accelerated growth— 1960 to the present

After many decades of slow but steady growth, a series of events began in the 1960s that were destined to change the face of special education. These events, as they continued through the 1970s and into the early 1980s, provided a visibility for the handicapped that would have been unbelievable in even the wildest dreams of advocates at mid-century. Many individuals and organized groups played a role in this change, but a variety of actions of the Congress were to provide the major push of the early 1960s, and one final action by Congress, the passage of Public Law 94-142 in 1975, was to set the stage for the situation as it exists today. More will be said about PL 94-142 in Chapter 2.

After some early legislation indicating that the Congress could indeed be motivated to encourage special programs for the handicapped, a major step in federal support of special education came in 1963 with PL 88-164, hailed by many as the ultimate in assistance for handicapped children and youth. President Kennedy, himself a strong personal advocate of assistance to the handicapped. signed this bill into law and soon afterward established the Division of Handicapped Children and Youth to administer all programs for the handicapped. This act indicated federal interest in all categories of handicap and firmly established the responsibility of the federal government with respect to this interest.

In addition to the establishment of important precedent, it appeared that Congress found a unique degree of satisfaction in passing legislation benefiting a group that did not contribute to campaigns, picket or demonstrate, or even possess any great power through control of voting blocs. It apparently "felt good" to do something beneficial just because it was beneficial. The next Congress, the Eighty-ninth, passed ten highly important laws, nine expressly for the handicapped and one, PL 89-10 (the Elementary and Secondary Education Act), that had profound effects on education in general, including education of the handicapped. Special education, as far as federal support was concerned, had arrived.

A number of factors contributed to this deluge of positive congressional action. The following are among the most important:

1. A number of major political figures, including President Kennedy, had an unusual personal interest in the handicapped because of handicapped individuals in their immediate families. Twenty years earlier the existence of handicapped family members might have been hidden, but increased objectivity about the handicapped, public relations efforts by major organizations concerned with the handicapped, and national concern about minority populations made it socially and politically acceptable to promote such causes.

2. Organizations such as the National Association for Retarded Children and the United Cerebral Palsy Associations, Inc., had become increasingly active in the preceding years, and leading national figures, particularly those in show business, had supported their efforts and had given the cause of the handicapped unusually high national visibility.

3. Professional organizations, led by the Council for Exceptional Children but including many more, had grown in power, recognition, and lobbying expertise.

4. Congress was venturing into new fields of involvement, and this appeared to be a fruitful one. Few would criticize efforts to assist the handicapped.

5. It is our personal knowledge that two or three individuals who were among the most influential in the world of business, banking, and economics and who knew each of the presidents, starting with President Eisenhower, well enough to call them on the phone and receive immediate personal attention, were promoting the cause of the handicapped. This was not a matter of party politics but of power and influence with Congress and the President, regardless of party.

In total, the federal government, through meaningful legislation and relatively adequate funding, gave special education tremendous impetus in the late 1960s. Along with this federal emphasis came efforts at the state and local level to encourage state legislators to pass more comprehensive legislation for the handicapped. In some states this took the form of broad-scale permissive legislation; in others, mandatory legislation; and in still others, it meant inclusion of a hitherto excluded category of handicap (for example, the trainable mentally retarded). Things were going well for proponents of better, more complete educational provisions for the handicapped. Special education was riding the crest of a wave of success.

Then, somewhere in the background, new voices were heard. For the most part these were voices of professional special educators, and their message seemed to run counter to the prevailing mood of the day. They were saying "Are these special efforts really doing any good? Is special education really effective, in terms of actual achievement, or is much of it a waste?" Specifically, they were asking if special education classes for the mildly (educable) mentally retarded were even *as* effective as retention in the regular class. Lloyd Dunn asked this question in such a manner as to shake some of the foundations of special education (Dunn, 1968). Because of Dunn's stature in special education, wide-scale reevaluation began soon thereafter and is still taking place. Dunn's comments were directed primarily at self-contained classes for the educable mentally retarded, but many confused the message and generalized his words to a broader scope of programs for the handicapped. Thus, for at least a few years, we seemed to have one group of special educators encouraging lawmakers at the state and federal level to pass laws and provide funds for special programs for the handicapped, whereas in the opposite corner we found those who said (or were interpreted as saying) that what we had was essentially negative and students would be better off without it.

Now, add to this confusion a series of court actions, specific litigation regarding special education classes and services to and for handicapped children. This litigation began to appear in earnest in the early 1970s, and although it took many forms, we will consider two major thrusts here. The first may be characterized as litigation in which it was alleged that special education classes (usually classes for the educable mentally retarded) lead to stigma, inadequate education, and irreparable injury. These were usually class action suits, that is, suits brought on behalf of specific plaintiffs and "all others similarly situated." Many of these suits were brought on behalf of black or Mexican-American children and were in part the result of placement of children in special classes on the basis of grossly inadequate evaluation. One example is the case of *Diana* v. *State Board of Education (California)*. This suit, used as the basis for many other similar suits, alleged that the

intelligence tests used for placement were culturally biased and that class placement based on these inadequate tests led to an inadequate education. In addition, this suit claimed that as a result, the stigma of mental retardation was suffered by children who were not mentally retarded. In the *Diana* case the plaintiffs sought relief from existing practices of identification and placement. They also sought compensatory damages.

Diana v. *State Board of Education* was settled out of court with the following points of agreement: (1) children whose primary language is not English must be tested in their primary language and in English; however, verbal questions, which by their very nature are unfair to children whose primary language is not English, cannot be used in testing such children; (2) all Mexican-American and Chinese children already enrolled in special education classes must be retested in accordance with the preceding principle; (3) every school district in the state must develop and submit to the court the school district plan for retesting and reevaluating Mexican-American and Chinese children presently in classes for the educable mentally retarded, and as a part of this plan they must show how they will place back into regular classes those children whom this reevaluation indicates were misplaced; (4) school psychologists must develop more appropriate testing devices and measures that will reflect Mexican-American culture; and (5) any school district that has a significant disparity between the percentage of Mexican-American children in regular classes and this percentage in classes for educable mentally retarded must submit an acceptable explanation for this discrepancy.

The *Diana* case is similar to many filed against the schools. Most were settled in a manner similar to that in the *Diana* case.

A second type of major litigation appeared

to be going in a different direction, that of demanding more special education classes and services for the handicapped in the public schools. The following description of two cases, one in Pennsylvania and the other in Washington, D.C., illustrates this effort (Gearheart and Litton, 1979, pp. 17-18). Although the first affected only the mentally retarded, the second specifically related to all handicapped and, because it was based on the United States Constitution, has ramifications for all areas of the United States.

Two major cases appear to have established the right of free access to public education for the school age trainable mentally retarded. The first, *The Pennsylvania Association for Retarded Children* v. *the Commonwealth of Pennsylvania*, questioned educational policies of the state of Pennsylvania, which led directly to practices that denied an appropriate education at public expense to retarded children of school age. This case was filed on January 7, 1971, by the Pennsylvania Association for Retarded Children on behalf of fourteen specifically named children and all other children similarly situated. This was a typical *class action* suit, filed in such a manner as to affect those fourteen children named, all others of a similar "class" now residing in the state, and all children similarly situated who will be living in Pennsylvania in the future.

Pennsylvania, like a number of other states, had compulsory school attendance laws, provided certain types of special classes for handicapped children within the public schools, and provided residential schools for some handicapped children. But within the Pennsylvania School Code, there were two specific ways in which the trainable mentally retarded child could be excluded from public education. First, if a qualified psychologist or personnel from a mental health clinic certified that a given child could no longer profit from public school attendance, the child could be excluded. Second, because the law provided that the local board of directors could refuse to accept or retain children who had not reached the mental age of 5 years, most trainable retarded were never admitted to the public schools. Even if a

child were not excluded under either of these two provisions, there was a third provision that permitted the local board to provide training outside the public schools, "if an approved plan demonstrates that it is unfeasible to form a special class."

The Pennsylvania Association for Retarded Children (PARC) set out to establish three main points in their case: (1) Mentally retarded children can learn if an appropriate educational program is provided, (2) "education" must be viewed more broadly than the traditional academic program, and (3) early educational experience is essential to maximize educational potential.

After considerable testimony by the state and by a variety of "expert witnesses," the case was won by the PARC. In a finalization of earlier decrees, the court ordered (on May 5, 1972) that each of the named plaintiffs be immediately reevaluated, and that each be provided free access to public education and training appropriate to his learning capabilities. It further ordered that all retarded persons between the ages of 6 and 21 years be provided such access and programming as soon as possible but in any event, no later than September 1, 1972.

The order and agreement also contained a number of added benefits for the retarded of Pennsylvania. The state department was made responsible for supervision of educational programs in state institutions, children served through homebound programs must now be automatically reevaluated every 3 months, and any district providing preschool education for other children must now provide preschool for the retarded.

The Pennsylvania Association for Retarded Children v. *Pennsylvania* suit, like many that were to follow, was settled on the basis of a *consent agreement*. This is an out-of-court agreement, usually formally approved by the court. In this suit, the state was ordered to provide free public education, appropriate to the learning capabilities of retarded children, and the consent agreement provided the working framework. To make certain that the consent agreement was carried out, the court established a time schedule for implementation and appointed two "masters" to oversee the total process.

A second case, *Mills* v. *the Board of Education of the District of Columbia*, is of unusual significance because it applied to *all* handicapped children. To a certain extent, it established a principle that tended to lead to the inclusion of all handicapped students in future class action suits. This case, like *PARC* v. *Pennsylvania*, led to a court order that required the public schools to provide for handicapped students even if they did not fit the educational mold. As in the Pennsylvania case, the court appointed masters to oversee the operation. Unlike the Pennsylvania case, which resulted in a consent agreement between the parties, *Mills* v. *District of Columbia* case was decided through a judgment of the court and was based on a constitutional holding.

These cases, and others initiated on behalf of other handicapped students, established the handicapped student's right to a free, appropriate public education and to protection from inappropriate assessment and classification procedures as well as the parents' right to be totally involved in educational planning. These court cases, and the fact that the decision almost always favored the position taken by advocates for the handicapped, undoubtedly played a role in the passage of PL 94-142, the Education for All Handicapped Children Act of 1975. This law, the culmination and capstone of all earlier efforts, provides for all these rights, and its passage led to the rapid passage of many similar state laws. PL 94-142 will be reviewed in some detail in Chapter 2 as we consider how services are delivered to handicapped students today.

SUMMARY

Handicapped students are first of all students; they need and have a right to an appropriate education at public expense. Their handicapping condition makes it imperative that we adjust and adapt educational offerings, but this is only consistent with the manner in which American society is learning to approach the question of any other minority group.

The philosophy of education for the handicapped presented in this chapter supports an emphasis of learning strengths and abilities and a deemphasis of labeling of handicapped children. On the other hand, education for many handicapped students *must* be adapted (that is, braille for the blind, adapted language systems for the severely hearing impaired, and others), and to provide such adaptations, we must speak objectively of the type and degree of handicap; thus some "labels" must be used at times. However, most handicapped students can be served effectively in the regular classroom *if materials and consultive assistance are provided*. All possible effort should be directed toward such participation in the regular class.

In the past the handicapped have been eliminated, ignored, made to work as indentured servants, and institutionalized, in that approximate order. There have been variations in different parts of the world and differences according to the various types of handicapping conditions, but these were the most common societal reactions to the handicapped until about 1900. Commencing soon after the beginning of the twentieth century, public school special classes became popular and commonly accepted. They represented a significant step in the right direction but before long were misused and overused, and thus some reform was needed. This reform began to take shape in the 1960s and was given a boost by court rulings that directed the public schools to educate the handicapped, but to do so in a manner that permitted them to be in the most nearly normal setting possible.

A number of significant federal legislative enactments culminated in the passage in 1975 of the Education for All Handicapped Children Act, PL 94-142. This act in effect formalized what a variety of litigative results and a number of more progressive state laws had been clearly indicating. The time for full

recognition of the educational needs of *all* students, regardless of handicap, level of intelligence, or cost of such education, had arrived. With this law came the requirement for education of the handicapped in the least restrictive environment, consistent with appropriate education. This law, and the events that preceded and accompanied it, thus led to the need to provide educational programming for many handicapped students in the regular classroom. In Chapter 2 we will further investigate PL 94-142, the provision of educational programs within the regular classroom, and the various results and influences of these programs. These first two chapters will set the stage for the remainder of this text, which is designed to assist the regular classroom teacher in successfully educating the handicapped student in the regular classroom.

REFERENCES AND SUGGESTED READINGS

Abeson, A. *A continuing summary of pending and completed litigation regarding the handicapped.* Reston, Va.: Council for Exceptional Children. (These summaries are issued periodically by the Council for Exceptional Children. Those issued after 1973 may be of particular interest in relation to topics discussed in this chapter.)

Ashcroft, S. C. The handicapped in the regular classroom. *NEA Journal*, November 1967, *56*, 33-34.

Birch, H. G., & Gussow, J. *Disadvantaged children.* New York: Harcourt Brace Jovanovich, Inc., 1970.

California State Department of Education. *An investigation of Spanish-speaking pupils placed in classes for the educable mentally retarded.* Sacramento: Author, 1969.

Christoplos, F., & Renz, P. A. A critical examination of special education programs. *Journal of Special Education*, 1969, *3*, 371-379.

Cruickshank, W., Paul, J., & Junkala, J. *Misfits in the public schools.* Syracuse, N.Y.: Syracuse University Press, 1969.

Dunn, L. M. Special education for the mildly retarded: is much of it justifiable? *Exceptional Children*, 1968, *35*, 5-22.

Gearheart, B. R. (Ed.). *Education of the exceptional child: history, present practices, and trends.* Scranton, Pa.: Intext Publishers Group, 1972.

Gearheart, B. R. *Organization and administration of educational programs for exceptional children.* Springfield, Ill.: Charles C Thomas, Publisher, 1974.

Gearheart, B. R., & Litton, F. *The trainable retarded: a foundations approach* (2nd ed.) St. Louis: The C. V. Mosby Co., 1979.

Itard, J. M. G. *The wild boy of Aveyron.* New York: Appleton-Century-Crofts, 1962.

Kanner, L. *A history of the care and study of the mentally retarded.* Springfield, Ill.: Charles C Thomas, Publisher, 1964.

Kott, M. G. The history of mental retardation. In J. Rothstein (Ed.), *Mental retardation: readings and resources.* New York: Holt, Rinehart & Winston, Inc., 1971.

Lilly, S. Improving social acceptance of low sociometric status, low achieving students. *Exceptional Children*, January 1971, *37*, 341-348.

Lowenfeld, B. *The visually handicapped child in school.* New York: The John Day Co., 1973. (A translation by Lowenfeld from Klein's *Guide to provide for blind children the necessary education in the schools of their home communities and in the circle of their families;* 1836; Rev. Ed., 1845.)

Pritchard, D. G. *Education and the handicapped: 1760-1960.* London: Routledge & Kegan Paul, Ltd., 1963.

Weintraub, F.: Recent influences of law regarding the identification and educational placement of children. *Focus on Exceptional Children*, 1972, *4*(2), 1-11.

Wolfensberger, W. *Normalization: the principle of normalization in human services.* Toronto: National Institute on Mental Retardation, 1972.

Wright, R. G. Special—But Not Separate. *Education*, May 1967, *87*, 554-557.

Zilboorg, G., & Henry, G. W. *A history of medical psychology.* New York: W. W. Norton & Co., Inc., 1941.

2 THE PRESENT FRAMEWORK FOR SERVICES TO THE HANDICAPPED

B. R. Gearheart

.In Chapter 1, we reviewed the basis on which present services to the handicapped have been established. We further noted that Public Law 94-142, The Education for All Handicapped Children Act of 1975, was the result of a variety of recognized factors and forces. PL 94-142 was actually an amendment of earlier legislation and "represents the standards that have ... been laid down by the courts, legislatures, and other policy bodies of our country" (Weintraub, 1977, p. 114). It is, then, a formalization of what should be considered accepted practice in providing handicapped students (and their parents) educational rights and equal protection of the law. A basic understanding of PL 94-142 is essential if we are to fully understand the concept of the least restrictive environment as applied to the requirement for free, appropriate education for all handicapped children and youth. The review of PL 94-142 that follows should help provide such an understanding.

PUBLIC LAW 94-142

The purpose of PL 94-142 is outlined in one comprehensive sentence from the Statement of Purpose section of the actual law. According to this statement, PL 94-142 is designed to assure that:

> ... all handicapped children have available to them ... a free appropriate public education which emphasizes special education and related services designed to meet their unique needs, to assure that the rights of handicapped children and their parents or guardians are protected, to assist states and localities to provide for the education of all handicapped children, and to assess and assure the effectiveness of efforts to educate handicapped children.

PL 94-142 specifically directs that certain handicapped children be served, including the (1) deaf, (2) deaf-blind, (3) hard of hearing, (4) mentally retarded, (5) multihandicapped, (6) orthopedically impaired, (7) other health impaired, (8) seriously emotionally disturbed, (9) learning disabled, (10) speech impaired, and (11) visually handicapped. The law is written so that it is clear that *all* special programs and services required by such handicapped students between the ages of 3 and 21 years should be provided. This mandate for services does not apply for children in the 3- to 5-year age range and the 18- to 21-year age range *if* such requirement is inconsistent with a state law or practice or any applicable court decree.

Services to be provided, as spelled out in the Rules and Regulations for the act, include (1) audiology, (2) counseling services, (3) early identification, (4) medical services, (5) occupational therapy, (6) parent counseling, (7) physical therapy, (8) psychological services, (9) recreation, (10) school health services, (11) social work services, (12) speech pathology, and (13) transportation (Federal) Register, August 23, 1977, pp. 42479-42480). This specific list of services, according to comments in the Rules and Regulations, was not intended to be exhaustive, but was included to indicate the broad scope of services encompassed in the intent of the law. The fact that these various sections of the federal regulations seem to make absolutely clear is that the public schools must furnish all services needed to provide an effective educational program for all handicapped students.

PL 94-142 has been discussed in professional journals in all areas of education, is regularly mentioned in law journals, has been reviewed in many popular magazines, and has been a topic of concern in top-rated national television programs and documentaries. In short, it has led to more general interest and concern than any other legislative enactment relating to handicapped students in the history of this nation. It was of sufficient concern to the National Education Association (NEA) that it led to an important NEA Resolution passed in 1978 (see p. 21).

NEA RESOLUTION 78-37 EDUCATION FOR ALL HANDICAPPED CHILDREN*

The National Education Association supports a free appropriate public education for all handicapped students in a least restrictive environment which is determined by maximum teacher involvement. However, the Association recognizes that to implement Public Law 94-142 effectively —

a. A favorable learning experience must be created both for handicapped and non-handicapped students.

b. Regular and special education teachers, administrators, and parents must share in planning and implementation for the disabled.

c. All staff should be adequately prepared for their roles through in-service training and retraining.

d. All students must be adequately prepared for the program.

e. The appropriateness of educational methods, materials, and supportive services must be determined in cooperation with classroom teachers.

f. The classroom teacher(s) must have an appeal procedure regarding the implementation of the program, especially in terms of student placement.

g. Modifications must be made in class size, using a weighted formula, scheduling, and curriculum design to accommodate program demands.

h. There must be a systematic evaluation and reporting of program developments using a plan which recognizes individual differences.

i. Adequate funding must be provided and then used exclusively for this program.

j. The classroom teacher(s) must have a major role in determining individual educational programs and should become members of school assessment teams.

k. Adequate released time must be made available for teachers so that they can carry out the increased demands upon them.

l. Staff must not be reduced.

m. Additional benefits negotiated for handicapped students through local collective bargaining agreements must be honored.

n. Communication must be maintained among all involved parties.

o. All teachers must be made aware of their right to dissent concerning the appropriate program for a student, including the right to have the dissenting opinion recorded.

p. Individual educational programs should provide appropriate services for the handicapped students and not be used as a criteria for the evaluation of the teacher.

*From National Educational Association. *Today's Education*, September-October 1978, p. 62.

The NEA Resolution effectively illustrates two important points regarding PL 94-142:

1. The fact that the NEA, the most influential teacher organization in the nation, developed a specific resolution regarding PL 94-142 indicates NEA's perception of its significant impact.
2. The breadth of the sixteen points included in the resolution indicates the complexity of the problems related to implementation of an appropriate educational program for all handicapped children and youth.

There are many specific requirements for educational programs for the handicapped in PL 94-142, but the goal of all such requirements is that we provide an appropriate education to handicapped students within the least restrictive environment. The various additional provisions and requirements felt to be essential to this major purpose include:

1. The requirement that school personnel develop and maintain an individualized educational program (IEP) for each handicapped student with provision for periodic revision as necessary.
2. Various policies and procedures that guarantee due process
3. Policies and procedures designed to protect the confidentiality of records
4. Initiation and maintenance of regular parent involvement and consultation
5. Testing and evaluation procedures that are nondiscriminatory

The rules and regulations for PL 94-142 are complex and lengthy. However, most of these requirements are the responsibility of special educators, and it must be certified that they are being followed by local school administrators. One requirement, however, becomes an immediate concern of the regular educator, for much of this requirement will be carried out in the regular class for most handicapped students. This is the requirement for an IEP for each handicapped student.

The individualized educational program (IEP)

The IEP for each student must include the following:

1. A statement of the present levels of educational performance
2. A statement of annual goals, including short-term instructional objectives
3. A statement of the specific educational services to be provided to this handicapped student and the extent to which such student will be able to participate in regular educational programs
4. The projected date for initiation and anticipated duration of such services
5. Appropriate objective criteria and evaluation procedures and schedules for determining, on at least an annual basis, whether instructional objectives are being achieved.

Most states have essentially these same regulations, although wording may vary, and some states have developed more detailed regulations. The IEP is a tool for management of the educational program and should ensure that each student is actually provided for individually. Other requirements of the law relating to the IEP are those designed to ensure parent participation, to make certain that parents understand the proceedings of IEP meetings (interpreters should be provided for parents who are deaf or whose basic language is not English), and guidelines for record keeping. Development of the IEP is primarily the responsibility of special educators; if, as the IEP is being drawn up, it is certain that the student will attend the regular classroom, the regular classroom teacher will usually be asked to assist. The IEP must reflect, in both objectives and content, the regular class environment; however, the teacher who receives a given student may or may not have been involved in the development of the original IEP. If, however, a teacher retains a student for any significant length of time, that teacher should be a part of any IEP reviews or redevelopment. That teacher also has the right, and the responsibility, to ask for conferences with various special education personnel if there are any questions or concerns about the content or meaning of the IEP.

The least restrictive environment

In speaking of the meaning of PL 94-142 for the regular classroom teacher, John Ryor, president of the NEA, noted that the key word in the provision for an "appropriate public education in the least restrictive environment" is *appropriate*. He further noted that "the phrase 'least restrictive environment' does not automatically mean that all handicapped students will be mainstreamed" (Ryor, 1977, p. 24).

A statement on the least restrictive environment, which may be viewed as especially significant because it was provided as a type of editorial comment in *Closer Look*, a newsletter of the *Parents' Campaign for Handicapped Children and Youth*, follows:

One of the basic principles of the new education law for handicapped children is the right of each child to be educated in the "least restrictive alternative" setting. It emphasizes the importance of learning in as normal an environment as possible. P.L. 94-142 makes clear that children should be removed from the mainstream of school life *only* if it really isn't possible for them to make it in regular classes (even with extra assistance). When a child *is* in a separate program, every effort should be made to provide experiences for give-and-take with non-handicapped peers.

That's the spirit—and the letter—of the law. Mainstreaming covers a wide variety of alternatives, and placement *should* be made on the basis of individual needs. For some, it means learning in a regular classroom with the help of resource teachers, or special kinds of aid. For others, it may mean spending most of their day in separate classrooms, with as much opportunity as possible to participate in regular school activities. For a few, it may still be necessary to live and learn in a residential setting—but close to home, with as many contacts with the real world as possible.

These are important decisions, and they must take into account many aspects of each child's needs and levels of ability. They are not fixed, unchanging plans; they should be evaluated and revised as children develop.

Underlying the philosophy of mainstreaming is the recognition of the growth in self-esteem, social skill and awareness that takes place when handicapped and nonhandicapped children have the chance to learn, play and grow together (*Closer Look*, 1978, p. 5).

We feel that this statement is unusually significant because *Closer Look* is an advocacy-oriented publication from *The Parents' Campaign*, an organization that is strongly dedicated to assisting parents in obtaining educational rights for their children. It has always supported the concept of maximum integration in the regular classroom, but in this statement carefully explains that all students may not be able to function in the regular classroom. Our concept of the least restrictive environment was briefly outlined in Chapter 1 (p. 3), but we have included this additional discussion because we believe it is extremely important for regular classroom teachers to understand the *real* intent of PL 94-142, rather than harboring misconceptions based on limited information and understanding. In one final attempt to address this concern, which has grown into a major problem in some parts of the nation and could be a threat to the entire issue of appropriate education for all handicapped students, we will summarize the major issues, focusing on myths and fallacies. This section is subtitled "boon or boondoggle?" in all seriousness, for this is a pertinent, serious question.

Mainstreaming and the least restrictive environment: Boon or boondoggle?

In concluding this consideration of PL 94-142, it is important to face one issue squarely.

That issue is whether the principle of the least restrictive environment and the resulting movement that has been called "mainstreaming" represent a major step forward or a giant facade. This issue must be addressed, for it appears that in some instances educators may have willingly made it the latter.

In a discussion of positive aspects of the IEP and the effective application of the least restrictive environment in principle in schools in Ohio, Cole and Dunn (1977) have outlined some of the problems as they encountered them in the schools. They point out that "the least restrictive environment clause offers more than one temptation to harried administrators" (p. 6). They remind us of the mounting budgetary problems of the schools and the manner in which taxpayers often vote down school levies. They then note that misapplication of mainstreaming can lead to keeping handicapped students in the regular class even if they should be in a special class program, "thus saving the school system the considerable extra expense of placing the child in a special classroom" (p. 6). They further indicate that "several superintendents in Ohio viewed this type of 'mainstreaming' as a realistic alternative" (p. 6). *The intent of PL 94-142 was that handicapped students be in the regular class when their needs can be best met in the regular class setting.* The various state statutes have a similar intent. *The fact is that students may be improperly retained in the regular class because of (1) good intentions on the part of poorly informed educators, (2) misunderstanding of the directive of the law regarding "parent involvement" (giving in to parent's expressed desire to keep the student in the regular class, even when the facts clearly indicate otherwise), or (3) mainstreaming to save money.*

Our concern is that this misunderstanding and misapplication not be permitted to continue. If they do continue, the entire future of appropriate education of the handicapped could be seriously endangered. The remaining chapters of this text are devoted to the role that the regular classroom teacher must play with the handicapped, but this effort will not be effective unless these are the "right" handicapped students. Table 1 provides an illustration of some of the facts and fallacies about mainstreaming and the least restrictive environment. These facts and fallacies must be fully understood for the remainder of this text to have pertinence and meaning.

STATE LEGISLATIVE ACTIONS

It was noted earlier that PL 94-142 did not "just happen." It was a result of many factors, including the influence of political figures such as John Kennedy who promoted much-needed legislation, parent and professional groups who lobbied for services, congressional interest, and research results (efficacy studies). The effects of litigation also had a tremendous impact on prevailing practices in special education. In addition, a number of state legislative enactments preceded the actual enactment of PL 94-142. These state laws varied in wording, but the intent was clear, and state education officials were directed to provide regulations for the implementation of these laws. Tennessee enacted such a law in 1972.

Tennessee Laws, Sec. 2B, Ch. 839, 1972. To the maximum extent practicable, handicapped children shall be educated along with children who do not have handicaps and attend regular classes. Impediments to learning and to the normal functioning of handicapped children in the regular school environment shall be overcome by the provision of special aids and services rather than separate schooling for the handicapped. Special classes, separate schooling, or other removal of handicapped children from the regular school environment shall occur only when and to the extent that the nature and severity of the handicap is such that education in the regular classroom, even with the use of supplemental aids and services, cannot be accomplished satisfactorily.

Table 1. Mainstreaming and the least restrictive environment—facts and fallacies

Commonly accepted fallacy	Fact
PL 94-142 and the principle of "mainstreaming" dictate that all handicapped students should be enrolled in the regular class for all, or at least part, of the school day.	Handicapped students should be enrolled in the regular class for as much of the school day as appropriate, given their unique needs. This may mean that they are in the regular class for all of the day, in a special class for all of the day, or anywhere on the placement continuum between these extremes. (See pp. 30-31.)
If the parent says "no" to a proposed plan that includes some special class programming, the school has no alternative but to retain the student in the regular class.	The parent(s) must be a part of all deliberations regarding the educational programming and may say "no" to a given plan. The school may decide to go along with the parent's stand, but when this does not work out, or in certain very clear-cut cases, school officials have the responsibility to initiate an appeals procedure in which outside authorities are involved in final determinations about placement.
The IEP is a "contract," and if the student does not reach the educational goals described in the IEP, the teacher and other school authorities may be liable to lawsuit for "breaking" or not living up to the contract.	The IEP is an educational management plan or tool. It does require good faith efforts to achieve the goals and objectives listed in the IEP, and the parent can ask for revisions, but federal regulations specifically note that the IEP does not constitute a guarantee that the student will progress at a specified rate or achieve specific academic levels.
If a student does not reach the goals and objectives outlined in the IEP, the teacher will be blamed by the administration at teacher evaluation time.	As noted above, the IEP is recognized in the federal regulations as a plan, not a contract. The local school district can establish whatever means of teacher evaluation it deems feasible, but the strong NEA stand on this issue (see item p of the NEA Resolution on p. 21) makes this highly unlikely.
Mainstreaming is less costly than providing services in a special class setting.	Mainstreaming may be either more costly or less costly than education in a special class setting. This depends on the needs of the student under consideration. In most cases, *given the provision of proper support services*, it will cost the same or perhaps slightly more.
Mainstreaming handicapped students will detract from the educational progress of nonhandicapped students.	There is little question that many students are limited in their understanding of the extent and nature of differences between individuals in society. Through mainstreaming they may learn to better understand and appreciate human differences, while recognizing important similarities. *If* the regular classroom teacher is assisted through special materials and alternative teaching strategies, *all* students may benefit academically. If such assistance is *not* provided, or if students who should be in special programs are placed in regular classes, nonhandicapped students may suffer academically.

One year later, the state of Colorado passed a legislative declaration with similar intent.

State of Colorado House Bill 1164, Sec. 123, 22, 2, 1973: Legislative declaration: The general assembly, recognizing the obligation of the state of Colorado to provide educational opportunities to all children which will enable them to lead fulfilling and productive lives, declares that the purpose of this article is to provide means for educating those children who are handicapped. It is the intent of the general assembly, in keeping with accepted educational principles, that handicapped children shall be educated in regular classrooms, insofar as practicable, and should receive supplementary services only when the nature of the child's handicap makes the inclusion of the child in a regular classroom impractical. To this end, the services of special education personnel shall be utilized within the regular school programs to the maximum extent permitted by good educational practices, both in rendering services directly to children and in providing consultative services to regular classroom teachers.

A number of other states passed similar legislation prior to the passage of PL 94-142, and the trend was unmistakable. Handicapped students were to be maintained within the regular classroom along with their nonhandicapped peers whenever possible. However, this then-new philosophy led to an obvious additional need. This was the need to provide better preparation for the regular classroom teacher, so that the handicapped student might benefit from this new practice, and other students would not be placed at a disadvantage. This need for additional preparation of the nonspecial education teacher is the subject of the following section.

Teacher preparation

An obvious prerequisite to successfully serving handicapped students in regular classrooms is the provision of specific preparation for general educators at the pre- and in-service levels. Surveys of practicing regular classroom teachers clearly indicated that they did not feel competent in working with handicapped students and that they needed specific preparation. This preparation may be provided to practicing teachers (in-service) or as a part of the requirements necessary to obtain a teaching credential (preservice).

Among the earliest efforts to provide general educators with the needed skills and competencies to work with handicapped students in the regular classroom, the Colorado legislature in 1972 earmarked two million dollars for the in-service training of regular teachers to acquaint them with the recently enacted mandatory legislation and to provide them with the necessary understanding, skills, and competencies to work with handicapped students in their classrooms. This appropriation was followed by similar amounts for two subsequent years to ensure that a large number of general educators would have the opportunity to participate in in-service offerings.

Some states require that practicing teachers receive in-service education concerning handicapped students. Other states have enacted specific legislation requiring that all teachers must receive specific preparation in techniques of how to work with handicapped students in regular classrooms to become certified. The following bills from the states of Missouri and Georgia are examples of legislation requiring that all general educators receive preparation in this area.

House Bill No. 370
77th General Assembly of the State of Missouri
Be it enacted by the General Assembly of the State of Missouri, as follows:
Section 1. 1. After July 1, 1976, no person shall be granted a certificate of license to teach in the public schools of this state as provided by section 168.021, RSMo, unless he has satisfactorily completed a course of two or more semester hours in the psychology and education of the exceptional child.

2. The course shall include instruction on identification of children with learning disabilities caused by neurological disorders, mental retardation and sociological factors. The course shall provide information on methods and techniques for teaching exceptional children, sources of referral and assistance to teachers and parents.

The State of Georgia*

Section 8A. Course in Education of Exceptional Children. (a) After July 1, 1976, any person granted a certificate as a teacher, principal, or guidance counselor, pursuant to Section 8 of this Act, shall have satisfactorily completed a course of five or more quarter hours, approved by the State Board of Education, in the education of exceptional children, or participate in a local system's staff development program designed to assist teachers in the identification of students with special needs.

In some states requirements for specific coursework and/or the number of required hours is specified, whereas other states indicate that part of a teacher's preparation must include aspects of dealing with handicapped students.

Sargent (1978), in examining the trend toward requiring regular educators to receive special preparation, surveyed all fifty state certification agencies to learn which states required or have such a requirement pending. He found that eighteen states and the District of Columbia had adopted requirements mandating preparation of regular classroom teachers. In addition, ten states had similar requirements pending.

It appears that the mandate to require specific preparation of general educators is well established. More than half of the states currently require or are in the process of requiring such preparation. It is safe to assume that others will follow with similar requirements.

In each state there are a number of colleges and universities that provide teacher

---

*Only the applicable section is quoted.

training leading to state certification. Some train large numbers of both elementary and secondary teachers, some specialize in or emphasize certain subject areas, but the majority have now been asked to prepare teachers to meet this new need. The way in which this preparation is provided varies considerably, ranging from the incorporation of this content into existing courses to specific courses that are tailored to the needs of general educators. It appears that a variety of approaches are being employed successfully. Our purpose in developing this text has been to provide a specific offering, tailored to the unique needs of regular educators. We will continue this chapter with a consideration of service delivery—that is, how we deliver special assistance and services to handicapped students—but will first take a quick look at the prevalence of handicapped students. This will provide a better concept of the magnitude of need for these special services.

PREVALENCE OF HANDICAPPED STUDENTS

The prevalence of handicapped individuals in the United States has been estimated, calculated, surveyed, enumerated, guesstimated, and reported over the years since the first federal employee was asked for such data for some type of report to Congress. The number cannot be determined with absolute accuracy; the discovery, each year, of students who have obviously been handicapped for some time (but have been previously unidentified) indicates that some handicapped individuals remain unidentified at any given time. One of the better ways to estimate the number of handicapped students is to determine the number in some of the states that apparently provide the most adequate services backed by the best state funding and apply percentages derived from those states to the national population.

Table 2 reflects a range of prevalence de-

Table 2. Prevalence of handicapped children in the United States

	Percent of population	Number of children ages 5 to 18*
Visually impaired (includes blind)	0.1	55,000
Hearing impaired (includes deaf)	0.5 to 0.7	275,000 to 385,000
Speech handicapped	3.0 to 4.0	1,650,000 to 2,200,000
Crippled and other health impaired	0.5	275,000
Emotionally disturbed	2.0 to 3.0	1,100,000 to 1,650,000
Mentally retarded (both educable and trainable)	2.0 to 3.0	1,100,000 to 1,650,000
Learning disabilities	2.0 to 3.0	1,100,000 to 1,650,000
Multihandicapped	0.5 to 0.7	275,000 to 385,000
	10.6 to 15.0	5,830,000 to 8,250,000

*Number of children based on 1982 population estimates.

rived from a composite of federal reports and other state-level data, using the methods suggested in the preceding paragraph. Overall, these should be considered relatively conservative data. The purpose of presenting these data is to provide a general idea of the magnitude of the problem, which should in turn indicate the critical need for appropriate programs and services for this handicapped population.

It is estimated that approximately half of these students have been identified and are receiving services (the percentage varies with handicapping condition). An important question is how well those students are presently being served in these programs. Since the regular classroom teacher is now an integral part of much of the programming for the mildly handicapped student, the question of quality service will be greatly influenced by these nonspecial educators. The following section will contain a relatively detailed description of *how* services are provided to handicapped students and will illustrate *the principle of a continuum of alternative educational provisions for the handicapped.* Provision of this wide variety of services is required by PL 94-142, and we believe it to be the only way in which

all handicapped students may be appropriately, effectively served.

SERVICE DELIVERY

Certain specific regulations from the Rules and Regulations for PL 94-142 provide the basis for much of our thinking in recommending the continuum of alternative placements. We will therefore make reference to these regulations before we initiate our discussion of the continuum of services. The boxed material on p. 29 lists the regulations regarding the least restrictive environment.

PL 94-142 thus requires that a continuum of alternative placements be made available to meet the changing, individual needs of all handicapped students. In years past, school districts have offered as few as two or three service delivery systems for their handicapped students. Such an approach demanded that the student be "fit into" the organizational plans offered. A program continuum provides a full spectrum of services that may be tailored to the individual needs of each student at any given time during his educational career. A program continuum for handicapped students is shown in Table 3.

The continuum of alternative educational provisions for handicapped children requires

RULES AND REGULATIONS FOR PL 94-142
REGARDING LEAST RESTRICTIVE ENVIRONMENT*

General

Each public agency shall insure:

(1) That to the maximum extent appropriate, handicapped children, including children in public or private institutions or other care facilities, are educated with children who are not handicapped, and

(2) That special classes, separate schooling or other removal of handicapped children from the regular educational environment occurs only when the nature or severity of the handicap is such that education in regular classes with the use of supplementary aids and services cannot be achieved satisfactorily.

Continuum of alternative placements

(a) Each public agency shall insure that a continuum of alternative placements is available to meet the needs of handicapped children for special education and related services.

(b) The continuum required under paragraph (a) of this section must:

(1) Include the alternative placements listed in the definition of special education (instruction in regular classes, special classes, special schools, home instruction, and instruction in hospitals and institutions), and

(2) Make provision for supplementary services (such as resource room or itinerant instruction) to be provided in conjunction with regular class placement.

Placements

Each public agency shall insure that:

(a) Each handicapped child's educational placement:

(1) Is determined at least annually,

(2) Is based on his or her individualized education program, and

(3) Is as close as possible to the child's home;

(b) The various alternative placements included are available to the extent necessary to implement the individualized education program for each handicapped child;

(c) Unless a handicapped child's individualized education program requires some other arrangement, the child is educated in the school which he or she would attend if not handicapped; and

(d) In selecting the least restrictive environment, consideration is given to any potential harmful effect on the child or on the quality of services which he or she needs.

*From section 121(a) of the Rules and Regulations for PL 94-142; *Federal Register*, *42*(163), August 23, 1977, p. 42497.

Table 3. A continuum of alternative educational provisions for handicapped children

	1	2	3	4
Regular class No assistance needed	Regular classroom and consultive assistance from special education	Regular classroom and consultation plus special materials from special education	Regular classroom and itinerant teacher services from special education	Regular classroom and resource room, resource teacher service from special education
	Regular classroom teacher—primary responsibility			
		Consultant, itinerant, resource room, special education teacher responsibility		

*Regular class teacher may (1) assist homebound/hospital teacher, (2) teach the child through telephone hookup or mode, direct and indirect service may be provided by special education.

that a full range of services be offered, a range from regular classroom placement to very intensive special education programming (Table 3). In the first four plans the student remains in a regular classroom for all or a majority of the school day, and his regular classroom teacher has primary responsibility for his program. In the first two plans the regular classroom teacher receives consultive assistance or special instructional materials from special education personnel, but the student does not work directly with special educators. In the third and fourth plans the regular classroom teacher retains primary responsibility, but special education personnel provide supportive or supplemental assistance to *both* the student and his teacher or teachers. The services provided by special education personnel may take place in the regular classroom or in a designated work area, such as a resource room.

In plans five and six the student attends a regular classroom part-time and a special class part-time. The amount of time spent in the regular classroom is dependent on the individual's ability to profit from regular classroom instruction. In plan five, the student may spend a near equal amount of time in each setting, whereas in plan six the student spends the majority of his day in a special class and is selectively included in regular classroom activities.

In plans seven, eight, and nine, comprehensive services needed by the more seriously involved or multihandicapped are provided. Plan seven involves service by specialized personnel in a school in which all students are receiving special assistance because of handicapping conditions. Plan eight may involve the regular classroom teacher, and instruction may be provided through electrical-electronic hookup with the regular classroom. Plan nine is for students with severe problems who require twenty-four–hour programming.

Although we agree that placement in regular classrooms is desirable for the majority of students, there are and will be students

5	6	7	8	9	
Regular class (half-time) and special class (half-time)	Special class in regular school some integration for at least some children	Special class in separate special day school	Hospital and homebound service	Residential or boarding school	No educational provision (This "no-service" condition is rapidly disappearing owing to recent court decisions.)
			*		
	Special classroom teacher—primary responsibility				

electronic equipment, (3) not be involved at all. If child is taught by regular class teacher through electrical-electronic

whose needs must be met through more segregated programs. The alternative program continuum does not assume that one type of program is better for *all* students. *An important basic assumption is that each and every student must be considered individually.* For one student, special class placement may be the least restrictive alternative, whereas another may be most effectively served in a regular classroom with or without special education services. Still another student may be most appropriately served in a residential or boarding school.

The alternative educational placement continuum must be flexible. It must be recognized that students' needs may change over time or as a result of corrective work (such as glasses, prosthesis, and hearing aid) or educational remediation. According to PL 94-142, students must be reevaluated annually to determine if they are able to move to another program. It is also possible that a student may make large skips from one type of program to another. Hopefully, most moves will be in the direction of the less restrictive settings.

Nature of services

Regular classroom and consultative assistance from special education. Students in this type of program are enrolled in the regular class on a full-time basis. Supportive assistance from special education personnel may involve observation of a student in his regular classroom, followed by consultation with the teacher to relate specific suggestions or procedures that may be helpful. The services of the special educator may be needed for only a limited time, or some problems may require repeated observations and consultation.

The special educator must be a master diagnostician to be able to analyze the problem and to develop meaningful educational recommendations. The key to this type of service is open communication between the regular teacher and the special educator. The regular teacher must feel comfortable in asking for assistance from this outside person and in trying out the recommendations offered. The special educator, by nature of his or her experience and preparation, should be competent in analyzing problems and offering tentative solutions to the identified problem in a way that regular teachers find helpful.

Regular classroom and consultation plus special materials. Services at this level may be essentially the same as those at the previous level except that specific materials may be recommended and tried. For example, the regular classroom teacher and special educator may agree on an approach that involves special resource materials. For instance, enlarged materials may be recommended for a partially seeing student or high-interest–low-vocabulary reading materials may be recommended for a student experiencing difficulty with the regular materials. It is possible in this instance that the special educator may provide the needed materials on a trial basis.

Regular classroom and itinerant teacher services. When served by an itinerant teacher, the student is enrolled in his neighborhood school, but he and his teachers receive direct assistance from special education personnel. The itinerant teacher plan with which most educators are familiar is that followed by public school speech specialists. This plan has also been used quite extensively by teachers of the visually impaired and hearing impaired in districts where there is only a limited number of these students.

Although there are variations in the manner in which this plan is implemented, the itinerant or traveling teacher will generally work with the students on a regularly scheduled basis (two or three times a week) or whenever necessary, depending on the student's needs at that particular time. The itinerant teacher will provide instruction in a designated area outside of the classroom or may meet with the student in his classroom. The itinerant teacher may also assume a helping or assisting teacher role by working with a small group of students who are in need of the same remedial work as the handicapped child.

In sparsely populated areas of the country, where schools tend to be quite small in total enrollment, it may be difficult to justify a full-time resource room program at one school, and because of long distances between schools it is equally difficult to justify busing students into a specific school so as to enlarge the population of students requiring special services. In this instance the resource/itinerant teacher plan would be the most appropriate approach.

As mentioned previously, this plan seems to be a viable service delivery system for some students with low-incidence handicaps such as visual impairment, hearing impairment, and crippling conditions or health impairments. The itinerant teacher plan does not seem to be as practical as the resource room plan (see following section) for students with learning disabilities, behavior problems, or limited intellectual ability because it does not provide intensive services on a daily basis.

Regular classroom and resource room. In this plan the student is enrolled in a regular classroom but receives supplemental or remedial instruction in a resource room. The resource room plan differs from the itinerant teacher plan in that the student is provided more specific assistance on a regularly scheduled basis (probably daily) from the resource teacher, and he has a specific room in which he receives this assistance. The way in which resource programs operate varies quite extensively. In some instances the resource teacher may serve the student on a temporary basis while completing assessment techniques and planning instructional strategies that may be carried out in the student's regular classroom. In this situation the student may go to the resource room for a brief period of time each day until assessment procedures have been completed and a program plan has been implemented. In most school systems, however, a placement or program planning committee will have reviewed a variety of information about any student referred for possible assistance in the resource room, and programming will be initiated only as this committee has indicated its feasibility (for the student) and its consistency with local school district policy. In all cases the parents must have been involved in such placement-planning committee deliberations and must have given express permission for resource room intervention.

The resource room teacher should have the time, the materials, and the specific training needed to find more effective ways to teach students with special needs. Her function becomes a dual one: to initiate alternative strategies and help the student find success in the resource room and to provide suggestions to the regular classroom teacher that may increase the odds that the student will find success in that setting.

Often the resource room teacher will provide valuable unofficial assistance to various teachers, sometimes in terms of general instructional ideas, but more often in relation to a specific student. This is one of the more highly effective functions of the resource room teacher, although in some states it must be done unofficially because state reimbursement guidelines restrict the number of students who may be served.

In recent years some resource teachers have been providing their services in regular classrooms rather than "pulling out" students. By assisting the student in the regular classroom, it is assumed that there will be greater transfer and maintenance than if programming is provided only in a special setting.

Students often perform in a very different way or at a different level in their regular classroom as compared to a small group situation in the resource room. By working with the students in their regular classroom, the regular teacher may gain greater insight into their needs. In addition, the regular classroom teacher and the resource teacher may be able to share ideas and materials and establish a stronger working relationship, a relationship that is accepting of individual teaching strategies, strengths, and weaknesses. One of the greatest gains in placing handicapped students in regular classrooms is that general and special educators may share their unique skills and competencies rather than working in isolation, a practice that occurred for many years. Although this in-classroom service is presently being employed on a limited basis, it should be given serious consideration if the nature of the problem is not so significant that it calls for very intensive work in the resource room.

Regular class and special class (cooperative plan). This plan is very similar to resource programs except that the student is actually enrolled in a special class but continues to attend a regular classroom for part of the school day. The basic difference between this and the resource room plan is that in the cooperative plan the student's homeroom is the special class. In the resource room plan, the student's homeroom is the regular classroom. The amount of time spent in the regular classroom would depend on his ability to profit from regular class instruction. This plan has been popular in past years; however, there is a definite movement toward resource rooms. Under the cooperative plan, both the regular teacher and the special education teacher have basic instructional responsibilities for these students. It is necessary to establish close lines of communication to ensure maximum carryover from one situation to the other.

Special class in regular school. Under this plan, the student receives his academic instruction from a special education teacher but may share luncheon facilities and attend school-wide activities such as assemblies, concerts, clubs, and athletic events with regular classroom students. In a few instances students may attend such classes as industrial arts, physical education, home economics, and music.

In the past, students classified as educable mentally retarded or educable mentally handicapped have often been served on this basis. There has been a definite move away from such programming except for the more seriously involved or multihandicapped. This type of service delivery has been seriously criticized because it has served to segregate these students.

Special class in separate day school. The special day school plan is generally designed for students who are very severely disabled or multihandicapped and need comprehensive special education services for their entire school day. Many of the students served in this plan would have been placed in a residential setting in years past, and would have had little or no contact with their family or community. The special day school permits a return to home and family at the close of each school day, and so moves the student in the direction of the least restrictive environment.

Often the special day school will offer all the needed services for these students, such as physical and occupational therapy, counseling, special vocational workshops, and the necessary adapted equipment. Although this type of service delivery has been criticized because of the degree of segregation it involves, there remains a need for such services for some students. A variation of this plan that meets some of the criticism just mentioned is a specially designed wing attached to a regular elementary or secondary school building.

Hospital and homebound service. Students with chronic conditions requiring long-term treatment in a hospital or in their homes receive special instruction from homebound-itinerant special education personnel. The nature of the educational program is dependent on the student's ability, level of achievement, prognosis of the condition, and likelihood of the student returning to school. Some students who are hospitalized or homebound because of a short-term illness may also be served on this basis. In this instance, the instruction would be closely related to the programming in his regular classroom and would be planned in conjunction with teachers of the classes to which he will return. In situations in which the student requires long-term care, a two-way communication system between the student's home and regular classroom may be set up. This system may employ a telephone or a videophone to reduce the isolation of being at home or in a hospital. This two-way telephone or videophone system provides an opportunity for full-time educational programming and maximum interaction with other students.

Residential or boarding school. Residential and boarding schools are the oldest type of educational delivery system. Historically, these schools were established for students who were visually impaired, hearing impaired, emotionally disturbed, or mentally retarded because local school districts did not offer the needed services. In these programs students may attend only during the nine-month school year or on a year-round basis, depending on the extent of the handicap. Because of the trend toward placing handicapped students in the least restrictive setting, these programs now tend to serve the more seriously involved and multihandicapped. In addition to educational programming, they can also provide twenty-four–hour-a-day comprehensive services required by many of these students.

Placement variables

When determining the least restrictive educational placement for a particular student, there are a number of variables that must be considered. In general, these variables fall into three categories: student, teacher, and administration. The following variables, although not inclusive, would be considered by professionals concerned with placement decisions for a particular student.

I. Student
   A. Chronological age
   B. Type and degree of impairment or disability
   C. Age at onset (birth or acquired)
   D. Level of achievement
   E. Measured intellectual ability
   F. Social maturity
   G. Presence of multiple handicapping conditions (thus the need for related, noneducational services)
   H. Ambulation or mobility (particularly important when considering crippled and other health impaired and visually impaired)
   I. Success of past and present placement
   J. Speech and language ability
   K. Wishes of student and student's parents

SPECIAL NOTE: The role of parents has changed significantly during the past several years. Before the passage of PL 94-142 parents were primarily passive consumers of service with limited input in the process. They were occasionally involved in program and placement decisions, but generally the nature of their involvement was as receivers of information from professionals, that is, "your child will be served here or there." Today, as a result of federal legislation that was a direct result of parental demands and litigation, they have become integral and active participants in educational decision making and in monitoring their child's acquisition of essential skills. This is evidenced not only by mandatory participation in due process procedures but also by parental involvement in the development of the student's IEP, discussed on p. 22 of this chapter.

II. Teacher

After preliminary placement determinations based on specific student characteristics have been made, the next step is to consider existing programs and services relative to the apparent needs of the student. In most cases, some variation of existing programs will be effective. Where this is not the case, the possibility of initiating new programs or of obtaining services by contract or by some type of tuition arrangement with another school district must be considered. There is little question but that the teacher(s) who actually contact the student will have a major influence on the students' success in the regular classroom. Some teachers readily accept the challenge of serving a handicapped student in their classroom whereas others have considerable difficulty in making the adjustments necessary to be effective with these students. Among the most important variables are the following:
   A. Professional preparation or in-service education concerning handicapped students (not a prerequisite but highly desirable)
   B. Previous experience with handicapped students (not a prerequisite but highly desirable)
   C. Willingness to work cooperatively with resource personnel and parents (resource personnel must be readily available)
   D. Flexibility with respect to scheduling, teaching assignments, number of students, and classroom structure
   E. Ability to assess individual learning needs, set goals and objectives, plan and implement teaching strategies, and evaluate student progress
   F. Acceptance of the basic premise that *all* students have the right to the most appropriate education in the least restrictive environment

III. Administration

A highly important variable is the degree of administrative commitment to serve all students, regardless of learning abilities or disabilities. The administrative staff, beginning with the superintendent through the building principal, must have a real commitment to developing the most appropriate, least restrictive alternatives. There are some indications that a very high correlation exists between administrative commitment to the concept of serving handicapped students in regular classrooms and the attitudes of teachers and students. In other words, if the principal is sincerely interested in serving *all* students, this has a very positive influence on the teacher's attitude toward these students. If, however, the principal's attitude toward handicapped students is essentially negative, this attitude is often exhibited by the teachers. The commitment must go beyond a desire to merely comply with federal or state regulations and must recognize the inherent abilities and potential of all students.

In the next few paragraphs we have provided three hypothetical cases illustrating the interaction of the preceding variables. We have also established tentative recommendations concerning placement based on these variables. Actual placement decisions in real cases would likely have considerably more information than provided here, but we believe these cases serve as illustrations of the use of significant variables in the placement decision.

Minicase A. Jerry is a 9-year-old totally, congenitally blind student who is achieving at the third-grade level. His measured intellectual ability is within the normal range. He relates quite well with his peers and is quite mature socially. He has no multiple handicapping conditions, and his orientation and mobility (travel) skills are adequate for his age. He has attended regular classrooms and received assistance from a resource teacher during his entire school career. He and his parents prefer that he be maintained in regular classrooms.

Where and how would this student be most effectively served at this time in his educational program, assuming that his district has available all the services listed in Table 3?

It is our opinion that Jerry would be most effectively served in a regular classroom coupled with concrete assistance from a resource teacher in a resource room. However, as he acquires greater skill in the use of special adaptive equipment, special reading and writing devices, and braille reading, consideration should be given to itinerant services. Naturally, any special preparation or previous experience of his regular classroom teacher, although not a prerequisite, would facilitate his movement to itinerant services.

Minicase B. John, 9 years old, is having difficulty both academically and behaviorally in his third-grade classroom. His reading achievement is middle first grade, and his math scores indicate first-grade level achievement. He acts out frequently during class time and gets into fights with his classmates. An individually administered test of intelligence places him in the bright-normal range of intellectual ability. He has had extensive medical examinations, and there is no indication of any physical or mental difficulty.

His achievement and behavior during kindergarten and first grade were slightly below average but within the normal range. He began to fall farther and farther behind during second grade.

The parents blame his difficulty on his past teachers and feel strongly that he should remain with his peers rather than be placed in a special class for children with behavior and learning disorders.

Where would John be most effectively served, assuming a full continuum of services?

It is our recommendation that John remain in his regular classroom and also be served in a resource room by a resource teacher for at least an hour to an hour and a half each day. Remedial efforts by the special education resource teacher should be directed at reading and math. As John acquires skills and desirable behaviors the amount of time spent in the resource room would be decreased, and hopefully he would be returned to full-time regular classroom placement. In addition, the resource teacher should work with the regular classroom teacher to provide techniques that will serve to reduce classroom behavioral problems. As the academic performance improves, behavior problems will likely improve also, but in the meantime the regular classroom teacher needs help. The final goal is assistance that will permit John to be successful in the regular classroom.

Minicase C. Karen is a 12-year-old moderately mentally retarded child. Her achievement level is at approximately the first-grade level. Her IQ has been variously indicated to be 40, 44, and 46. Although she is socially immature, she is outgoing and friendly and enjoys being with almost anyone. In addition to her retarded mental development, she has cerebral palsy, a serious speech disorder, and must use a wheelchair to get around. She attended a special school for retarded cerebral palsied students for several years. Her parents would like her to attend a school closer to their home.

Where would this student be most effectively served, assuming that a full continuum of services is available?

The most effective program for Karen at this time probably would be a special class for trainable retarded students. Ideally, this classroom should be located in a regular school building so that Karen may have some interaction with nonhandicapped students.

We recognize that some students who are functioning at a level similar to Karen's are being served in regular classrooms for part of their school day; however, it is believed that every effort must be made to maximize all educational efforts and that special educators are best prepared to provide the most effective program for a student with Karen's degree of mental retardation and related handicaps in speech and mobility.

TOWARD LEAST RESTRICTIVE ALTERNATIVES

In the following sections of this chapter we will briefly discuss what we believe to be the reasons why many handicapped students can and should be served in the least restrictive setting—the regular classroom.

Positive changes in regular classrooms

There have been many significant changes during the past several years that allow greater participation by handicapped students. The use of individual behavioral objectives, the increasing popularity of and knowledge about diagnostic-prescriptive teaching, and greater cooperation between general and special education are a few of the positive changes that have occurred. Open classrooms are gaining popularity throughout the United States, and it is interesting to note that many instructional practices and strategies being promoted today are similar to those used in better special education programs. These include (1) learning centers, (2) programmed and self-instructional materials, (3) application of the principle that each student should move at his own learning rate, (4) use of peer teachers and tutors, (5) highly motivating instructional materials such as talking calculators, and (6) continuous evaluation as part of a diagnostic-prescriptive teaching model. It has finally been recognized that there are considerable differences between students who are placed in a common room under the assumption that the group is, in fact, homogeneous. Teachers have recognized that heterogeneity is inevitable, that all students are different, and that each must be provided with the most appropriate instructional program to accommodate their unique learning styles, abilities, disabilities, and interests. Teachers are finding that cooperative learning experiences between students promote greater achievement, higher self-esteem, greater social skills, and more social acceptance and friendship between all students, including those who are handicapped. Several years ago, when educational programs offered a "lock-step" approach, handicapped students would have failed, but today it is possible that many of these students can achieve the needed success in regular classrooms.

Advantages to nonhandicapped students. Often, regular classroom teachers are concerned that a handicapped child enrolled in their classroom may detract from the education of the nonhandicapped students. On the contrary, there are indications that the non-handicapped students learn as much if not more when a handicapped child is in their classroom. As indicated previously, the use of peer teachers and tutors has proved to be viable and effective. Each student has a great deal to offer others and by teaching students to teach others, all will be advantaged. Another obvious advantage of educating handicapped students in regular classrooms is that students need to be exposed to differences in individuals, not for purposes of "feeling sorry for" another individual but to gain respect for and appreciation of human differences while recognizing inherent similarities. Students must be exposed to racial, ethnic, intellectual, and psychological differences if they are to reach their full personal potentials.

It is our opinion that perhaps today's adults were "disadvantaged" to some extent because when they were in school they did not have the opportunity to know classmates who were handicapped or different. This disadvantagedness may be observed in many ways. For example, why are there so many prevalent misconceptions about disabled individuals expressed by adults today? Could it be that they had limited opportunities to learn about differences in individuals? Is it because they never sat next to a braille-reading classmate or a classmate in a wheelchair? Are the less-than-desirable attitudes often reflected by today's society an indication of our lack of experience with different persons? We owe nonhandicapped students the opportunity to work and play with individuals who are different if we are to provide them with the best possible education—an education that must include more than purely academic skills.

Advantages to teachers. It has been encouraging to observe changes in teacher preparation and competency during the past several years. There is little question that today's teachers are the best prepared and, in general, the most competent ever.

The trend to include as a part of every teacher's professional preparation specific coursework and/or skills and competencies to work with handicapped students will greatly increase their ability to work with handicapped students and special educators. After many years of isolation, general and special educators are beginning to assume cooperative teaching roles. Each discipline has unique skills and competencies that must be shared, and both are beginning to look for insight and specific suggestions on how to best meet the needs of all students. Regular classroom teachers now have the opportunity to provide cooperative learning experiences for themselves and their students, including those who present a special challenge.

Teachers must have challenges to grow personally and professionally. A handicapped child presents one such challenge. We have had considerable experience with regular classroom teachers who express concern when they are informed that they will have a handicapped student in their classroom. Certainly, this situation may present a serious threat to a teacher who has not had previous experience or preparation in how to work with such students. However, it has been very encouraging to observe these same teachers grow personally and professionally and at the end of the year indicate that it was one of the most exciting and challenging experiences of their teaching career. Often such teachers ask if they may have another handicapped student the following year. What initially may be seen as a serious threat often turns into a very positive growth experience. Teachers benefit from such growth experiences, and they need to work with students who are different. Very often the methods and instructional techniques used with a handicapped student may be used with other students. The challenge of working with students of different abilities—intellectual, physical, or both—may keep teachers from "teaching at" students. With only minimal help they may learn to serve as a facilitator who will provide each student with the opportunity to reach his fullest potential.

Advantages to handicapped students. In the preceding paragraphs we have reviewed potential advantages of placement of the handicapped in the regular classroom. We must also be certain that there are actual advantages for the handicapped student.

Certain questions remain as to when, how, and under what conditions we should integrate the moderately and severely handicapped with nonhandicapped students. PL 94-142 requres that we have special classes and even residential settings as available alternatives, and we may conclude that some students require such separate settings. For the most part, we may assume that it will be the severely handicapped, and in some cases the moderately handicapped, who will require more separate settings. The mildly handicapped, when appropriate assistance is provided to the regular classroom teacher, are another matter. There are certain questions that may assist us in our consideration of advantages for these students. Two such questions follow: (1) Does it seem reasonable to educate the mildly handicapped in a physically isolated setting during their school career and then, on completion of their education, ask them to compete in a nonhandicapped society? (2) Would we ask an individual learning to drive an automobile to complete his driver training without actually driving on the streets with other cars?

If our purpose is to provide handicapped students with the opportunity to reach their maximum potential and to become contributing members of society, we must provide them with an *equal* educational opportunity, an opportunity to be educated with their nonhandicapped peers in the least restrictive educational environment. When this is at all possible, it is the best way to prepare them to live as successful adults in an integrated society.

SUMMARY

Education of the handicapped within the regular classroom is the obvious trend of the day. Past experience with other procedures for serving the handicapped leads us to be cautious about predicting practices for the next forty to fifty years, but federal legislation would seem to ensure the principle of education in the least restrictive environment for at least a decade or two. PL 94-142 is now in force, and all but one or two states have indicated their intention to comply with its requirements. In a number of states, the state legislature has directed that all regular classroom teachers receive some degree of formal training that will prepare them to educate handicapped students in the regular classroom with greater skill and effectiveness.

Some disagreement remains as to how the principle of the least restrictive environment shuld be implemented, but we feel certain that the intent of the law is that responsibility for the handicapped should be shared by general and special education personnel. When regular classroom teachers and special education personnel share their unique skills, competencies, and insights, it is not only an advantage to all students but a very positive growth experience for teachers—an experience they must have if they are to continue to grow personally and professionally.

In this chapter we have outlined a plan for providing services to handicapped students that requires the use of a "continuum of alternative educational provisions." We have described how this concept should be applied and have emphasized the need for *individual* planning. We have reviewed the requirements for an individualized educational program (IEP) for each handicapped student, outlined a number of common fallacies regarding the least restrictive environment, and presented what we believe to be the facts with respect to these misconceptions. The principle of the least restrictive environment, applied through the provision of an individualized educational program and implemented through serving students in the appropriate place(s) along the continuum of alternative educational provisions, is the basic rationale of this text. All of the chapters that follow are dedicated to a further discussion of how the regular classroom teacher may carry out her role in this total process.

REFERENCES AND SUGGESTED READINGS

Adamson, G., & Van Etten, G. Zero reject model revisited: a workable altenative. *Exceptional Children,* 1972, *38,* 735-738.

Alexander, M. Let me learn with the other kids. *Learning,* March 1973, *1,* 18-21.

Beery, K. *Models for mainstreaming.* San Rafael, Calif.: Dimensions Publishing Co., 1972.

Birch, J. W. *Mainstreaming: educable mentally retarded children in regular classes.* Leadership Training Institute/Special Education, University of Minnesota, 1974.

Brenton, M. Mainstreaming the handicapped. *Today's Education,* March-April 1974, *63*(2), 20-25.

Chaffin, J. D. Will the real "mainstreaming" program please stand up! (or . . . should Dunn have done it?). *Focus on Exceptional Children,* October 1974, *6,* 1-18.

Christopherson, J. The special child in the "regular" preschool: some administrative notes. *Childhood Education,* December 1972, *49*(3), 138-140.

Closer Look. Editorial statement on the "least restrictive alternative setting." Washington, D.C.: Parents Campaign for Handicapped Children and Youth, December 1978, 5.

Cole, R., & Dunn, R. A new lease on life for education of the handicapped; Ohio copes with 94-142. *Phi Delta Kappan,* September 1977, *59*(1), 3-6.

Deno, E. N. (Ed.). *Instructional alternatives for exceptional children.* Reston, Va.: Council for Exceptional Children, 1973.

Deno, E. N. Special education as developmental capital. *Exceptional Children,* 1970, *37,* 229-237.

Dunn, L. M. *Exceptional children in the schools: special education in transition.* New York: Holt, Rinehart & Winston, Inc., 1973.

Gallagher, J. J. The special education contract for mildly handicapped children. *Exceptional Children,* 1972, *38,* 527-535.

Grosenick, J. K. Integration of exceptional children into regular classes: research and procedure. *Focus on Exceptional Children,* October 1971, *5,* 1-8.

Hayes, J., & Higgins, S. Issues regarding the IEP: teachers on the front line. *Exceptional Children,* January 1978, *44*(4), 267-272.

Hendrickson, B. Mainstreaming: teachers make mainstreaming work. *Learning,* October 1978, *7*(2), 104-110.

Kavanagh, E. A classroom teacher looks at mainstreaming. *The Elementary School Journal,* March 1977, *77*(4), 318-322.

Klein, J. W. Mainstreaming the preschooler. *Journal of the National Association for the Education of Young Children,* 1975, *30,* 317-326.

Kolstoe, O. P. Programs for the mildly retarded: a reply to the critics. *Exceptional Children,* 1972, *39,* 51-56.

Kreinberg, N., & Chou, S. (Eds.). *Configurations of change: the integration of mildly handicapped chil-*

dren into the regular classroom. Eugene, Ore.: Far West Laboratory for Educational Research and Development, 1973.

Lilly, S. A training based model for special education. *Exceptional Children,* 1971, *37,* 745-749.

Martin, D. L. Are our public schools really ignoring the very children who need the schools most? *The American School Board Journal,* 1975, *162,* 52-54.

Martin, E. W. Some thoughts on mainstreaming. *Exceptional Children,* November 1974, *41,* 150-153.

Molloy, L. The handicapped child in the everyday classroom. *Phi Delta Kappan,* January 1975, *56*(5), 337-340.

NEA Resolution 77-33, Education for all handicapped children. Adopted 1977 by the National Education Association.

NEA Resolution 78-37, Education for all handicapped children. Adopted 1978 by the National Education Association.

Payne, R., & Murray, C. Principals' attitudes toward integration of the handicapped. *Exceptional Children,* 1974, *41,* 132-135.

Ryor, J. Integrating the handicapped. *Today's Education.* Washington, D.C.: National Education Association. September-October, 1977, *66*(3), 24.

Russo, J. R. Mainstreaming handicapped students: are your facilities suitable? *American School and University,* October 1974, *47,* 25-32.

Sapon-Shevin, M. Another look at mainstreaming: exceptionality, normality, and the nature of difference. *Phi Delta Kappan,* October 1978, *60*(2), 119-121.

Sarason, S., & Doris J. Mainstreaming dilemmas, oppositions, opportunities. *The Exceptional Parent,* August 1977, *7*(4), 21-24.

Sargent, L. State certification requirements. *Journal of Teacher Education,* November/December 1978, *29*(6), 47.

Theobald, J., & Gickling, E. Mainstreaming: affect or effect. *The Journal of Special Education,* Fall 1975, *9*(3), 317-328.

Turnbull, H. The past and future impact of court decisions in special education. *Phi Delta Kappan,* April 1978, *59*(8), 523-526.

Van Etten, G., & Adamson, G. The fail-save program: A special education continuum. In E. N. Deno (Ed.), *Instructional Alternatives for Exceptional Children.* Reston, Va.: Council for Exceptional Children, 1973, 156-165.

Weininger, O. Integrate or isolate: a perspective on the whole child. *Education,* November/December 1973, *94,* 139-146.

Weintraub, F. J. Editorial comment in Abeson, A., & Zettel, J. The end of the quiet revolution: the education for all handicapped children act of 1975. *Exceptional Children,* *44*(2), October 1977, 114.

Weintraub, F. J., & Abeson, A. New education policies for the handicapped. *The Education Digest,* September 1974, *40*(1), 13-16.

Weintraub, F., & Abeson, A. New education policies for the handicapped: the quiet revolution. *Phi Delta Kappan,* April 1974, *55*(8), 526-529.

3 STRATEGIES AND ALTERNATIVES FOR EDUCATING THE HEARING IMPAIRED

Ronald Stewart

Although special educators have been serving hearing impaired students for many years, such students have not been educated within the regular classroom setting on a nationwide basis until the past ten to fifteen years. Certain predictable problems may result from impaired hearing, and in order to work successfully with hearing impaired students, regular classroom teachers should have a basic understanding of the nature of hearing impairment and its relationship to learning. Such understanding may perhaps be best gained by reviewing the role of hearing, commencing at birth.

Listening is an important learning tool that is used from the time a child is born. An infant learns to discriminate between loud and soft, high and low, and disturbing and pleasant sounds. He also learns to determine the direction, distance, and meaning of sounds. He analyzes the human voice and differentiates his babbling and crying from the sounds of others. Sometime between the ages of 12 and 24 months, as a result of his previous language experiences, he begins to learn to speak and develop his own language. It is obvious that if the child has a hearing impairment his speech and language development will be delayed. Underdeveloped speech and language is the greatest limitation imposed by a hearing impairment. The student's delayed speech and language will influence his ability to develop communication skills such as reading, writing, listening, and speaking. As a result, these skills will develop at a slower rate than those of the normally hearing child (see p. 119). The hearing impaired student will have the most difficulty in the language arts areas, such as reading, English, spelling, and writing, because of their relationship to speech and language development. The extent of difficulty will depend on the student's language level or command of the language, degree of hearing loss, and age at onset.

The student is not necessarily conceptually handicapped; however, he may have difficulty learning the label or language used to describe the concept. For example, the concept of buoyancy may be understood by the student but he may have difficulty in writing, saying, or spelling the word *buoyancy*. He may have much less difficulty with science, math, or other nonlanguage arts programs. Math, with the exception of story problems, is conceptual in nature. Science may also be thought of as conceptual rather than primarily related to the language arts. In contrast, the reading process involves associating meaning with sounds and written symbols. A hearing impairment seriously limits the association between sounds and written symbols; therefore, reading may be an area of considerable difficulty for these students, particularly for the young child who is in the process of acquiring reading skills. He *can* learn to read; however, a very well-planned program must be offered—a program that reflects close cooperation between the regular teacher and the special education resource/itinerant teacher. Although language development is very important to success in school, the hearing impaired student is able to learn and profit from instruction in the regular classroom.

In addition to academic difficulties that may result from a hearing loss, two other limitations may be imposed by impaired hearing. The first limitation may be characterized by inability to hear and appreciate good music. Some such limitations cannot be overcome, but must be compensated for in a manner that is acceptable to the individual. A second limitation is that which may be imposed by society. Such societal limitations, characterized by negative or demeaning interactions with others, such as parents, teachers, siblings, and friends, may lead to self-imposed social limitations and restrictions. Teachers may play an important role in reducing this latter type of limitation.

In instances where a hearing impairment has been identified, there are a number of methods and techniques the regular classroom teacher can use that may be beneficial to the hearing impaired student. In order to better understand these methods and techniques, we will also consider various other aspects of programs for the hearing impaired as they are administered in the public schools. In this chapter we will review the following considerations:

1. Nature of hearing impairment
2. Methods of identifying a student with a hearing impairment
3. Referral procedures
4. Appropriate classroom modifications and adaptations for the hearing impaired student in the regular classroom
5. Role and responsibility of special education resource/itinerant personnel

NATURE OF HEARING IMPAIRMENT
Types of hearing impairment

There are two major types of hearing impairment, and different degrees of hearing loss are associated with each of these two types. One type of hearing impairment affects the loudness or intensity with which a person hears speech. This type of loss is known as a *conductive* hearing loss and is caused by interference with the transmission of sound from the outer to the inner ear. The other type affects the frequency, intelligibility, or clarity of the sounds the person hears. A *sensorineural* loss is associated with damage to the sensory end-organ or a dysfunction of the auditory nerve.

An example that roughly illustrates the two types of hearing loss and with which most people are familiar is the radio. One dial on the radio controls the volume or loudness of the sounds. By turning the volume down, we can simulate what it is like to have a hearing loss affecting the loudness with which we hear sounds. If we can hear the sounds, we can understand them; they are not distorted.

The tuning dial, which controls the frequency of signals, may be used to illustrate the second type of hearing loss. If the radio is not tuned in correctly, the sounds are not clear and are difficult to understand. Often words are not complete. A sentence such as "He sat at his desk at recess" may sound like "e a a iz de."

Measurement of hearing

Hearing *acuity* (sharpness or acuteness of sensory discrimination) is measured by an instrument known as a *pure tone audiometer*. An audiometer produces sounds at varying intensities (loudness) and frequencies (pitch). An *audiologist*, when administering an audiometric examination, systematically presents a series of carefully calibrated tones that vary in loudness and pitch. The results are charted on a graph called an *audiogram*, which provides an indication of the person's ability to hear each tone at each of the presented frequencies. The *audiometric evaluation* assists in determining the extent and type of hearing loss so that the proper remedial or medical steps may be taken.

The unit of measurement used to express the intensity of sound is the *decibel* (dB), and the frequency is expressed in *hertz* (Hz). If an individual has a hearing loss, it is indicated in decibels; the more significant the loss, the larger the number value. For example, a 60 dB loss is a greater loss than a 25 dB loss. In addition to information concerning the extent of the loss in decibels, it may be helpful to have information concerning the frequency at which the loss occurs. The Fig. 5 audiogram on p. 45 indicates a severe hearing loss of an 11-year-old student.

To better understand the nature of hearing loss, we can consider the following common environmental sounds expressed in intensity (decibels):

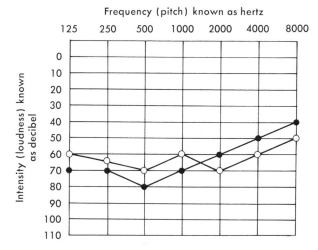

AUDIOGRAM

Frequency (pitch) known as hertz

Decibels	Sounds
140	Threshold of pain
120	Threshold of feeling
100	Riveting machine at thirty feet
80	Loud radio or phonograph music in a home
60	Average restaurant sounds or normal conversation
40	Outdoor minimum in a city
20	Very quiet conversation
0	Threshold of hearing

Severity of hearing impairment

Often, attempts to systemically classify hearing acuity in relation to actual hearing efficiency or functional ability do not account for a number of outside factors such as motivation, intelligence, social maturity, and family background. These variables may have a definite influence on the individual's functional ability. Two individuals with the same measured hearing loss will not necessarily have the same type and/or degree of difficulty in academic or social settings.

Although it is difficult to classify degrees of hearing impairment on the basis of severity, it is necessary to have a classification system

tem that provides some insight into the degree of loss and the resulting implications. The following system is quite commonly used by educators:

Mild	27 to 40 dB
Moderate	41 to 55 dB
Moderately severe	56 to 70 dB
Severe	71 to 90 dB
Profound	91+ dB

Mild: 27 to 40 dB. A person who has a hearing loss between 27 and 40 dB has a mild hearing loss and is likely to have difficulty with faint or distant speech. Students with mild losses may need favorable seating; may benefit from speechreading instruction, vocabulary, language instruction, or a combination of these; and may need speech therapy.

Moderate: 41 to 55 dB. A hearing loss in the 41 to 55 dB range is usually classified as a moderate loss. This individual can understand conversational speech at a distance of three to five feet. This student will probably need a hearing aid, auditory training, speechreading, favorable seating, speech conversation, and speech therapy. The extent of services provided by the resource/itinerant specialist may vary considerably, depending on the student's actual achievement in the regular classroom.

Moderately severe: 56 to 70 dB. The individual with a moderately severe hearing impairment has a hearing loss in the 56 to 70 dB range. For the student with a moderately severe loss, conversation must be loud to be understood. His speech will probably be defective, and he may have a limited vocabulary. This student will have difficulty in group and classroom discussion, can use all the services usually provided students with mild and moderate losses, and, in addition, will require specific assistance from the resource/itinerant teacher in the language arts areas.

Severe: 71 to 90 dB. A person who has a hearing loss between 71 and 90 dB has a severe loss and may not be able to hear a loud voice beyond a distance of one or two feet. He may be able to distinguish some environmental sounds and will have difficulty with consonant sounds but not necessarily vowels. He will need all the services required by hearing impaired students with less severe losses and many of the techniques used with deaf students.

Profound: 91 + dB. Individuals with a hearing loss of more than 91 dB have a profound impairment. Although this individual may be able to hear some loud sounds, he probably will not rely on hearing as the primary learning channel. This student will likely need all the previously mentioned services and possibly more intensive services from the resource/itinerant teacher of the hearing impaired. The profoundly hearing impaired student will require special assistance with emphasis on speech, auditory training, and language; however, he may be able to attend regular classes on a part-time basis or attend classes that do not require language skills.

• • •

Considerable caution must be exercised in using this classification system, because students with nearly identical losses may function differently. In addition to using caution with classification systems, educators must also exercise care in predetermining the extent of special education services needed in relation to the degree of loss. Experts in this field do not agree on the relative importance of various degrees of loss. In any individual case, a variety of other information must be carefully considered. The characteristics of need may be defective speech, with substitutions, omissions, or distortions; reading problems; immature language patterns; a lower level of abstraction; and perhaps lower interpersonal relationships (Northcott, 1972). Some students with severe losses may be readily integrated into regular classrooms, whereas a student with a less severe, or moderate, loss may need extensive special education services for the majority of his school day.

IDENTIFICATION OF STUDENTS WITH IMPAIRED HEARING

Although not always recognized by the regular classroom teacher, a particular student's learning or behavior problems might result from a hearing loss. The teacher could misjudge the student as being mentally retarded, emotionally disturbed, or having some type of specific learning disability. In other instances the teacher *may* feel the student's problems are caused by some failure in her methods of teaching. Until the teacher recognizes that the student's problem may be the result of a hearing loss, she could waste a great deal of time on fruitless remedial measures. Therefore, it is very important for the regular classroom teacher to be aware of some common behaviors that indicate a hearing loss. The following are the most common behaviors and medical symptoms that *may* indicate a hearing loss.

Behavioral indications

Lack of attention. One such behavior is an apparent lack of attention. If the student does not pay attention, it is possible that he cannot hear what is being said. Another possibility may be that the student hears sounds but they are so distorted that it is difficult for him to understand. Consequently, he tunes them out or does not make the effort to attend to them.

Difficulty in following directions. An unusual amount of difficulty in following oral directions is another possible indicator of hearing impairment. The student who has little difficulty with written directions and considerable difficulty with oral directions may have a hearing loss. Also, if a student often loses his place in oral reading assignments, it could be because he has difficulty hearing what the others are reading.

Turning or cocking of head. A behavior that may indicate the student has a hearing loss is an unusual amount of cocking the head to one side. The student may need to turn one ear toward the speaker to hear more adequately. In addition, the student with a hearing loss may make frequent requests for repetitions.

Acting out, stubborn, shy, or withdrawn. Have you ever tried to listen to a speaker who was talking so softly you had difficulty hearing him? You could see his lips move but were unable to hear what was being said. Remembering that frustrating experience may help the teacher understand why a student with a hearing loss may be stubborn, disobedient, shy, or withdrawn. If the student is unable to hear, personality and behavior problems may arise. He may compensate for his inability to hear by acting out in the classroom. Other hearing impaired students may compensate by withdrawing, acting stubborn, or being shy.

Small-group achievement best. If the student seems to do his best work in small groups or in a relatively quiet working area, this may be an indication of a hearing loss. More success with tasks assigned by the teacher at a relatively close distance or in an uncluttered auditory area (as compared with tasks assigned at a distance or in a noisy situation) may also be an indication.

Disparity between expected and actual achievement. A possible indication of a hearing loss is a disparity between expected and actual achievement. Obviously, there may be many reasons for a student not achieving in a manner consistent with his ability, but the teacher should be aware that one of the reasons may be a hearing loss.

Reluctance to participate in oral activities. A less extreme behavior sometimes characteristic of the hearing impaired student may be a reluctance to participate in oral activities. Another possible identifying characteristic of the student with a hearing loss is an apparent lack of a sense of humor. The student who often does not laugh at a joke may not be hearing the joke.

Dependence on classmates for instructions. Another indication of which the teacher should be aware is the student who watches his classmates to see what they are doing before he starts working. He may not have fully heard or understood the directions given and will look for a cue from his classmates or teacher.

Medical indications

So far we have been concerned only with *behavior* that may indicate that a student has a hearing loss. There are also medical indications of a hearing loss that should not be ignored by the teacher. These include frequent earaches, fluid running from the ears, frequent colds or sore throats, and recurring tonsillitis. These physical characteristics must be brought to the attention of the school nurse and the parents, who should be urged to contact their physician.

A SUSPECTED LOSS

If a loss is suspected, the teacher should be certain to list the specific behavior(s) or medical indications that lead her to believe there may be a hearing loss and should immediately refer the student to the school nurse, speech specialist, or audiologist. Any of these professionals will be able to do preliminary screening. If there is an indication from this screening that a student has a hearing impairment, the student should be referred to a physician who specializes in diseases of the ear (otologist).

If the direct services of a school nurse, speech specialist, or audiologist are not available, the student should be referred to the school counselor, principal, or directly to the student's parents. The teacher may have to assume a leadership position in the referral process; she may have to check to be certain that subsequent referrals have been made. Often a referral will be made, but for any of a variety of reasons, no further action is taken. The teacher should make sure that there has been appropriate follow-up.

In a hypothetical case, let us assume the teacher observes some behavior that makes her suspect that a student has a hearing loss. The teacher refers the student to the nurse, speech therapist, or audiologist, who finds that a hearing loss is present. The student is then referred through the parents to an expert for a more extensive examination. The otologist may find an accumulation of wax or some other obstruction in the ears, infected tonsils or adenoids, or some other abnormality that may be medically corrected. In this instance hearing can be restored and the student returned to school without any educational modifications or adaptations. However, many referrals do not result in medical correction, and as a result, a hearing aid may be recommended. Now what happens to the student? Should he be placed in a special class, or can he continue in his regular class? Every effort should be made to keep the student with his peers. Of course, recommendations regarding placement must be very carefully considered during individual staffing for

the student. The following are some advantages for hearing impaired students offered by regular classroom placement:

1. An opportunity to continue relationships with hearing classmates, which will reinforce the feeling that he is more like other students than not like them. He will gain, or maintain, a feeling of belonging.
2. An exposure to a greater variety of language styles.
3. The need to keep his speech and language patterns at a more intelligible level. Often when hearing impaired students are grouped together in the same class, they do not develop or maintain a high level of speech and language. A regular classroom also provides normal, age-appropriate speech, language, and other social models.
4. The need to establish a wider variety of communication techniques. The hearing impaired student may have to modify his communication skills if he is not understood by his classmates. This may necessitate a reexamination of his communication skills.
5. An opportunity for the student to compete academically with hearing classmates. The academic pace is faster, and general achievement level expectations are raised. However, in the interests of professional objectivity, we must note that this may be the major reason why some students *cannot* participate with success in the regular classroom.
6. Regular classroom participation prepares the student to function in a hearing world, and all individuals interacting with the student must constantly remind themselves that the ultimate objective is for each student to function as independently as possible in a hearing society.

Another advantage of regular classroom placement, although not related only to the hearing impaired, is that hearing students have an opportunity to become acquainted with someone who is different. This must be seen very positively, particularly today when many students do not have the opportunity to mix with children of different ethnic backgrounds or races or with students who are disabled. It is our opinion that most individuals benefit from the opportunity to meet and associate with individuals who are different from themselves.

Placement and/or retention of the hearing impaired student in the regular class works very well for some students and is essentially unsuccessful for others. As noted in the preceding paragraphs, we believe that retention in the regular classroom is the best procedure, *if it is effective in meeting prescribed educational goals.* One of the more important factors is the attitude and readiness of the regular classroom teacher; promoting this readiness is the major purpose of this text. However, it must be recognized that a number of interrelated factors are at work when we attempt to plan a program for the hearing impaired. In a comprehensive study of mainstreaming of the hearing impaired, Nix (1976) identified the following guidelines and components for successful mainstreaming placement:

1. Early identification of the hearing loss and enrollment in a family-oriented special education program
2. On diagnosis of impaired hearing, amplification immediately provided
3. Use of hearing aid during all waking hours
4. Minimal disparity between hearing classmates and the hearing impaired students in:
   a. Listening age
   b. Developmental age (social, emotional, and physical)
   c. Language age
   d. Academic skills
   e. Reading achievement level
5. Average or above-average intellectual ability
6. An outgoing personality
7. Expressive and receptive auditory-oral communication skills at a level sufficiently high to anticipate reasonable success in the regular classroom
8. The ability to profit from large group instruction when new material is presented
9. Supportive parents and family
10. A full complement of supportive specialists available to assist the student and his family in areas such as counseling, monitoring the placement, and providing necessary remediation.

SUGGESTIONS FOR THE REGULAR CLASSROOM TEACHER

The student with impaired hearing may be served in the regular classroom with a number of specific modifications and adaptations. These modifications and adaptations are easily made and do not require substantial teacher time or classroom adjustments.

Obtaining complete information about the student

Complete information should be obtained prior to taking a hearing impaired student into the class; be certain that there is sufficient information concerning (1) the nature of the loss, (2) the amount of residual hearing, and (3) the ways in which the student communicates. A few brief private sessions with the student should be arranged so that a comfortable relationship and communication process can be established. Because the speech of a hearing impaired student may be defective, these sessions may familiarize the teacher with the student's unique speech patterns. The teacher may also find it very helpful to discuss the student's speech needs with the speech specialist or special education resource person. Most of this information concerning the student can be obtained from the special education resource personnel in the school or school district.

Using a "listening helper" or "buddy"

The use of a "listening helper" or "buddy" can be of considerable assistance to the hearing impaired student. This peer may sit next to the hearing impaired student to ensure his turning to the correct page or taking notes or for other appropriate assistance in areas such as adjusting to a new class or school or participating in activities such as physical education. The buddy may clarify something the teacher has said by repeating it while facing the hearing impaired student or by writing it down.

At the upper elementary and secondary levels the listening helper or buddy may assist in note taking by simply making a carbon copy of his notes. This allows the hearing impaired student to concentrate fully on what the teacher is saying.

The listening helper or buddy may be rotated weekly or monthly, or a few classmates may volunteer for an extended period of time. Some caution must be exercised so that the helper or buddy provides assistance only when needed; otherwise, the very purpose of the integrated educational experience may be defeated. If the helper provides assistance when it is not necessary, the hearing impaired student may become overly dependent on his classmates—a dependency that must be carefully avoided.

Hearing aid—care and maintenance

The regular classroom teacher should have a basic understanding of the use and limitations of the student's hearing aid. A hearing aid is not a complicated piece of equipment. The aid helps compensate for the hearing loss by amplifying sound. It cannot replace the natural ability of the ear and the student who wears an aid should not be expected to hear normally.

There are several things that can be checked by the regular classroom teacher if the student does not seem to be hearing well because of a malfunction in the hearing aid. Although it is not the primary responsibility of the regular classroom teacher to troubleshoot hearing aid problems, it may be helpful to be aware of a few minor factors that may cause malfunctions so that the resource teacher or the parents may be alerted. The following should be checked:

1. Make sure the battery is not dead.
2. Determine if the battery is installed properly, with the positive and negative terminals in the proper position.
3. Check the cord to see if it is worn or broken or if the receiver is cracked.
4. Be sure the plug-in points are not loose. Check both the hearing aid and the receiver.
5. Check the ear mold to make sure it is not obstructed by wax and that it is inserted properly. An improperly fitted ear mold can cause irritation and feedback (squeaky sounds).
6. Keep a fresh battery at school (changed at least monthly, even though it may not have been used) so the child does not have to go without his hearing aid on the day the battery goes dead. Often the resource/itinerant teacher will have an extra supply of batteries and will assist in determining where other problems might exist.

There are some additional considerations that the regular teacher must be aware of with respect to proper care and maintenance of hearing aids.

1. Do not get the hearing aid wet.
2. Serious damage may result from leaving it in extremely hot or cold places.

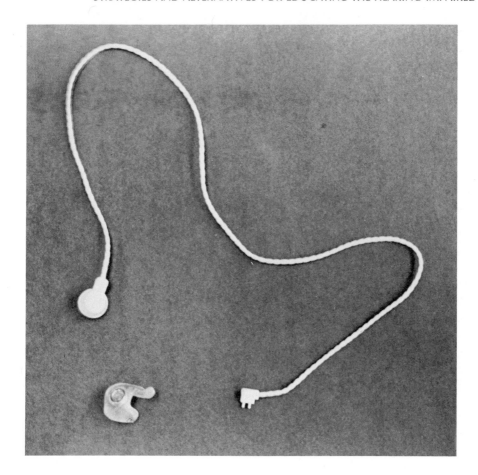

3. Always turn the aid off before removing it from the ear. Removing the aid without turning it off will cause a squeal.

4. Do not allow the student to wear the hearing aid microphone too close to the receiver; if this is done, the aid will make unusual noises. If the student has a unilateral loss (one ear), the hearing aid should be worn on the opposite side of the receiver.

5. Do not take the aid apart and attempt to repair it. This should be done by a hearing aid dealer.

Facilitating speechreading

Although most hearing impaired students have some remaining or residual hearing, special efforts must be made to facilitate speechreading because the student may not hear all the sounds in his environment. The student must learn to closely observe lips, facial gestures, body gestures, and other environmental clues to fully understand what his teacher and classmates are saying. The following factors should be considered by the regular teacher:

1. Allow the student to sit where he can make the most of what he hears and

sees; sometimes a younger child will need guidance in this area. Remember, the hearing impaired student listens with his eyes as well as his ears. The student should be within five to ten feet of the speaker. Do not, however, have him sit so close that he constantly has to look up. To aid the student in becoming a more proficient speechreader, change the seating arrangement from time to time to give him practice in watching different speakers in the classroom from different positions. Seating arrangements may depend on the classroom organization. If the class is small, arranging the desks in a semicircle and seating the hearing impaired student on the end facilitates speechreading. In a lecture situation, placing the student near the front of the room off to one side allows him to readily read the speech of classmates and teacher(s). Seating arrangements must remain flexible to ensure that the student can observe and participate in class activities.

2. Seating should be arranged so that the student does not have to look into a light source. Do not stand in front of windows; this makes speechreading very difficult. Do not stand in a dark area or an area where there may be shadows. Generally, speechreading is easier when the light source is behind the student.

3. Try to face the group when speaking, and when members of the class are speaking, encourage them to face the hearing impaired student. Many of us frequently turn our back to the class and talk when writing on the board. The teacher should stay in one place as much as possible when giving oral examinations or while lecturing, so that when the student looks up the teacher will be in the same general location. Oral examinations requiring a written response may also cause considerable difficulty for the hearing impaired student. The student may be writing a response while the teacher is giving the next item, and the student may miss several items. Overhead projections and transparancies work extremely well for all students. In general, visual aids are effective with the hearing impaired student.

4. Do not exaggerate gestures. Exaggerated gestures may cause considerable confusion. Use gestures, but keep hands and any objects away from the face whenever possible. Beards and mustaches sometimes distract from the lips or make them difficult to see.

5. Provide a good pattern of speech for the student; distinct articulation is more helpful to the hearing impaired student than speaking louder. Speech patterns, however, should not be exaggerated.

6. Ask questions of the student occasionally to make certain he is following the discussion. When presenting a new word or asking a question, repeat it if it is not understood the first time, speaking directly at the student. If he seems to miss the term or request, rephrase what was originally said and ask him a question; for example, "This is a stapler." "How could you use a stapler?" "Who would use a stapler often?"

7. Certain words are not easily understood through speechreading; therefore, encourage the student to ask questions or have statements repeated if he does not understand.

8. When isolated words are presented, such as in spelling, the words should

be used in context. Spelling tests may also be given by providing the contextual words of the sentence on a sheet of paper and replacing the spelling word with a blank space. In this way the student will have the necessary contextual clues. Remember, many words appear alike on the lips and sound alike, for example, beet and bead. Other examples are meal and peal, safe and save, and pie and buy.

9. When presenting new vocabulary words, present the multiple meanings for these words; some words have more than five meanings. This can be very difficult for the hearing impaired student because his vocabulary may not be sufficient to understand the multiple meanings.

10. Chewing movements should be avoided as much as possible. If students are allowed to chew gum, this may make speech reading very difficult, since they may not be able to differentiate between chewing and speech.

11. When referring to an object in the room, it may be beneficial to point to it, walk over to it and touch it, or actually manipulate the object. This may put the object into the context of the discussion and support what is being discussed. When the teacher is speaking directly to the student or calling for the student's attention, it may be helpful to call the student's name or speak directly to him. In nearly all instances, instruction that combines both visual and auditory cues is more effective with the hearing impaired.

Facilitating desirable speech habits

An essential component of educational programming for the hearing impaired student is speech training. The student's ability to

monitor his language may be seriously limited by his hearing impairment, thereby limiting his expressive language abilities.

Often the speech therapist working with the student will have clearly established goals and objectives related to the student's speech patterns and general articulation. The regular classroom teacher plays an important role in facilitating good speech habits. Reinforcement of therapy goals and objectives in the student's classroom is essential if the needed carry-over and maintenance in everyday situations are to be expected. The following suggestions may facilitate carry-over and maintenance.

1. Encourage the student to use the dictionary to aid in pronunciation of difficult words. This would naturally depend on the age and reading level of the student.

2. Encourage the student to participate in oral discussions, and expect him to use complete sentences when speaking. Be careful, however, not to "emotionally load" the situation. If proper speech is insisted on and the student is demeaned in front of the entire class for incorrect usage or incomplete sentences, the student may be discouraged from participating in any oral discussion. Be careful not to "nag" the student. Often, correction of a mispronounced word may be accomplished by a brief conference at the end of the period or day. Some teachers have had success with keeping a list of words, with the correct pronunciation, and giving them to the student without any verbal mention. He should also be encouraged to participate in conversation, reading, storytelling, and creative dramatics.

3. The teacher should not be afraid to talk with the student about his hearing loss. The hearing impaired need to be told when they are speaking too loudly or too softly. The teacher can do a great deal to keep the student from developing dull or

expressionless speech habits by speaking with him honestly and openly.

4. Praise and encourage the student when he has correctly pronounced a previously difficult word. The child will need a great deal of encouragement and success if he is to accomplish this very difficult task.

5. Provide a relaxed language environment. The more relaxed and casual the speech and language styles of the teachers and students, the better the opportunity for language acquisition.

Discussing new materials or assignments ahead of class time

Whenever possible, the teacher should briefly discuss topics ahead of time that are to be presented later in class. This may be accomplished by providing the student with an outline of the material to be discussed. Sometimes prereading of assignments is very helpful. Another suggestion worthy of consideration is to provide a list of key vocabulary words that deal with the new material on the board or a piece of paper. When giving an assignment, write it on the board in addition to giving it orally. The student's listening helper may check to see that he has the correct assignment.

Being aware of student fatigue

Hearing impaired students may fatigue more easily than other students, and teachers should be aware of this potential problem. This may be particularly noticeable in young children near the end of the day, but it will be a factor for all hearing impaired students. The fatigue should not be interpreted as boredom, disinterest, or lack of motivation. The fatigue is due in part to the continuous strain of speechreading, using residual hearing, and the constant watching required to keep up with various speakers while participating in the classroom activities. It may be helpful to vary the daily schedule so that the student is not required to attend to academic

subjects for an extended period of time. However, he should be expected to complete all assignments. The teacher should also be aware that the hearing impaired student may hear better on some days than on others. Some students may experience *tinnitus* (hearing noises within the head), which may result in nervousness or irritability.

Facilitating interaction

The hearing impaired student may have a tendency to be shy and withdrawn if he is not fully aware of what is going on in the class. Opportunity for him to interact should be provided; however, do not push him into peer group relationships. Remember to keep the general classroom noise level down when providing specific instructions or directions. The hearing impaired student's hearing aid amplifies all sounds including classroom noises.

Discussing the nature of hearing impairment

Hearing students often do not understand the nature of a hearing impairment or the limitations imposed by it. Mini–in-service sessions may be held to explain the exact nature of a hearing loss through simulation activities or discussions. The resource/itinerant teacher and speech specialist are valuable persons to consider when such activities are being planned. They may bring to the class a variety of hearing aids and allow the students to listen through them to gain a better understanding of how they work.

The hearing impaired student should be encouraged to participate in these mini–in-service sessions, but it is generally a good idea to consult with the student prior to the actual demonstration to be certain he does not feel that he is being exploited. The time spent in such activities often can do a great deal to clear up many misconceptions and possible misunderstandings concerning the student's abilities and limitations.

District audiovisual personnel and equipment

Audiovisual equipment and personnel can be of particular value to the teacher who has a student with a hearing impairment in her class. Overhead projectors can greatly enhance the achievement of the hearing impaired student. As the teacher lectures she may put important notes or key vocabulary words and phrases on the overhead projector. An overhead projector allows the teacher to maintain eye contact with the students while writing on the projector. In general, supplementary diagrams, pictures, and tangibles should be used as often as possible. Often the complete narrative script to a filmstrip or audiotape accompanies the materials and, if available, should be given to the hearing impaired student.

Many educational films have been captioned so they may be used by the hearing impaired student in the regular classroom (see Appendix A). The resource or itinerant teacher of the hearing impaired may provide the teacher with a detailed listing of available materials.

The use of these modified and adapted instructional materials will not interfere with the education of the normally hearing students; in fact, they will facilitate their achievement.

Grading

The hearing impaired student should not be graded differently from the other class members. The resource/itinerant teacher may want to add a special note to the report card to indicate his progress on resource room activities, such as speechreading and auditory training.

• • •

These suggestions to regular classroom teachers are certainly not all-inclusive, but they do represent the areas of greatest concern. It would be helpful to periodically review and discuss them with the resource/itinerant teacher. It is the classroom teacher's use of ingenuity and creativity that is instrumental in modifying and adapting curriculum, materials, and teaching strategies to make this a successful experience for everyone.

The most important consideration, above all other suggestions or techniques, is the attitude of the teacher. The teacher is the single most important variable. She must be understanding, but not sympathetic. She should treat the hearing impaired student as nearly as possible like any other student in the classroom, being fair and truthful, not lenient, in reporting his progress. *The handicapped student should be treated as a student who is able, who is an individual, and who, incidentally, has impaired hearing.*

There has been considerable controversy among educators of the hearing impaired concerning the most appropriate method of communication for these students. Some have advocated the manual method, which employs American Sign Language (a series of gestures representing words or concepts), fingerspelling (finger positions representing individual letters of the alphabet, used to spell out words), or both. Others have defended the oral/aural method, which makes use of oral and auditory training and speechreading. A third general approach, called total communication, combines the manual and oral/aural modes according to the abilities, interests, and needs of the hearing impaired student. It appears that the oral/aural and total communication systems are being used most effectively in programs where hearing impaired students attend regular classrooms.

Students enrolled in a total communication program may use interpreter/tutors to assist them in their regular classroom. The interpreter/tutor is usually located just outside the direct line of sight from the student to the teacher, slightly facing the student, thereby allowing the student to directly speechread

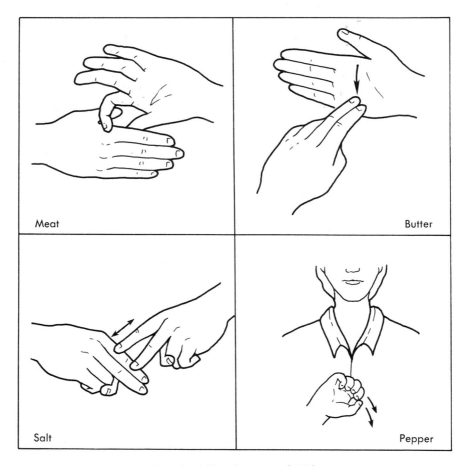

Meat

Butter

Salt

Pepper

American Sign Language (ASL).

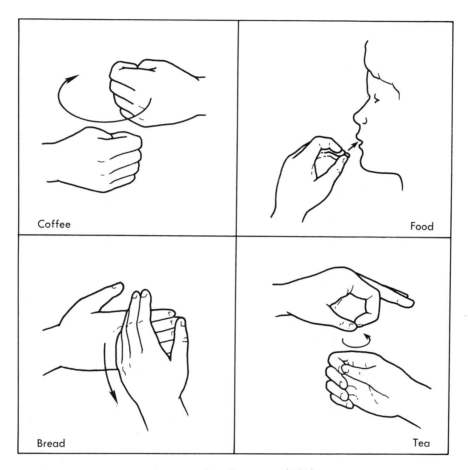

American Sign Language (ASL).

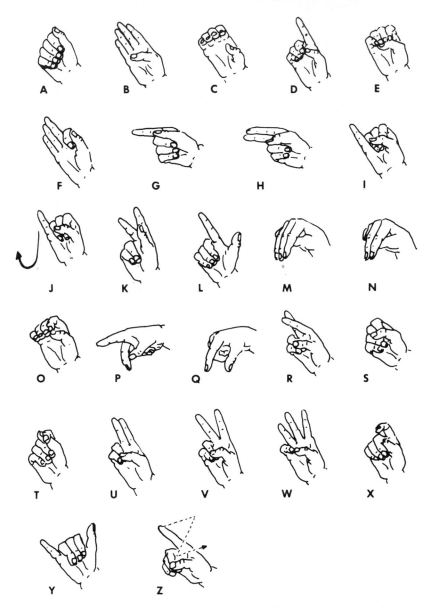

Manual alphabet used by the deaf of North America (From Litton, F. W.: Education of the trainable mentally retarded, St. Louis, 1978, The C. V. Mosby Co.).

the teacher or the interpreter. The interpreter repeats what the teacher is saying through signs, fingerspelling, and nonvocalized speech. He may paraphrase or modify what the teacher is saying if the student is not familiar with the words or concepts being used by the teacher. Interpreter/tutors are not teachers but they must be experts in total communication. They must pass a proficiency examination and may have to be certified in some states. Some caution must be exercised to avoid a dependency relationship between the interpreter/tutor and the student, so that the interpreter/tutor is used only when necessary. Students who do not have good speech reading skills and might not be able to participate in the regular classroom may be able to do so with the assistance of an interpretor/tutor. It is imperative that every idea that may help a student make maximum progress be fully investigated.

ROLE OF RESOURCE/ITINERANT TEACHER

The roles and responsibilities of special education resource/itinerant personnel will vary extensively, depending on the age or grade level of the hearing impaired students served, number of children, geographic area (number of teachers or buildings served by itinerant teacher), and the local school district policy concerning specific responsibilities. In some school districts the resource teacher's responsibilities relate only to a limited number of students in one building and their role is well established, whereas in other districts the resource personnel may serve a number of buildings and their role may be quite varied.

In the following paragraphs we will briefly review a few of the responsibilities of special education resource/itinerant personnel.

Cooperation

The key to a successful educational program for the hearing impaired is a cooperative working arrangement between the regular teachers and the resource teacher. They must establish a working relationship that will enhance the education of the hearing impaired student. The ability of the resource teacher to relate to other staff members in a meaningful way is paramount. The regular teacher must feel free to ask for assistance, whenever needed, without reservation. The

resource teacher should be allowed to observe in the regular class at any time, not in a judgmental manner but as a helper. If the working relationship between the regular classroom teachers and the resource teacher is one of mutual respect and understanding, the student's education will be greatly enhanced. They should jointly plan educational strategies, modify and adapt materials, and have an ongoing dialogue centering around the hearing impaired student's unique needs. They must recognize that there are no "experts," that neither is self-sufficient, and that when working with each other, open communication is the key.

Placement

The resource teacher often shares in the responsibility for placement of the hearing impaired student. In most programs a student is studied and staffed by a team. The team is generally composed of the principal, the resource teacher, speech specialist, school psychologist, school social worker, audiologist, director of special education (or a representative from his office), a member of the medical profession, the regular classroom teacher, and the student's parents. The staffing team carefully studies past performance and problem areas and makes recommendations concerning educational programming and placement.

Although the staffing team makes recommendations concerning placement, the ultimate decision as to which teacher the student should be placed with often rests with the principal and resource teacher. The principal has information concerning the unique competencies of each teacher, the teachers' willingness and attitude toward accepting a student with a hearing loss, and their ability to work cooperatively with resource personnel. The principal knows which teachers will see this experience as a new and exciting challenge. The principal may recommend several teachers who would meet the preceding criteria; however, the next step would be for the resource teacher to informally interview these teachers, observe in their classrooms, and discuss in greater detail the nature of the new challenge. The resource teacher must observe carefully to determine the general position of each teacher in the room, the quality of the lighting, the teacher's rate of speech and type of voice, the visibility of the lip movements, and the visual aids used. These factors must be carefully reviewed prior to placement because they are important in facilitating the speech and language of hearing impaired students. In addition, the resource/itinerant teacher would be responsible for evaluating students' readiness for regular classroom placement, success, and progress. Assessment of student progress must be an ongoing process, subject to change as the students' needs dictate.

Orientation/in-service

Depending on the geographical area to be served (one or more schools), resource/itinerant teachers may be responsible for the in-service education of regular classroom teachers in one or several buildings. Often the resource/itinerant teacher is called on to acquaint a building staff with the rationale underlying integrated placement of the hearing impaired. The nature of the in-service session may be quite general and relate only to the philosophy of integrated education, or it may be specifically related to techniques for modifying and adapting curriculum, materials, and teaching strategies.

Although it is not necessary for regular teachers to know the manual alphabet, they often are interested in learning it. In this instance the resource/itinerant teacher may conduct in-service programs for teachers and/or students or arrange for classes to be taught by another person. (For a more detailed discussion concerning the provision of specific information to nonhandicapped students, see Chapter 10.)

Another role often assumed by the resource teacher is to provide selected journal articles, readings, or topics of special interest in relation to a particular student's problem or to specific teaching techniques (see Appendix B). The orientation and in-service efforts of the resource personnel are an ongoing responsibility that must be taken seriously. The way in which the resource personnel sell themselves, the program, and the students will have a tremendous influence on the effectiveness of the program.

Demonstration teaching

Special educators have traditionally served their students in what might be termed "pull-out" programs. That is, they pull the students out of the classroom and work with them in a special resource room. This practice, although it may be necessary in some instances, is totally unnecessary and even undesirable in other situations.

If we are to fully appreciate the potential of integration or mainstreaming, we should attempt to involve special educators in regular classrooms wherever possible. This practice can greatly facilitate the communication between special and general educators and overcome many of the misunderstandings between them. The expertise held by both professions can be shared in the most meaningful way through the actual teaching of students. Special educators can increase their knowledge concerning large group instruction and the limitations imposed in modifying and adapting materials, curricula, and teaching strategies. Regular classroom teachers can increase their competency in working with the hearing impaired student by observing the resource person work with large and small groups. At times, the resource teacher could assume an aide or tutor role not only with the hearing impaired student, but also with small groups of students who are having problems with a difficult concept or assignment. This is not a new concept;

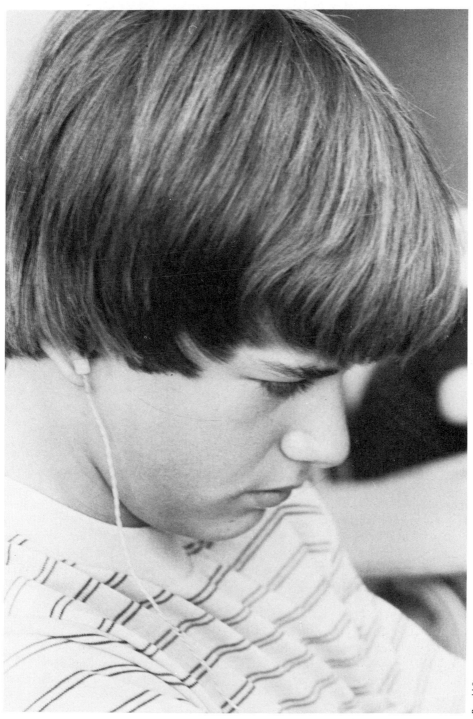

some resource teachers have been assuming a helping or assisting role with regular teachers for some time. Unfortunately, the number has not been significantly large.

The resource teacher may also demonstrate a particular teaching strategy. For example, if the resource teacher has asked the regular teacher to use an overhead projector to teach a science or social studies lesson, it would be desirable for the resource teacher to actually demonstrate the use of the projector by teaching the lesson. This method may be employed in giving a spelling test or in any other teaching technique. It is also possible for the resource teacher to assist in teaching a unit on the anatomy and physiology of the ear or a unit on hearing as one of the senses to acquaint all students with the nature of a hearing loss. The resource teacher may actually conduct or assist in conducting mini–in-service sessions with the students concerning the nature of a hearing loss, the benefits of a hearing aid, or any other topics that may be of interest to the hearing students.

Procuring, modifying, and adapting materials

The resource teacher may assist the regular teacher in modifying or adapting materials for the hearing impaired student. For example, she may provide outlines or vocabulary lists that are about to be introduced into the regular classroom. Many times the regular teacher does not have time to modify materials, and this service can be a tremendous help. If neither the regular teacher nor the resource teacher has the necessary time, volunteers or teacher aides may be most helpful in this area.

If activities are planned far enough in advance, many times the resource teacher may obtain captioned films, slide-tape presentations, or other tangible teaching materials to be used by the regular teacher.

Serving as liaison between medical personnel, therapists, and regular teacher

The resource teacher, by nature of her professional preparation and experience, generally has a very good understanding of medical aspects, audiology, and speech therapy. She may serve as the liaison between these disciplines and the regular teacher. She may interpret the exact nature of the hearing loss in relation to medical and audiological evaluations and provide specific suggestions related to the unique characteristics of hearing efficiency for a particular student. It is hoped that information concerning the individual's functional ability would be emphasized rather than medical/quantitative information. In addition, she may interpret the student's development of language and its influence on learning. She may also serve as an extension of the speech specialist by reinforcing those speech sounds that may reasonably be expected of the student and identifying those that are in need of further therapy. In some instances the resource teacher may serve as the follow-up agent for the hearing impaired student or for students who have been referred for medical examinations.

Assessing hearing aid effectiveness

The resource teacher can assist in evaluating many aspects of hearing aid problems and hearing aid effectiveness. She can routinely check all aspects of hearing aid operation by checking and replacing worn out batteries and, in general, troubleshooting any other problems. Many resource teachers obtain a tester for use in the building or make arrangements for assistance from a local hearing aid dealer.

A more important role of the resource teacher is to assess hearing aid effectiveness in the classroom situation, particularly if the student has just recently been fitted with an aid. She can appraise the effectiveness of the aid by evaluating changes in the way the student handles everyday situations. She should look very carefully for the following: (1) increased social interactions, (2) changes in voice quality and articulation, (3) increased language skills, (4) reactions to sound and amplification, and (5) increased educational achievement. In addition, the resource teacher should observe to see if the student is turning the volume down or completely turning it off; this may be an indication of an improperly fitted aid. Systematic longitudinal evaluation of a student's hearing aid effectiveness is an important role of the special education resource teacher.

Teaching special skills

There are a number of special skills that should be routinely provided by resource personnel. The specific skills will vary depending on the grade level of the students. At the primary level, the resource teacher may have responsibility for reading instruction or she may supplement the material presented in the student's regular class. The reading material used by the resource teacher may be the same as that used in the regular class, except that the resource teacher will spend considerably more time on comprehension, questioning, and related language activities. At the intermediate level the resource teacher will probably supplement regular classroom instruction by emphasizing phonetic and comprehension skills or by introducing new vocabulary words prior to their introduction in class. Hearing impaired students may need to be taught "in" words that are popular with their classmates.

In addition to supplemental instruction, the resource teacher may work on a number of other areas, such as individual and small-group auditory training, vocabulary development, comprehension, questioning, speech-reading, and speech correction.

In some instances, the resource/itinerant teacher is an integral part of routine class-room activities and has specific instructional responsibilities with hearing students who have instructional needs similar to the hearing impaired. In other settings the resource/itinerant teacher will employ a preteach, teach, postteach strategy (Birch, 1973). Using this approach, the resource/itinerant teacher introduces a particular concept, area of study, or special vocabulary prior to its introduction in the student's regular classroom. The particular area of study is then taught by the regular classroom teacher. Following such instruction the teacher communicates with the resource teacher or with the student, discussing any unique or special problems that may need to be followed up by the resource teacher.

The exact nature of the resource teacher's role will depend on the age or grade level of the students, the number of students, and the extent of hearing impairment. Generally, the role involves tutoring or supplemental instruction, the introduction of new materials or skills, and instruction in highly specialized skills related to hearing impairment.

Counseling

The resource teacher, by nature of her specialized preparation and experience, may assist the regular teachers in counseling the hearing impaired student and the student's parents. This counseling may relate to routine academic matters, such as parent-teacher conferences, or to specific problems imposed by a hearing impairment, such as interpersonal relationships, language and speech problems, or vocational interests.

Assistance with vocational education programs

The resource teacher will assist in planning and implementing work-study, vocational education, and vocational rehabilitation services for hearing impaired students in secondary school. The resource/itinerant teacher may be responsible for actually initiating these services or may contact others who will initiate them.

As mentioned previously, the role and responsibility of resource personnel will vary considerably. The key to successful resource services is communication between the regular teachers and the resource personnel.

SUMMARY

For many years it was believed that nearly all hearing impaired students needed an essentially separate special educational program. Recently, however, these students have been having considerable success in the least restrictive setting—the regular classroom. The need for special services in auditory training, vocabulary development, comprehension, questioning, speechreading, and speech correction still must be provided on a routine-scheduled basis.

Younger students and students with severe and profound losses will require greater amounts of special education service during their early school years and may attend regular classes on a very limited basis. After they have acquired the necessary skills, they may attend regular classrooms for increasing amounts of time, but nearly all will need supportive assistance from special education resource/itinerant personnel during their entire school career.

Recent improvements in hearing aids and the increased use of these aids have contributed to the increase in the number of students who can successfully participate in regular programs. In addition, the development of captioned films and other media has had a very positive influence on the education of the hearing impaired. Tutor/interpreters are being used with increasing frequency and are assisting these students a great deal. As a larger number of hearing impaired students are integrated into regular classrooms and as professionals continue to more effectively analyze and share information and expertise about these students, integration/mainstreaming may reach its fullest potential for these students.

In this chapter we have reviewed the nature of hearing impairment, the limitations imposed by such impairment, identification procedures, and methods of referral. Alternative teaching strategies to be considered by the regular classroom teacher were discussed, and very specific suggestions were offered that should facilitate the education of hearing impaired students. In addition, the role and responsibility of special education resource/itinerant personnel was reviewed, and it was emphasized that the key to successful programming for these students is a cooperative working arrangement between regular classroom teachers and special education personnel.

Students with impaired hearing must be exposed to different language styles. They must establish a variety of communication techniques, and continually reexamine and modify these communication skills to keep their speech and language at an intelligible level. A regular classroom provides normal age-appropriate speech, language, and social models. Perhaps the most important advantage is the opportunity for these students to establish and continue relationships with hearing individuals—the opportunity for participation in the hearing world.

REFERENCES AND SUGGESTED READINGS

Alexander Graham Bell Association for the Deaf. Guidelines for an integrated program. *Volta Review*, February 1964, *66*, 87-88.

Alexander Graham Bell Association for the Deaf. Guidelines for pre-school programs for hearing impaired children, 3-6 years. Washington, D.C.: Volta Bureau, 1967.

Ashcroft, S. C. The handicapped in the regular classroom. *NEA Journal*, November 1967, *56*, 33-34.

Athey, J., & Vernon, M. The Holcomb plan: a creative

approach to mainstreaming deaf and hard of hearing children. *Instructor*, 1977, 5, 136-137.

Birch, J. W. *Hearing impaired children in the mainstream*. Reston, Va.: Council for Exceptional Children, 1975.

Bitter, G. B., Johnston, K. A., and Sorenson, R. G. *Integration of the hearing impaired: educational issues*. Washington, D.C.: U.S. Office of Education, Bureau of Education for the Handicapped, 1973.

Bitter, G. B., & Mears, E. G. Facilitating the integration of hearing impaired children into regular public school classes. *Volta Review*, 1973, 75, 13-22.

Bothwell, H. What the classroom teacher can do for the child with impaired hearing. *NEA Journal*, November 1967, 56, 44-46.

Brackett, D. Communicative interaction of preschool hearing impaired children in an integrated setting. *Volta Review*, 1976, 78, 276-285.

Braddock, M. J. Integrating the deaf and hard of hearing students. *Volta Review*, October 1962, 64, 500-501.

Bruce, W. Social integration and effectiveness of speech. *Volta Review*, September 1960, 62, 368-372.

Bruininks, R. H., & Kennedy, P. Social status of hearing impaired children in regular classroom. *Exceptional Children*, February 1974, 40, 336-342.

Carruth, K. J., Kryeger, A. H., Lesar, D. I., & Redding, A. J. Possible effects of integration of the deaf within a typical vocational school setting. *Journal of Rehabilitation of the Deaf*, 1971, 4, 30-41.

Carver, R. L. A parent speaks out on integration in the schools. *Volta Review*, 1966, 68, 580-583.

Classroom teacher's guide for the hard of hearing. Garden Grove Unified School District, 10331 Stanford Avenue, Garden Grove, Calif., 17 pages.

Cohen, O. P. An integrated summer recreation program. *Volta Review*, April 1969, 71, 233-237.

Community College of Denver provides integrated programs. *Volta Review*, 1971, 73, 190.

Connor, L. E. The oral education of deaf children. *Voice*, November 1968, 11, 3-12.

Connor, L. E. Integration. *Volta Review*, 1972, 74, 207-209.

Culhane, B., & Curwin, R. There's a deaf child in my class. *Learning*, October 1978, 111-117.

Dale, D. M. *The deaf child at home and at school*. London: University of London Press, 1967.

Delaney, P. A. Is it a hearing problem? *Grade Teacher*, March 1972, 89, 17-19.

DeSalle, J. Some problems and solutions: high school mainstreaming of the hearing impaired. *American Annals of the Deaf*, 1976, 121, 533-536.

Dixon, C. C. Integrating . . . a positive note. *Hearing and Speech News*, 1968, 36, 16,18.

Eichstadt, C. Signing: communicating with hearing impaired individuals in physical education. *Journal of Physical Education and Recreation*, 1978, 49, 19-21.

Elser, R. P. The social position of hearing handicapped children in the regular grades. *Exceptional Children*, 1959, 25, 305-309.

Fallis, J. The key to integrated learning for children who are hearing impaired. *Volta Review*, 1975, 77, 363-367.

Ford, F. C. Reactions of the hearing impaired child to school situations. *Peabody Journal of Education*, November 1968, 46, 177-179.

Formaad, W. Help for the child with impaired hearing, *NEA Journal*, December 1965, 54, 45-47.

Freeman, G. G. Innovative school programs: the Oakland School's plan. *Journal of Hearing and Speech Disorders*, August 1969, 34, 220-225.

Frick, E. Adjusting to integration: some difficulties hearing impaired children have in public schools. *Volta Review*, 1973, 75, 36-46.

Garrett, C., & Stovall, E. M. A parent's views on integration. *Volta Review*, 1972, 74, 338-344.

Gildston, P. Hard of hearing child in the classroom: a guide for the classroom teacher. *Volta Review*, 1962, 64, 239-245.

Gonzales, B. R. Breaking the fear of placement for the hearing impaired. *Journal of the Rehabilitation of the Deaf*, October 1969, 3, 22-28.

Hedgecock, D. Facilitating integration at the junior high level. *Volta Review*, March 1974, 76, 182-188.

Johnson, A. L. Supportive instruction for hearing impaired students. *Volta Review*, March 1968, 70, 184-188.

Johnson, J. C. *Educating Hearing Impaired Children in Ordinary Schools*. Washington, D.C.: Volta Bureau, 1962.

Kennedy, P. Social status of hearing impaired children in the regular classroom. *Exceptional Children*, February 1974, 40, 336-341.

Kodman, F., Jr. Educational status of hard of hearing children in the classroom. *Journal of Speech and Hearing Disorders*, August 1963, 28, 297-299.

Kowalsky, M. H. Integration of a severely hard of hearing child in a normal first grade program; a case study. *Journal of Speech and Hearing Disorders*, 1962, 27, 349-358.

Leckie, D. J. Creating a receptive climate in the mainstream program. *Volta Review*, 1973, 75, 23-27.

Leigh, D. The deaf child enrolled in a hearing school. *Volta Review*, 1963, 65, 312.

Lewis, D. N. Lipreading skills of hearing impaired children in regular schools. *Volta Review*, 1972, 74, 303-311.

Lexington School for the Deaf. Giving deaf children

needed experience with the hearing world. *Audiovisual Instruction*, November 1969, *14*, 98-99.

Lloyd, L. L. Have you a pupil with a hearing handicap? *Instructor*, 1962, *72*, 62, 136.

McCauley, R., Bruininks, R., & Kennedy, P. Behavioral interactions of hearing impaired children in regular classrooms. *Journal of Special Education*, 1976, *10*, 277-280.

McGee, D. I. The benefits of educating deaf children with hearing children. *Teaching Exceptional Children*, 1970, *2*, 133-137.

Meecham, S. R., & VanDyke, R. C. Pushing back the walls between hearing and hearing impaired children. *Volta Review*, 1971, *73*, 359-364.

Miller, A. S. Academic preparation to insure adjustment into classes with hearing students. *Volta Review*, 1964, *66*, 414-425.

Monagham, A. Educational placement for the multiply handicapped hearing impaired child. *Volta Review*, September 1964, *66*, 383-387.

Nix, G. W. *Mainstream education for hearing impaired children and youth.* New York: Grune & Stratton, Inc., 1976.

Northcott, W. H. Candidate for integration: A hearing impaired child in a regular nursery school. *Young Children*, 1970, *72*, 367-380.

Northcott, W. H. An experimental summer school: impetus for successful integration. *Volta Review*, 1970, *72*, 498-507.

Northcott, W. H. Integration of young deaf children into ordinary education programs. *Exceptional Children*, 1971, *38*, 29-32.

Northcott, W. H. A hearing impaired pupil in the classroom. *Volta Review*, 1972, *74*, 105-108.

Northcott, W. H. (Ed.). *The hearing impaired child in a regular classroom: preschool, elementary, and secondary years.* Washington, D.C.: Alexander Graham Bell Association for the Deaf, 1973.

O'Connor, C. D. The integration of the deaf in schools for the normally hearing. *American Annals of the Deaf*, 1961, *106*, 239-245.

O'Connor, C. D., & Connor, L. E. Study of the integration of deaf children in regular classrooms. *Exceptional Children*, 1961, *27*, 483-486.

Oregon State Department of Education, Division of Special Education. *ABC's in ways the regular classroom teacher can aid the hard of hearing child.* Salem, Ore. Author, 1967.

Paul, R. L. Resource room for hard of hearing children in the public schools. *Volta Review*, 1963, *65*, 200-202.

Paynter, D. H. *The role of the principal assigned to hard of hearing classes.* Garden Grove, Calif.: Garden Grove Unified School District, 1971.

Pollock, M. B., & Pollock, K. C. Letter to the teacher of a hard of hearing child. *Childhood Education*, January 1971, *47*, 206-209.

Reich, C., Hambleton, D., & Houldin, B. The Integration of Hearing Impaired Children in Regular Classrooms. *American Annals of the Deaf*, December 1977, *122*, 534-543.

Regular classroom teacher's manual for aurally handicapped children. Garden Grove, Calif.: Stanford Elementary School, 1969.

Rister, A. Deaf children in a mainstream education. *Volta Review*, 1975, *77*, 279-290.

Roberts, W. Regular school teachers' views of integration. *Voice* (Montreal Oral School), November 1968, *11*, 13-17.

Rosenthal, C. Social adjustment of hearing handicapped children. *Volta Review*, 1966, *68*, 293-297.

Rudy, J. P., & Nace, J. G. *A transitional integrative program for hearing impaired students.* Newark, Del.: Sterck School for the Hearing Impaired, 1973.

Salem, J. M. Partial integration at the high school level. *Volta Review*, January 1971, *73*, 42-46.

Sheeline, A. Integrating deaf children into public schools. *Volta Review*, 1971, *73*, 370-373.

Schwartz, M. G. Deaf child in my hearing class. *Volta Review*, 1964, *66*, 627-630.

Silverman, S. R. The hard of hearing child: how the classroom teacher can recognize and help him. *NEA Journal*, 1950, *39*, 136-137.

Stuckless, E. R. *A notetaking procedure for deaf students in regular classes.* Rochester, N.Y.: National Technical Institute for the Deaf, 1969.

Sykes, G. Tips on note-taking. *Volta Review*, April 1965, *67*, 307-309.

Tudyman, A. Public school problems in educating hard of hearing children. *Hearing News*, October 1952, *20*, 5-8.

VanWyk, M. K. Integration, yes, if . . . *Volta Review*, February 1959, *61*, 59-62.

Vaughn, G. R. *Education of deaf and hard of hearing adults in established facilities for the normally hearing.* Pocatello, Idaho: Idaho State University Press, 1967.

Watson, F. J. Use of hearing aids by hearing impaired pupils in ordinary schools. *Volta Review*, 1964, *66*, 741-744.

Weiss, J. T. Integrating the hearing handicapped. *Instructor*, 1968, *78*, 102.

Woodburn, V., & Schuster, M. Mike was our first deaf student. *Today's Education*, 1978, *67*, 77-78.

4 STRATEGIES AND ALTERNATIVES FOR EDUCATING THE VISUALLY IMPAIRED

Ronald Stewart

The visually impaired were first among handicapped students to be systematically placed in regular classrooms, and many of the service delivery systems used today with other handicapping conditions were modeled after successful programs for the visually impaired. Because of the limitations imposed by this condition, students with impaired vision do not have ready access to the same educational materials as other students; thus the primary features of programming for the visually impaired relate to modification and adaptation of educational materials.

The visually impaired student may be considered on the basis of medical, legal, educational, or functional definitions, but our emphasis will relate to educational and functional ability. For our purposes the visually impaired student may be defined as one whose vision is limited to such an extent that he may require educational modifications and adaptations. If the student can read printed material, either enlarged print or standard print with the use of special magnification devices, he will be classified as partially seeing or a print-reader. Students whose visual impairment is so severe that they must use materials other than print (such as braille and taped materials) will be classified as educationally blind or as braille-readers.

Although there is a trend toward educational or functional definitions, there are a number of state and local school programs that continue to define students on the basis of medical or legal aspects. Generally these definitions are used for eligibility for services or materials from state or federal agencies or for reimbursement purposes from state departments of education. The most common classification used relating to visual acuity (measurement of visual ability) divides the visually impaired into two groups, the partially seeing and the legally blind. The definition for legally blind, given by the National Society for the Prevention of Blindness (1957), is as follows:

A legally blind child is one who has central visual acuity of 20/200 or less in the better eye after correction; or visual acuity of more than 20/200 if there is a field defect in which the widest diameter of the visual field subtends an angle distance no greater than 20°.

Ratios such as 20/20, 20/70, and 20/200 are used to express visual acuity. These numbers correspond to the size of symbols or letters on the Snellen chart, each relating to the standard distance at which a person with normal vision can comfortably read the symbols or letters. For example, if an individual can read the twenty-foot–sized symbol or letter on the chart at twenty feet, the measured acuity would be 20/20, or normal vision. If an individual can only read the symbol representing the seventy-foot letter or larger on the Snellen chart, his distance visual acuity would be indicated as 20/70. If the only letter that can be read is the largest, the two hundred–foot letter, then the individual's measured distance visual acuity is 20/200.

An individual's distance visual acuity is indicated by these figures, but they do not provide information concerning near-point vision (the ability to see at close distances, such as while reading). Not only do these definitions exclude information about near-point vision, but there is considerable variance between individuals with the same measured acuity. For example, two students may have 20/200 measured acuity, but one may be able to read printed material, whereas the other may have to read braille.

The preceding discussion of the various types of visual impairment and the definitions used for differing purposes will serve as the introduction to this area of handicap. In the remainder of this chapter we will consider a number of major concerns, including (1) identification of the visually impaired,

(2) educational programming, (3) the continuum of services required for the visually impaired, (4) suggestions to regular classroom teachers, and (5) the role and responsibility of the resource/itinerant teacher.

IDENTIFICATION OF THE VISUALLY IMPAIRED

Students with severe visual impairments are usually easily identified prior to enrollment in school. There are, however, some students whose impaired vision has gone undetected for many years. The student's impairment may be detected by routine visual screening during the primary grades, or it may not be detected until the student is in the fourth or fifth grade, when subject matter requires extensive visual work such as reading and map study. This delay in identification may be attributed to the nature of academic tasks required up to this level or to poor vision screening procedures during the student's early elementary years. Many screening programs are carelessly conducted; the procedures may be inaccurate or not carried out on a routine basis. In addition, tests for near-point vision (ability to read at twelve to eighteen inches) are required by only a very few states. Most screening programs are concerned with the student's distance vision (ability to see at twenty feet). Although vision screening procedures are improving, it must be recognized that these procedures, at best, are only a screening process and will not identify all students with impaired vision.

When considering the problems associated with vision screening procedures, the role of the regular classroom teacher in identifying students with vision problems cannot be overemphasized. The teacher has the opportunity to observe the student in a variety of settings, under a variety of conditions, and may be in the best position to identify visual difficulties. Therefore, it may be helpful for the regular classroom teacher to be aware of behaviors and observable signs that could indicate a visual problem.

Visual behavior
1. Rubs eyes excessively
2. Shuts or covers one eye; tilts head or thrusts head forward
3. Sensitivity to light
4. Difficulty with reading or other work requiring close use of the eyes
5. Squinting, blinking, frowning, facial distortions while reading or doing other close work
6. Holds reading material too close or too far or frequently changes the distance from near to far or far to near
7. Complains of pain or aches in the eyes, headaches, dizziness, or nausea following close eye work
8. Difficulty in seeing distant objects (preference for reading or other academic tasks rather than playground or gross motor activities)
9. Tendency to reverse letters, syllables, or words
10. Tendency to confuse letters of similar shape (o and a, c, and e, n and m, h and n, and f and t)
11. Tendency to lose place in sentence or page
12. Poor spacing in writing and difficulty in "staying on the line"

Observable signs
1. Red eyelids
2. Crusts on lids among the lashes
3. Recurring styes or swollen lids
4. Watery eyes or discharges
5. Reddened or watery eyes
6. Crossed eyes or eyes that do not appear to be straight
7. Pupils of uneven size
8. Eyes that move excessively
9. Drooping eyelids

If any of these behaviors or signs are observed in a student, he should be referred immediately to the school nurse, principal, or the individual responsible for vision problems. Additional tests might be conducted to determine if the student should be referred to an eye specialist for a more extensive evaluation. After some determination is made concerning needed services, the teacher may have to serve as the catalyst or advocate to ensure that the recommendations are not lost in a file somewhere and that the needed services are provided.

Teachers may find it helpful to have information concerning the role and capabilities of the various eye specialists in the community to make the necessary referral or to provide information to parents. Occasionally, the classroom teacher may need to confer with one of these specialists; therefore, a brief description is provided here:

ophthalmologist (or oculist) a medical doctor who specializes in the diagnosis and treatment of diseases of the eye. This physician is also licensed to prescribe glasses.

optometrist a highly trained person who specializes in eye problems but does not possess a medical degree. This individual is licensed to measure visual function and prescribe and fit glasses. If disease is suspected, a referral will be made to an ophthalmologist.

optician a craftsman who makes glasses and fills the prescriptions of ophthalmologists and optometrists.

orthoptist a nonmedical technician who directs prescribed exercises or training to correct eye muscle imbalances and generally works under the direction of an ophthalmologist.

EDUCATIONAL PROGRAMMING

As mentioned previously, the integration of students with other handicapping conditions is a relatively recent trend, yet students with vision impairments have been integrated or mainstreamed into regular classrooms for more than half a century. Early professionals recognized that students with vision impairments could be educated with their sighted peers with only minor modifications and adaptations and that the limitations imposed by a visual disability did not require a special curriculum.

Materials need to be provided in different media or in modified or adapted form so that the student will be able to learn through sensory channels other than vision. For example, if the student is not able to read printed material, this material would be provided through the tactual (touch) or auditory channels. If the student can read printed material only with considerable difficulty, the material may be enlarged or the student may use magnification devices. The primary nature of special education services for visually impaired students relates to the modification and adaptation of educational materials.

The curriculum for students who are visually impaired is the same as it is for their sighted peers; however, in addition to the regular curriculum they require many "plus factors." In other words, the student will have, for example, reading, math, and social studies, but in addition he may need braille instruction, orientation and mobility (travel) training, typewriting, and training in the use of the abacus. Generally, the "plus factors" are taught by the resource/itinerant teacher and are not the responsibility of the regular classroom teacher.

CONTINUUM OF SERVICES

There is a very definite need for a full continuum of services for students with impaired vision. The following variables should be considered when placement options are being studied: (1) age, (2) achievement level, (3) intelligence, (4) presence of multiple handicapping conditions, (5) emotional stability, (6) nature and extent of eye condition, (7) wishes of students and parents, (8) recommendations of staffing team, and (9) availability of services. Naturally, each student should be considered individually, but there are some general placement considerations that should be taken into account. For example, there seems to be a relationship be-

61 **Care of the ears.** There are some important things you should know about taking care ... too.

You sho... things ... eardrum. The... anyth... germs to get through ... may ... eas... le ear. Repeated colds an... yo... may cause loss of hearing. inf... thing to remember in was... our ears is, "Never use any... finge... ler than your litt... clean ... your ears ... by a washcloth"

properly, you should see yo... He knows how to wash ou... safely.

When you have a cold, blow your nose carefully ... way to do this is to h... ndkerchief over both ... e and blow very g... hard, you may se... d from the nose i... leads to the mid... this tube in the p... This liquid has g... may start an infection ... ear.

Loud noises or sl...

79

Ronald Stewart

a   b   c   d   e   f   g   h   i   j

k   l   m   n   o   p   q   r   s   t

u   v   w   x   y   z

In braille each letter is represented by a pattern of raised dots within a six-dot cell. Additional combinations include letter sequence, numbers, punctuation, and words.

tween the age of the student, the nature and extent of the visual impairment, his level of achievement, and the amount of direct special education service and instruction needed. If the child is a young braille-reader (ages 5 to 9), resource/itinerant assistance will be needed on a routinely scheduled daily basis to provide the needed instruction in braillle reading and other areas requiring the specialized services of the resource/itinerant teacher. During the child's early education, he may spend an hour to an hour and a half each day with his resource teacher. When he has developed braille-reading skills and a familiarity with all the necessary tangible apparatus, he may attend his regular classroom for increasing amounts of time. If the student is able to read printed materials, with or without an aid, it will not be necessary to spend as much time with the resource/itinerant teacher. The student at the secondary level generally does not require a great deal of direct service from the resource/itinerant teacher.

SUGGESTIONS TO REGULAR CLASSROOM TEACHERS

The suggestions that follow may be used for the student who is either a braille- or a print-reader, as many of the techniques and modifications are the same for either group. These suggestions may be categorized as follows: (1) adapted educational materials and equipment, (2) educational environment, (3) orientation and mobility, (4) alternative teaching strategies and adaptations, and (5) general considerations. Although it is difficult to determine proper placement for some suggestions, we believe they will be more easily conceptualized if grouped into these general areas.

Adapted educational materials and equipment

As mentioned previously, the primary nature of educational programming for the visually impaired relates to the modification and adaptation of educational materials. Most of these materials are available from private agencies at no cost to the student. Over the many years of service to the visually impaired an extensive array of very helpful materials has been developed.

It is not practical to review all the adapted material and special equipment available for students with impaired vision, since there are several hundred different types. Most of these materials are directed at increasing the student's learning through sensory channels other than vision. The following listing of materials indicates the many different types:

Geography aids
  Braille atlases
  Molded plastic dissected and undissected relief maps
  Relief globes
  Landform model (a set of three-dimensional tactual maps illustrating forty geographic concepts)

Mathematics aids
  Special slates to be used in computation
  Abacuses
  Raised clockfaces
  Geometric area and volume aids
  Wire forms for matched planes and volumes
  Braille rulers
  Talking calculators

Writing aids
  Raised-line check books
  Signature guide
  Raised-line writing paper
  Longhand writing kit
  Script letter sheets and boards

Reading aids
  Optacon (a device that converts printed material to either a tactual or auditory stimulus)

Miscellaneous aids
  Audible goal locators, which can be used as a goal, base, object locator, or warning device
  Special braille or large-type answer sheets
  Science measurement kits (containing such items as thermometers, spring balances, gram weights, and gravity specimens)
  Sports field kit (raised drawings of various sports playing fields or courts)
  Simple machine kits, including working models of simple machines such as pulleys and levers, including plane, wheel and axle
  Childrens games, such as Rook, Rack-O, Scrabble, bingo, cards, checkers, and Parcheesi
  Adapted sports equipment (audible balls)
  Braille clocks, wristwatches, and timers

The American Printing House for the Blind* has a very extensive offering of adapted materials and educational equipment. In addition, the American Foundation for the Blind* has an "Aids and Appliances Catalog" from which materials may be ordered. There are several other agencies that have special materials available. The majority of the states have established instructional materials centers serving as registries and depositories for materials, loaning materials to school districts as needed. These state instructional materials centers will assist in locating specific materials and may even reproduce them in the desired format, that is, large type, tape recording, or braille (see Appendix C for list of instructional materials centers).

It is generally not the responsibility of the regular classroom teacher to obtain materials unless a resource/itinerant teacher is not available. The resource/itinerant teacher is familiar with all the agencies that provide adapted materials and equipment and with the procedures used to acquire these materials. In the event that selected materials are not available from any of the agencies, it is necessary that the resource/itinerant teacher reproduce these materials or make some provision for them to be prepared by community volunteers. For example, a particular reading text may not be available in modified form because it has only recently been published. After all agencies have been queried, including the state instructional materials center for the visually impaired, the resource/itinerant teacher may have the text reproduced in large type, tape-recorded, or transcribed into braille by community volunteers or by a salaried aide who has the necessary special skills.

In addition to textbooks and special adapted materials that may be available from an agency, there is always a need for teacher-made materials used on a day-to-day basis,

---

*American Printing House for the Blind, 1839 Frankfurt Avenue, Louisville, Ky. 40206.

*American Foundation for the Blind, 15 West Sixteenth Street, New York, N.Y. 10011.

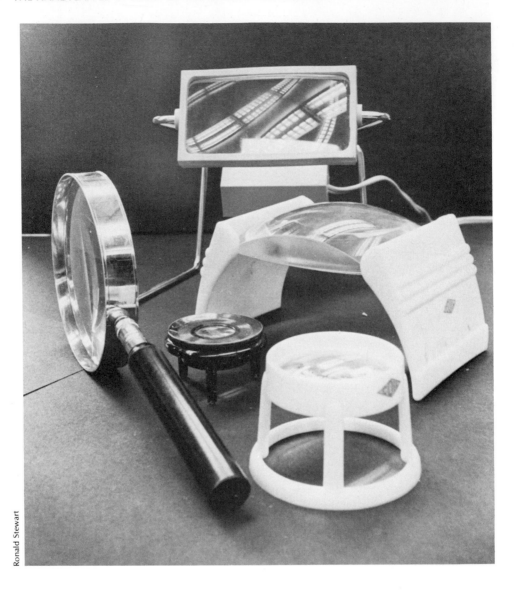

Ronald Stewart

such as teacher-made tests, work sheets, and special games or activities. These must be reproduced in the desired format by the resource/itinerant teacher or by specially trained aides or volunteers because it is essential that the student's materials be the same as those of his peers. Advanced planning and a special communication system must be implemented with the resource/itinerant teacher, which will provide for an explanation of the nature of the needed materials and allow sufficient time for their reproduction. This is usually accomplished by leaving the desired materials in the resource/itinerant teacher's mailbox, establishing a routine conference between the regular teacher and the resource/itinerant teacher, or sending the material with the student when he meets with the resource/itinerant teacher.

Occasionally the regular classroom teacher may have to modify needed materials. For example, if mimeographed materials are being prepared for class distribution, it may be necessary to darken the letters or figures with a felt-tipped pen so they can be seen more esaily by the partially seeing student. Usually, materials duplicated in purple cause considerable difficulty for the visually impaired; therefore, if possible, use black stencils to ensure the desired contrast. It may also be of value to consider preparing handout materials in primary or enlarged type for all students, since they, too, are able to read enlarged materials more easily.

Educational environment

Although not a major concern, there are several environmental or classroom modifications that will facilitate the education of students with impaired vision. Preferred or open seating allows the student to sit wherever he is most comfortable. When the teacher is using the chalkboard, when a movie or filmstrip is being shown, and when the teacher is demonstrating a particular concept using tangible materials, the student should be allowed to move as close as necessary.

The student's seating should be arranged for best possible lighting conditions. This does not imply that all partially seeing students should be in bright or highly lighted areas. Some visual impairments require no special lighting, whereas others require lower levels of illumination. The resource/itinerant teacher or the report from the student's eye specialist should be of particular value in this area. The teacher should not stand with his back to a bright light source such as a window, since the student will be looking directly into the light. Writing on a chalkboard where there is considerable glare should also be avoided.

Safety while traveling independently in the classroom can be a problem if doors are not completely open or closed. Often the visually impaired student may think the classroom door is open, because of auditory and other cues, only to find it only partially open. Keeping the door completely open or closed is difficult to accomplish with thirty other students in the classroom, but it should be attempted.

Teachers who have a visually impaired student in their class are sometimes reluctant to change the classroom seating or position of desks, tables, and other items because they are afraid the student may become disoriented or sustain an injury. The physical arrangement of the room should be changed as often as necessary, but the visually impaired student must be oriented to the changes. This should take only a few minutes of formal orientation and a few minutes of independent exploring by the student, followed by a brief question-and-answer session concerning the new arrangement. Other students in the class can be of some assistance by directing the visually impaired students through the new arrangement or describing it to them. The noise level of the classroom should be kept reasonably low, since the visually impaired student must depend on his auditory skills for a great deal of his educational program. Braille-reading students need open space and shelves at the side of the room, since braille materials are very large and bulky, and they may need room for their braillewriter, typewriter, books, and other materials.

Orientation and mobility (independent travel)

The ability of a visually impaired student to move about independently is one of the

most important factors in his total educational program. Programming efforts should be directed toward academic and social development, but if the area of travel is neglected, the student may be denied the opportunity to move freely and independently in his school and community. In view of the relative importance of independent travel, an overview of the nature of training, the major modes of mobility, and the role of the regular classroom teacher will be presented.

The terms *"orientation"* and *"mobility"* are interrelated because mobility cannot be achieved unless the individual is oriented. *Orientation* refers to an individual's use of his remaining senses to establish his position and relationship to objects in his environment. *Mobility* refers to the individual's movement from one point in his environment to another. In other words, mobility is getting from point A to point B, whereas orientation involves the individual knowing his location, the location of his objective, and the most efficient way to reach the objective.

The regular classroom teacher is not responsible for formal training in orientation and mobility. The nature of this training is very specialized and should be conducted by an orientation and mobility specialist or by the resource/itinerant teacher. It is important, however, that the regular classroom teacher understand the nature of the training and the major methods or modes of independent travel. The five modes of travel used by visually impaired individuals are (1) the sighted guide, (2) the long cane, (3) dog guides, (4) electronic devices, and (5) independent travel without any assistance or devices.

One of the first techniques taught is the use of the *sighted guide*. It is an efficient way to "orient" an individual to an unfamiliar area and is also a viable mobility technique. It involves the visually impaired individual grasping a sighted person's arm just above the elbow. He will place his thumb on the outside and his fingers on the inside of the guide's arm and will walk about one half step behind the guide. In effect, the visually impaired person is "reading" the sighted individual's arm or elbow, and any movement of the guide's body and arm will be communicated to the student. By following approximately one half step behind, the student will know when the guide is stepping up or down, turning left or right, and so on. There are some additional methods related to the efficient use of this technique that would be taught by the resource/itinerant teacher or orientation and mobility specialist, but this is the essence of the sighted guide technique.

Use of the *long cane* is the most common systematic method of travel. The age at which a student is introduced to and provided formal training in the use of the cane is dependent on the student's maturity, need for more independent travel, and ability to profit from rather extensive one-to-one training. The decision to initiate this formal training in the use of a cane is made after careful consideration of the aforementioned factors. Generally, instruction in the use of the cane is not started until age 14 or 15, but some students have succeeded in learning cane techniques as early as age 11 or 12. There are many types of canes, but the most common are made of aluminum or fiberglass and are approximately one half inch in diameter. Some have a crook for balance and easy placement, and others have a golf club–type grip. The tip of the cane is usually made of steel or nylon.

The third mode of travel is the *dog guide*. Generally, a dog guide is not recommended until the student is at least age 17 or 18. Prior to this age the student may not have the maturity to handle a dog properly nor the need for more independent travel. Often young visually impaired students indicate an interest in obtaining a dog guide as a pet or com-

Ronald Stewart

panion but not necessarily for independence in traveling. For obvious reasons the dog guide should not be considered a pet, but rather a partner in achieving independent travel. Contrary to popular opinion, only a relatively small percentage of the visually impaired use dog guides. Specific informa-tion concerning dog guide agencies, such as cost and nature of training, may be provided by either the resource/itinerant teacher or the orientation and mobility specialist.

The *electronic mobility device* is the fourth mode of travel used by the visually impaired. A number of devices are available; they are used as a primary mobility tool or as a supplement to other devices such as the long cane. Although it is encouraging to see research being conducted in this most important area, it does not seem that any one device will meet the needs of all individuals. Some of the devices enhance hearing efficiency, some detect obstacles, others enable the individual to walk in a straight line, whereas others are directed at revealing the specific location of obstacles in the environment.

The fifth method of travel, *independent travel* without any assistance or device, is probably the method most commonly used by younger students. There are, however, certain basic skills that are prerequisite to other modes and are designed to achieve efficient and safe travel. These basic skills are taught at a very early age and are essential if the student is to achieve independent travel in his school and community. A few of the basic techniques that would be taught by the resource/itinerant teacher or orientation and mobility specialist are as follows:

1. Upper hand and forearm—protection for head and upper body from half-open doors, walls, and so on.
2. Lower hand and forearm—protection for lower body and location of desks, tables, and so on.
3. Trailing—following lightly over a straight surface with back of fingertips to locate specific objects or to get a parallel line of direction.
4. Direction taking—using an object or sound to establish a course of direction toward or away from an object

Patterns of familiarization, geographical directions, hearing acuteness for travel, sound localization, and the use of residual vision should be developed with the assistance of the resource/itinerant teacher or orientation and mobility specialist.

The type of mobility aid or device to be used, whether it be cane, dog, or electronic device, is totally an individual matter and should be given very careful consideration by the student, his parents, and others after extensive thought and planning in cooperation with the resource/itinerant teacher or orientation and mobility specialist.

It is highly desirable that the regular classroom teacher be aware of the nature of training provided by special education personnel so that she can reinforce concepts and specific techniques being taught. The teacher is generally able to observe the child in a variety of settings, under a variety of conditions, and at different times of the day, as well as being able to provide information to special education personnel concerning the transfer and maintenance of a desired concept or skill. It is not uncommon for a student to demonstrate efficiency with a particular skill when working with the resource/itinerant teacher, but be unable to transfer this skill when he returns to his classroom.

The teacher should be as specific as possible when giving directions to the student. For example, do not say to the child "Go down to Mr. Jones' office, which is about halfway down corridor number three." Instead, provide very specific directions such as "Go to Mr. Jones' office, which is on the right side of corridor number three, two doors past the water fountain." Directions in the classroom should also be specific. It would not be sufficient to say "Your science project is on the shelf in the back of the room." Instead, you might say "Your science project is on the shelf in the back of the room, three feet to the left of the sink, at the back of the shelf."

All the students should be acquainted with the proper procedures used in serving as a sighted guide. The resource/itinerant teacher or orientation and mobility specialist may want to attend or actually conduct this type of mini–in-service session. The students may want to wear blindfolds to gain a better un-

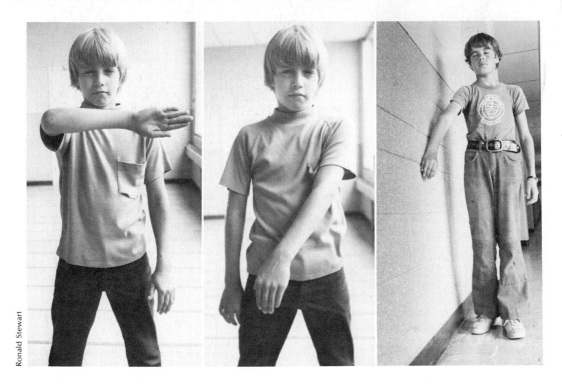

Ronald Stewart

derstanding of traveling without sight. Some caution should be exercised here so that the students do not develop a sympathetic attitude but rather an objective understanding of travel techniques used by the visually impaired.

Alternative teaching strategies and adaptations

It is generally not necessary for the regular classroom teacher to significantly change teaching strategies to accommodate a visually impaired student. However, it may be helpful to consider a few suggestions that have been found to be effective. Whenever possible, instruction should be initiated at a concrete level. It should start with concrete materials, moving more to the abstract as the student develops the concept. The use of manipulative, tangible, or auditory materials is preferred to totally verbal instructions or lessons. Although a model of an object may be necessary, the real object or situation is much preferred. For example, if a science lesson is concerned with simple pulleys, an actual pulley should be provided if possible. The resource/itinerant teacher is a valuable asset in this area and may be able to assist in obtaining the actual object or may make a model similar to the one needed.

"Learning by doing" and "teaching by unifying experiences" are certainly not new concepts to regular classroom teachers. These concepts, however, are particularly important to the student with impaired vision because he may not have the same experiential background as other students of the same age. Whenever possible, the visually impaired student should be allowed to actually experience "doing it" rather than just verbally explaining the process. Closely related to this is the need to unify or integrate experiences and concepts as often as possible. A young child may not be able to relate one isolated concept to another because he may not have had any previous experience with the particular concept.

When writing on the chalkboard, the teacher should be certain to explain verbally the concept or actual writing being presented. In general, any highly visual instructions or lessons should be supplemented with verbal explanation. This can become routine with a little effort and practice.

In art, emphasis should be placed on tactual activities such as clay modeling, finger painting, weaving, paper sculpture, and collage whenever possible. It is important that the student have the experience of carrying out the process involved in an art project; the end product should be deemphasized. By completing the process, in whatever medium, the student can achieve the same objectives as his peers.

Lessons in physical education or gross motor activities should be demonstrated by physically taking the student through the activity. For example, if a particular tumbling routine is being taught, the instructor may want to actually move the student through the correct movements rather than merely explain the process. A discussion of specific techniques for modifying physical education may be seen on p. 110.

Testing procedures may have to be modified for the visually impaired. Reading braille or large type takes considerably longer than reading standard print, and it may be necessary to either extend the amount of time for completion of the test or reduce the number of items. Of course, this would depend on whether the purpose of the test was speed or power; if the purpose is speed, the visually impaired student may have considerable difficulty. The administration of the test may also have to be modified; for example, it may be necessary to (1) administer the test orally,

(2) tape the test in advance and have the student type his answers, or (3) send the test home with the student and have the parent read the test while the student types or brailles his answers. Of course, some students require little or no modifications and would be able to take the test with the other students. Achievement tests administered at the beginning and end of the school year, because of their relative importance and the amount of time needed to complete them, may have to be administered by the resource/itinerant teacher or an aide. The regular teacher should be certain to consult with the resource/itinerant teacher in advance to consider these and other options for testing.

The visually impaired student who is partially seeing may become fatigued if tasks involving close visual examination are required for long periods of time. It may be helpful to vary activities as much as possible. This can be accomplished by alternating listening activities, close visual activities, and motor activities. The student should be encouraged to take short breaks from activities requiring prolonged periods of visual work whenever possible.

Teachers often express considerable concern when informed that they will have a braille-reading student in their classroom. Actually, it is not necessary for the teacher to know braille because the resource/itinerant teacher will write or print whatever the student has written directly above the braille dots. For example, if the student completes an assignment and turns it in to the regular teacher, the teacher should forward it to the resource/itinerant teacher, who will write in the student's responses and return it to the regular teacher. At the upper elementary, middle school, and secondary levels, the student may complete his assignment on a conventional typewriter (discussed on p. 85).

General considerations

When speaking to the visually impaired student during class discussion, the teacher should be certain to use the student's name because he may not know that the teacher is looking at him. For example, "Don, what is the answer to problem 16?" This would also be helpful when the teacher enters a room. The teacher should address the student by name and identify herself to let him know who has entered the room. Similarly, if the student enters a room where the teacher is alone, she should provide some indication that she is there, either by speaking to him directly or by some other auditory clue.

Established standards for grading or discipline should not be altered for the visually impaired student. When an assignment has been given or a classroom rule established, the visually impaired student should be expected to adhere to the same procedures as the other students. If the teacher employs a double standard, one for the class and another for the visually impaired student, the other students will be quick to recognize the difference and may resent the visually impaired student. This resentment may have a very adverse effect on their interpersonal relationships; the other students may identify the visually impaired student as the "teacher's pet" and subsequently reject him.

The student with impaired vision may not be able to see the teacher's facial gestures or smile when he has completed an assigned task successfully or look of displeasure when he has not. Physical contact, a pat on the back or a touch on the arm, may be necessary. Of course, the teacher should only praise the student when the job has been well done, not just because it was done by a visually impaired student.

Unless the eye specialist has indicated that the student should not use his vision, every effort must be made to increase the student's visual efficiency. If the visually impaired student has some remaining or residual vision, encourage him to use it to the fullest extent possible. It is not unusual for a student's measured visual acuity to remain the same over a period of years while his visual performance actually increases.

Somewhat related to this area is the use of low-vision or optical aids (such as magnifiers and special glasses). Students who use these aids should be encouraged to do so whenever appropriate. The regular classroom teacher should observe whether the device seems to be helpful, how often it is used, and under what conditions. Naturally, this information should be shared with the resource/itinerant teacher who, in turn, may share this information with the student's physician or low-vision aids specialist.

A "buddy" may be assigned by the teacher to assist the visually impaired student with, for example, highly visual assignments, orientation to a new school building, physical education activities, and emergencies such as fires. The use of a "buddy system" is a desirable approach to peer teaching or assistance regardless of whether or not there is a disabled student in the classroom.

The regular teacher should reinforce concepts taught by the resource/itinerant teacher, orientation and mobility specialist, or any other personnel working with the student. Communication between disciplines is essential if we are to see the needed transfer to every possible situation. One individual in the school environment may be emphasizing particular skills (such as using a particular magnification device, traveling independently, and typing), and another, being unaware of these efforts, will miss the opportunity to reinforce and ensure transfer and maintenance.

The needs for independence, freedom of movement, and play are as important for the student with impaired vision as for his sighted classmates. Approximately 130 years ago, Samuel Gridley Howe, a noted educator of the visually impaired, offered the following general rules in working with these children (Buell, 1950):

Never check the actions of the child; follow him, and watch him to prevent any serious accidents, but do not interfere unnecessarily; do not even remove obstacles which he would learn to avoid by tumbling over them a few times. Teach him to jump rope, to swing weights, to raise his body by his arms, and to mingle, as far as possible, in the rough sports of the older boys. Do not be apprehensive of his safety. If you should see him clambering in the branches of a tree be assured he is less likely to fall than if he had perfect vision. Do not too much regard bumps on the forehead, rough scratches, or bloody noses; even these may have their good influences. At the worst, they affect only the bark, and do not injure the system like the rust of inaction.

It is quite natural for a teacher who has not had previous experience with the visually impaired or with any handicapped students to be somewhat overprotective and to be concerned that these students will injure themselves on playground equipment or in traveling around the school building. However, every effort should be made *not* to underestimate their capabilities. The teacher's responsibility to the student with impaired vision is the same as for other students—to assist him in developing socially, emotionally, physically, morally, and educationally.

ROLE AND RESPONSIBILITY OF THE RESOURCE/ITINERANT TEACHER

The role and responsibility of the resource/itinerant teacher varies from school district to school district and at times within a single district. The exact nature of the resource/itinerant teacher's assignment will depend on the following factors:

1. Geographic distance to be traveled between schools. Some teachers are responsible for only one school, whereas others may have responsibilities extending to two or three schools. In some rural areas the resource/itinerant teacher may travel to several communities.
2. Number of students and teachers to be served.
3. Age of students; generally, the younger the student, the more need for direct service.
4. The number of braille-readers and print-readers. This can vary extensively; generally, the braille-reading student will require considerably more direct services.
5. Availability of orientation and mobility instruction. If an orientation and mobility specialist is not available, the resource/itinerant teacher may be responsible for this instruction.
6. Availability of paid or volunteer braille transcribers, large-print typists, and tape transcribers.
7. Availability of adapted and special materials. In states in which an instructional materials center for the visually impaired is available, the acquisition and distribution of educational materials can be greatly facilitated.

Resource/itinerant teachers generally provide services on the basis of direct or indirect service. Direct service involves working directly with the visually impaired student on a one-to-one basis or in small groups. Indirect service involves working with individuals other than the student, such as the child's teacher, administrators, medical personnel, and parents. The extent to which the resource/itinerant teacher works directly with the student would depend on the preceding variables. Most resource/itinerant personnel will provide both direct and indirect services.

Although it is sometimes difficult to clearly establish that one type of service is direct and

Ronald Stewart

another indirect, the following discussion of specific responsibilities will relate to the type of service provided.

Direct service to students

As mentioned previously, there are a number of "plus factors" that must be provided in addition to regular curricular offerings such as reading, math, and social studies. These plus factors would be provided by the resource/itinerant teacher.

Specialized instruction in reading. The resource/itinerant teacher will provide the needed instruction in braille reading and writing and the use of slate and stylus. The amount of time required for instruction in these special skills will depend on the age of the student. More time will be required for a younger braille-reading student because he will be developing these specialized skills during his elementary school years, whereas the student at the secondary level may have already developed these skills. Braille instruction should be provided on a daily scheduled basis for the first three years of the student's education or until he develops the necessary competency. After the student is relatively proficient at braille reading and writing, it may not be necessary for the resource/itinerant teacher to work with the student on a daily basis.

If a student is a print-reader, the amount

of instruction will usually not be as great as for a braille-reader. However, if the student uses low-vision aids (magnification devices), it may be necessary to provide specific instruction in their use.

Instruction in listening skills. It has been estimated that forty-five percent of our time in communication is spent in listening activities and that approximately two thirds of a student's school day is spent in activities related to listening. Listening is one of the most significant avenues of learning for the visually impaired student. He must rely on his auditory channel more than his sighted classmates. As a result, systematic instruction in listening activities must be provided. Instruction in listening should include a variety of listening situations, such as environmental, formal presentations, informal conversations, and audio reading required by using talking books and tape-recorded materials.

Instruction in the use of adapted or special equipment and aids. Specialized instruction in the use of equipment and aids such as tape recorders, tape players, and talking-book machines will be necessary for the visually impaired. Special mathematical computation devices such as the abacus and talking calculator and instruction in the use of special maps will also be required. Generally, instruction in the use of this equipment will be introduced as the need arises rather than systematically scheduled as with braille instruction.

Development of visual efficiency. Through systematic instruction the visual efficiency of a low-vision student can be increased. Special techniques and materials to determine the amount of visual efficiency and specific techniques to increase visual ability are available. Constant visual stimulation provided through a sequentially planned program can increase the visual efficiency of many students. This instruction should be provided by the special resource/itinerant teacher on a routine basis. The resource/itinerant teacher may also observe the student in the regular classroom to determine if the student is using his vision as much as possible.

Instruction in writing. Instruction in handwriting for a partially seeing student should be initiated at the same time as it is introduced to his sighted classmates. It may be necessary, however, for the resource/itinerant teacher to provide supplemental assistance in this area. The braille-reading student will want to gain some proficiency at handwriting so that he can sign his own name and make brief notations. Special handwriting aids and instruction will be necessary to achieve this skill.

Typing, using an electric typewriter (if available), is routinely taught to visually impaired students. Since their handwriting may be difficult to read and braille writing can only be read by a few individuals, typing can be a boost to their written communication skills. Instruction is generally initiated at about the fourth grade level. Often, typing is taught to the student along with spelling assignments because there is considerable repetition in both subject areas. As the student increases his typing proficiency he can complete more and more assignments with the aid of the typewriter. The adapted approach to instruction is known as "touch typing" and employs a special system that does not require vision. Naturally, accuracy is emphasized rather than speed, since it will be difficult for the student to check his work. Instruction in this area is usually continuous throughout the student's upper elementary and secondary school years.

Instruction in techniques of daily living. To function effectively as a responsible and contributing member of society requires more than just being able to complete the required academic tasks such as reading and writing. Often a visually impaired individual does not know how to carry out all the activities of independent living such as personal grooming, housecleaning, cooking and serving food, and home repair. These specific activities of daily living must be part of the visually impaired student's school curriculum. Many of these activities could be provided in a home economics course at the secondary level, but often the home economics teacher is not familiar with the ways in which these activities should be modified or adapted or with the special equipment available. Often these techniques are taught after school, in the evening, or in Saturday programs; but in the event they are not offered at these times, they may have to be provided during school hours by the resource/itinerant teacher independently or in cooperation with others.

Instruction in orientation and mobility. The extent to which the resource/itinerant teacher is responsible for direct instruction in orientation and mobility will depend on whether an orientation and mobility specialist is available. If available, the specialist will be responsible for formal instruction; if not, the resource/itinerant teacher will assume this responsibility. There are, however, certain basic or "precane" skills that may be taught by the resource/itinerant teacher. In addition, the resource/itinerant teacher will be responsible for familiarizing or orienting the student to a new classroom or school building and supplementing the instruction of the orientation and mobility specialist. Throughout the student's educational program, orientation and mobility should be systematically provided.

Student and parent counseling. Many resource/itinerant teachers assume responsibility for student and parent counseling and for seeking appropriate professional counseling when needed. They may work with the student for several years, whereas the student's regular teachers may only be in close contact with the student for one year. Resource/itinerant teachers are acquainted with the unique problems imposed by impaired vision and their relationship to adjustment and social and emotional growth. They may also be in the best position to discuss personal problems, interests, and projected vocational plans.

Although the primary responsibility for reporting student progress rests with the regular classroom teacher, the resource/itinerant teacher should attend parent-teacher conferences to report the student's progress in the special areas. Often it is necessary for the resource/itinerant teacher to meet separately with the student's parents to interpret special programming efforts or other special problems that may be related to the student's visual impairment.

Supplementary or introductory instructions. Because it may take longer for the student to complete an assignment or because the assignment may be highly visual, it is often necessary for the resource/itinerant teacher to supplement the instruction of the regular classroom teacher. For example, if the process of "carrying" in mathematical addition is being introduced, the resource/itinerant teacher may want to introduce the use of a special mathematics aid that would be of assistance, or she may want to supplement the regular classroom teacher's instruction by using a special "mental mathematics" technique.

Often the resource/itinerant teacher will want to introduce a particular concept prior to its actual introduction in the regular classroom. For example, a unit on the solar system may have considerably more meaning to the visually impaired student if the resource/itinerant teacher provides a model of the solar system and actually introduces the unit to the student. In physical education it is often necessary to orient the student to special equipment, games, or activities prior to the physical education period so that the student acquires a basic understanding of the concept and so that the physical education instructor will not have to take a disproportionate amount of time to introduce the concept. Supplemental or introductory instruction can play a very important role in the education of the visually impaired child in a regular classroom.

Indirect services

Services provided to individuals other than the student are considered indirect services. As mentioned previously, there are a number of variables determining the nature and extent of indirect services provided. The following discussion provides an overview of indirect services that might be provided by a resource/itinerant teacher.

Preparation of materials. If the needed educational material is not available from any agency in the desired format and all sources have been queried, it may be necessary to have a paid or volunteer transcriber-reproducer prepare the material. The resource/itinerant teacher would serve as the liaison between the classroom teacher and the transcriber-reproducer to ensure that the material is in the needed format and that it is completed in sufficient time.

Many day-to-day materials such as teacher-made tests, work sheets, and special projects obviously would not be available from outside agencies; therefore, it would be the responsibility of the resource/itinerant teacher to have these materials prepared or prepare them herself. The type of material needed would be quite varied, ranging from a teacher-made mathematics test to a geologic survey map of the county.

Often it is not practical or possible to have a text brailled on relatively short notice, or because it may only be used once. In this event, the resource/itinerant teacher would assist in arranging for the material to be read aloud by another person. The use of "readers" is a technique used frequently by secondary school students, and if used properly, it can be a tremendous advantage to the visually impaired student.

Acquisition of materials. The acquisition of educational materials such as braille or enlarged-type texts, tapes, and tangible apparatus is one of the primary responsibilities of the resource/itinerant teacher. These materials must duplicate the content of the materials being used by the other students and must be obtained in the shortest possible time. There are several well-established procedures that will be used by the resource/itinerant teacher to obtain the needed material in the needed format without duplication of efforts. These procedures involve checking national and state agencies and volunteer groups prior to the actual transcription or production of the desired material.

Conducting in-service sessions. The resource/itinerant teacher may be responsible for the in-service education of regular teachers and administrators. She may be expected to acquaint a building staff with the rationale underlying integrated placement of the visually impaired student if the staff has not had previous experience with these students. The nature of the in-service education may be quite general and relate only to the philosophy of integrated education. In other instances it may be directed at a small group of teachers who will have the student in their classes and would specifically relate to techniques for modifying and adapting materials or teaching strategies.

The resource/itinerant teacher may conduct mini—in-service sessions with a group of students to acquaint them with the nature of impaired vision to ready them for a visually impaired classmate. At other times, student in-service sessions may relate to the special materials and techniques that will be used.

Another in-service role often assumed by the resource/itinerant teacher is to provide select journal articles, readings, or films for regular classroom teachers. These readings or materials would be directed at providing the needed competencies to more effectively work with the visually impaired student.

Assuming responsibility for coordination of outside services. The resource/itinerant teacher often assumes responsibility for providing and coordinating many other services needed in addition to classroom activities. The resource/itinerant teacher may coordinate orientation and mobility services, or therapeutic recreation and leisure activities. She may also assist in planning and implementing work-study or vocational education programs. In general, her role is one of student advocacy—by providing all needed services and programs necessary for the student's complete educational and social development.

Assisting in adapting or modifying activities. The resource/itinerant teacher may assist the physical education, art, music, home economics, or industrial arts teacher in adapting or modifying a particular lesson or activity. If the resource/itinerant teacher has established a routine and ongoing communication system with all teachers, it is relatively easy to anticipate an activity that may need modification or adaptation. The resource/itinerant teacher may offer specific suggestions on how to change the activity in such a way that the visually impaired student can meet the objective of the lesson. Sometimes it is desirable for the resource/itinerant teacher to actually attend the activity to assist the student or his teacher.

Interpreting medical information. Often the resource/itinerant teacher is expected to serve as a liaison between medical personnel and the regular classroom teachers. She may be asked to interpret medical reports and to explain the nature of the eye condition and the limitations imposed by it. In addition, she must share information concerning seating arrangements, lighting requirements, and levels of visual expectation for the partially seeing student. She may also be asked to evaluate the suitability of materials to be used, particularly in the areas of clarity of pictures, type size, spacing, and margins.

SUMMARY

Most students with severe visual impairments are identified prior to enrollment in school. There are, however, a significant number whose impaired vision goes undetected even during their school years. Teachers must be aware of signs and behaviors that may indicate visual loss and be prepared to make the necessary referrals. In this chapter we have examined the educational needs of visually impaired students and provided detailed suggestions for modifying and adapting classroom methods and materials to better meet their needs. In addition, the role and responsibility of resource/itinerant personnel was reviewed, providing the regular classroom teacher with insight into their specific function.

The key to the successful integration of visually impaired students is communication between the regular classroom teacher and the resource/itinerant teacher. An open and ongoing communication system that will provide for sharing of information concerning students' needs, interests, problems, and abilities must be established. Each professional must share his unique expertise and competency with the others to provide the best possible program for these students.

Although many specific suggestions of assistance to the regular classroom teacher have been offered, some care must be exercised so the student does not become so *special* that he becomes the "teacher's pet." If this occurs because we have attempted to do too many special things for him, we have defeated the very purpose of an integrated program.

In many respects, the visually impaired

student is easier to teach in the regular class than any other type of handicapped student, for he is very likely to do well academically and may cause little, if any, management problems with regard to behavior. On the other hand, there are indications that in the past we have focused too much on academic behavior to the detriment of teaching techniques of daily living; the regular classroom teacher, along with the parents, must play the major role in this area. The visually impaired student must be deliberately treated more normally and less like a handicapped individual in all possible classroom interactions. This may be the major challenge to the regular classroom teacher when planning the best possible program for the visually impaired.

REFERENCES AND SUGGESTED READINGS

Alonso, L. What the teacher can do for the child with impaired vision. *NEA Journal*, November 1967, *56*, 42-43.

Barber, G. A. Teaching the blind: the resource room approach. *Education*, February 1960, *80*, 333-336.

Barry, E. Resource program for the visually handicapped. *California Education*, May 1966, *3*, 6-8.

Bateman, B. Sighted children's perceptions of blind children's abilities. *Exceptional Children*, September 1962, *29*, 42-47.

Bruce, R. E. Using overhead projector with visually impaired students. *Education of the Visually Handicapped*, May 1973, *5*, 43-46.

Buell, C. Motor performance of visually handicapped children (Unpublished doctoral dissertation, University of California, Berkeley, 1950).

Buell, C. Is vigorous physical activity feasible for blind children in public schools? *Journal of Health, Physical Education, Recreation*, February 1969, *40*, 97-98.

Buell, C. How to include blind and partially seeing children in public secondary school vigorous physical education. *Physical Education*, March 1972, *29*, 6-8.

Deahl, T., & Deahl, M. Integrating partially sighted children in the classroom, *Instructor*, October 1973, *83*, 142-143.

Forman, E. The inclusion of visually limited and blind children in a sighted physical education program. *Education of the Visually Handicapped*, December 1969, 113-115.

Freund, C. Teaching art to the blind child integrated with sighted children. *New Outlook for the Blind*, 1969, *63*, 205-210.

Haack, J. The visually handicapped: in your classroom? *Instructor*, March 1966, *75*, 62-64.

Hall, C. Introducing sighted children to visual handicaps: a short program description. *Education of the Visually Handicapped*, Fall 1976, *7*(3), 91-94.

Hathaway, W. *Education and health of the partially seeing child*. New York: Columbia University Press, 1959.

Helping the partially seeing child in the regular classroom. Pittsburgh, Pa.: Pittsburgh Branch of Pennsylvania Association for the Blind, 1967.

Hoffman, H. W. Exceptional child: 10 ways to help the partially sighted. *Teacher*, September 1972, *90*, 140-141.

Jacobson, I. Getting ready for vision screening. *Instructor*, October 1973, *83*, 143.

Johansen, G. Integrating visually handicapped children into a public elementary school physical education program. *Journal of Health, Physical Education, Recreation*, April 1971, *42*, 63-64.

Johnson, P. R. Physical education for blind children in public elementary schools. *New Outlook for the Blind*, 1969, *63*, 264-271.

Johnson, Y. *A blind child becomes a member of your class*. New York: American Foundation for the Blind, 1961.

Jones, C. R. Art for the blind and partially seeing. *School Arts*, 1961, *60*, 21-22.

Jones, J. W., & Collins, A. P. Trends in program and pupil placement practices in the special education of visually handicapped children. *Education of the Blind*, 1965, *14*, 97-101.

Jose, R. T., & Rosenbloom, A. A., Jr. The role of the low vision assistant in the care of visually impaired persons. *New Outlook for the Blind*, January 1975, *69*, 20-24.

Laufman, M. Blind children in integrated recreation. *New Outlook for the Blind*, 1962, *56*, 81-84.

Marsh, V., & Friedman, R. Changing public attitudes toward blindness. *Exceptional children*, January 1972, *38*, 426-428.

Moor, P. M. *A blind child, too, can go to nursery school*. New York: American Foundation for the Blind, 1952.

Morin, A. Waukegan finds advantages in the itinerant teacher plan. *Sight Saving Review*, Spring 1960, *30*, 33-35.

Napier, G., Kappan, D. L., Tuttle, D. W., Schrotberger, W. L., & Dennison, A. L. *Handbook for teachers of the visually handicapped*. Louisville: American Printing House for the Blind, 1975.

National Society for the Prevention of Blindness. *Vo-

cabulary of terms relating to the eye, Publication No. 172. New York: Author, 1957.

Nezol, A. J. Physical education for integrated blind students. *Education of the Visually Handicapped*, March 1972, *4*, 16-18.

Pelone, A. J. *Helping the visually handicapped child in a regular class*. New York: Teachers College, Columbia University Press, 1957.

Poppelen, V. D. Blind triumph in a seeing school. *Arts and Activities*, April 1968, *63*, 21.

Randolph, L. G. Don't rearrange the classroom! Why not? *Education of the Visually Handicapped*, October 1970, *2*, 83-86.

Scholl, G. *The principal works with the visually impaired*. Reston, Va.: Council for Exceptional Children, 1968.

Scholl, G. Visually handicapped children in the regular classroom. *Teacher*, February 1978, *95*(6), 79-82.

Skinner, D. The partially sighted child in the regular classroom. *Special Education—Canada*, March 1970, *44*, 26-28.

Stephens, T. M., & Birch, J. Merits of special class, resource, and itinerant plans for teaching partially seeing children. *Exceptional Children*, February 1969, *35*, 481-484.

Tait, P. E. Believing without seeing: teaching the blind child in a regular kindergarten. *Childhood Education*, March 1974, *50*, 285-291.

Tomasek, D. Teaching the blind to type, *Rehabilitation Gazette*, 1976, *18*, 13-14.

Trevena, T. M. Integration of sightless children into regular physical activities. *Journal of Health, Physical Education, Recreation*, June 1970, *41*, 42-43.

Winkley, W. M. Public high school or residential high school for blind students. *Education of the Visually Handicapped*, December 1972, *4*, 86-87.

Workshop: teaching blind children, first take them out of special classes. *School Management*, September 1967, *2*, 15.

5 EDUCATIONAL MODIFICATIONS FOR CRIPPLED AND OTHER HEALTH IMPAIRED STUDENTS

Ronald Stewart

One of the most heterogeneous categories in special education is the area of crippling conditions and other health impairments. Students grouped under this broad category range from the cerebral palsied (a condition commonly associated with secondary or multiply handicapping conditions) to the student with asthma, those handicapped as a result of an accident, and the child born without a limb. One student may have limited use of his arms but have good use of his legs, another may have use of all extremities but have considerable difficulty breathing, and another may be generally weak because of a progressive condition. One may be completely mobile in the classroom, another mobile with the use of crutches, and still another confined to a wheelchair. In the sections that follow, a number of suggestions are made that relate to specific conditions. There are, however, some general areas that should first be considered.

The primary focus of programming for students with crippling conditions is modification and, as much as possible, the elimination of physical barriers. The term "least restrictive environment" in PL 94-142 is primarily concerned with the appropriate placement for handicapped students. This term has special meaning when applied to students with crippling conditions. The least restrictive environment for these students implies appropriate academic placement, but suggests additionally that the physical environment of the building and classroom be given careful consideration.

The mere presence or placement of a handicapped student in the classroom and accomplishment of assigned academic tasks may represent only a small part of the individual's total educational need. Independent ambulation is an important factor in the student's total development, possibly more important to the student than many of the academic challenges presented in the classroom. Movement is essential not only for the obvious reasons of maintaining and improving motor function, but also for facilitation of important psychosocial interactions. The teacher should be aware of the effects that lack of movement has on the student and his interaction with peers. The school and classroom should be arranged to enable student movement to all areas. Independent ambulation must be given priority if the student is to be allowed an equal opportunity to grow socially, educationally, and emotionally.

Because of the diversity of problems presented by this population, a complete continuum of educational services must be offered, ranging from full-time special class placement for the multiply handicapped or severely physically disabled to full-time regular class placement for those able to function and achieve in that environment. Children who are temporarily disabled by infectious diseases or accidents may receive hospital or homebound instruction. The primary goal or direction of educational services should be the inclusion of these students in regular classrooms wherever possible. Today it is possible for more children to be educated in regular classes than in years past because of the reduction of architectural barriers, as required by the Rehabilitation Act of 1973 (Section 504). School buildings built around the turn of the century were typically multilevel buildings with many stairs and second-story entrances, whereas today's schools are generally one-level structures, much more accessible or adaptable for the child with limited mobility. However, even more modern schools often require modification. Some modifications include bathroom stalls made wider and deeper, sinks and water fountains lowered to enable individuals in wheelchairs to use them, classroom doors widened to accommodate wheelchairs, and blackboards lowered and hinged to allow someone in a wheelchair to write comfortably.

There are many variables contributing to the increasing number of physically disabled students who attend regular classes. One factor is the changing nature of the population served. Because of advanced medical and technological procedures, many students are not as seriously disabled as students with the same condition were thirty years ago. For example, in the past, children born with congenital heart defects were seriously disabled, generally for life, whereas today most of these defects can be surgically corrected, and the child may live without serious restrictions. Changes in treatment procedures for conditions such as asthma, diabetes, and heart defects allow these students to participate in nearly all activities. Students are fitted with artificial limbs much earlier today than they were previously. Congenital defects such as clubfoot can generally be corrected early, and the child can participate fully in nearly all endeavors. Many students who might have attended special schools in years past are now attending regular public schools with minor modifications and adaptations.

The following information on disabilities and related adaptations is presented on the basis of medically derived or defined conditions. Although there are disadvantages to discussing a condition on the basis of medical diagnosis rather than educational implications, it is hoped that through this approach teachers will seek specific suggestions concerning educational procedures on the basis of a particular disability. For example, if a child has epilepsy, teachers are encouraged to seek information concerning the nature of the condition, the treatment procedures, educational implications, and the unique management techniques that must be employed.

As mentioned previously, this is an extremely heterogeneous population. There are more than two hundred possible conditions included in the category; however, we will discuss only the conditions most commonly found in regular classrooms. This chapter is presented in a different format than other chapters in that educational implications are summarized after discussion of each condition rather than at the end of the chapter.

ALLERGIES

Nature of condition. An allergy is an adverse sensitivity or intolerance to a specific substance that may not be a problem to other individuals. When an allergic student comes in contact with the substance to which he is sensitive, he develops a reaction or an irritation. The reaction may take many forms, such as sneezing, watering eyes, runny nose, tiredness, itching, or a rash. The student may react to a number of different substances. Among the most common are inhalants (pollen, smoke, dust, and perfumes, for example), foods (eggs, chocolate, wheat, pork, strawberries, nuts, and citrus fruits, for example), infectious agents (bacteria and fungi, for example), substances that come in contact with the skin (poison ivy, poison sumac, fur, leather, animal hair, and dyes, for example), and drugs (vaccines, serums, and antibiotics, for example).

Treatment procedures. The first step is to determine the cause of the allergy. The physician may prescribe medication for temporary relief; but generally, he will carefully study the student's medical history, home surroundings, eating habits, and so on to determine which allergens the student is sensitive to. He may conduct specific allergy tests such as skin tests on the arm or back to determine substances to which the child reacts. He may also suggest a series of shots to desensitize the student to a particular substance. The student with allergies can participate fully in nearly all educational programs. The teacher may, however, assist in identifying the specific sensitivity, particularly if the student seems to have more difficulty when at school. If an allergic reaction is suspected, this should be reported to the student's parents or school nurse, since treatment can do a great deal to ease the effects of the condition. In addition, there is a tendency for students with allergies to develop asthma, and this should be avoided if at all possible.

Educational implications. Some students may miss school because of their condition, particularly during early fall or in the spring when ragweed pollen levels are highest. Missing school and associated problems should not greatly interfere with the educational process except for being a nuisance to the student. It is the teacher's responsibility to make certain the student completes missed assignments. It may also be necessary to provide additional instruction or establish a peer teaching arrangement.

Although it is an individual matter, some students with allergies fatigue more easily than other students while participating in physical activities. As a result, they may withdraw during recess or physical education while their classmates continue. This must be observed very carefully, since withdrawal may have serious social and emotional resultants. Because physical fitness is an important component of treatment, the teacher may assist by modifying or adapting the activity so that the student is encouraged to participate as much as possible. The teacher should also carefully observe to see if there is any change in the student's condition as a result of activity and report this information to the parents or physician. The student must learn how to live with the limitations caused by allergies and develop a life-style that allows him a maximum amount of freedom.

ASTHMA

Nature of condition. Asthma usually results from an allergic state that causes an obstruction of the bronchial tubes, the lungs, or both. When sensitivity flares into an attack, an excessive amount of mucus is produced, and there is a spasm of the bronchial musculature. As a result, breathing becomes difficult, and the student may lose his color, wheeze, and perspire excessively. The attack may last for a few minutes, for hours, or for days.

An asthma attack can be a frightening experience because of the labored breathing and other behaviors. The attack may be brought on by a specific sensitivity to an allergen, by exposure to excessive physical activity, or it may be an emotional reaction. The influence of emotional factors is not well established. Some authorities believe that emotional factors play an important role in asthma, whereas others believe there is little or no relationship.

Treatment procedures. Treatment procedures are similar to those for allergic individuals. Adrenaline administered by injection or by inhalation usually gives relief for brief periods; however, since asthma is a chronic condition, long-term treatment procedures must be employed.

Educational implications. Students with asthma should be treated as normally as possible. Caution must be exercised to avoid overprotection from routine classroom activities. If care is not practiced, the student may become an asthmatic or emotional cripple. The teacher should be aware of the factors that precipitate an asthma attack and have information concerning the proper course of action should an attack occur. Management of students with asthma should include attention to psychological factors that may aggravate the condition. The teacher should also be aware of possible side effects or behavioral changes that may be related to prescribed drugs being used by the student. Teachers are in a unique position to observe the student during a variety of activities throughout the school day. They can provide a positive learning atmosphere,

Ronald Stewart

an atmosphere that promotes growth, acceptance, and independence. Information provided by the teacher may be very helpful to parents or the physician in determining subsequent treatment procedures.

There has been research recently concerning the extent to which asthmatic students should participate in physical activities. In years past, it was believed that these students should be excluded from physical education or physically exerting activities. The results of the recent research clearly indicate that there are many beneficial effects of exercise and activity in relationship to long-term care and treatment of asthma (Seligman, Randel, and Stevens, 1970; Scherr and Charleston, 1958). Many of the

limitations formerly placed on these students may have done more harm than good. Generally, the student will regulate himself—if he runs too long, he may start wheezing and naturally will rest. Physical restrictions may have adverse psychological effects, which are as great a danger as the physical problem itself. A good general rule to follow with any health impairment, including asthma, is to check with the parents or physician to determine more specifically what the individual student can and cannot do.

ARTHRITIS

Nature of condition. Although arthritis is primarily a condition that occurs in adults, it can begin at any age. The most common form of arthritis in students is called *juvenile rheumatoid arthritis*. It may have a very sudden onset, or it may be a slow, gradual disease, with quite variable effects and complications. In some instances it may only last a few weeks or months and not seriously limit the student. In other cases it may be a chronic condition that continues throughout the student's life, becoming worse as time goes on. Rheumatoid arthritis attacks the joints of the body, and may involve many organs, such as the heart, liver, and spleen. There may be a skin rash, inflammation of the eyes, retardation of growth, and swelling and pain in the fingers, wrists, elbows, knees, hips, and feet. As the disease progresses, the joints may stiffen, making movement very difficult and painful. *Osteoarthritis*, or the wear-and-tear type of arthritis, is generally confined to one joint and does not affect the whole body.

Treatment procedures. The major aim of treatment is to allow the student to live as normally as possible. Many times students with arthritis become "care-cripples." In other words, they are overprotected and not allowed to participate fully in the activities of home or school. Juvenile arthritis is self-limiting, and the student will ordinarily use good sense in determining whether he should participate in an activity.

Treatment procedures are generally highly individualized because no two cases are exactly alike. Because of the variance between patients and their individual response to drugs, the drugs prescribed by the physician may be different in each case. Generally, aspirin is the single most effective drug used in the treatment of arthritis because it reduces pain and inflammation of the joints and is among the safest drugs on the market. Usually, large amounts are prescribed on a routine basis, and dosage must be continued even after the swelling and pain have subsided. Special exercises may be prescribed

and will involve putting the joints through a full range of motion to prevent joint deformity and loss of strength in the muscles. Heat treatments may also be prescribed to enable joints to move more smoothly and with less pain. Heat treatments take a variety of forms and may be carried out at home or in a clinic. Surgical procedures are also used to prevent and correct deformity caused by this disease. For some children, splints, braces, or plaster casts are prescribed to subdue inflammation and protect the joint or joints from becoming frozen.

Educational implications. The educational modifications necessary for the student with juvenile arthritis depend on his age, severity of condition, independent travel ability, and range of motion in the arms, hands, and fingers. This student probably will not need special curricular methods or materials in the academic areas. However, if the joints in his upper extremities are severely involved, he may need writing aids, adapted paper, or special pencils. It is likely that he will have the most difficulty with walking since the knees, ankles, and hips may be more involved than the upper body, and as he travels he may experience considerable pain. As a result, it may be well to consider somewhat limited movement for many of these students. However, some students may experience increased joint stiffness during prolonged immobility and may need to get up and walk to relieve the discomfort. This, of course, depends on the individual, since many students will not experience this difficulty to any great extent. Some students may need an individualized physical education program or a program carried out by a physical therapist, whereas others may need very little modification in their physical education program.

Teachers should watch for any changes in vision, because eye disease is commonly associated with rheumatoid arthritis. In particular, pain in the eyes or light sensitivity may indicate the need to be seen by an ophthalmologist. It is generally recommended that the student be checked for changes in vision at least every six to nine months.

Although it is not certain, there does seem to be some evidence that emotional stress is related to attacks of arthritis (Abruzzo, 1971; Cobb and Stanislav, 1966; Decker, 1967). This does not imply that the teacher should modify academic and social standards but does dictate that the teacher be aware of the general emotional climate and its possible effects on the child.

The teacher should be aware of other implications for the arthritic child. For example, the child may miss a considerable amount of school when he has attacks. Faulty posture habits should be avoided, since good body alignment and posture are important in reducing the effects of arthritis. Activities such as extensive and prolonged writing may need to be avoided because they may be painful for the student. It may also be necessary to give the student extra time to get to and from classrooms and extra time for completing assignments.

The student must learn to live with arthritis and accept the limitations imposed by it. An understanding teacher can do a great deal to assist the student in living with this condition.

AMPUTATION

Nature of condition. A missing limb may be a congenital condition, or the limb(s) may have been amputated as a result of trauma, disease, or infection. In nearly all instances, the student will be fitted with an artificial arm or leg (prosthesis). Generally, the student with a congenital condition will be fitted with the prosthesis very early and will have adapted to it by the time he begins school. The prosthesis may be made of wood, metal, or plastic. Plastic materials are being used with greater frequency today because they are light; this is a factor that may influence the student's functioning.

Educational implications. Students with a prosthesis are usually able to function at nearly normal capacity and will require very little educational modification. The extent of modification, however, depends on the age of the student, the site of the amputation (the higher on the extremity, the more severe), and the child's adjustment to the disability.

There are a few factors of which the regular classroom teacher should be aware to ensure the best educational programming. The following suggestions should be considered:

1. Because of growth, a student's prosthesis will rarely fit for more than one year. As a result, the teacher must be certain the student is using the prosthesis effectively and that it fits properly. The student will visit the prosthetist for routine adjustments and fitting.

2. The teacher should have general information, particularly for a younger student, concerning the basic mechanics, proper fitting, and maintenance of the prosthesis. This information may be obtained from the student, the student's parents, the resource/itinerant teacher, or by visiting a prosthetist. If the student feels comfortable in discussing his prosthesis, it would be of great social and psychological value for him to explain its function to the entire class. Of course, this depends on the age of the other students and the extent to which the student has adjusted to the amputation.

3. Proper exercise is very important for the child, particularly in the joints around the amputation. Physical education activities and games may be adapted or individualized to ensure maximum fitness and exercise. It is

not uncommon to read or hear about individuals with amputations who not only participate, but excel, in competitive athletic events. Many individuals with lower extremity amputations participate and compete successfully in activities such as bowling, snow skiing and waterskiing, golf, and even football.

4. Postural habits must be carefully observed to ensure that the student does not develop spinal curvatures such as scoliosis (lateral curvature of the spine resulting in a C-shaped curve). The student may develop habits such as using only one side of his body, causing postural problems. Postural problems can limit his body mechanics and general functioning. If the student has a lower extremity amputation, the teacher must observe to see that unusual gait or ambulation problems do not develop.

5. Proper hygienic principles must be exercised in the care of the stump. It should be kept clean and allowed to air for brief periods. Although these practices will typically be conducted at home, the teacher should be aware of this need.

6. Some students with amputations may use modified or adapted equipment such as pencil holders, page turners, or other reading and writing aids. Many of these materials are available from commercial sources, others may be easily adapted or made by the teacher. The resource/itinerant teacher may be of assistance in modifying materials and equipment.

7. Curricular modifications may also be necessary. For example, typing may be taught using a one-handed method with very little modification. A book of instructions that may be read by both the student and the typing instructor is available from Southwestern Publishing Company in San Francisco and is entitled *Type With One Hand*, by Nina K. Richardson. The resource/itinerant teacher should have information concerning this type of material. The occupational therapist is a valuable resource person and should be consulted when questions arise. The occupational therapist can assist in modifying equipment and materials and can plan and initiate activities that will facilitate maximum functioning for the student. Amputations in children are generally not as troublesome as they are in adults because children are more tolerant and adaptable. They generally can participate in regular classrooms very successfully with only minor modifications and adaptations.

DIABETES

Nature of condition. Diabetes is a metabolic disorder wherein the individual's body is unable to utilize and properly store sugar. This condition is a result of the inability of the pancreas to produce a sufficient amount of the hormone *insulin*.

Although diabetes is most frequently seen in adults, it does occur in younger students and can become a serious problem if the proper treatment procedures are not adhered to. Symptoms indicative of diabetes that classroom teachers should be aware of are unusually frequent urination, abnormal thirst, extreme hunger, changes in weight (generally a rapid loss), drowsiness, general weakness, possible visual disturbances, and skin infections such as boils or itching. If a child indicates any of these symptoms, the school nurse and the student's parents should be contacted as soon as possible. Prompt medical diagnosis and treatment are essential in the care of the diabetic student.

Treatment procedures. If diabetes is diagnosed, treatment procedures will probably involve daily injections of insulin, adherence to a rather strict diet to maintain the correct sugar level, and a balance between exercise and rest. Generally, students with diabetes can have a happy childhood and adolescence, and can do almost everything their peers do, except fill up on sweets, and they must maintain a balance between the previously mentioned variables.

To most of us, the thought of daily injections may seem like a serious proposition, but to the student with diabetes this will become a very routine matter. The injections are generally administered at home and become as routine as other hygienic practices, such as bathing or brushing teeth. Often the student and his parents will attend a clinic that will teach them how to manage daily activities such as injections, diet, exercise, care of the feet (this can be a definite problem because of poor circulation), and the changes in life-style that are necessary to accommodate the condition. As a result of these clinics, the student will know a great deal about his condition and will know how to manage it.

Educational implications. There are several potential problems the classroom teacher should be aware of, such as an insulin reaction (hypoglycemia) and diabetic coma. An insulin reaction may result from anything that increases the metabolic rate, such as too much exercise, too much insulin, too little food, or nervous tension. It may occur anytime during the day but most often occurs before meals or after strenuous exercise. For instance, an insulin reaction may occur if the student refuses to finish his breakfast; the usual dose of insulin may become unbalanced by the reduced food intake. Emotional tension about school or personal problems may have variable effects. Occasionally, tension may cause the blood sugar level to fall below normal, resulting in an insulin reaction.

The insulin reaction may follow a stereotyped pattern for each individual, so it is important to consult with the student or his parents to determine what these signs may be. Often, general irritability may be the first sign. One student may be despondent and cry readily, whereas another may be exuberant or belligerent. The student may be hungry, perspire excessively, tremble, be unable to concentrate, and complain of being dizzy. These symptoms may vary in duration and will often disappear after the student is provided with a sugar cube, pop, candy, raisins, fruit juice with sugar, or any other carbohydrate. Generally the symptoms will disappear after ten to fifteen minutes. If they do not, the student's parents or physician should be called.

The opposite of an insulin reaction is a diabetic coma. Although fairly rare, it does occur and can be serious if not treated immediately. A diabetic coma is the result of failure to take insulin, an illness, or neglect of proper diet. In this instance the student has too much sugar and must have an injection as soon as possible. Generally it is slow in onset, and the following symptoms may be observed: thirst, frequent urination, flushed face, labored breathing, nausea, and vomiting. These symptoms should be reported to the parents, school nurse, or student's physician as soon as possible. Treatment will involve rest, injection of insulin, and possible hospitalization. Table 4 summarizes the various causes, symptoms, and what to do in cases of diabetic coma and insulin reaction. *Specific instructions from the physician always take precedence over any such generalized instructions*, but these guidelines might be called "what to do until you hear from the physician."

There are several additional factors that that should be considered:

Table 4. Diabetic coma and insulin reaction: causes, symptoms and a guide to proper action*

	Insulin reaction† (rapid onset)	Diabetic coma (slow onset)
Causes	Too much insulin Not eating enough food An unusual amount of exercise Delayed meal	Too little insulin Failure to follow diet Infection, fever, emotional stress
Signs to watch	Excessive sweating, faintness Headache Hunger Pounding of heart, trembling, impaired vision Irritability Personality change	Increased thirst and urination Weakness, abdominal pains, generalized aches Loss of appetite, nausea and vomiting
What to do	Give the child sugar or any food containing sugar (fruit juice, candy) Call the doctor Do not give the child any insulin	Call the doctor at once Keep the child warm and allow him to lie down Give the child fluids without sugar

*Adapted from *Care of the child with diabetes.* by the Ames Company, Division of Miles Laboratory, Inc., Elkhart, Indiana: Author, 1977, p. 15.
†Also known as hypoglycemia (low blood sugar level).

1. Check with the student's parents to see if he should have a midmorning snack. If so, help him be as inconspicuous as possible about it. It may also be advisable to schedule the child for an early lunch period.
2. Very active or strenuous physical activities might be avoided immediately before lunch.
3. Keep candy, raisins, or sugar handy in case the student needs them.
4. Be certain to inform special or substitute teachers that there is a student in the class with diabetes and indicate what they should do in case of insulin reaction or diabetic coma.
5. Above all else, do not panic about having a student with diabetes; proceed calmly with the necessary steps if he has an insulin reaction or goes into a coma. For the vast majority of the time, he may be treated like any other student in the class.

Students with diabetes should be expected to participate in all normal school activities unless specific restrictions have been advised by the physician. The student must learn to live with his condition and to accept the limitations imposed by it. He must develop a life-style that will allow the greatest possible freedom and still maintain the necessary balance between diet, rest and activity, and medication.

EPILEPSY

Nature of condition. Epilepsy is not a disease in itself, but it is a sign or a symptom of some underlying disorder in the nervous system.

Convulsions, or seizures, are the main symptoms in all types of epilepsy. The seizures occur when there are excessive electrical discharges released in some nerve cells of the brain. When this happens, the brain cannot function properly for a short time, and it loses control over muscles, consciousness, senses, and thoughts. The loss of these functions is only temporary, and the cells work properly between seizures. The most common types of seizures are (1) grand mal, (2) petit mal, and (3) psychomotor or temporal lobe. Seizures may occur at any age, in any race, in both sexes, and in any individual. Approximately seventy-five percent of all epileptic seizures begin before the age of 25. Epilepsy occurs in one out of every fifty children.

Grand mal seizures are the most severe form of epilepsy. When a grand mal seizure occurs the individual loses consciousness, falls, and has general convulsive movements. Breathing may be very labored, the student may shout or produce a gurgling sound, and saliva may escape from the lips. The seizure may last for several minutes, and afterwards the individual may be confused or drowsy. He will not recall what happened or what was said to him during the seizure, and he may be very tired and want to sleep for a short time.

Petit mal seizures are generally short in duration, lasting from five to twenty seconds. They are most common in children and can occur as often as one hundred times a day. Often this student may be accused of being a daydreamer because he will lose contact with what is happening in the classroom during the seizure. The student may become pale, he may stare into space, his eyelids may twitch, or he may demonstrate slight jerky movements. After the seizure the student will continue with his activities almost as though nothing had happened, because he probably will not be aware that he had a seizure. Petit mal seizures have a tendency to disappear before or near puberty, but may be replaced by other types such as grand mal.

Psychomotor or *temporal lobe* seizures are the most complex because they not only affect the motor system but also affect the mental process as well. The seizure may last from a few minutes to several hours. During the seizure the individual may chew or smack his lips or appear to be confused. In some instances, the individual may carry out purposeless activities such as rubbing arms or legs, may walk, and may pick at or take off clothing. Some individuals may experience fear, anger, or rage. After the seizure they will probably not remember what happened and will want to sleep.

Identification. It is not difficult to identify the child who has grand mal seizures; however, teachers should be watchful for a number of other signs that indicate petit mal or psychomotor epilepsy, conditions that can elude detection for some time. Repeated occurrences of two or more of the following signs may indicate the presence of these forms of epilepsy: (1) head dropping, (2) daydreaming or lack of attentiveness, (3) slight jerky movements of arms or shoulders (tic-like movements), (4) eyes rolling upward or twitching, (5) chewing or swallowing movements, (6) rhythmic movements of the head, (7) purposeless movements or sounds and (8) dropping things frequently. If any combination of these signs is observed, be certain that the school nurse and the student's parents are contacted to ensure that a proper medical examination is obtained. Seizures can be controlled through the use of anticonvulsant medication and every effort should be made to seek the proper medical services when epilepsy is suspected.

What to do if a student has a grand mal seizure. As mentioned previously, there are many misconceptions concerning epilepsy, including the presumption of mental retardation, brain injury, or insanity. But there is a greater amount of misinformation about what should be done when an individual has a grand mal seizure. A grand mal seizure can be a frightening experience for the teacher unless she is well prepared and knows exactly what to do. The Epilepsy Foundation of America suggests that the following steps be taken in the event of a grand mal seizure:

1. Remain calm. Students will assume the same emotional reaction as their teacher. *The seizure itself is painless to the child.*

2. Do not try to restrain the child. Nothing can be done to stop a seizure once it has begun. It must run its course.

3. Clear the area around the student so that he does not injure himself on hard objects. Try not to interfere with his movements in any way.

4. Do not force anything between his teeth. If his mouth is already open, a soft object like a handkerchief may be placed between his side teeth. Under no circumstances should a hard object such as a spoon, pen, or pencil be used; more harm may result from this than if nothing were used.

5. Turn the head to one side for release of saliva and place something soft under the student's head.

6. It generally is not necessary to call a physician unless the attack is immediately followed by another major seizure or if the seizure lasts more than ten minutes.

7. When the seizure is over, let the student rest if he needs to.

8. The student's parents and physician should be informed of the seizure.

9. Turn the incident into a learning experience for the entire class. Explain what a seizure is, that it is not contagious, and that it is nothing to be afraid of. Teach the class understanding toward the student—not pity—so that his classmates will continue to accept him as "one of the gang."

After the seizure and short rest, the student can generally carry on routinely. The way in which the teacher and the students react to the seizure is very important. If the teacher overreacts, it can have a very negative effect on the student with epilepsy and on other children in the class. However, if the teacher has prepared and informed the students concerning what to do in the event of a seizure, a potentially traumatic and upsetting experience can be a routine matter.

There is some controversy concerning whether a student's previous history of seizure behavior should be discussed with the class prior to a potential seizure. It is possible that a seizure may never occur in class. On the other hand, if students are informed of the nature of this condition and other similar conditions as a part of their general education, it may reduce the stigma of epilepsy and provide helpful information for everyday living.

Educational implications. Of the three most common types of seizures, it is difficult to establish which can cause the most severe educational problems. It is generally thought, however, that grand mal is probably the most serious because of possible bodily injury, and because it is so widely misunderstood. Petit mal seizures can seriously limit the child's achievement because he may miss a great deal of the material being covered during a seizure and because he may be labeled a behavior problem. Although psychomotor seizures are relatively uncommon in children, they too would impose serious limitations on school achievement and adjustment. It must be recognized that all three are serious, and minor modifications and adjustments may need to be made to accommodate the student with any of these conditions.

Special curricular modifications are not necessary for students with epilepsy. Their academic program and materials will be the same. However, there are several factors that should be taken into consideration by the teacher. The extent to which a student's seizures are controlled will determine the extent to which the following factors and suggestions should be considered. If the seizures have been controlled for several years, it will not be necessary to make many special provisions. However, if the seizures are not well controlled or if epilepsy has only recently been diagnosed, many of these factors will assume additional importance:

1. One of the most important considerations is to treat the student with epilepsy the same as the other students. The teacher's open mindedness and candor concerning the nature of the condition and the way she reacts during and after a seizure will determine how the other students react.

2. The teacher may want to discuss the condition with the student to obtain more complete information concerning how he feels about the condition, the extent of seizure control, and any individual aspects that need to be considered.

3. If the student takes medication for the control of seizures during the day, the teacher should participate by seeing that he gets it. The teacher may also be asked to carefully observe and record the student's behavior in regard to his reactions to the medication. Occasionally, the anticonvulsant drugs used to control epilepsy produce side effects such as lethargy or irritability. Such indicators should be brought to the attention of the parents and/or physician, since such effects may indicate the need for a reduction in dose or a change to another drug.

4. The teacher should not lower the level of expectation or set up protective devices that would single out the student with epilepsy. This must be avoided if the child is to develop a feeling of self-worth and a healthy personality.

5. School personnel, including other teachers, should be oriented to the nature of epilepsy and procedures employed in the event of a seizure.

6. In general, the student with epilepsy can participate in nearly all school activities. There are, however, some activities that probably should be avoided. Contact sports (boxing and football, for example), which may result in head injury, and activities where there is increased danger in the event of a seizure (rope climbing, for example) should be avoided, as should activities involving excessive fatigue. It is also recommended that the student with epilepsy not swim alone because of the possibility of a seizure. It is difficult to generalize about activities in which a student should not participate because it is a very individual matter. The student's parents and physician should be consulted to determine which activities should be avoided.

7. Free information is available from the Epilepsy Foundation of America.*

---

*The Epilepsy Foundation of America has a program entitled "School Alert" that presents a basic educational program for classroom teachers, school nurses, and others in recognizing epilepsy and techniques of management in the school and classroom. The program provides educational materials, literature, posters, and other aids that can be adapted for a variety of age levels and situations. In addition to School Alert, this agency offers services such as monthly publications, technical assistance to public and private agencies, training and placement services, research and training grants, fellowships, and conferences and workshops. For information concerning School Alert or any of the many available services write the Epilepsy Foundation of America, 1828 L. St., N.W., Washington, D.C. 20036. A listing of agencies concerned with crippled and other health impaired individuals appears in Appendix C.

Using materials from a national agency such as the Epilepsy Foundation will familiarize the class with procedures that should be employed in the event of a seizure. Students can be assigned specific responsibilities so that care of the student with epilepsy is a routine matter. If the class is prepared for seizures, it may not be a disturbing experience.

The greatest limitation imposed by epilepsy is not the condition itself but rather the misinformation, antiquated attitudes, and, in many cases, consistent rejection in a society that fears what it does not understand.

Congress was concerned enough about rampant misinformation that in 1975 it established a National Commission for the Control of Epilepsy and Its Consequences. Public education was indicated as the top priority of the commission, and a national information center was established to provide specific information concerning this widely misunderstood condition.

CEREBRAL PALSY

Nature of condition. Cerebral palsy is not a progressive disease but a group of conditions that may seriously limit motor coordination. Of the serious crippling conditions cerebral palsy is the most common. Several years ago, polio was the number one crippling condition among children; today, cerebral palsy has replaced it. Cerebral palsy is most frequently present at birth, but it may be acquired anytime as the result of a head injury or an infectious disease, for example. It is characterized by varying degrees of disturbance of voluntary movements resulting from brain injury. Since there may be varying degrees of brain injury, the majority of the students will have multiple handicapping conditions, such as hearing impairments, visual difficulties, language disorders, and speech problems. Depending on

the severity of this condition some cerebral palsied students will attend special schools or special classes, which provide the comprehensive educational and therapeutic services needed. There are, however, a number of students with mild or moderate cerebral palsy who may attend regular classes for part or all of their school day.

The two most common types of cerebral palsy are *spastic* and *athetoid*. Spastic cerebral palsy is characterized by jerky or explosive motions when the student initiates a voluntary movement. For example, in a severe type, if the student is asked to draw a line from one point to another he may demonstrate erratic or jerky movements such as

The student with athetosis also has difficulty with voluntary movements, but controlling the movement in the desired direction is an added problem. In other words, this child would demonstrate extra or purposeless movements. In drawing a line from one point to another, he may have considerable uncontrolled movement, such as

Educational implications. The degree of involvement and severity of the condition may vary considerably; therefore a full continuum of educational services is needed. The severity will dictate where the student would best be served, but the emphasis should be placed on providing as "normal" an educational environment as possible. Wherever practicable, students with cerebral palsy should attend regular classes with their nondisabled peers. Classroom modifications will vary according to the individual needs of the student. Some will need no modifications, whereas others may need some minor adjustments.

Often an interdisciplinary approach is required in the care and treatment of the cerebral palsied. It may be necessary for some students to be served on a routine and continued basis by a physical, occupational, or speech therapist or a combination of these. If these therapies are initiated early, they may not be needed as frequently during the upper elementary and secondary school years. Therapy sessions may be attended during the school day or after school hours.

The physical therapist is primarily concerned with the lower extremities and will direct attention to posture, movements, and the prevention of contractures (permanent muscle shortening because of lack of neurostimulation and muscle use). It is necessary for the regular teacher to have a basic understanding of treatment procedures so that she may reinforce desirable movements and postural habits. The occupational therapist is primarily concerned with the upper extremities and with activities such as buttoning, tying shoes, eating, or any of the routine activities required in daily living. Many of these routine activities may be seriously limited for the cerebral palsied student because of the lack of muscle coordination. It is important that the regular teacher have information concerning the skills being taught so that she may reinforce them in her classroom. Often the occupational therapist may assist in modifying and adapting educational materials to be used by the cerebral palsied student. The services offered by the speech therapist will also need to be reinforced by the teacher to ensure carry-over and maintenance of desired speech habits.

If the student with cerebral palsy is placed in the proper educational program, it should not be necessary to offer a curriculum different from his peers; however, it may be necessary to modify or adapt materials and equipment so that he may participate more fully in classroom activities. The extent of the necessary modifications will vary considerably. For example, some students have limited use of their hands and arms but have no difficulty getting around. As a result of the variance between individuals, it is difficult to offer specific suggestions. The following list of materials and equipment is provided as examples of ways that modifications may be made:

1. Pencil holders made of clay, Styrofoam balls, or plastic golf balls may be helpful for students with fine motor coordination difficulties.

2. Adapted typewriters may be useful for the student with fine motor coordination difficulties or the student with very weak muscles. Electric typewriters are generally preferred; a keyboard guard placed over the keys may be necessary for some students. A pencil, rather than the fingers, may be used to strike the keys if the involvement is very serious. Hand calculators may be used in arithmetic computation if the student has considerable difficulty writing.

3. Some students may be so severely involved that communication is seriously limited. These students may have average to high intellectual ability but because of poor motor coordination have considerable difficulty with speech. For these students, a language board may be necessary. A language board is a simple lap board with key words, phrases, and an alphabet on which the student points to the desired word or phrase. Although this form of communication is very slow, it is much better than not being under-

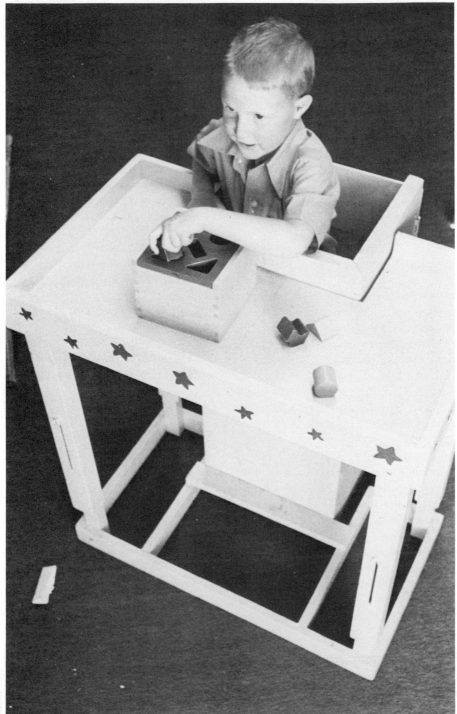

stood or not having any way to communicate.

4. Page turners are useful for students with limited arm use. The turner may be attached to the head, elbow, or hand. A rubber "thumb" such as those used by office workers may also make page turning easier.
5. Weights (such as a small sandbag or bar bells) placed on the wrist or hand are used to eliminate random or uncontrolled movements.
6. Book holders that can be adjusted to any angle may be helpful for some students.
7. Paper holders may be necessary for students who have the use of only one arm or very limited use of both arms. A clipboard to hold the paper in position may be fastened to the desk, or a piece of unbleached muslin cloth may be attached to the desk and sprayed with a nonskid fluid. It may be necessary to tape down the paper while the student is writing on it. A large rubber band may also be used to hold the paper down.
8. Stand-up tables are necessary for many students with cerebral palsy. Since a considerable amount of time is spent sitting, provisions should be made to allow them to stand for parts of the school day. This is needed to prevent muscle contractures, provide proper circulation, and maintain desired postural habits. Since standing unaided may be difficult, a stand-up table may be purchased or built inexpensively to provide the needed support while the student is standing. An individual standing table should normally include a tray for a work area approximately two feet square. A base of the same size should be used to avoid tipping over. The height of the table may be changed by raising or lowering the foot platform.

These are only a few of the modifications and adaptations that may be made. It is essential that the teacher remain open and flexible in trying a variety of aids to meet the unique needs of the student with cerebral palsy. The teacher will not have to modify and adapt materials and equipment alone, since the therapists and resource/itinerant teacher will provide assistance when needed.

One of the most important factors to be considered by the regular teacher is that this child should be accepted as an individual. It is important to allow the student to carry out his own tasks. It may take him considerably longer than the other students to complete an assignment, because of the motor involvement, but he must be allowed to complete it independently.

SPINA BIFIDA

Nature of condition. Spina bifida is a serious birth defect in which the bones of the spine fail to close during the twelfth week of fetal development. As a result, a cyst or sack is present in the area of the lower back when the child is born. This protrusion is generally surgically treated during the child's first 24 to 48 hours of life. The extent of the disability resulting from this condition varies enormously. Some will have little or no disability, whereas others have varying degrees of paralysis of the legs and incontinence (lack of bowel and bladder control). In addition to the degrees of paralysis and incontinence, the child may have impaired autonomic nervous system functioning (absence of perspiration) and absence of sensation below the level of the spinal defect. In some respects this condition is similar to other crippling conditions that cause degrees of paralysis in the legs, but it is complicated by the lack of bowel and bladder control. Due to the deficiency of nerve fibers, the student may not be able to tell when his bladder is full. The bladder may overflow, and the student may not be aware of the situation until he sees the wetness through his outer clothing. There is a threat of infection from residual urine in the bladder, and the student may also have difficulty with bowel control.

There are surgical procedures that can assist in accommodating this condition, or artificial devices may be worn to collect the urine. The student may also regulate his fluid intake and adhere to a systematic voiding schedule. Generally, the student will be able to take care of his toileting needs, but younger children may need some assistance from a classroom aide, volunteer, parent, or resource/itinerant teacher.

Educational implications. It is important for the teacher to work closely with medical personnel and especially the school nurse to ensure proper health care. The teacher must also maintain a close working relationship with physical and occupational therapists to meet the student's ambulation needs and activities of daily living. Last, but certainly not least, the teacher should discuss the student's special needs and problems with the parents. The teacher should be aware of the symptoms of urinary infection: increased temperature, flushed skin, and excessive perspiration. The parents or the school nurse should be contacted if any of these symptoms occur. Infections can generally be avoided with proper care, but in the event of infection the student may have to be hospitalized, necessitating absence from school. A flexible scheduling procedure providing specific times for toileting needs should be implemented.

Teachers should be aware of problems associated with the lack of sensation in the legs. The lack of sensation can lead to skin or pressure sores. Problems imposed by wearing braces or using a wheelchair should also be considered. It may be necessary to reposition the student or ask him to sit up straight during the school day to prevent postural problems and muscle contractures.

If not handled properly, the psychosocial limitations imposed by this condition can be very serious. This may seem a trivial matter, but it is a very real concern expressed by many spina bifida students. The student may bear the brunt of others' laughter or joking because of odor or an "accident." The teacher should also be aware that factors such as excitement or spicy foods can cause a problem and should allow the student to leave the classroom suddenly if an "accident" occurs.

The problems imposed by poor ambulation skills must be taken into consideration by therapists and teachers. However, this factor would not be any more significant for the child with spina bifida than for the child with cerebral palsy or any other major crippling condition.

Inasmuch as the child with spina bifida has good use of his upper body, arms, and hands, the educational modifications necessary are minimal. These children can profit from regular classroom attendance and instruction with only minor modifications and adaptations.

MUSCULAR DYSTROPHY

Nature of condition. Muscular dystrophy is a progressive condition in which the muscles are replaced by a fatty tissue. Although there are several types, the most common and most serious type, Duchenne, occurs in children. Duchenne, or childhood muscular dystrophy, is generally a fatal disease characterized by a slow deterioration of the voluntary muscles ending in a complete state of helplessness.

The age at onset is generally between the child's first and sixth year and rarely occurs after the child's first decade of life. Early signs of the condition include a tendency to fall easily, clumsiness in walking, difficulty in climbing stairs, and difficulty in rising from the floor. There is a steady progressive decline in the child's ability to walk. He falls more frequently and eventually will need crutches to move about. As he continues to lose his strength it will be necessary to move from crutches to a wheelchair. Later, nearly all large muscles will be involved and he will be bedridden. During the later stages, he may be unable to raise his arms, sit erect, or hold his head up. Fortunately, the small muscles of the hands and fingers maintain some strength even during the most advanced stages.

Educational implications. The regular classroom offers obvious educational advantages as compared to a school or special class for students with crippling or health impairments. In addition to the educational advantages, there are many recreational and social factors offered by regular school attendance. During the early stages of muscular dystrophy, very few modifications and adaptations will be necessary, but as the condition progresses there will be need for some modifications. Eventually, the student may not be able to attend any educational program and will have to receive homebound instruction; however, every effort should be made to maintain the student with muscular dystrophy in regular classrooms as long as possible.

Muscular dystrophy imposes a set of contradictions. On one hand, it is known that it is generally fatal, and on the other, we ask the student, his parents, teachers, and others to carry on as though he were going to live a rich and full life. This apparent contradiction must be dealt with; guidance and counseling services can do a great deal to accommodate the acceptance of this conflict. There is little question that if the child and parents are to accept this contradiction, ongoing counseling must be offered. Counseling programs should be conducted in cooperation with the student's parents, brothers and sisters, therapists, teachers, and physicians.

It is important that the student attend adapted physical education classes and maintain a balance between diet, activity, and rest, since there is a tendency for the child to become overweight. He should be encouraged to participate as fully as possible in recreational and physical activities. Although the effects of the condition cannot be stopped by physical activity, there is some indication that it may assist in delaying some of the debilitative effects. Some caution must be exercised, however, as the student may become very easily fatigued. He should be allowed intermittent periods of rest as needed.

Several studies have been conducted to determine if mental retardation is associated with muscular dystrophy. There have been no indications that there is a greater incidence of mental retardation in students with muscular dystrophy than in the population as a whole. A large number of research studies have also attempted to identify particular personality characteristics that might be associated with muscular dystrophy. Although some researchers have found personality patterns unique to these students, others have not been able to do so; therefore it is reasonable to assume that differences in personality may be attributed to something other than the muscular dystrophy. If there is no mental retardation or particular personality configuration that may be associated with muscular dystrophy, then achievement and adjustment in school should be similar to that of other students. Perhaps the most important role of the teacher is to stimulate these students academically, recreationally, and socially as much as possible and to expect as nearly as possible the same of these students as of others.

ADAPTING PHYSICAL EDUCATION

The student with a crippling condition or health impairment can often successfully participate in nearly all curricular areas. One area, however, that presents special problems is physical education. If the physical educator has had previous experience or special preparation in this area, he often makes the necessary adjustments to accommodate these students with little difficulty. If the physical educator has not had previous experience or preparation, a student with limited ambulation or a health impairment may present a special problem. As mentioned previously, activity is essential for these students, perhaps even more so than for students without a disability. Nonhandicapped students will routinely get the necessary activity, whereas students with physical problems may be overprotected and not afforded the opportunity to be active. In general, there are at least four ways that physical education activities can be changed to allow greater participation for these students:

1. Change the way all students participate
2. Change the way one player of each team participates
3. Modify the equipment
4. Make special allowances for the handicapped student

The following suggestions are not intended as a comprehensive or detailed program but should be considered when attempting to modify or adapt programs for students with crippling conditions or health impairments:

1. Consider minor rule modifications of the game or contest.
2. Ask the students how to adapt a game or activity. Some physical educators have had considerable success in asking all of the students to identify ways to modify or adapt an activity.
3. Schedule opportunities for rest. Fatigue may be a factor for the handicapped student. The number of points required to win a game can be reduced, quarters may be shortened, or required distances may be reduced.
4. Use larger balls, larger pieces of equipment, or change equipment—lighter balls, lighter racquets, lower baskets, etc.
5. Use more players on a team, reducing the individual responsibility and activity.
6. Change the way the entire class plays the game—all players on knees, sitting on the floor, use only one hand, or use scooter boards.
7. Have one person on each team assume a functional disability—using a wheelchair, crutches, etc.
8. Create a special role for the handicapped student and one other student on the other team—hand out a baton at the end of a relay, catch a basketball after a goal is made and return it to the shooter.
9. Plan a backup activity in the event that the primary activity does not work.
10. Use as many activities as possible that the handicapped student can do.

We are not advocating that activities be modified every day; this may seriously limit the needed activity of the nonhandicapped students. We are suggesting, however, that consideration be given to these suggestions and that attempts be made to meet the unique needs of *all* students.

Participation in a regular physical education program can have many benefits and should be encouraged as much as possible. Regular physical education, however, should not preclude the need for physical therapy provided by a physical therapist or for special individualized or adapted physical education provided by a specialist. The regular physical educator is also strongly encouraged

1. Assuming responsibility for coordination of referrals from teachers, administrators, and school health personnel. Coordinating initial information on the student's readiness to attend an integrated program. Assisting in program planning and staffing. If the staffing team suggests regular classroom placement, the resource/itinerant teacher will begin specific planning to determine the best possible school and teacher or teachers, transportation, and availability of therapies.

2. Coordinating information between medical agencies, therapeutic services, parents, and teachers. Often the resource/itinerant teacher serves as the liaison between the agencies serving the student and regular teachers and parents. For example, medical services may make specific suggestions concerning the care of a student with a health impairment, and it may be necessary for the resource/itinerant teacher to interpret these recommendations to either the parents or the student's regular classroom teacher.

3. Interpreting occupational, physical, or speech therapy to the student's teacher or teachers. The therapist may make recommendations concerning activities, methods of ambulation, or ways to modify materials in the regular classroom. It is the responsibility of the resource/itinerant teacher to interpret these recommendations and to assist in carrying them out. It is also necessary for the resource/itinerant teacher to obtain up-to-date evaluations, recommendations, and changes in treatment procedures.

4. Assisting the therapist in actual therapy sessions to more fully understand the treatment priority and the methods used to correct or prevent an undesirable behavior or ambulation pattern.

5. Observing the student in classroom, playground, or school community to ensure that desired ambulation patterns are being transferred and maintained outside of therapeutic settings.

6. Assisting the regular classroom teacher in spot-checking braces, crutches, and wheelchairs and observing to see if equipment is functioning properly.

7. Observing specific students in classrooms and offering suggestions on ways to modify and adapt equipment and materials so that the student may participate fully in all activities.

8. Assisting in modifying architectural barriers and physical restrictions, such as removing desk bottoms for wheelchairs and providing adjustable chairs and stand-up tables when needed.

9. Arranging special transportation to and from school and to any special activities.

10. Keeping abreast of current technological advances and new materials and equipment that may facilitate integration of these students.

11. Supplementing and reinforcing instruction of the regular classroom teacher or the physical education teacher in selected areas. It may be necessary, for example, to tutor a student in an academic area in which he cannot complete assignments as rapidly as the other children. Some resource/itinerant teachers have also had considerable success in working with small groups of students in the regular classroom.

12. Providing guidance and counseling to regular teachers through in-service meetings with an entire school staff or individually. In some instances the resource/itinerant teacher may con-

duct mini–in-service sessions or small group discussions with students concerning a particular disability.

13. Coordinating volunteer services or classroom aides used in the regular classroom. This role may involve the selection, training, placement, and scheduling of aides for activities such as assisting in physical education, physical therapy, toileting, or adapting materials.

14. Assisting in planning recreational activities and leisure skills during school hours and possibly after school hours and weekends.

15. Assisting in planning and implementing work-study, vocational education, and vocational rehabilitation services for secondary students. The resource/itinerant teacher may have to serve as the catalyst to ensure that these services are offered and that there is continuity of services.

16. Detailing for each student what is expected in such emergencies as fire drills. Although this is not a serious problem, it is often a concern expressed by teachers and administrators when a student's ambulation is limited.

In general, the resource/itinerant teacher plays a helping and assisting role in working with the student, teachers, administrators, parents, therapists, and all others involved in the care and education of the handicapped child. This role is a combination of student advocacy and of facilitating needed individualized services.

SUMMARY

This chapter is organized differently than other chapters in that discussion is presented on the basis of a particular disability or condition. This is not intended to mean that the suggestions offered are related only to that particular condition; in fact, many suggestions are equally appropriate to other conditions. For example, the need for an adapted physical education program is not unique to students with allergies or asthma but is equally appropriate for students with arthritis or epilepsy. As a result, teachers are encouraged to consider all the suggestions, regardless of their immediate interest. The role and responsibility of resource/itinerant personnel was reviewed, and it was emphasized that the regular classroom teacher should work very closely with the special educator and with the students' parents.

The modifications and adaptations for a student with a crippling condition or health impairment who attends a regular classroom may be very minimal. Perhaps the most important factor for the regular classroom teacher to understand is the influence of her attitude on the attitudes of handicapped and nondisabled students alike. The following adage indicates the need for an objective attitude:

What you think of me,
I will think of me,
What I think of me,
WILL BE ME

If the student's teachers, parents, siblings, and friends perceive him in a negative way, he may assume that attitude about himself. If, on the other hand, others important in his environment see him positively, he probably will also see himself in this way. He may come to see himself not as a disabled individual but first and foremost as an individual who has many abilities and who, incidentally and lastly, is disabled.

REFERENCES AND SUGGESTED READINGS

Abruzzo, J. L. Rheumatoid arthritis: reflection on etiology and pathogenesis. *Archives of Physical Medicine and Rehabilitation*, January 1971, 52, 30-39.

American Academy of Pediatrics Committee on Children with Handicaps. The epileptic child and competitive school athletics, *Pediatrics*, October 1968, *42*, 700-702.

Best, G. *Individuals with physical disabilities—an introduction for educators*. St. Louis: The C. V. Mosby Co., 1978.

Bigge, J. *Teaching individuals with physical and multiple disabilities*. Columbus, Ohio: Charles E. Merrill, 1976.

Blakeslee, B. *The limb-deficient child*. Berkeley: University of California Press, 1963.

Buchanan, R., and Mullins, J. Integration of a spina bifida child in a kindergarten for normal children. *Young Children*, September 1968, 339-343.

Cobb, S., and Stanislav, K. The epidemiology of rheumatoid arthritis. *American Journal of Public Health*, October 1966, *56*, 1657-1663.

Collier, R. N., Jr. The adolescent with diabetes and the public schools—a misunderstanding. *Personnel and Guidance Journal*, April 1969, *47*, 753-757.

Conine, T., and Brennan, W. T. Orthopedically handicapped children in regular classrooms. *Journal of School Health*, January 1969, *39*, 59-63.

Deahl, T., and Deahl, M. The orthopedically handicapped. *Instructor*, 1971, *80*, 34.

Decker, J. L. Closing in on rheumatoid arthritis: the number one crippler. *Today's Health*, June 1967, *45*, 44-47, 71.

Drash, A. Diabetes mellitus in childhood. *Journal of Pediatrics*, June 1971, *78*, 919-937.

Ducas, D. Winning the battle against asthma. *Today's Health*, August 1967, *45*, 28-32.

Dunn, L. M. Education for children with epilepsy. *Rehabilitation Record*, January-February 1967, 4-7.

England, G. O. Treating 'C.P.'s' as persons. *Cerebral Palsy Review*, July-August 1964, *25*, 10-11.

Finnell, C. Despite cerebral palsy—I have the chance to try. *Today's Education*, November 1970, *59*, 74-75.

Forsythe, W. I., and Kinley, J. G. Bowel control of children with spina bifida. *Developmental Medicine and Child Neurology*, February 1970, *12*, 27-31.

Gault, P. L. Care of the child with meningitis. *RN*, October 1969, *32*, 44.

Harlin, V. K. Experiences with epileptic children in a public school program. *Journal of School Health*, January 1965, *35*, 20-24.

Haskell, S. H., and Anderson, E. M. The education of physically handicapped children in ordinary schools. *Irish Journal of Education*, Summer 1969, *3*, 41-54.

Haskell, S. H. Physically handicapped children: special or normal schooling. *Slow Learning Child*, November 1969, *16*, 150-161.

Hill, M. L., Shurtleff, D. B., Chapman, W. H., and Ansell, J. S. The myelodysplastic child—bowel and bladder control. *American Journal of Nursing*, March 1969, *69*, 545-550.

Holley, L. The physical therapist: who, what, and how, *American Journal of Nursing*, July 1970, *70*, 1521-1524.

Kalk, L. What teachers need to know about diabetes, *Diabetes in the News*, Summer, 1978, *7*(4), 1-10.

Klein, R. A., and Hummel, L. The hemophiliac: an exceptional child. *Journal of School Health*, June 1967, *37*, 303-306.

Livingston, S. What the teacher can do for the student with epilepsy. *N. E. A. Journal*, November 1966, *65*, 24-26.

Lord, D. W., and Root, H. F. Brighter future for children with diabetes. *Parents Magazine*, November 1966, *41*, 70-71 and 156-158.

Martin, J. W. Attitudes toward epileptic students in a city high school system. *The Journal of School Health*, 1974, *28*, 144-146.

Merley, F. Toward a normal life. *Science News*, August 1968, *94*, 163.

Mitchell, M. M. Occupational therapy and special education. *Children*, September-October 1971, *18*, 183-186.

Moore, M. L. Diabetes in children. *American Journal of Nursing*, January 1967, *67*, 104-107.

Noon, E. F. Don't be afraid of the child with epilepsy. *Instructor*, 1968, *78*, 57.

Patthoff, C. J. Insulin reaction. *Today's Health*, October 1969, *47*, 74.

Puthoff, M. New dimensions in physical activity for children with asthma and other respiratory conditions. *Journal of Health, Physical Education, Recreation*, September 1972, *43*, 75-77.

Robins, H., and Schaltner, R. Obstacles in the social integration of orthopedically handicapped children. *Journal of Jewish Community Services*, Winter 1968, *45*, 190.

Russo, J. R. Mainstreaming handicapped students: are your facilities suitable? *American School and University*, October 1974, *47*, 25-32.

Sauer, L. W. Heart diseases in children. *PTA Magazine*, November 1967, *66*, 29-30.

Scherr, M. S., and Charleston, L. F. A physical conditioning program for asthmatic children. *Journal of the American Medical Association*, 1958, *168*(15), 1196-2000.

Schwartz, A., and Lieberman, M. Integrating the orthopedically handicapped child into the Center. *Jewish Community Center Program Aids*, Summer 1963.

Seligman, T., Randel, H. O., and Stevens, J. J. Conditioning program for children with asthma. *Physical Therapy Journal*, May 1970, *50*, 641-647.

Semans, S. Principles of treatment in cerebral palsy.

Journal of the American Physical Therapy Association, July 1966, *46,* 318-325.

Soldwedel, B., and Terrill, I. Sociometric aspects of physically handicapped and nonhandicapped children in the same elementary school. *Exceptional Children,* May 1957, *23,* 371-383.

Solow, R. A. Psychological aspects of muscular dystrophy. *Exceptional Children,* October 1965, *32,* 99-103.

Stratch, E. H. Rehabilitation of young spina bifida children. *Rehabilitation,* April-June 1969, *69,* 17-20.

Sugar, M., and Ames, M. D. The child with spina bifida cystica: his medical problems and habilitation. *Rehabilitation Literature,* December 1965, *26,* 362-366.

Swack, M. J. Training special education teachers in physical therapy techniques by means of programmed demonstrations. *Exceptional Children,* April 1967, *33,* 529-534.

Waleski, D. The physically handicapped in the regular classroom. *Today's Education,* December 1964, *52,* 12-16.

West, W. L. Occupational therapy: philosophy and perspective. *American Journal of Nursing,* August 1968, *68,* 1708-1711.

Winnick, J. P. Planning physical activity for the diabetic. *Physical Educator,* March 1970, *27,* 18-20.

6 SPEECH PROBLEMS

Assistance with speech production problems for public school students represents one of the oldest generally recognized areas of service for the handicapped. However, of all the services for various handicapping conditions discussed in this text, those for speech have historically been more likely to be administratively separate from the rest of special education. Until the past five to ten years (and the rapid development of programs for learning disabled students) it was more likely that the regular classroom teacher would have contacted the speech specialist than any other special educator, for it was common to have at least one or two students from each elementary class receiving speech services. This contact, however, was often different from contact with other special educators. The speech specialist usually served the schools on an itinerant basis, providing the needed services and then leaving for the next school. Because the speech specialist was required to be on the move constantly, and because of the very specialized nature of their services, there was often little meaningful contact between the speech specialist and the regular classroom teacher, except in unusual cases. Teachers were grateful for the help received by their students but seldom asked the speech specialist for additional assistance or suggestions.*

Gerald Freeman, Director of the Oakland Schools Speech and Hearing Clinic in Pontiac, Michigan for the past twenty years, notes that "although the concept of interdisciplinary cooperation between teachers and speech/language specialists is not new, frequently these professionals have failed to interact effectively to achieve their common goals" (1977, p. 1). He further notes that some teachers tended to delegate total responsibility for a student's verbal communicative needs to the speech specialist, as though such needs were not directly connected with academic achievement. In turn, speech specialists did not properly establish the essential value of their role with the classroom teacher. The coming of the type of joint planning required by new legislative mandates and the expansion of roles of speech clinicians into the area of language disorders has made it essential that the speech specialist know more about the teaching process and that the teacher know more about the skills and potential contributions of the speech specialist.

The role played by the speech specialist will vary from district to district and may be indicated by the various titles held by specialists in this profession. It might seem logical that the role and function of these individuals would vary with title. This is not necessarily the case. Although the addition of the word "language" to their titles in many areas of the nation over the past ten years does reflect a trend toward working with language disorders, other factors may more often determine their function. In

---

* Up to this point in this chapter, we have used the term "speech specialist" to refer to the professional who provides services in this area. The preferred term today appears to be "speech/language specialist" or "speech/language pathologist," but the terminology may vary considerably in different areas. Historically, the first term other than speech teacher that found favor on any large national scale was "speech therapist." Then came "speech clinician," "speech pathologist," or "speech specialist." The more recent terminology (speech/language specialist) reflects an apparent desire to be free from a primarily clinical or medical connotation, and to emphasize that the domain of this professional group includes both speech and language. Another title sometimes used is that of "communication disorders specialist" but this can be easily confused with the learning disabilities specialist, who also works with communication disorders. In the remainder of this chapter, when it is necessary to refer to the professional who provides speech/language services, we will use the title speech specialist.

some states, speech specialists will be involved to a great extent with programs for learning disabled students. In others they will not. In some states they will work with speech or language problems of mentally retarded students. In others they will not. In some geographical areas they will work with bilingual students to a considerable degree. In others they will not.

The regular classroom teacher should know that although the speech specialist is usually well trained and highly competent, he or she is often not trained as a *teacher* and may not be as aware of the problems of teaching reading, mathematics, and various subjects as other special education personnel. However, the speech specialist is much more knowledgeable about the effects that deviations and disorders of speech and language have on the total communication process. This knowledge, plus skills in the remediation of speech defects and language disorders, makes the speech specialist a highly important source of information and assistance, both in direct remedial efforts and as a consultant for more mild problems.

To assist the regular classroom teacher to better understand the speech and language disorders, we will first consider how speech and language normally develop and then look at the major types of speech problems. A more complete understanding of these topics should alert the teacher to the problems that may exist in the classroom and provide the basis for a better, more effective working relationship with the speech specialist. Following these basic areas of concern, we will consider the role of the speech specialist, and some of the ways the regular classroom teacher can assist students with speech and/or language problems. With the requirement for more total input in determining staffing for students thought to be handicapped, it seems likely that other staff members will now be able to learn more from the speech specialist and, in turn, that the speech specialist will become better acquainted with the total educational process.

SPEECH AND LANGUAGE: HOW THEY NORMALLY DEVELOP

Because they usually develop so easily, speech and language are often not appreciated for the near-miracle they represent. Philip Dale, commenting on research in language development, indicates that most children "learn how to talk without any difficulty at all. In a sense, we are never going to discover any astonishing new facts: *this* is the fact that we are trying to explain" (1976, p. 1). Perkins believes that "human infants apparently begin life as cryptographers innately equipped biologically to 'crack' society's communications code within a few years. No other hypothesis offered so far comes close to explaining a baby's extraordinary capacity to decipher speech" (1977, pp. 99-100). Weiss and Lillywhite characterize the learning of speech and language as "possibly the most . . . complicated accomplishment of the human organism" (1976, p. 46). Other authorities who speak to this topic have similar impressions.

These comments from authorities in separate but related professional disciplines succinctly summarize the "miracle" of speech and language. Perhaps the automatic, without-apparent-effort nature of speech and language development is the reason many educators are poorly informed about these skills, which are basic to the entire academic process. Whatever the reason, such knowledge is essential when we deal with those students who are not progressing normally in speech and language. Therefore, we will briefly review the *normal* development of speech and language as a basis for considering what to do with students with speech and language problems.

A very generalized explanation of how a

child learns language skills is that they are acquired through listening and imitation. Such imitation is apparently encouraged when a child learns that language is of value to get what he or she wants, be it attention, adult approval, toys, or food. This general theory is supported by the fact that deaf children have serious problems with language, presumably because they cannot hear and thus cannot imitate.

Despite the many mysteries surrounding the acquisition of speech and language, there are certain "knowns." Among those things we do know is the fact that speech and language are learned behaviors and that they seem to follow the laws that apply to other types of learned behavior in lower animals and humans. We know that although similarities exist between the more than one thousand languages spoken by humans, there are highly significant differences; there is little apparent logic as to why each race or culture has its specific language patterns. We also know, by observation, that these patterns are perpetuated as children learn the language spoken around them to comnicate their needs and desires.

If a child is to speak normally, and thus to develop language, certain abilities must be present. He must have the ability to hear, have normal or near normal speech mechanisms, and have adequate (normal or near normal) brain and central nervous system functioning. If he cannot hear or has impaired hearing, he does not receive accurate auditory input to imitate; this results in slow speech development, faulty articulation, or both. (For a description of this problem, see p. 43 relating to the hearing impaired.) If he does not have normal or near normal speech organs, he may be unable to articulate in a manner that is acceptably imitative of others. (This *may* be correctable through surgery; see p. 130.) If his central nervous system is to some degree dysfunctional, he

may not be able to receive the proper sensory input, make the necessary associations, or coordinate the muscles of articulation. If he is mentally retarded, his speech and language development may not follow normal patterns of development. The type of neural dysfunction and the degree of mental retardation will have significant effects on the type and degree of speech and language problem.

If a child has normal abilities, normal environmental stimulation, and opportunity to learn, the development of speech will follow a predictable developmental pattern. For most children the first sounds uttered following birth are those accompanying the first exhalation. The newborn child exhales, coughs out accumulated amniotic fluid, and in so doing produces the so-called birth cry. Very soon, however, real crying begins, and this develops into the characteristic crying that parents learn to interpret in terms of specific wants and needs. This may be considered primary communication, but it is not speech. At least three distinctive types of crying seem to be common to all very young babies: a cry that says, "I'm not comfortable!" (wet or too warm, for example), a cry that says, "I'm in pain!" and a cry that says, "I'm hungry—feed me."

These first primitive attempts at communication may appear to be primarily one-way (from the child to anyone who may hear), but in fact they are preliminary to other meaningful sounds to which most parents respond, thus triggering more sounds from the child. This is the start of meaningful two-way communication and provides the base for later speech.

Babbling, a stage recognized by most authorities who document the development of speech and language, may begin as early as the age of 6 weeks, but may occur as late as 10 to 12 weeks. Once viewed by some as an all-important step in the *language* development process, it seems more likely that it is a kind of vocal exercise. Babbling consists of combinations of syllables in some sort of random, meaningless (as far as we can tell) order. It is apparently a milestone in prespeech vocalization, and it is important that the parent babble or talk back to the child. In addition to the reinforcement the child receives from the parents' returned babbling, there is an obvious element of pleasure that all children seem to derive from hearing their own babbling. If the child cannot hear his own babbling because of a hearing impairment, he is not reinforced to continue babbling and thus begins a series of events that may result in severe retardation in speech and language development.

Most authorities recognize the existence of one or perhaps even two other stages following babbling before the child produces his first actual words. A two-stage process may include "lallation," a stage when the child begins to deliberately imitate sounds, although not producing words, and "jargon," a stage following the lalling stage, in which there are additional noticeable patterns of speech rhythm (Schreiber, 1973). These two stages then lead to the production of the first actual word. Other authors might group these two stages together and call them the jargon stage, or the "vocal play" stage. Whatever these are called, these stages may be relatively short or several months long. In either case, it is likely that many children will actually say their first word by the time they are 1 year old, although some may not speak a distinguishable word until many months later. A few months' difference at this point is not critical. The exact time at which the first word is spoken is less important than giving the child every opportunity to proceed through the requisite developmental steps with the necessary environmental support. This includes, but is not limited to, (1) a maximum of personal interaction with the child—not "smothering" but including the child in a maximum of activities and settings consistent with his other physical needs and limitations, (2) a careful evaluation of the adult speech surrounding the child to make certain it provides a good model, and (3) a concerted effort to *talk* to the child, using a variety of words, facial expressions, and voice inflections at a level at which the child may be maximally stimulated. This includes deliberate inclusion of the child in conversations when small groups of individuals are together in the presence of the child. If these steps are followed and the child receives a maximum of love and care, he has been given the best possible chance to develop normal speech in later childhood.

After the child develops the ability to say single words, he will soon move on to two-word sentences. However, this does not usually occur until he uses what may be properly called one-word sentences. Although a single word may be used simply to express strong feelings (for example, "daddy," when the child sees daddy coming in the door), it may also be used regularly to comment on some object or event in the environment ("daddy" as he points to daddy's hat—obviously saying "that is daddy's hat"). In the normal course of development in this beginning stage of language, the use of a two-, three-, or four-word sentence may be encouraged if other adults in the environment respond; "yes, that is daddy's hat" or simply "daddy's hat."

Linguistic experts have studied the "most common first fifty words" for many years, and yet have only cautious theories as to the exact process whereby the child selects from the vast array of words in his environment those words he first chooses to use. It appears that the names of food, clothing, animals, and toys, along with "mommy" and "daddy," are among the earliest words for most children. In addition, words describing actions, such as "give," "bye-bye," and "down," which may also be demand words, are commonly learned at an early age. Whatever the words, the suggestions given previously relating to maximizing personal interaction, providing a good model, and talking to the child will, if adjusted to the child's level, be of value throughout the preschool years. It may be tempting at times to shut the child off since he seems to be talking ceaselessly, but if speech can be directed and encouraged, the payoff will be better language development and at least slightly increased odds of success in the areas of reading and language arts after he enrolls in school.

It is almost certain that during the preschool years children will exhibit speech characteristics that would be viewed as speech problems requiring correction if they were in existence several years later. Articulation problems abound with almost all young children. These are simply a reflection of partially developed speech production and a partially trained ear for sounds and words. Nonfluencies will undoubtedly develop, some of which could be interpreted as stuttering, but most will vanish if parents accept them for what they are—a part of the developmental process of most children. The existence of certain normal nonfluencies is emphasized by many authors because the efforts of some parents and teachers to correct nonfluencies appear to be an important causal factor in stuttering. Too much reaction to normal nonfluencies by parents and well-intentioned but uninformed teachers may promote rather than reduce stuttering (see pp. 128-130 for further discussion).

In this brief consideration of how speech and language normally develop we have not attempted to consider some of the theoretical debates among language experts as to what mechanism in the human brain permits the individual to expand his vocabulary from 200 or 250 words at 2 years to 2,500 words or more at 6 years. Nor have we considered the mysteries of how a young child develops an understanding of the rules of phonology and morphology (building words from sounds; that is, from phonemes and morphemes) and of syntax (arranging words into phrases and sentences). As noted by Perkins, "How these grammatical rules are acquired . . . is one of life's great mysteries." However, the real mystery may be "how . . . a two-year-old baby learns rules that his parents do not understand well enough to make explicit" (Perkins, 1977, p. 100). Let us simply note that the sequence described in the preceding paragraphs is the one followed by the vast majority of young children, and in most of these children it leads to the development of speech and language that may be readily understood and that provides the basis for verbal communication, reading, and thinking. When speech and language are underdeveloped or defective, it will almost always lead to academic problems in school, especially in reading. In the case of more serious problems, there is an apparent correlation with problems in thinking, because it appears that for the most part humans think in terms of language.

This discussion was provided as a basis for consideration of speech problems that may occur in students enrolled in the regular class. Some of these students may have other handicapping conditions, but for many, a speech problem is the basic difficulty. In the following section we will consider the major speech problems and suggestions for remediation.

MAJOR SPEECH AND LANGUAGE PROBLEMS AND SUGGESTIONS FOR REMEDIATION

In this section we will consider three identifiable categories of speech problems:

(1) *articulation*, (2) *voice*, and (3) *stuttering*, plus one catch-all category, *other nonfluency problems*. In addition, we will discuss certain difficulties that are more appropriately called *language problems*. We will emphasize those difficulties that are most subject to assistance on the part of the regular classroom teacher and will also consider some that are primarily the responsibility of the speech specialist. The regular class teacher must be aware of the former so that he or she may provide the proper assistance whenever possible. The regular classroom teacher must also be aware of the more complex or difficult speech problems so that the student may be referred for specialized help, and so that (as is the case with stuttering) the teacher does not become engaged in efforts that are actually counterproductive.

When considering speech problems, a very obvious first question to be asked is, "When is a *difference* in speech sufficiently different or significant to consider it a *handicap?*" The various authorities appear to

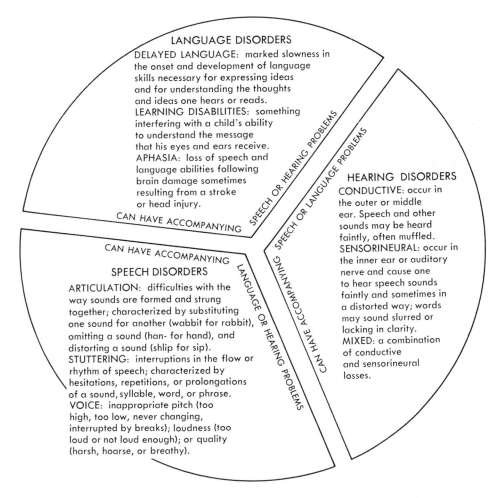

From public information materials of the American Speech and Hearing Association; reproduced with permission.

agree that a speech problem may be called a handicap if (1) it interferes with communication, (2) it causes the speaker to be maladjusted, or (3) it calls undue attention to the speech itself as opposed to what the speaker is saying. Stated another way, if the speech causes communication problems (for example, unintelligibility) or if it causes negative reactions on the part of the speaker or the audience, it is considered a speech problem. Note that the preceding relates to the effects of the speech, not to the physiology of speech production. The speech specialist is concerned with helping the student produce speech in the most normal manner possible; using speech effectively in normal communication in a manner that permits the speaker to concentrate on what he is saying, not how he is saying it. The preceding generalization also applies to language disorders, which are often, although not always, related to speech problems. Before proceeding with the discussion of speech and language problems, it would be well to consider the manner in which speech, language, and hearing problems may interrelate. This interrelationship is illustrated on p. 123 and indicates why the regular class teacher may be working with one or more of three special education specialists in some cases. These specialists—in the areas of speech, learning disabilities, and hearing impairment—should make the final decision as to who is primarily responsible for providing suggestions and classroom assistance. That responsibility and interrelationship will be specifically spelled out in the Individualized Educational Program (IEP) for the student involved.

Articulation problems

In most textbook discussions of speech problems, articulation difficulties are mentioned first. The reasons for this may be many, but chief among them are the facts that these are the most common speech er-

rors, and they are sufficiently obvious that they are easy to describe. Add to this the fact that so many young children exhibit such errors, and the rationale seems clear. These facts led to practices in the 1950s and 1960s that are now undergoing change.

In those days of rapidly growing speech programs in the public schools, speech specialists spent the majority of their time with students who were experiencing articulation problems. This practice has slowly changed so that today, in some schools, regular class teachers do a majority of the remediation of minor articulation errors. This does not mean that articulation difficulties should not be referred to the speech specialist. If 5-, 6-, or 7-year-old children have problems that seem to be interfering with their academic progress or are leading to social problems, they should be referred. The teacher needs to be attentive to the speech used by her students and try to make objective evaluations of the need for assistance. Overreferral is undesirable, but teachers must also be careful to not get used to a student's speech problems to the point that they are ignored, even though an outside observer can see that these problems are leading to academic or social difficulties. The fact is that many students *do* simply outgrow their articulation problems. This is why fewer young children with minor articulation problems are seen by speech specialists today. On the other hand, some who outgrow their problems do so because of assistance provided by parents and regular classroom teachers who know what to do. In many cases, evaluation by the speech specialist followed by management suggestions implemented by the regular classroom teacher and the parent is the combination that proves most effective. In many ways, this is the best sort of arrangement, and the role of the regular classroom teacher in this partnership is the premise of this text.

Articulation errors are those involving

omissions, substitutions, distortions, or additions when pronouncing (articulating) words. The following are examples of articulation errors:

Substitution: "wun" for run, "dat" for that, "wabbit" for rabbit, "thum" for some
Omission: "pay" for play, "cool" for school, "ift" for lift, "da y" for daddy
Distortion: "shled" for sled
Additions: "buhrown" for brown, "cuhow" for cow, "puhlease" for please, "sawr" for saw

Certain generalizations that are applicable in nearly all cases of articulation error therapy may be used as guidelines for remedial efforts. First, *the student must hear the error.* In most cases the letter or letters are pointed out to him in writing or in print, so that there is no question just what letter or letters are under consideration; then, he must learn to hear the sound—as properly articulated by the teacher or speech specialist. Often he must learn to listen for the sound in initial, medial, and final positions; then, he must learn to differentiate between the sound properly articulated and the sound as he articulates it. One way this may be done is through the use of a tape recorder. The teacher may deliberately mispronounce the sound, and on the playback the student may learn to discriminate the error sound from the correctly produced sound in varying phonetic contexts. After this stage, recordings of both the student and the teacher may be made to assist in recognizing the varying sounds. Other methods or materials may be used to enable the student to recognize differences between accurate and inaccurate articulation of speech sounds. Learning to *hear* errors is an absolute prerequisite to any further work with articulation problems and is sometimes called *ear training* or *auditory training.*

Second, *reduction or elimination of known causal factors should be attempted.* This is not possible in all cases, but the provision of a good model and the expectation of good articulation can be encouraged in the classroom and in the home. Parent conferences are required to explain the speech goals, and parents may sometimes be quite sensitive to the idea that they may have helped cause the problem, even if it is not stated this way. Perhaps the best way to approach parents is to indicate that we cannot always determine the cause of speech problems, but that we do know good speech models are essential as part of the remedial scheme.

After being absolutely certain that the student can hear the difference between articulation and misarticulation of the sounds in question, *it is necessary that the child learn to produce the correct sound.* This may be accomplished through games, exercises, behavior shaping (using approximations of the right sound production and slowly approaching the correct articulation), or any method that seems appropriate to the age and interests of the child. Many young children see little reason to change their speech patterns; this applies to all speech correction but perhaps most often to articulation problems. They seem to get by, and unless they are embarrassed by the reactions of others, they may not care. In some instances we must *make them care enough to hear articulatory differences,* and then motivate them to learn to make the correct sound. Reward systems may be of considerable value in accomplishing this step.

A fourth step is to *have the student incorporate the newly learned, accurately articulated sound in familiar words.* Even though the student learns to hear the difference between accurate and inaccurate articulation and to produce the required sound, until it is regularly used in language he has not overcome the problem. When an individual has had months or years of practice in saying the sound incorrectly, it takes a fair amount of repetition to develop new speech habits and patterns. Here again, motivation is highly important; with young children, games are often valuable.

In addition to the preceding overall rules for remediation, one general rule must be carefully observed by the regular classroom teacher. *If the student is being seen by a speech specialist, the teacher should consult with the specialist to be certain that any special efforts in the classroom are complementary, not contradictory, to efforts of the speech clinician.*

In addition to the activities previously mentioned, certain other tools or materials that may be used effectively by both the speech specialist and the regular classroom teacher include the following: (1) reading stories in which accurate articulation is modeled is a good technique, particularly with younger children; (2) word rhyming is an effective approach with some students; and (3) puppetry is an excellent way to overcome self-consciousness, which may be a serious deterrent to successful speech remediation for some children.

Teachers, as well as parents, must remember that children develop language as an imitative function. Teachers, as professionals whose primary responsibility is the welfare of the student, have a very special reason to provide a good model of correct articulation and broad language usage. The *teacher's articulation* and the *teacher's language patterns* have a dramatic effect on the students for whom she is responsible; the teacher should be constantly aware of this effect.

Regular efforts to promote speech improvement for all students in the class and individualized efforts to assist specific students with known articulation problems are the two ways in which regular classroom teachers are most likely to become involved with speech and speech problems. These are the areas in which the teacher is most likely to achieve significant success. The preceding discussion of articulation problems should provide sufficient information for the teacher to get started. It should also make it difficult for the conscientious teacher to ever again say, "I just don't know enough about speech correction to even make a start at helping Jimmy," If a speech specialist is available, *try to obtain help from her* and *work with her if she is seeing the child in question.* If there is no specialized help, start from the base of the preceding information and do additional reading in some of the suggested readings listed at the close of this chapter; the positive results may be surprising.

Voice problems

Voice disorders, according to Perkins (1977), are only about one eighth as common as articulatory disorders. He also notes that "therapy of vocal disorders has plagued speech pathologists more because we have known better what is wrong with a voice than how to make it right" (Perkins, 1977, p. 390). For the regular classroom teacher, voice disorders require very different consideration than articulation disorders in that the teacher's role is immediate referral to the speech specialist if such problems are suspected. If there is no speech specialist available, referral to the school nurse and the parent is in order.

In advising parents about various speech problems, Schreiber advised: "The minute you think you notice something wrong with your child's voice, start counting. If whatever it is hasn't gone away by the third day, take him to the doctor" (1973, pp. 127-128). This is not to indicate that every child with a voice disorder needs an immediate medical examination, but rather that if a significant change is noted (other than the voice changes usually experienced at puberty), there is the possibility of medical problems, some of which may require immediate treatment to prevent serious complications. This is not likely in the majority of voice problems but should be viewed as a possibility and treated accordingly.

Voice disorders are generally considered to include disorders of pitch, intensity, quality, and flexibility. For the most part, these problems do not have the same kind of direct effect on the learning of basic skills as, for example, serious articulation problems may have. In fact, unless they are very different from the norm, they are often accepted as part of the uniqueness of the individual. The following descriptions of these four types of voice disorders are presented so that the teacher may have an overall view of voice disorders and a base from which to consider the need for referral, either to the speech specialist or, through the parents, to the physician.

Pitch problems seldom cause any serious difficulty to the speaker, with the exception of the high falsetto voice in the upper-teenage or adult male. For girls and women a various levels of pitch are accepted, with some women considered to have "sexy" voices if the pitch is low and feminine voices if the pitch is high. For men, the problem may be different. Despite a number of recent societal changes in concepts of masculinity and femininity, there is a stubborn persistence of the belief that men should have a voice that is of low or medium pitch. Therefore, a boy with a high-pitched voice that apparently is continuing into his upper-teenage years may benefit from therapy to help him lower the pitch. Sometimes pitch can be lowered, and sometimes it cannot; the matter is usually a sensitive one, but if assistance can be provided, it may help greatly in the social arena.

Voice intensity, too loud or too soft, is not often a problem in and of itself, but very loud speech may mean that the individual does not hear his own voice distinctly and should serve as a cue to recheck the possibility of a hearing problem. The teacher should also note that if a child speaks indistinctly (as opposed to too softly) and is asked to *speak up*, the result may be even more unsatisfactory than before. In speaking up, many students with indistinct speech will give voice to very loud vowel sounds, which will even further drown out the weaker consonant sounds. Therefore the teacher (or speech specialist) must work on more precise consonant production.

Voice quality is the most common voice disorder of the four major types. Three types of voice quality problems are breathiness, harshness, and nasality. Harshness or breathiness may be caused by vocal abuse (such as occurs at a hard-fought football game) or may be the result of infection or inflammation of the vocal cords. These temporary problems usually go away after a few days of vocal rest. A more serious problem is that which occurs as a result of continued vocal abuse, causing growths to develop on the vocal cords. Such benign growths are fairly common among singers and, to some extent, among those who do a great deal of public speaking. These too may go away with vocal rest or if the individual receives therapy to assist in more normal voice production. It is also possible that such growths are malignant; thus the advice to seek prompt medical attention mentioned at the start of this discussion is applicable to older students and of course to adults. Malignant growths cause the same type of voice quality problem as benign growths; the only way to check out this possibility is through referral to a qualified specialist. The teacher should be alert for voice disorders and should be particularly alert for rapid changes in voice quality, especially hoarseness or breathiness. If the teacher is in doubt, an immediate referral to the speech specialist or physician is in order.

The fourth type of voice problem is a *flexibility disorder*. The most common flexibility problem is exhibited by the monotone speaker. This problem may result from many different causes, such as physical tiredness, emotional difficulties, voice pitch too near the top or the bottom of the vocal range, or a hearing problem. If the voice is very unpleasant because of a flexibility disorder and the problem persists, referral to the speech specialist is the proper course of action. Seldom is the regular class teacher in a position of technical knowledge and skill to assess and attempt to remediate this type of problem on her own.

In summary, voice problems may be of a minor nature and may be properly overlooked. An exception is the case of unusual voice *changes,* particularly those typified by hoarseness, harshness, or breathiness. If these persist, even for a few weeks, referral to a speech specialist or physician is recommended. Most voice disorders are of such nature that if the teacher is to be involved in remedial efforts, it should be under the direct supervision of the speech specialist.

Stuttering and other nonfluency problems

Stuttering represents about the same percentage of all speech difficulties as voice disorders, and has been a major target of speech practitioners and researchers for many years. In fact, the amount of professional effort directed toward stuttering as compared to the incidence of stuttering is considerably greater than in other areas of speech difficulty. Every few years, someone develops a "cure" for stuttering that is alleged to be almost certainly effective. Thus far in the history of such cures, each has been effective only for those individuals for whom it works. For many, many other stutterers, these various new approaches have failed. This is not to indicate that the stutterer cannot be helped or that there never can or will be a generally applicable approach to

help all stutterers. We will review approaches that appear to work with some stutterers and review the underlying rationale for each, but for the present there is no single procedure that can be called the best approach in all cases.

One reason stuttering has received so much attention is that it is such an obvious disorder. Another reason is that it is, in many instances, a debilitating disorder. Although there is continuing debate as to the cause of stuttering, theories fall into two major groups: organic and behavioral. Van Riper (1978) believes that stuttering has many origins. Organic theories propose a variety of neurological causations for stuttering, ranging from older theories relating to lack of cerebral dominance to those that liken stuttering to epileptic seizures. In many of these theories the fact that stutterers do not always stutter is accounted for by postulating a constitutional weakness of one of the types just mentioned that tends to "give" under pressure.

There are a number of nonorganic or behavioral theories concerning the causes of stuttering, and they have been assigned different titles as various authorities have revised them to fit the results of continuing research. The following three major theories will be presented without label or title:

1. Stuttering is a result of the fact that important individuals in the student's early life label normal disfluencies "stuttering." In response, the child focuses on these disfluencies, attempting to eliminate them. Overreaction, fear, tension, and anxiety lead to these disfluencies being maintained long beyond the time when they would normally be abandoned and thus they become actual stuttering.

2. Stuttering is the result of an unusual need, on the part of the child, to be listened to. In trying to maintain listeners' attention, normal disfluencies

that might otherwise be overlooked by both speaker and listener lead to more and more frustration. As the speaker struggles to become more fluent (due to internal drives, not outside influence) tension and frustration lead to continued disfluency.

3. Stuttering is the result of a need to satisfy anal or oral desires, infantile tendencies, or high levels of hostility. These in turn are the result of inadequate or unsatisfactory relationships with parents and may be related to various Freudian theories of child-parent conflict.

Various combinations or permutations of the foregoing theories may be constructed to form additional theories, but for the non-specialist, these indicate the thrust of stuttering theories. Although therapists may insist that their particular approach is based on a specific theory and feel that recognition of the cause is highly important, in practice all therapies are notable for their high rate of failure.

On the bright side, it is generally recognized that certain suggestions or guidelines seem to be applicable to most existing theories. The suggestions that follow indicate an attitude that must be adopted by the teacher and others who deal with students who stutter.

1. Do not mention the stuttering; try to reduce the student's awareness of this problem.
2. Minimize those settings and situations that appear to cause increased stuttering.
3. Minimize conflict of all types when possible.
4. Encourage speaking when all is going well, and immediately minimize demands to communicate when stuttering becomes more pronounced.

Primary, or beginning, stutterers may overcome the problem if those around them play their role properly. For secondary or confirmed stutterers, major goals may be acceptance of stuttering as a part of the language pattern and learning to stutter more easily or "gracefully." There exists a considerable degree of agreement on certain facts about stuttering. The following "facts" appear to be accepted by a large majority of authorities.

1. Stutterers rarely, if ever, stutter while singing.
2. Stutterers rarely stutter while speaking in unison or in synchronization with a rhythmic beat.
3. Stutterers rarely stutter while alone, or while swearing.
4. Stuttering cannot always be induced, even in those who stutter regularly.
5. Stutterers tend to stutter on the same words when reading and rereading the same passage. They may *not* stutter on these *same words* in other sentences.
6. Stutterers tend to be able to predict their stuttering.
7. Time pressure seems to be a factor in causing and/or increasing stuttering.
8. Stutterers cannot be shown to be biologically different from nonstutterers.
9. Stutterers can learn to hear how their speech flows and understand what normal fluency means; they just cannot *attain* such fluency.
10. Many cases of stuttering (more than 75% by some estimates) simply disappear without any identifiable, provable reason.

For the regular classroom teacher, knowledge of the above facts, plus application of the guidelines presented earlier in this section, provides the best available guide to action while awaiting the results of referral to professional speech specialists. After the student has been seen by the speech specialist, the only way to proceed is to follow the recommendations provided by the specialist. Stuttering is sufficiently complex that the teacher should *not* follow the temptation to try out some new cure featured in the Sunday newspaper or even in some professional journal. Once the speech specialist has entered the scene, the teacher should persist in efforts to obtain specific instructions from the specialist and should follow such instructions carefully.

Other types of speech problems

Certain other types of speech problems that deserve consideration include those related to *cleft lip or cleft palate, cerebral palsy, and hearing loss.* Cleft lip and cleft palate problems vary in effect on speech, depending on the depth of the cleft and the success of surgical procedures. Since midcentury, most children born with a facial cleft of any severity have been treated surgically during the first 2 or 3 months of life. Cleft lip, after surgical treatment, seldom causes any serious speech problem, but cleft palate is not often completely corrected surgically. The effects of cleft palate commonly include articulation errors and problems with nasality. Correction of these physiologically based speech problems is usually best left to the speech clinician. As a result of all of the related problems, students with cleft palate may tend to avoid speaking and may eventually become retarded in vocabulary and overall language development.

Speech problems relating to cerebral palsy may result in speech that is quite difficult for the listener to understand, although a small percentage of cerebral palsied students (perhaps twenty-five to thirty percent) do not have significant speech problems. Speech problems among the cerebral plasied vary for a number of reasons, but primarily in relation to the type of cerebral palsy and degree of involvement. For the most part, the teacher should try to give the cerebral palsied student with speech problems sufficient time to try to communicate as needed for class purposes. Speech therapy for the cerebral palsied is best left to the speech clinician.

Speech problems relating to hearing loss are discussed in Chapter 3 and are not mentioned here except to note that speech and language problems are to be expected in the student with a hearing loss. In a similar manner, students who are mentally retarded will probably have problems with delayed speech, vocabulary development, and grammatical usage.

There are a number of physiological causes of speech problems, such as faulty dentition and abnormal laryngeal structure. Under the direction of a speech clinician, the classroom teacher may be of great assistance in nearly all such cases.

Language difficulties

It appears that all the leading theorists who have researched the relationship between the development of language and cognitive development agree that such a relationship exists. They do not, however, agree on the nature of that relationship. In relation to certain specific tasks such as learning the concept of conservation of liquids, Bruner suggested "that training children to use language appropriate to the demands of the task would improve their performance on it" (Dale, 1976, p. 262). In a contrasting point of view, Piaget believes that language reflects, rather than determines, cognitive development. Either belief may apply in certain cases, but regardless of which is "more correct," there is agreement that cognitive development and language development are related. Since one major task of educators is maximizing cognitive development, and language and cognitive development are apparently closely related, language difficulties are an important target for the educator.

Assuming that language difficulties *are* a problem that may lead to handicaps in learning, we must then agree on some way to further define or classify them. Egland (1970) points out that the language problem subarea of speech correction may include more loosely classified and poorly defined terms than any other recognized subarea. Certain disorders are believed to relate to specific physiological causation and may be called central nervous system disorders. These would include such classifications as dyslexia and aphasia and are relatively severe problems with which the regular classroom teacher should have expert help. (The term dyslexia is sometimes used very loosely to indicate almost any remedial reading problem. We are referring here to severe, specific dyslexia.) Most of these disorders of language may also be considered learning disabilities, and they will be considered in a general way in the chapter on learning disabilities. In this section we will limit our discussion to more general, nonspecific language problems and delayed speech development. It is important to remember that in many cases the problems first recognized in relation to poor language development are multifaceted and deserve the attention of a competent, interdisciplinary diagnostic team. Therefore, when the teacher is considering language problems, particularly if there seem to be many pieces of the "puzzle" missing as the observations are recorded and assessed, it is best to refer to a source having good interdisciplinary resources.

Language problems are the most difficult problems of speech to diagnose with certainty. In contrast to stuttering for example, where the diagnosis can be made with certainty, even the experts may not agree on whether a given student actually has a language problem. This is made all the more complex by the degree to which a language problem diagnosis must relate to an evaluation of many other facets of the student's environment. Earlier, we emphasized the importance of articulation as it relates to the student's effective communication. Spoken language is the major means whereby children communicate; it provides the basis for reading, writing, and a foundation of information essential to the development of further knowledge. It is used for social and, to some degree, technical purposes. Spoken language has value and meaning only as society gives it value and meaning, but for the human species, it is valued above almost all else.

Language differences have been the topic of much debate in recent years; we have recognized, for example, that some ghetto language, although abnormal by middle-class standards, is quite normal in its home setting. At this point in time, no one can safely predict what direction this particular issue will take. If we reconsider the definitions of speech problems, we see that language problems should be considered significant if they interfere with communication, if they cause the speaker to be maladjusted, or if they cause problems for the listener. Outisde the ghetto, extremes of ghetto language may well cause problems for the listener, who simply would not understand much of what the speaker is saying. This, in turn, will cause problems for the speaker. This problem and that of teaching bilingual (for example, Spanish speaking) students to communicate in standard English create problems other than "how-to-do-it." There are questions of preservation of culture, individual rights, and school district policy. We cannot make pronouncements that will apply in all settings, but must comment that these are real problems and that teachers should use all their available influence (through teacher organizations and legislative influence, for example) to encourage local schools to take an official position and to make some provision for the specialized programs and curriculum adjustments required by students with these unique needs.

Before considering delayed speech and various ways in which the teacher may work to prevent or correct language problems in the classroom, we should be reminded that some language problems are related to other causal factors and may be taken care of, at least in part, in programming directed at these more basic factors. One prime example is that of the hearing impaired. If the hearing impaired student does *not* have problems with language, it is considered highly unusual. This topic was considered in Chapter 3 and will not be further pursued here. However, it must be remembered that students with mild hearing impairments may have been bypassed in screening procedures and that language problems may be the clue to identification. Therefore, *if a child has a language problem, the teacher should immediately check to make certain he has had a recent audiological examination.* If he has not, this should be the first order of business, and the teacher should pursue this with vigor. Two other conditions that often lead to language problems are mental retardation and learning disabilities. Some mildly mentally retarded students show only a small degree of language development problems, but in general, they will tend to have language development below expectations for their chronological age. The lower the intellectual level, the lower the language level is likely to be. With the learning disabled, the picture is not so clear-cut. If the learning disability is the type that is closely related to spoken language, there will be definite language problems. If the learning disability is related almost totally to reading ability and visual channel problems, the student may have average or above average spoken language. In fact, the large discrepancy between spoken language level and ability to decode written language is one of the indicators of learning disability in many cases.

Delayed speech, considered here as a type of language problem, is mentioned as a separate category in some texts in the field of speech pathology. Schreiber (1973), in a guide intended mainly for parents, indicated that one of the more common causes of delayed speech may be lack of need for the child to talk; other causes may be a bilingual home or the fact that the student is a twin (and thus used to communicating more without speech). If parents attempt to anticipate the student's every need, so that he need not ask for much, it may delay his speech. Or, if parents literally believe that children should be seen and not heard, this may delay speech. Fortunately, children with such parents usually play with other children in the neighborhood; here they have the opportunity and the need to speak to be a successful part of the group. The term "delayed speech" is often used to refer to the speech patterns of hearing impaired and mentally handicapped children, but it does not mean the same thing as delayed speech in children who have adequate hearing and normal or above normal mental ability. For parents who become overly concerned with the fact that their 2½ -year-old child does not speak and thus wonder if something is basically wrong, it is well to cite the case of Albert Einstein, who did not speak until after his third birthday. It is a somewhat different situation if the child comes to school at age 5 years and still has seriously delayed speech. This may require special attention, and planning should start with a complete physical checkup to eliminate the possibility of structural defects. If there are no such disabilities and the intellectual level appears to be at least normal, then environmental background should be reviewed. In all cases the teacher should supply every possible opportunity for use of language but should not use undue pressure tactics. Sometimes we find students with speech patterns that are two to three years behind that which would be predicted from chronological age, intellectual level, opportunity to learn, and other such factors. After complete examination by a team of specialists from all disciplines, the only answer may be *delayed speech—unknown etiology*, which simply means we do not always know the causes of delayed speech. After seeing such a case, it may be tempting to conclude that we should just deal with the delayed speech in all cases, rather than go through the cost and effort of various evaluations. This is an unacceptable decision, for in many cases the examination results in the discovery of causes that may be treated directly, and in some cases the problem may be remedied relatively quickly.

If causes are known, they should be carefully considered when planning remediation of delayed speech. If the student has not had sufficient language experience, then we should provide it for him. This may include games in which language development plays an important role. If the student likes to listen to tapes, it may mean listening to stories that will broaden his vocabulary and widen his language experience. Rhymes may be of value, or sentence-building exercises may be appropriate, depending on the particular case. Parents may be given specific exercises or activities, and it may be well to review such things as the role they should play in monitoring television programs to broaden language experience and in taking time to really talk to their children, even if time is limited.

Most of the preceding suggestions and activities are obviously more applicable with younger students. At the secondary level, it is doubtful whether the parent can play such a major role, but even here the provision of reading material that is interesting and that stimulates further language development may help. Parents must sometimes be reminded that even though their children do not *appear* to be noticing what the parents do, they may be providing more of a model than they suspect. Their reading habits, their language usage, and their values may have a direct effect on their children. The teacher may have a positive effect by virtue of the way assignments are given and the manner in which good language usage is rewarded. This requires planning that permits rewarding one student for a language level that would not be considered satisfactory for another student, but this is the essence of individualization.

The key words in such planning and teaching are exposure, encouragement, variety, opportunity, and innovation. Interest must be stimulated and maintained. A reward system must be established, be it through grades, praise, or privileges, that encourages the student to maintain effort. As previously stated, more severe language problems are the province of specialists in speech or learning disabilities. Less severe problems must be dealt with by the regular class teacher or they may not be dealt with at all. The potential benefits for the student are considerable, but in many instances, the student is not fully aware that change or additional development is needed. He is functioning at his present level, and unlike such problems as stuttering, the difficulty may not be obvious. This is all the more reason for educators to play their proper role in this area of concern.

ROLE OF THE REGULAR CLASSROOM TEACHER

Suggestions about how the teacher may assist in cases of recognized articulation problems, voice disorders, stuttering problems, and language problems have been included in the discussions of each of these areas earlier in this chapter. In cases where there is a speech specialist available within the local school district, such advice should be sought and followed. In certain instances, such as obvious changes in voice quality that persist and are not obviously connected with a cold or throat infection, prompt action should be taken, as outlined on pp. 126 to 128. One question that will continue to be a concern to most teachers, who do not want to be accused of being "chronic overre-ferrers", is when to ask for help. There are no pat answers to this question, but the following points may serve as general guidelines, to be modified as local practices dictate.

1. For the new teacher, who is not experienced in evaluating potential speech problems, overreferral may actually be the best practice. With experience, the number of referrals may be reduced without the risk of overlooking students who require assistance.

2. If the speech specialist is available for conferences with teachers (and he *should* be, either on an informal or a formal, scheduled basis), new teachers may find it of value to confer with him regarding potential referrals in order to learn more about what type of information is needed and who should or should not be referred. Such conferences usually turn out to be informal inservice training sessions and as such are of great value. The number of such conferences can be reduced as the teacher gains experience.

3. When it appears that the speech or language difficulty might relate to other problems such as hearing impairment or mental retardation, the teacher should check all records and talk with previous teachers (when possible) to determine if these possibilities have been investigated. The matter of a recent audiological evaluation must especially be pursued in the case of possible hearing impairment.

When the services of a qualified speech specialist are readily available, the student should be referred to the specialist if any doubt exists concerning a speech problem. Then, if the problem is one requiring specific assistance, the speech specialist will do his part and will provide suggestions to the teacher. The teacher's role will depend on the type and extent of the problem. Activities that will support the clinician's efforts will be suggested, and some "don'ts" along with positive suggestions will help determine the teacher's role. Even in an ideal setting there may be problems if the teacher is uninformed regarding speech problems, for experience indicates that some teachers, like some parents, may adjust to speech problems to the point that they no longer hear them. Therefore, each teacher must be aware of certain more obvious identifying characteristics of each disorder. In other words, a child with an articulation disorder will either be omitting, substituting, distorting, or adding certain speech sounds. Other major speech disorders also have certain unique characteristics, as described in the preceding sections of this chapter.

Careful observation of the problem as it presently exists should be considered along with information concerning potential problems in later life that each speech problem may generate. In settings in which the speech specialist is overloaded with cases (a common situation), the teacher may expedite matters if he can describe the type and extent of the problem accurately. It is not enough to say the child lisps. There are many other factors, such as how consistently it occurs, whether it occurs mainly under pressure or when the child is tired, whether it is noticed by other children, and so on. In each of the speech problem categories, there are specific points to note that will help the teacher, or the teacher and the specialist in conference, to decide what to do next.

In summary, the role of the teacher may have several different aspects, and the degree to which the teacher is involved depends on the grade level at which she teaches and the availability of adequate services from a speech specialist. In most settings the teacher must be deliberately aware of speech problems, must refer serious cases to the speech specialists, must assist—at the direction of the speech specialist—in the classroom program of students with whom the speech specialist is working, and must be alert for every opportunity to promote better speech production by all children in her classroom. The teacher must also be aware of the effect of her own speech and language patterns on the children she teaches, this influence being especially important at the lower grade levels. To fulfill the preceding responsibilities, the teacher must know how to listen (to be able to refer accurately) and how each type of speech problem may handicap the child in the educational-academic and social settings. With such knowledge and understanding, the regular classroom teacher can become a part of a valuable working partnership with the speech specialist, and all students will benefit.

ROLE OF THE SPEECH SPECIALIST

The speech specialist is the orchestrator of school speech and language services and as such provides direct services to students with severe or difficult problems, while providing advice to teachers who serve students with milder problems. Speech programs comprise identification, evaluation, and remediation and are highly dependent on good cooperative working relationships between speech specialists and regular classroom teachers. The American Speech and Hearing Association recommends that speech and language programs be organized along a continuum that extends from a communicative development component to a communicative disorders component (Healey, 1974).

With respect to communicative development, the speech specialist must serve to make teachers and parents aware of factors that help students develop good communicative skills, especially those factors that can be a part of the regular classroom or home environment. Many of the suggestions provided earlier in this chapter would be a part of any such program, along with efforts to construct a total curriculum for the school that will automatically ensure a maximum of the type of experiences that promote good communicative skills in all children. This program is primarily developmental and pre-

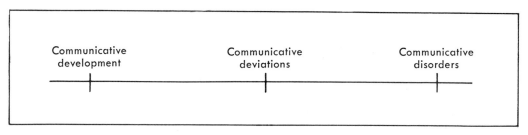

The comprehensive speech and language program continuum

ventative in nature, and the speech specialist may have minimum visibility in such programs once they are well established in a school.

Communication deviations may be viewed as mild to moderate speech or language deviations and include many types of articulation problems. Speech specialists continue to work directly in this phase of the total program but will, when possible, provide instructions to the regular classroom teacher and leave much of the direct effort to be carried out in the regular classroom. Where regular classroom efforts are not successful, the speech specialist will again intervene directly as required.

Communication disorders, as viewed by many of today's speech specialists, are those sufficiently severe to demand intensive direct service. This area of service involves a great deal of cooperative effort between the speech specialist and the regular classroom teacher and requires by far the greatest time investment of the speech specialist. The speech specialist must assist the teacher to "tune in" to situations in the regular classroom in which various class proceedings, including certain standardized academic tests, are greatly affected by lack of speech or language ability. The specialist must determine the most effective ways to improve the student's speech or language and must involve the teacher in such remediation, providing assistance in required carry-over activities in the classroom.

Speech specialists may serve in special schools, in clinic centers in large school districts, or in special programs for the physically handicapped, the cerebral palsied, or the multiply handicapped. In this case, a specialist may be assigned to a single school on a full-time basis. Often the specialist serves a case load of sixty to eighty students; however, effectiveness of service is reduced if the case load is more than forty to fifty.* The speech specialist will, of necessity, modify his scheduling and operational tactics in accordance with the needs of the schools served, but in all public school settings the purposes of the speech program can be realized only as the specialist and the regular classroom teacher develop a process whereby each can contribute to meeting the speech and language goals established for the *individual student*.

SUMMARY

Speech specialists have provided remedial services as part of the public school program for many years and, to a limited extent, regular classroom teachers have been involved in related efforts in the regular classroom. The events of the past ten to fifteen years, especially the passage of Public Law 94-142 in 1975 and the requirement for more specific individual planning and planned cooperation between specialists and regular classroom teachers, have led to the initiation of a great deal more cooperative planning and programming. This, in turn, has made it necessary for the regular classroom teacher to become better informed about speech and language problems and what to do to assist students who are experiencing such problems.

In this chapter, we have included a discussion of articulation, voice, stuttering, and language problems. Articulation problems are the most common and provide the most fruitful area for assistance in the regular classroom. Articulation problems have a variety of causations, but most can be ap-

---

*As the type of services provided by speech specialists evolve in the direction of serving only more serious or severe cases, some states have officially limited caseloads to maximums of twenty-five or thirty students. This means that the regular classroom teacher *must* serve many students with mild speech problems.

proached by (1) making certain the child hears the error, (2) reducing causal or contributive factors, (3) assisting and encouraging the child to learn to make the correct sound, and (4) planning so that the newly learned, accurately articulated sound is incorporated into familiar words and used regularly. A highly important rule to be applied to the correction of articulation problems and to all other remedial efforts carried out by the regular classroom teacher is that *if the child is being seen by a speech specialist the teacher should consult with the specialist to make certain that classroom efforts are consistent with and complementary to the specialized efforts provided in therapy.* The speech specialist should contact the teacher, but if this does not happen the teacher should contact the specialist.

Voice problems, for the most part, are of such a nature that if they require therapy, it should be provided by the speech specialist. The role the regular classroom teacher should assume is that of referring the student to the speech specialist and, in the case of a child who undergoes a very rapid voice change (such as unusual harshness or breathiness), referring the student to the speech specialist, the physician, or both.

Stuttering therapy is best left to the speech specialist, but the teacher should consider the following guidelines unless specifically told otherwise by the specialist: (1) do not mention the stuttering—try to overlook it; (2) minimize settings that appear to cause increased stuttering; (3) minimize all types of conflict; (4) encourage speaking when the student is speaking fluently; and (5) reduce or minimize demands, as unobtrusively as possible, when stuttering becomes worse.

Speech and the development of language are sufficiently complex that they are often called the "miracle of human development." They represent one major function of hu-

mankind that is not duplicated by the lower animals, and to a great extent the question of how speech and language actually develop remains unanswered. We can "map" the steps taken in normal development—a procedure presented in abbreviated form in this chapter—but how the brain and neurological system actually take these steps remains essentially a mystery.

A certain degree of variation in speech and language development exists between students, and delayed language development is not necessarily indicative of a serious problem. However, we do know that such a delay *may* be a signal of future problems, and providing adequate opportunity to develop speech and language affords good, if only partial, insurance against later difficulties. Parents and teachers must work together to provide an environment in which students are encouraged to exercise existing language skills and are provided opportunities to acquire new skills as required by their age and developmental level.

The remediation of language disorders beyond assisting the student who is experiencing some sort of simple language delay is beyond the scope of what may normally be expected of the regular classroom teacher. Language development efforts with the mentally retarded and the hearing impaired must be carefully coordinated with all other facets of the students' programs. Students from culturally different settings will often have more language problems than students from major ethnic and cultural groups and should receive assistance in developing better English language usage; however, this may be best accomplished through special curriculum offerings that are planned to assist with standard English while protecting the child's right to maintain another culture or language. In remediation of most language problems, careful planning of enriched language experiences and employment of all possible motivational techniques form an effective start. With language problems, the teacher should double-check to make certain that the student has had a recent audiological evaluation, because hearing impairments are sometimes overlooked for years.

The major thrust in all speech and language programming should be one of a team effort to assist the student who is experiencing difficulties. When the student has no hearing impairment or mental retardation, the team is the speech specialist and the regular classroom teacher. If other handicapping conditions exist (hearing, mental retardation, or others) other professionals should become team members as appropriate. For both planning and implementation, parents are the final team members who must not be forgotten. Students with speech and language problems experience them throughout their waking hours, and efforts must be directed at this total need and not only at the situations when the teacher is in direct contact with the student. With such complementary efforts, goals will be reached more quickly and all will benefit proportionally.

REFERENCES AND SUGGESTED READINGS

Black, M. *School speech therapy: a source book.* Pittsburgh: Stanwix House, Inc., 1970.

Broman, B., & Shipley, S. Language development. *Instructor,* October 1969, 79, 132.

Cazden, D. *Child language and education.* New York: Holt, Rinehart and Winston, Inc., 1972.

Dale, P. *Language development: structure and function* (2nd ed.). New York: Holt, Rinehart and Winston, Inc., 1976.

Dixon, C. Speech problems—how and when to step in. *Grade Teacher,* February 1968, 85 (6), 51-52.

Egland, G. *Speech and language problems: a guide for the classroom teacher.* Englewood Cliffs, N.J.: Prentice-Hall, Inc., 1970.

Freeman, G. *Speech and language services and the classroom teacher.* Reston, Virginia: Council for Exceptional Children, 1977.

Fundula, J. Applied awareness: speech improvement in an elementary classroom. *Teaching Exceptional Children,* Summer 1973, 5, 190-194.

Healey, W. *Standards and guidelines for comprehensive language, speech, and hearing programs in the schools.* Washington, D.C.: American Speech & Hearing Association, 1974.

Hendrick, J. *The whole child: new trends in early education.* St. Louis: The C. V. Mosby Co., 1975.

Karnes, M. *Helping young children develop language skills: a book of activities.* Washington, D.C.: Council for Exceptional Children, 1968.

Perkins, W. *Speech pathology: an applied behavioral science* (2nd ed.). St. Louis: The C. V. Mosby Co., 1977.

Sacco, P. How do you help the stutterer? *Instructor,* June-July 1974, 83, 35.

Schreiber, F. *Your child's speech.* New York: Ballantine, Books, Inc., 1973.

Travis, L. *Handbook of speech pathology and audiology.* New York: Appleton-Century-Crofts, 1971.

Van Riper, C. *Speech correction: principles and methods* (6th ed.). Englewood Cliffs, N.J.: Prentice-Hall, Inc., 1978.

Weiss, C. & Lillywhite, H. *Communicative disorders: a handbook for prevention and early intervention.* St. Louis: The C. V. Mosby Co., 1976.

Wiig, E., & Semel, E. *Language disabilities in children and adolescents.* Columbus, Ohio: Charles E. Merrill, 1976.

A special introduction to Chapters 7 and 8

In the first edition of this text, we attempted to combine our considerations of mild mental retardation and learning disabilities into one chapter. We noted the following in that chapter:

> We believe that both mental handicap (or mental retardation) and learning disabilities are real, significant handicapping conditions. We feel that they are different and, in some cases, relatively easy to identify. However, in other instances, particularly with younger children, they are extremely difficult to differentiate. We will discuss mental handicap and learning disabilities in this one chapter and will attempt to indicate how they are alike and how they are different. In addition, we will indicate methods and procedures that may be of value with both types of handicap plus methods and procedures that may be more appropriate for only one of these handicapping conditions.

We are now convinced that the combination chapter was an error, that it apparently caused confusion. Thus this second edition has two separate chapters, one on mental retardation and one on learning disabilities. However, we still emphasize that in cases of *mild* mental retardation and learning disabilities, it *may* be difficult to differentiate between the two, especially with young children. It also remains true that in *some* cases, methods and procedures that are appropriate for one of these conditions may also be appropriate for the other. We must hasten to say that in some instances, methods that are appropriate for one condition may be entirely inappropriate for the other.

B. G. and M. W.

7 EDUCATION OF THE MENTALLY RETARDED

From Chinn, P. C., Drew, C. J., and Logan, D. R.: Mental retardation: a life cycle approach, St. Louis, 1975, The C. V. Mosby Co.

Ten to fifteen years ago, the regular classroom teacher was unlikely to have extended dealings with the educable mentally retarded student once that student was identified. The standard process formerly involved identifying these mildly mentally retarded students and then providing a separate, adapted, full-day program in a self-contained special class. This has changed radically in a matter of a very few years, so that today "most of the children within this category . . . are mainstreamed" (Kelly and Vergason, 1978, p. 48). As noted in Chapter 1, students enrolled in classes for the educable mentally retarded were the subject of numerous court suits. In many cases, the reason for such litigation was that a number of these students had been improperly diagnosed and were not actually mentally retarded. There were also serious concerns about disproportionate numbers of minority students in these classes and about the stigma attached to "mental retardation." With such confusion, even on the part of the special education "experts," we may properly wonder what we should believe. A number of important questions must be answered. These include the following: (1) How do we know who is mentally retarded? (2) How were such errors in diagnosis and placement made with so many students? (3) If there are all these questions and uncertainties, can we be certain that any given student is mentally retarded? (4) Is there really such a thing as a mentally retarded student? (5) If there are some students who are really mentally retarded, what is the best educational program for them? All these questions have been asked many times, and there remains considerable debate about many of them. We will attempt to answer them, or at least pose what we believe are the most acceptable tentative answers in the light of present evidence. First, however, we will define, and briefly discuss, the condition called mental retardation.

THE NATURE OF MENTAL RETARDATION

Mental retardation has been defined in various ways in the past, and differing state regulations and identification practices have led to some degree of confusion. For many years it was only necessary to show that a student had scored below a certain cutoff point on an individual test of intelligence to permit identification of him as mentally retarded or mentally handicapped. The Stanford-Binet or the Wechsler Intelligence Scale for Children (WISC) were the standard tests for determining a student's IQ.

In most states, parents were consulted; at least this was written into the regulations. Upper IQ limits for such identification varied from state to state, but the most common upper limits for inclusion in such programs were IQs of 70, 75, or 80. State officials had the responsibility to monitor these programs to be certain that students with IQs above the upper limits were not included. In a few states, there was mention of adaptive behavior, that is, the way the student functions in social settings other than the academic, as another criterion for classification as educable mentally retarded (EMR), but this was often not followed. In summary, then, to be identified as EMR, an IQ of 50 to 70 (or 75 or 80) was essentially all that was required.

The next level of mental retardation below EMR is commonly called trainable mentally retarded (TMR). The TMR, like the EMR, were identified primarily with respect to IQ; the upper IQ limit for this category corresponds to the lower limit for the EMR. Ten years ago, a majority of the states did not regularly provide public school programs for the TMR, and if they did, they were completely separate programs. Today, more and more public schools provide for the TMR, and in some states at least part of the program may be provided in the regular classroom. However, this tends to be a very small part of the school day, except perhaps for very young children who are borderline EMR-TMR, and the major concern of the regular classroom teacher (with respect to students who are mentally retarded) is that of educational programming for EMR students.

With the coming of Public Law 94-142 and its accompanying regulations, at least two measures are required for a diagnosis of mental retardation. These two measures are (1) results of an individual IQ test and (2) corroborating evidence on a measure of adaptive behavior. In addition, school functioning in both academic and social areas should support these measures. The following definition of mental retardation is the most recent and most widely accepted, and is supported by the regulations of PL 94-142 and by almost all state regulations (Grossman, 1977, p. 5):

Mental Retardation refers to significantly subaverage general intellectual functioning existing concurrently with deficits in adaptive behavior and manifested during the developmental period.

This definition, accepted by the American Association on Mental Deficiency (AAMD) has received widespread acceptance by the various disciplines involved with the mentally retarded. As for levels of mental retardation, Table 5 indicates the two levels that may be of significance to the regular classroom teacher.

In practice, many regular classroom teachers teach EMR students for a part or nearly all of the day. In all cases, there should be planned assistance, both in teaching strategies and materials, from a resource or consulting teacher with specialized training and competencies in this area. Not many regular classroom teachers are asked to teach the TMR; however, there are a few areas of the nation where integration for a very limited part of the day is being tried. In most instances where there is integration of the TMR (beyond a few hours per week for purposes of socialization), the students being integrated are more like EMR than TMR in those characteristics important to educational practices. Therefore, our focus in this chapter will be on the EMR student.

Despite the general acceptance of a definition of mental retardation and recognition of the mild (educable) level, some questions remain about the EMR. In part, this is a result of the factors mentioned previously (litigation, misuse of special classes, and so forth) but also relates to another very important factor. In the past the mentally retarded had for the most part been considered permanently mentally retarded. Recent efforts have indicated that IQ as measured by the best available tests of intelligence can sometimes be increased. This is often true of minority children but also relates to the white, middle-class child who, for some

Table 5. Levels of mental retardation as determined by individual tests of intelligence

	Obtained IQ*	
Level of mental retardation	Wechsler scales	Stanford-Binet
Mild (educable or EMR)	69-55	67-52
Moderate (trainable or TMR)	54-40	51-36

*It will be noted that these IQ limits are different from those mentioned on p. 141. The previously mentioned limits were those typically included in state regulations several years ago. The limits shown here are being used in a growing number of states.

reason, has not developed to his full intellectual potential. Intelligence, as measured by intelligence tests, is *not* a static fact of life, and in some cases (although not necessarily all) can be changed. Thus some, perhaps many, students who are called mentally handicapped may simply have underdeveloped, normal-range intelligence.

With all these factors in mind, it seems appropriate that we clarify our beliefs about retarded students before further discussion of how the regular classroom teacher may most effectively deal with these students. The following statements reflect our beliefs:

1. Many students who have been identified as mentally retarded have been mislabeled on the basis of inappropriate or biased tests, insufficient data, or both.

2. Many students who might be viewed as mildly mentally retarded can be assisted to develop intellectually and cognitively to approach the level of normal mental ability.

3. There are "true" educable mentally retarded children (just as there are more severely mentally retarded children—a fact few will deny), and they may occur in all races, ethnic groups, and socioeconomic levels.

4. The EMR students should be identified by multiple criteria, including (a) level of functioning in social situations, (b) level of language development, (c) functioning on an individual test of intelligence (full-scale or global IQ, plus consideration of patterns of subtest scores), (d) emotional maturity, and (e) academic achievement. Ethnic, cultural, social, and economic background must also be considered.

5. Many EMR students can be effectively educated in the regular class for the major part of the day if the teacher receives assistance with materials and specific methods.

6. Students who score at the lower end of the range often ascribed to the EMR (those who have a measured IQ of 50 to 60, with other indicators supporting this measure) may require a special class program for a major part of the school day.

7. Most EMR students are likely to benefit from a special work-experience–type program at the secondary level.

IDENTIFICATION OF EMR STUDENTS

Although the lower levels of mental retardation are almost self-identifying and such identification usually takes place long before school entrance, the EMR student may not be identified for several years. Later identification will more likely occur with those near the upper end of the EMR range. Under the accepted concept of the least restrictive environment, *if* a student is functioning in such a manner that he can remain within the regular classroom setting with no additional support services, *there is no reason to identify him or her as mentally retarded.* In fact, if he is functioning satisfactorily in the regular class, his adaptive behavior is most likely within the normal range. Given the definitional requirement that the individual be significantly subaverage in *both* measured intelligence and adaptive behavior, he would not be considered mentally retarded even with an IQ within the range of mild mental retardation. This set of conditions does not represent the usual situation, but it is important to know that these conditions sometimes exist.

Characteristics

Identification is closely related to knowledge of the characteristics of mental retardation; thus we will review a number of signs usually associated with mild mental retardation. The following characteristics, and certain subcharacteristics that relate to and grow out of these, will more often be found in the EMR students than in age peers of normal mental ability. It is not likely that all these characteristics will be found in all EMR students, but some combination of these characteristics are found in most EMR students. These characteristics are highly interrelated (for example, below average language ability and academic retardation), and all are related to the below normal level of mental functioning of the EMR students.

Sensory and motor coordination handicaps. Although many EMR students have no visual or hearing impairments, there tend to be more such impairments among the mentally retarded population than among the total population of children of the same age. In a similar manner, there is more likelihood that EMR students will have less well-developed motor skills, although many will have average motor ability and some will have above average motor ability.

Low tolerance for frustration. Low tolerance for frustration is regularly mentioned in relation to EMR students in academic settings established for age-peers of normal or above normal intellectual ability. It is altogether possible that it is the result of academic expectations beyond their capability, and content and concepts for which they are not ready, rather than some sort of "built-in" characteristic.

Poor self-concept. The cumulative effect of failure in academic and social situations may contribute to a low self-concept. The EMR student may lack confidence because of previous experiences and may not be willing to attempt new tasks because of failure. Their past experiences and the effect of lower expectations may contribute significantly to their lower self-esteem.

Short attention span. These students may demonstrate a relatively short attention span. This may be due to their failure in past academic efforts, to the inappropriateness of present academic expectations, or to auditory or visual distractions in the classroom. Each of these factors can limit a student's ability to attend, and in combination the effect may be quite serious.

Below average language ability. Although language ability that is below average might indicate hearing impairment, learning disability, lack of opportunity to develop language, or other causal factors, the EMR student will almost always have below average (for age) language ability. The only exception that we have seen to this generalization has been with upper borderline students in situations in which well-informed, highly motivated parents have invested unusual efforts at the preschool level. In such cases, these children may enter school with normal language ability. Usually it will slowly become lower than that of the normal peer group, as other children have opportunity to grow in this area.

Below average ability to generalize and conceptualize. Below average ability to generalize and conceptualize is at least partially measured by most individual tests of intelligence and thus is to be expected in most EMR students, since intelligence test results are a significant part of the base for determining mild mental handicap. It is useful for the classroom teacher to think in terms of the student's abilities in these areas, but care should be taken to avoid confusion between ability to generalize or conceptualize relating to what is read and ability to generalize or conceptualize in other settings. (A learning disabled student with a serious reading problem may appear to be unable to conceptualize if reading is the base for conceptualizations. However, he may be able to conceptualize quite well if the initial information is given verbally. In contrast, the EMR student will have a tendency to have difficulty with generalization and conceptualization in a variety of settings.)

General academic retardation. The EMR student will usually be academically retarded in such areas as reading, arithmetic, and spelling. If he is retarded academically in, for example, reading only, but is normal or above normal in arithmetic ability, he probably is not mentally retarded.

Play interests below those of age peers. A play interest below those of age peers is not always observed but is apparent in enough cases to deserve mention. Many types of play are related to an ability to understand rules and to integrate cause-effect factors and relationships. Whereas a particular activity may "stretch" the mental ability of most other children of a given age, the mildly mentally handicapped child will likely not understand. He may therefore turn to more simple play activities or to younger children.

The term "educable" implies that the individual can, with proper educational opportunity, become a self-supporting, participating member of society. It is likely that the reader knows of mildly mentally retarded individuals who appear to contradict this statement. They apparently cannot support themselves and certainly do not seem to be capable of contributory participation in society. In nearly every case of this type that we have seen over the years, the reasons for this inability were either (1) the existence of other handicapping conditions (in addition to the mild mental handicap) or (2) inappropriate or insufficient educational opportunity. Very often it was a combination of these factors.

The amount or degree of mental retardation must be measured through an individual test of intelligence such as the Wechsler Intelligence Scales or the Stanford-Binet test. Such tests may be suspect with minority or bilingual students, but if the test is given by a well-trained and experienced diagnostician, the fact that the test is not measuring adequately is usually evident. In this case, the tests should be considered invalid. If valid test results can be obtained, a second characteristic must be investigated. This characteristic, adaptive behavior, is also sometimes called "street behavior," indicating the manner in which the student is able to function in the everyday requirements of living. These include but are not restricted to such things as getting to and from school (walking or using the school bus, for example), functioning as a member of a peer group, following simple instructions, and being able to discuss with peers and adults common day-to-day topics of interest. Some might characterize adaptive behavior as the ability to function with peers without standing out as different. Of course, many nonmentally retarded youngsters may have subaverage adaptive behavior, but by definition mental retardation means performing considerably below average in academic areas, having a significant deficit in intellectual functioning (as reflected by an individual test of intelligence), and having subaverage adaptive behavior. If these conditions are met, then we will tentatively consider the student mentally retarded.

Referral for special assistance

If a given student is having significant educational difficulties and exhibits a number of the characteristics outlined previously, some consideration should be given to referring him for further evaluation. In almost all school districts such referral involves the completion of a special referral form that requires the recording of a variety of data. In addition to name, grade, sex, and similar identifying data, most forms require information on level of academic achievement by subject area, data on behavior, performance in situations such as class discussions, responses to information presented through media other than reading, and a listing of both strengths and weaknesses.

Many times an objective, systematic listing of such data leads to a recognition that, given the strengths listed, the student is probably not mentally retarded, and it may indicate an alternate course of action without further referral. If the referral is continued, other school personnel will gather additional information that will permit the consideration of many factors and variables. In the case of suspected mental retardation, this will always include individual measures of intelligence and adaptive behavior. If there is any question whatsoever regarding the results of these tests, especially the individual test of intelligence, additional measures must be employed. After gathering and considering all pertinent information, holding a conference with the parents and involving them in the identification process, and carefully considering all alternatives, the student may, with parental agreement, be placed in a special program for EMR students. "Placed" should mean placement at the point on the continuum of services (see pp. 30-31) consistent with the most appropriate educational assistance provided within the least restrictive environment.

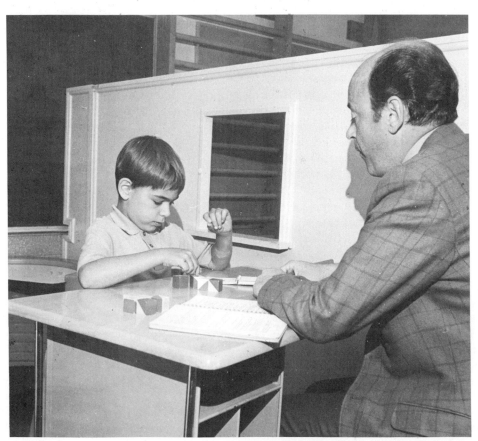

From Gearheart, B. R.: Learning disabilities: educational strategies, St. Louis, 1973, The C. V. Mosby Co.

RESPONSIBILITIES OF SPECIAL EDUCATION PERSONNEL

The responsibility of the special educator in programming for the EMR student will vary widely with respect to degree of mental retardation, the existence of other handicapping conditions, and the age or grade level under consideration. A variety of types of service should be available, although in reality this variety is *not* available in every community. Where it is not, the effect of PL 94-142 has generally been to increase the variety of services in the direction of a total continuum. The discussion that follows is based on the existence of at least a moderate range of services, but not necessarily the extremely broad range available in some of the larger, more progressive programs in the nation.

At the lower grade levels (first and second grades), suggestions and the provision of some special materials may permit the student to remain full time in the regular classroom. If the handicap is greater in degree (lower level of intelligence, other handicapping conditions, or very inadequate experiential background), part-time placement in a resource room may be of value. In this setting the student will receive much more individual help in developing basic reading and numbers skills, and the resource room teacher will attempt to determine those approaches that will provide maximum growth when the student is back in the regular class. Many of these students will later be able to come back to the regular class on a full-time basis; however, some will need to move into a part-time, special class program if the resource room setting proves to be insufficient to provide for unique educational needs. A few students may continue in a part-time special program throughout their school years, but every effort should be made to achieve maximum integration in the regular class.

For EMR students who continue to have significant academic difficulties, more years in school mean a growing discrepancy between their level of achievement and that of their age peers. The use of high-interest, low-vocabulary materials will permit the teaching of many essential concepts, but some curriculum modification becomes inevitable if education is to remain meaningful. If a child receives the benefit of several years of special programming that helps others to return to the regular class but is of much less help to him, by age 12 or 13 a more special program must be considered. Such a program should focus on learning the social skills required of adults and habits, attitudes, skills, and understandings that will maximize his ability to obtain and retain employment. In conjunction with this emphasis on employability, special efforts to assist him to become a knowledgeable consumer and a responsible parent and citizen must be initiated. Such programs are often called prevocational at the junior high level and vocational, work-study, or work-experience at the senior high level. Involvement with sections of the regular class program remains, with emphasis on such classes as driver education, typing, metalwork, body and fender work, and various semiskilled trades as deemed individually appropriate. The vocational rehabilitation counselor from the state rehabilitation services agency can assist in a number of ways, including arrangements for special vocational school training, payment of employers for training functions, and others as seem advisable. At the high school level, a work-study coordinator should be employed to assist in arranging and supervising off-campus work activities.

For the mildly mentally retarded for whom initial special programming does not lead to nearly complete reintegration into the regular class, the amount of special programming required will likely increase as the student progresses through school. This will happen for some, but for others there will be a type of remedial effect that permits functioning within the regular classroom. The major emphasis of the special educator who works with the mildly mentally handicapped student for whom the remedial effect is not significant is that of a modified curriculum promoting the learning of essential, age-level concepts within the framework of a learning vehicle appropriate for the student's academic skill level.

When the original move to return a large number of students from EMR classes was first initiated, there were many students in such classes who had been placed there inappropriately. Some were minority students who were not actually mentally retarded, others were emotionally disturbed, and still others were learning disabled. A few were students who needed a good remedial program, but provision of services through special education was less expensive for the local district because they received state funds for special education and not for remedial programs. Thus there were many such students who, with other educational adaptations, could function without special education assistance.

During this same time period, the upper IQ limits of mental retardation were lowered (the borderline range was eliminated) and for identification as mentally retarded, a measure of adaptive behavior was added to the requirement of subaverage IQ. This resulted in a decrease in the number of students identified, since both of these changes led to a more restricted concept of mental retardation.

Since it is now *less likely* that we will inaccurately identify students as mentally retarded, and since the upper limits of mental retardation have been lowered, *it is now more likely that those students identified as EMR will need specialized assistance, in*

addition to that which may be provided by the regular class teacher. Although the purpose of this text is to assist the regular classroom teacher in doing her part in this process and to promote the concept of the appropriate, least restrictive environment, we urge the teacher to be aware of the need for special assistance and to demand such specialized assistance as part of the approved Individualized Educational Program (IEP) required by PL 94-142 and state regulations. *To do any less would be in contradiction to both the spirit and the letter of PL 94-142 and to all that we know about the needs of handicapped students.*

SUGGESTIONS FOR THE REGULAR CLASSROOM TEACHER

A great deal of what the regular classroom teacher can do to provide maximum learning apportunities for the EMR student is directly related to understanding the type and degree of learning handicap. On the other hand, although mental retardation is usually discussed in terms of level, that is, mild (educable) or moderate (trainable), these students—like all other students—have unique learning styles and capabilities that may vary greatly, even among students with precisely the same IQ. *This individual variation is highly important and must not be overlooked in our discussion of the more generalized approaches that may be of value in teaching EMR students.*

In addition, we must again point out that a number of the teaching ideas that are of value with the learning disabled may be of value with EMR students. We will specifically point out a few of these ideas in the remainder of this chapter, but do not want to duplicate all this information. In practice, the teacher should at least consider the ideas presented in the following chapter for possible use with EMR students.

In the subsections immediately following

we will consider teaching suggestions and ideas that may be related to the characteristics of mental retardation outlined on pp. 143-145. These characteristics do not "identify" the mentally retarded, and all EMR students do not exhibit all these characteristics. However, if they do (and it is likely that they *will* exhibit a number of them), the following suggestions should be of value.

Sensory and motor coordination handicaps

EMR students who have visual or hearing impairments may be assisted in the manner outlined in Chapters 3 and 4. Certain modifications may be needed, but these will vary with individual differences.

Motor coordination problems may take the form of general, delayed development, that is, motor ability characteristics of children of somewhat younger chronological age (Johnson, 1975). There is also some tendency to have more difficulty with complex motor skills that require the integration of more than one motor skill component, but generalized lower level ability is seen more often. Since certain motor skills may be prerequisites for academic tasks (such as writing), it is important that the teacher do everything possible to provide special opportunities for development of such skills. It is equally important that the teacher not attempt to require any student to perform tasks for which the child does not have the prerequisite skills.

Simplified programs of games and specific motor exercise in areas of deficiency have proved to be worthwhile in various research studies (Cratty, 1971). Unlike some other skill areas, motor development may be approached through direct practice (exercise), although too much emphasis on one specific area of difficulty will reduce the child's enthusiasm for the task. Games such as bean-

bag throw and hopscotch, jumping games, games that promote eye-hand coordination, and other games as consistent with individual needs are of value. If motor coordination is a problem, it should be approached very directly. Special education resource teachers and physical educators are often of great assistance in establishing a specific plan of action.

In addition to the need to develop specific motor skills as prerequisites to academically related tasks, there is evidence that improved physical performance may contribute to a success syndrome and have carry-over effects as the child's self-concept is improved through successful competition in physical activities. This appears to be particularly true of boys (Cratty, 1969). The important point to remember is that motor skill development is amenable to improvement through practice; planned physical activities with the mildly mentally handicapped have been successful. The special education resource teacher should provide the main source of more specific assistance in determining deficits and in planning remediation.

Low tolerance for frustration

It is commonly recognized that some children are more easily discouraged and give up more quickly than others. This characteristic is often observed in the mentally handicapped. The teacher should make every effort to understand the cause of the child's inability to handle frustration. In doing this the teacher should confer both with parents and with other teachers. It is important to look beyond the immediate incident in our attempts to understand the cause of a student's behavior. What is observed in the classroom may be directly related to what happens in the home or on the playground. For example, the student may have been scolded for being late for breakfast that morning; the mother may have asked the stu-

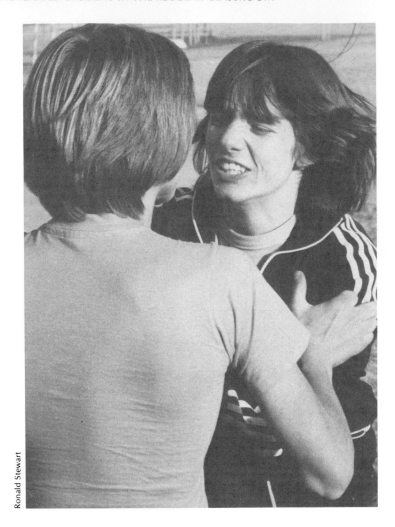

Ronald Stewart

dent why he could not dress himself as quickly as his little sister; he may have been the last to be chosen or he may have been teased or ridiculed by his peers on the playground. What the teacher observes in the classroom may be just one event in a long sequence of events accounting for the student's striking out at the teacher or giving up on a lesson.

If the teacher understands the student's environmental influences outside the classroom, the nature of the handicap, and its manifestation in easy frustration, she can make better decisions in eliminating frustrating situations in the classroom. Although there are no magic formulas or easy answers to dictate decisions or judgments, there are certain suggestions that may be of value.

The student should be assigned work that is within the level of his ability. Modified assignments do require extra teacher time but they pay off in learning and in time saved with respect to handling the classroom problems that result from reactions to frustration. Activities should be shifted frequently, always ending before the student becomes fatigued. The school setting should provide for group experiences so that the EMR student may share in group success, but the teacher should not assume that a skill has been learned until the student can use it independently.

EMR students will experience frustrating situations all their lives; this is a reality of life even for those of normal intelligence. An awareness of the EMR students' relatively low tolerance for frustration, together with careful planning may reduce the number of potentially frustrating situations that serve no purpose. However, at other times, it may be necessary for the student to experience difficulty and frustration, since these are essential to the growth of any individual.

Poor self-concept

In most cases, students learn that there are times when they cannot perform at the level that others expect. If that difference is marked and persistent, the student may acquire a poor self-concept. When a student is told repeatedly that he is a slow learner, he behaves as a slow learner. Since an EMR student is continually confronted with a disparity between expectation and performance, he almost invariably develops low self-esteem and may set up defenses against further failures. For example, he may be reluctant to attempt new tasks or repeat those he has already failed. The teacher must seek new ways to develop a basis for appraisal that leads to some feeling of success on the part of the student. This development is crucial not only for academic success but also for the overall quality of the student's adjustment to society.

Obviously, it would be desirable to reverse the process by which a poor self-concept is formed. For example, responsible behavior is more apt to occur if the teacher treats the student as if he were responsible.

But caution must be exercised here. An EMR student will not behave normally simply because he is treated as if he were not handicapped. Recognition should be given whenever possible, but only when actually earned. The student should be praised for small accomplishments and always for work well done.

Persistence, even in a task not satisfactorily completed, should also be recognized. As the student begins to demonstrate increasing signs of self-confidence, the realities of failure should be allowed to enter the picture. Occasional failure plus an understanding of why failure occurred is important for everyone. The student must learn to recognize his own ability to make judgments through participation in vicarious experiences. For example, the student should learn to read part of a story and guess what logical ending it might have. The events in such a story or an experience like a field trip can be identified, discussed, and evaluated in terms of relative importance.

The improvement of the student's self-concept can be accomplished not by removing failure from experience, but by controlling it. The student can then learn to cope with failure and understand why it occurs, thus reducing the possibility of repeated failure in the future. This procedure is highly important as a prerequisite to increased academic success.

Short attention span

The EMR student may find it easier to maintain attention on and, later, to recall those things that are concrete rather than abstract, familiar rather than remote, and simple rather than complex. Teachers should seek to make their language and ideas as concrete, familiar, and simple as possible. Any teacher can, with conscious effort, tie new experiences to the familiar. Shorter assignments and frequent review are also of value with many EMR students.

Concrete application should be used whenever possible. For example, the question, "If I have two apples and three oranges, how many pieces of fruit would I have altogether?" may lead to a meaningful answer of "five." This concrete example allows the problem to be visualized with relative ease. The student might not be able to immediately answer the abstract question, "How much is two plus three?"

The EMR student may have more difficulty understanding the relationship between (to continue our mathematical illustration) mechanical computation and the principle of addition. He may learn how to add, subtract, multiply, and divide, but have difficulty understanding the principles of these functions. He may not know when to perform one rather than the other.

The extent to which the student is able to attend to an assigned task may be directly related to whether he comprehends or is interested in the task. If he does not understand the task or is not interested, he may leave the scene in some way—by doodling, daydreaming, talking to a classmate, or by other even more annoying practices. At times the student may demonstrate his lack of understanding or interest by teasing, fighting, or throwing something. Whenever possible, the teacher should give assignments that are geared to a familiar level of understanding. In addition, she should shift activities before the student becomes fatigued and should attempt to give only one set of directions at a time.

EMR students may also be distracted by conflicting auditory or visual information. A classroom that is cluttered with highly distracting visual material (bulletin boards and pictures, for example) may negatively influence the student's attention span. A noisy classroom will decrease any student's ability to attend. These factors should be seriously considered by classroom teachers, since many students, not only those with limited ability, may be distracted by excessive visual or auditory clutter.

In many instances attention may be increased dramatically by providing more interesting materials presented on a concrete level. Awareness of this possibility and some of the simple steps that may help reduce problems with attention span are very important to success with the EMR students.

Below average language ability

The mildly mentally handicapped student may have difficulty in language development. If we were asked to read the word "bonto" most of us would pronounce it in the same way. In addition, if we heard it pronounced, most of us would spell it in the same way. But how would we define it? The definitions would vary widely. An EMR student may have learned to read in a very similar manner. Although he has a functional speaking vocabulary, it may be very restricted, and his reading vocabulary may have developed as an almost totally separate function. Although it may appear to be a "reading" vocabulary, it may actually be only a "pronunciation" vocabulary. A very limited speaking vocabulary, plus below average ability to handle most abstract concepts, may lead the EMR student to this type of "word-calling" without meaning. Language experiences—tied to meaningful situations—must be broadened. Teachers must create opportunity for verbal expression; they must use frequently encountered words again and again. New ideas should be related to the concrete rather than the abstract. And, to repeat an earlier generalization, students must tie new experiences to familiar ones.

Language development requires *experience,* and EMR students require *more* experience with language to develop a given level of language ability than students with average or above average intellectual ability. One final complicating factor is that if earlier school experiences and provisions have been inconsistent with the child's level of readiness, he may be even more retarded in language development than his intellectual level would predict. A further complication is the effect of bilingual or bicultural influences.

The teacher must be alert to every possible opportunity to broaden the student's language experience. He must utilize incidental opportunities and must provide structured, concretely oriented experiences that are consistent with the student's interest and appropriate to his present level of language development. Teachers must be particularly careful to provide such opportunities at the secondary level, not just for younger students.

Below average ability to generalize and conceptualize

Two related abilities, generalization and conceptualization, are among the more significant factors measured by an individual test of intelligence. Therefore, by the very nature of mental retardation, when we deal with the EMR student, we are dealing with lower ability in these two areas. These students may have difficulty in seeing the commonality between two similar situations; they may be unable to generalize one set of conditions or rules to another similar situation. A young student may quickly recognize the plus sign in a mathematical equation but have difficulty understanding that the word "and" (as in "6 and 7 equal 13") has the same meaning as the plus sign. He may learn the rules governing behavior in the cafeteria line but have difficulty relating the same rules to another situation, such as the recess line.

The teacher should attempt to integrate mechanical and conceptual skills into the lessons whenever possible and point out to the student how one principle may apply to other academic or social situations. By actual practice in generalization and conceptual skills, the student will acquire a repertoire of experiences that provides for maximum development of these abilities. *This ability to generalize and conceptualize is critically important as the basis for skills that relate to successful employment and participation in the adult world. But such skills are regularly overlooked or underemphasized in favor of specific facts or improvement in basic skills such as reading. It is very doubtful whether, for example, an increase of one year in basic reading level will be as important to the student as development of the ability to generalize in social situations or conceptualize the requirements of various job-related tasks.*

Play interests below those of age peers

The regular classroom teacher must be aware of lowered play interests so that he may assist the student in overcoming problems in this area. This problem may be directly related to the student's poor motor coordination or difficulty in following the rules of games played by his age mates. Teachers may provide assistance by interpreting or modifying game rules and activities to enable the student to participate fully.

It should be reemphasized that an *awareness* by the teacher of this problem is perhaps the most important step in remedying it. By recognizing the problem, teachers may do a great deal to facilitate more normal play activities with age peers. This characteristic may not be a problem except as interaction with younger children inhibits growth in other areas (language development and social skills appropriate to age, for example), or interferes with the development of age-appropriate social skills.

SUMMARY OF SUGGESTIONS RELATED TO CHARACTERISTICS

Some of the suggestions provided in the preceding subsections (relating teaching ideas to characteristics) may be generalizable throughout various subject areas. They will not be applicable in all settings or situations but the following summary may be of value for quick reference. The page notation will permit a review of the context in which the suggestion was given and provide guidance to other possible applications.

1. Do not attempt to require student to perform tasks for which he/she does not have the prerequisite skills (p. 149).
2. Simplify games and specific motor skills as much as possible (p. 149).
3. Assign work within the ability level of the student (p. 150).
4. Modify assignments if/as necessary (p. 150).
5. Utilize group experiences as frequently as possible (p. 151).
6. Be aware of low tolerance for frustration and attempt to reduce potentially frustrating situations (pp. 150, 151).
7. Be aware of student's poor self concept because of previous failure experiences (p. 151).
8. Structure new tasks in such a way that student may have greater likelihood of success (p. 151).
9. Give recognition whenever possible, but only when earned (p. 151).
10. Reinforce persistent efforts (p. 151).
11. Use concrete rather than abstract examples (pp. 151, 152).
12. Shorten assignments (p. 151).
13. Gear assignments to familiar level of understanding (pp. 151, 152).
14. Be aware of distractability (pp. 151, 152).
15. Use highly motivating materials as often as possible (p. 152).
16. Create opportunities for verbal expression (pp. 152, 153).
17. Be aware of bilingual and bicultural influences (p. 153).
18. Attempt to integrate mechanical and conceptual skills into lessons and point out how a principle may apply to other situations (p. 153).
19. Provide more frequent review (p. 151).
20. Control failure experiences; try to use them as learning experiences (p. 151).
21. Attempt to broaden language usage, but be careful to use simple language to explain new concepts (p. 153).

Where ideas and suggestions such as these are not effective, the special education consultant or resource teacher should be contacted for additional ideas and suggestions. In some instances, alternate approaches will be a part of the official IEP and thus may be spelled out to some considerable degree in that document. Where there is no alternate program specified and where no real source of meaningful help is available (this situation should *not* exist, but it *does* in some areas), we would suggest the possible use of one specific approach if the basic need is in reading. This approach, the simultaneous visual-auditory-kinesthetic-tactile (VAKT) method, is discussed in Chapter 8 (pp. 175 to 181). The simultaneous VAKT, or some variation of this approach, has been of value in a number of EMR programs we have observed. Its value may lie in the use of alternate learning channels, or perhaps in the use of stories that are meaningful because they are originated by the student. It is worth trying if other avenues are not effective.

Finally, we should note that many of the suggestions provided here have more application at the elementary than at the secondary level. Efforts to improve generalization and conceptual skills must be emphasized at all levels. The VAKT method has been used with success in the secondary school, but because the educational emphasis for many EMR students should change sometime during the junior high school years and should definitely be different during the senior high school years, we will provide a separate consideration of secondary programming.

SECONDARY SCHOOL PROGRAMS FOR EMR STUDENTS

When EMR adolescents are able to proceed through an adapted version of the regular secondary school program with at least modest success, this is undoubtedly the best plan. In practice, it seems that by the age of 14 or 15 years most students who were formerly a part of an elementary EMR program are either (1) more like nonhandicapped students than earlier seemed to be the case, and thus able to profit from some of the established "regular" programs with a minimum of special help, or (2) even less able to function effectively in the academic programs established for nonhandicapped students than was the case at the elementary level.

In the first situation, everyone concerned should be delighted, especially the regular classroom teachers who have worked with these students. In some cases, the existing vocational education program may be of value, either through inclusion of some EMR students in regular vocational education classes, or through the establishment of a separate class section for EMR students. When regular programs cannot be modified or adapted to be appropriate for the student, it is not necessarily because the schools did not provide the best possible program. Rather, it may be the effect of *cumulative educational retardation,* a direct and expected result of mental retardation. In most such instances the best alternative program may be some variety of work-study plan.

Hallahan and Kauffman (1978) indicate that work-study programs "are becoming more and more common in secondary classes for mildly retarded students." Brolin encourages a broad view of career orientation and provides, in his text, *Vocational Preparation of Retarded Citizens* (1976), both philosophical perspectives and practical guidance as to how to best prepare mentally retarded persons for maximum occupational effectiveness. For most EMR students, this means complete self-support, *if the right education and work training is provided.* This approach was earlier advocated in a full-length text by Kolstoe and Frey (1965), and its acceptance has grown steadily since that time. It is interesting to note that although special programs for EMR students have been under a great deal of active criticism since the late 1960's (as documented elsewhere in this text), little of this criticism has been directed toward work-study type programs. Perhaps this is because they have tended to be quite effective.

The regular classroom teacher will not be the primary manager or implementer of such programs, but may play a role by providing class instruction in areas such as typing, automobile mechanics, home economics, driver education, and other practically oriented secondary school subjects. Assignment to these subjects will ordinarily be on an individual basis, although all EMR students will probably take the driver education course. The special education teacher will often try to ensure maximum readiness on the part of the student for certain programs, and will need help and guidance from the regular classroom teacher who receives the student for one of these classes.

The five major phases of a typical work-study program, as described by Mercer and Payne (1975), are (1) vocational exploration, (2) vocational evaluation, (3) vocational training, (4) vocational placement, and (5) follow-up.

In this sequence students (1) become familiar with the nature of various occupations and the required skills; (2) are provided guided experience with job skills, thus permitting instructors to determine abilities and preferences; (3) receive broad training in a wide variety of vocational areas; (4) are assisted with placement in an actual job; and (5) are assisted with any on-the-job difficulties that may arise. Vocational rehabilitation counselors, employed by rehabilitation services agencies, play a considerable role in this process, especially the last two steps.

This work-study process is carried out with many variations, but the goal is the same in all instances. The role of the regular classroom teacher will vary with the ability level of the students under consideration and the availability of special education and rehabilitation personnel, but for the most part it will be the teachers who teach vocationally related subjects who will be most involved. This type of program has received even more acceptance since the recent emphasis throughout public education on career education. Although special educators and rehabilitation personnel will retain primary responsibility for these programs, regular classroom teachers may have increasing contact with this program.

SUMMARY

Mental retardation is among the more widely recognized handicapping conditions, but despite a great deal of concentrated medical and psychological research, much about mental retardation remains a mystery. However, after years of variability (especially from state to state), the *definition* of mental retardation is becoming fairly well standardized throughout the nation. By nearly unanimous agreement, mental retardation is now defined in terms of IQ *and* adaptive behavior, with an individual not considered mentally retarded unless he is sufficiently below average in *both* of these behavioral areas; low IQ alone is *not* sufficient for a diagnosis of mental retardation.

For the regular classroom teacher, the level of mental retardation of most concern is mild (educable) mental retardation. In some instances teachers may deal with the level of moderate (trainable) mental retardation, but at present this is the exception to the rule. The focus of this chapter was on the needs of the educable mentally retarded (EMR) student.

In a statement of beliefs about EMR students provided to establish a framework for this chapter, we indicated the following: (1) there has been, in the past, considerable misidentification of students as EMR due to inappropriate tests, insufficient data, or these and other causes combined; (2) some students who could possibly be identified as EMR may be assisted to improve their mental functioning to the level of normal mental ability; (3) despite the problems reflected in the two preceding statements, there *are* actual EMR students and these students require special educational planning. We further noted that (4) all students identified as mentally retarded, regardless of level of retardation, must be identified by multiple criteria; (5) many educable mentally retarded may be educated for at least part of the school day in a regular class; and (6) most EMR students will, at the secondary level, benefit from a special work-study type program.

EMR students may share a number of general characteristics, but the only three that are present in every case are the significantly lower-than-average IQ, significantly lower-than-average adaptive behavior, and educational/academic retardation. Other characteristics that are often observed are coordination problems, low frustration tolerance, poor self-concept, short attention span, poor general language ability, below average ability to generalize and conceptualize, and play interests below those of age peers. These characteristics are overlapping and interrelated.

In this chapter we reviewed referral procedures, the responsibilities of special education personnel, and suggestions that may assist in providing maximum educational opportunity for the EMR student in the regular classroom. In addition, a separate discussion of secondary programming for the

EMR student, emphasizing the value of work-study programs, was given. It was also noted that some of the classroom suggestions for the learning disabled, provided in the following chapter, may be of benefit to some EMR students.

In parts of the nation, when the word was first given that the regular classroom teacher was to be responsible for the EMR students, some teachers panicked. Most of these teachers, after a few years of experience with EMR students, now realize that the task is not impossible. They have learned to modify teaching approaches and to focus on individual differences. They have also found that the special education resource teacher can be of genuine assistance. In the process, teachers have developed new skills, and nonhandicapped students also be receiving more appropriate, individualized programs.

REFERENCES AND SUGGESTED READINGS

Birch, J. *Mainstreaming: educable retarded children in regular classes*. Reston, Va.: Council for Exceptional Children, 1974.

Brolin, D. *Vocational preparation of retarded citizens*. Columbus, Ohio: Charles E. Merrill, 1976.

Bruininks, R., Gross, H., & Rynders, J. Social acceptance of mildly retarded pupils in resource room and regular classes. *American Journal of Mental Deficiency*, January 1974, *78*, 377-383.

Cratty, B. *Perceptual-motor behavior and educational processes*. Springfield, Ill.: Charles C Thomas, Publisher, 1969.

Cratty, B. *Active learning*. Englewood Cliffs, N.J.: Prentice-Hall, Inc., 1971.

Drew, C., Hardman, M., and Bluhm, G. (Eds.). *Mental retardation: social and educational perspectives*. St. Louis: The C. V. Mosby Co., 1977.

Dunn, L. Special education for the mildly retarded: is much of it justifiable? *Exceptional Children*, 1968, *35*, 5-22.

Ellis, N. Memory processes in retardate and normals. In N. Ellis (Ed.). *International review of research in mental retardation* (vol. 4). New York: Academic Press, 1970.

Fernald, G. *Remedial techniques in basic school subjects*. New York: McGraw-Hill Book Co., 1943.

Fisher, K. Effects of perceptual-motor training on the educable mentally retarded. *Exceptional Children*, November 1971, *38*. 264-266.

Grossman, H. *Manual on terminology and classification in mental retardation*. Baltimore, Md.: Garamond/Pridemark Press (American Association on Mental Retardation), 1977.

Guerin, G., & Szatlocky, K. Integration programs for the mildly retarded. *Exceptional Children*, November 1974, *41*, 173-179.

Hallahan, D., & Kauffman, J. *Exceptional children: introduction to special education*. Englewood Cliffs, N.J.: Prentice-Hall, Inc., 1978.

Haring, N., & Krug, D. Placement in regular programs: procedures and results. *Exceptional Children*, 1975, *41*. 413-417.

Hurley, R. *Poverty and mental retardation: a causal relationship*. New York: Random House, 1970.

Iano, R., Ayers, D., Heller, H., McGettigan, J., & Walker, V. Sociometric status of retarded children in an integrative setting. *Exceptional Children*, January 1974, *40*, 267-272.

Johnson, G. The education of mentally retarded children. In Cruickshank, W., & Johnson, G. (Eds.). *Education of exceptional children and youth* (3rd ed.). Englewood Cliffs, N.J.: Prentice-Hall, Inc., 1975.

Kelly, L., & Vergason, G. *Dictionary of special education and rehabilitation*. Denver, Co.: Love Publishing, 1978.

Kolstoe, O., & Frey, R. *A high school work-study program for the mentally retarded*. Carbondale, Ill.: Southern Illinois University Press, 1965.

McMillan, D., Jones, R., & Meyers, C. Mainstreaming the mildly retarded: some questions, cautions, and guidelines. *Mental Retardation*, 1976, *14*(1), 3-10.

Mercer, C., & Payne, J. Programs and services. In Kauffman, J., & Payne, J. (Eds.). *Mental retardation: introduction and personal perspectives*. Columbus, Ohio: Charles E. Merrill, 1975.

Neer, W., Foster, D., Jones, J., & Reynolds, D. Socioeconomic bias in the diagnosis of mental retardation. *Exceptional Children*, September 1973, *40*, 5-13.

Sheare, J. Social acceptance of EMR adolescents in integrated programs. *American Journal of Mental Deficiency*, May 1974, *78*, 678-682.

Shneour, E. *The malnourished mind*. New York: Doubleday & Co., Inc., 1975.

Tonn, M. The case for keeping mentally retarded children in your regular classroom. *American School Board Journal*, August 1974, *161*, p. 45.

8 EDUCATION OF THE LEARNING DISABLED

Learning disabilities are of much more recent vintage than mental retardation, if we are to measure the existence of conditions by their mention in professional journals, research reports, and the like. Classes for the learning disabled in the public schools are a phenomenon of the 1960s and 1970s and continue with great strength into the 1980s. But is this condition really all that new? Certainly not; rather, it was not widely recognized until the last half of this century. Even today there are those who will debate the existence of learning disabilities.

The term "learning disabilities" has often been called an "umbrella" definition, and this is perhaps the simplest way to visualize it. As will be seen, the term includes a number of conditions that were previously viewed as being quite distinct, and from our vantage point (having followed the concept as it has developed in the public schools) it is a category that is most valuable insofar as it provides an administrative entity which permits school personnel to serve students who badly need special help. We will proceed to a definition of this term and further discussion of what it means before considering how to assist the learning disabled student.

THE NATURE OF LEARNING DISABILITIES: DEFINITION AND DISCUSSION

Mental retardation, visual impairment, and hearing impairment are so named in relation to the *cause* of problems in learning. They may therefore be called *causally oriented definitions*, indicating that the condition is the cause of learning problems. The *results* of these conditions (that is, learning problems) do not appear in the names of the conditions. *Learning disabilities are named to reflect only the result, not the cause.* Therefore, the condition of learning disabilities is defined in terms of what a student can or cannot do and focuses primarily on academic performance.

The definition of learning disabilities is primarily one of *exclusion*. This is because many of the effects that we might call learning disabilities may be a result of other handicapping conditions. This is not particularly unusual in that, for example, both mental retardation and hearing impairment will probably cause significant problems in language development. But in cases of mental retardation and hearing impairment, we can pinpoint the *cause* of learning problems, and so there is less chance for confusion than with learning disabilities. Learning disabilities are defined in terms of the manifested educational effects, and can be considered as such only when these effects are *not* primarily the result of mental retardation, hearing impairment, or other specified conditions. Thus the "exclusion" feature of the definition.

With this brief introduction to learning disabilities, we will present what we believe to be a middle-of-the-road definition of the term. It is a composite of definitions in use in various states, but is most similar to the federal definition used in Public Law 94-142. We have attempted to simplify the definition slightly and have added a few explanatory comments.

Students with learning disabilities exhibit a disorder in learning, which may be manifested as a problem in reading, writing, spelling, arithmetic, talking, thinking, or listening. Usually this involves processes relating to language usage (either spoken or written). To be considered a learning disability, there must be a significant discrepancy between the individual's actual achievement or performance and his apparent ability to achieve or perform. Learning disabilities include disorders that have previously been called dyslexia, dyscalculia, agnosia, minimal brain dysfunction, and others in which the preceding condition of significant discrepancy is met. The category of learning disabilities is *not* meant to include learning problems in which the *primary* or basic cause is mental retardation, visual or hearing impairment, emotional disturbance, or environmental disadvantage.

Certain problems are posed by this or any other definition of learning disabilities. One of the major problems results from the fact that it is very difficult to determine what degree of learning problem is sufficient to lead to the decision that a learning disability exists. Some writers have suggested that as many as twenty or thirty percent of all school age children have a learning disability. We believe that these percentage estimates are *much* too high for the concept of learning disabilities intended by those who initiated the term; they are so high that specialized educational assistance for learning disabled students who are in need of help is endangered by such thinking. If so many students have this need, it is no longer "special," but is "usual" or "normal." In addition, from a practical point of view, legislators cannot be expected to provide special funds for this high a percentage of students. We would therefore suggest that those students who seem to meet the criteria and who represent perhaps two to three or in some unusual stiuations even four or five percent of the school age population should be considered learning disabled.

A second problem with this definition is that it excludes students with other primary handicapping conditions. For example, a student with a moderate hearing impairment, if we interpret this definition literally, cannot be thought of as learning disabled. We believe that the two should not be confused (which was the intent of the definition) but that it is quite possible for the hearing impaired student to have an additional problem that *is* a learning disability and is in no way related to the hearing impairment. This stu-

dent needs the help that may be provided through *both* kinds of programs.

The environmentally disadvantaged are excluded from most definitions of learning disabilities because learning problems that originate because a student has not been *exposed* to educational opportunity are quite different from, for example, learning difficulties in those who have had a chance to learn. This is a valid point, but we are concerned that some have interpreted this to mean that the culturally disadvantaged or the culturally different *cannot* have learning disabilities. We believe that the student raised in a substandard learning environment in the ghetto or the bilingual student may just as likely have a learning disability as a middle-class, white child and deserves the benefit of special programming if he needs it. These two issues and the needs they generate should not be confused, but the fact that *one* exists should not automatically exclude the possibility of the other.

A number of additional points could be made regarding the problem of an acceptable definition of learning disabilities, but the preceding discussion should provide at least a minimal understanding of the problem (for a more detailed consideration, see Gearheart, 1976).

We do not propose that we can formulate a totally acceptable definition for learning disabilities; however, we can outline our frame of reference to indicate the basis for our discussion of learning disabled students.

1. Many students with very mild problems that give every indication of being temporary have been improperly called learning disabled.

2. The term "learning disabilities" has been too often used as a convenient and more socially acceptable way to relabel some educable mentally retarded (EMR) students.

3. Although many have broadened the

definition of learning disabilities to include too many students, it would be just as unacceptable to narrow the definition (as some have proposed) to include only those for whom we can find definite signs of neurological impairment.

4. Although many learning disabled students have perceptual problems, attempts to make the term "perceptually handicapped" synonymous with "learning disabled" have led some educators to believe that all learning disabilities are perceptual handicaps. Thus they have ignored the existence of disabilities in other areas.

These four points, the discussion of the definition of learning disabilities preceding them, and the six principles for planning and programming for learning disabled students (pp. 170 to 173) should, in total, provide a practical conceptualization of learning disabilities.

CHARACTERISTICS OF THE LEARNING DISABLED

Although the major common factor among those students considered learning disabled by a majority of authorities is a significant discrepancy between apparent ability to learn and actual level of learning, certain other characteristics occur with above average frequency. It is highly unlikely that any one student could exhibit all these characteristics (some, in fact, are contradictory to others), but the following are likely to be seen in the learning disabled student.

Hyperactivity. Hyperactivity is generally recognized as a common characteristic of learning disabilities. There are many different theories as to the *why* of hyperactivity, and some debate as to how much activity constitutes hyperactivity, but most authorities agree that the condition often exists in learning disabled students. Keogh (1971), in a discussion of causes, proposed three major

hypotheses: (1) neurological impairment, (2) information acquisition difficulties (based on the fact that the unusual amount of motor activity interferes with accurate information acquisition), and (3) decision-making process problems (indicating that the hyperactive student makes decisions too rapidly, before he can acquire enough information to make the best possible decision). Regardless of the actual cause, the student who is unable to focus on any one activity for long is placed at a disadvantage in the traditional learning situation.

Hypoactivity. Hypoactivity, or lethargy, is of course the opposite of hyperactivity in its behavioral manifestation. Although not found in as many cases as is hyperactivity, it is recognized as a characteristic of some learning disabled students. It should be noted that both hyperactivity and hypoactivity are descriptions that indicate that the individual is not reacting to the environment (usually we think of reactions to *sensory* stimuli) in a normal manner. And, if a student does not react normally, it is likely that his learning may be impaired.

Incoordination. Lack of coordination is another characteristic very commonly mentioned by nearly all authorities in the field of learning disabilities. It is true that some highly coordinated students may have learning difficulties, but by and large, those students who are identified as learning disabled according to multiple criteria are below average for their age in coordination. There may be a number of explanations for this, including the fact that normal motor skills are necessary for the early childhood exploration that developmental theorists believe is the foundation for later learning. The student with learning disabilities is often slower to develop the ability to throw or catch a ball, to skip, or to run. He is also likely to have difficulty in writing and other fine motor skills. He may be generally clumsy; he may stumble or fall frequently. Some coordination problems are related to an inability to properly assess position in space, to problems with balance, or to both.

Perseveration. A student may perseverate, or repeat persistently, in almost any behavioral area, but this is more often seen in writing or copying. A student may copy a word over and over again involuntarily. He may also perseverate in oral response. This behavior should not be confused with voluntary repetition, for with perseveration it seems that the student repeats almost as if some other hand were moving his hand (in the case of written perseveration) or some other mind were causing him to perseverate orally. In writing, this may be seen in cases where the task requires copying the same figure or letter two or three times in a row. The student may then go on to repeat the same configuration over and over until he runs out of space.

Overattention or attention fixation. A student who cannot shift his focus of attention in a normal manner will have just as much difficulty in learning as one who cannot focus on any object or activity for a normal length of time. Such a student may regularly focus on some object in the room or outside the window and literally be unable to notice the teacher's attempts to obtain his attention. He shuts out other sensory signals, even those that call attention to something he would very much like to do. It is not a matter of *choosing* to shut out other signals, but rather of involuntary overattention. This problem, and the problems inherent with hyperactivity (as these two conditions often overlap) may be more difficult to handle in open-concept classrooms. Modifications of classroom settings to deal with these problems are often required.

Perceptual disorders. Perceptual disorders might include disorders of visual, auditory, tactual, or kinesthetic perception. The student with visual perceptual problems may not be able to copy letters correctly or perceive the difference between a hexagon and an octagon. He may reverse letters or produce mirror writing. The student with auditory perceptual problems may not perceive the difference between various consonant blends or between the front doorbell and the first ring of the telephone. All these perceptual problems may at first make the student seem to be lacking in sensory acuity (that is, seem to have a visual loss or be hard of hearing), but when acuity checks out as normal, the possibility of perceptual disorder must be considered.

Memory disorders. Memory disorders may include either auditory or visual memory. Memory is a highly complicated process and is not fully understood, although various individuals have established theories that seem to explain the observable facets of memory. In case study reports we hear about individuals who cannot remember where the window is or on which side of the room their bed is placed, even though it has been there for months. In others we hear of students who cannot repeat a simple sequence of three words immediately after hearing them. These types of memory deficit seriously affect the learning process.

Differentiating learning disabilities from other problems

Some of the preceding characteristics are exact opposites (for example, hypoactivity and hyperactivity), and some are overlapping (for example, overattention and perseveration). In combination, problems such as these lead to difficulties in symbolic processes. Some of these characteristics go almost unnoticed until the student is asked to complete school tasks; thus we see why it is difficult to identify mild learning disabilities until the age of 5 or 6 years.

Care must be taken not to overpredict on

the basis of this type of characteristic alone. Many students have problems at some time early in life with copying or writing letters backwards. In most cases this is *not* a sign that the student has a learning disability. However, if the difficulty persists and there are a number of other problems, it may be time to look at the student more carefully. In a similar manner, because students differ in energy levels, some are much more active than others. The term "hyperactive" has been used too much and too loosely, and it is easy to make inaccurate assumptions based on activity level. When one sees a *really* hyperactive student—often called a "wall climber"—one then knows what hyperactivity is. A great deal of caution must be used with the concept of hyperactivity, but it is, in fact, a symptom or characteristic of many learning disabled students.

Those who have engaged in additional reading in this area, especially in some of the medically related areas, will note that most of the characteristics just discussed are also commonly listed as characteristics of individuals who have brain injuries. The fact is that many learning disabled students have a number of characteristics associated with brain injuries but have no known, verifiable injury, and have nothing in their health history to lead to suspicion of brain injury or insult. Educators are not qualified to diagnose brain injury, and many physicians hesitate to do so unless there has been, for example, an accident in which the brain injury was subject to visual examination. When dealing with learning disabilities, we are dealing with unusual learning behavior, not the causes of that behavior. Nevertheless, the extent to which learning disability characteristics overlap those of brain injuries must be recognized.

In the final analysis, only one characteristic may be attributed to *all* learning disabled students. That characteristic is the existence of a significant educational lag or discrepancy between expected and actual achievement. Various definitions supported by a wide range of authorities may add other limitations, but all have this component either implicitly or explicitly included. We will conclude this consideration of the characteristics of the learning disabled by calling your attention to the comparison of two boys shown on p. 164, which illustrates some of the differences between learning disabilities and mild mental retardation.

REFERRAL FOR SPECIAL ASSISTANCE

Although in many ways similar to mild mental retardation in outward manifestations, learning disabilities are quite different in other ways. One way they are different is the manner in which learning disabilities may remain "hidden" for many years, especially if the student is above average in intelligence. In these cases the student is apparently able to compensate through intact learning channels for disability that exists in other learning channels. For example, a student might have serious difficulties in accurately gaining information through the auditory channel, but with a high level of intelligence and effective learning through the visual channel be able to learn and appear to be "normal" in most respects. In this case, we might be tempted to ask, "Why interfere if he is learning normally?" Part of the answer is that learning that places a student within the "average" group for his age is not necessarily normal learning.

If a student's ability is such that he should be in the top five percent of the class, then achievement at the fiftieth percentile is not normal. We may be tempted to "leave well enough alone," but a 12-year-old student with an IQ of 140 may quite possibly be a learning disabled student if he is doing only

Jim	**Mark**
Age: 9 years	Age: 9 years
Grade: 3	Grade: 3
Years in school: 4½	Years in school: 4½
Reading achievement: 1.6 (grade equivalent)	Reading achievement: 1.6 (grade equivalent)
Group IQ score: 75	Group IQ score: 75

The preceding descriptions of Jim and Mark are obviously identical until the IQ as indicated by an *individual* test of intelligence is considered. Then it is found that:

Full-scale WISC IQ: 68	Full-scale WISC IQ: 102

Through the individual test of intelligence it is found that Jim is very likely a borderline EMR youngster, whereas Mark is probably a learning disabled student. Additional data are then gathered.

Arithmetic: 1.8 (grade equivalent)	Arithmetic: 3.2 (grade equivalent)

Generally, the EMR student will have basic skills in mathematics that are at about the same level as his reading skills, although sometimes they will be higher if they mainly involve rote memory. In contrast, many learning disabled students who have severe problems in reading may do near grade-level work in mathematics as long as reading is not required. The reverse may also be true of the learning disabled student; he may do satisfactory work in reading but have significant problems in mathematics. It is the inconsistency in performance between various academic areas and various types of activities that characterizes the learning disabled student. Additional information about the boys' abilities in classroom interaction, apparent ability to learn from peers, and ability to conceptualize follows:

In classroom interaction regarding relationships of planets and the sun, Jim had real difficulty in following the idea of relative movement. Jim can follow class discussion as long as concepts are simple but has difficulty in making generalizations. Jim's speaking vocabulary is better than his reading vocabulary, but it is still far below the class average.	In classroom interaction regarding relationships of planets and the sun, Mark was one of the first in the class to really understand. In most topics related to science, if no classroom reading is involved, Mark does very well. On a verbal level, he conceptualizes and generalizes well. Mark's reading vocabulary (words he can recognize in print) is no better than Jim's; however, his spoken vocabulary is up to the class average in all respects and is above average in science areas.

Often the learning disabled student has a performance profile (in such areas as reading achievement, arithmetic achievement, vocabulary, ability to generalize, and ability to conceptualize) that is characterized by many ups and downs. He sometimes (or in some academic areas) seems quite average, or perhaps above average, but in some areas he may be even less able than some EMR students. It is possible for a learning disabled student to be low in *all* areas of achievement and class interaction, but this is unusual. In contrast, the performance profile of the EMR student is usually relatively flat.

as well as those 12-year-olds with average intelligence. With proper assistance he may well improve his achievement to a level commensurate with his ability. Of course he may *not* be learning disabled. He may have adequately developed learning abilities and simply not be motivated, or he may have well-balanced basic abilities, but these abilities may be severely underdeveloped due to very poor educational opportunities. As noted at the start of this section, this type of learning disability may often remain "hidden"; the student may remain unidentified and unserved.

It is the responsibility of the regular classroom teacher to be alert for the possibility that students may be learning disabled and to refer such students for help when it seems appropriate. Specific referral procedures vary from district to district, but there will usually be a special referral form to be completed by the regular classroom teacher. In addition to name, age, grade, and sex, most referral forms will ask questions about (1) grade level in academic areas (usually means grade equivalent on a standardized achievement test), (2) data on behavior (interpersonal relations with other students and with teachers, for example), (3) specific reading strengths and deficits (for example, word attack skills, memory for words, and ability to read orally), (4) ability (related to others in class) in class discussion and interaction, (5) strengths and weaknesses in nonacademic areas, (6) any unusual family data that might be pertinent, and (7) a summary of any methods or approaches that were unusually successful, or total failures for the student.

Many school districts now encourage the teacher to have a conference with the learning disabilities specialist assigned to the building before actually completing such a referral form. Such a conference may have one of two main results: (1) after learning more about learning disabilities or as a result

of objective discussion with an outside person, the teacher may realize that there is almost no chance that the student is learning disabled and thus not refer him, or (2) because of additional insights gained through questions asked by the specialist, the referral will contain much more valuable information.

Students should be referred when appropriate, but overreferral should be avoided if at all possible. Since parents must be contacted to gain additional information and to obtain permission for further assessment, the matter of referral must not be approached lightly. If a student is referred when there is no need, the parents may become upset, and many people will spend time and effort needlessly. This is one of the reasons a conference with the learning disabilities specialist *prior to actual referral in cases that seem questionable* is a good practice.

In addition to referrals based on the teacher's everyday experience with a student, referrals may be initiated as a result of some type of screening procedure. A variety of screening devices may be used to assist in identifying the learning disabled student. One such device may be found in Appendix E. This particular screening form may help in identifying the learning disabled and, in some cases, mentally retarded students; like all screening procedures, it *does not identify a student as learning disabled or mentally retarded, but rather permits an organized framework within which to better consider such possibilities and provides a basis for deciding whether or not to further pursue the referral procedure.*

This type of screening instrument is useful as a guide to assist the regular classroom teacher in objectifying his observations and in enumerating pertinent related factors. We have known teachers who were about to refer a student for consideration for special education assistance, but after completing a data form similar to that shown in Appendix E they realized that the student was really quite normal except for perhaps one personality component, which was the real basis for the referral. Therefore, in addition to being of value as the starting point for possible specialized assistance, at times the referral forms, screening forms, or scales may be of value to the teacher as a structure through which a student's strengths and weaknesses may be systematically summarized and analyzed.

There are many ways the learning disabled student may receive additional assistance in the public schools. In mild cases the regular classroom teacher may be able to provide meaningful and stimulating opportunities for learning with suggestions from a resource or itinerant teacher. In other cases, some time may be needed in a specialized setting. In either case the student must be officially identified as learning disabled to be eligible for placement in a program for learning disabled students. This placement is essential in most states because it is the only procedure through which the local school can receive the special reimbursement from the state that pays a great deal of the costs of learning disability programs. The question of official identification is briefly addressed in the following section.

Identification as learning disabled

For reasons that should be clear in light of the preceding discussion of the definition of learning disabilities and the varied characteristics related to this condition, identification of learning disabled students is not as clear-cut as identification of visually impaired, hearing impaired, or mentally retarded students. In fact, it is a more subjective identification than that for any other handicapping condition, with the possible exception of emotional disturbance. Despite

many similarities in identification procedures between states, there are also wide differences. There are even differences within states, although regulations governing identification are usually statewide regulations. The simple fact is that the category we call learning disabilities includes, by definition, a widely divergent group of disabilities. Thus there is no practical way to establish a "tight" identification procedure without excluding some of the very students for whom the programs were established.

The result of these factors is that learning disabilities are usually identified by a consensus of a group of professionals who must understand the definition and the purpose of the program sufficiently well to make good decisions. There are certain general considerations that must be observed, but within these limits identification is a matter of expert opinion. The identification procedure is usually specific with respect to the kind of data being considered, and if certain other handicapping conditions are present and are apparently major contributors to the educational difficulties, then the student may not be identified as learning disabled. Academic retardation, when actual performance is significantly below ability to perform, seems to be a requirement in all states.

For students (other than those who need medical referral) who have only very mild problems, identification as learning disabled may have more disadvantages than advantages. *Identification can be justified only if it permits some educational provision and assistance that would not be provided without such identification.* In most cases, if the regular classroom teacher is sensitive to the unique educational needs of students with mild learning problems and has the knowledge, materials, and techniques to effectively assist them it may be best to forget all about labels. However, the more severe the learning problem, the more likely it is that help from outside the classroom will be needed. For these students, comprehensive, carefully conducted identification procedures are essential.

RESPONSIBILITIES OF SPECIAL EDUCATION PERSONNEL

In this chapter, as in the chapter on mental retardation, we will discuss the responsibilities of special education personnel before examining the role of the regular classroom teacher in dealing with learning disabled students. It is hoped that this mode of presentation will enable more meaningful consideration of the principles and practices in the latter section.

The primary special education personnel who provide service to learning disabled students are diagnosticians and teachers. Those who provide various diagnostic or assessment services may be called diagnosticians, diagnostic specialists, psychologists, psychometricians, assessment specialists, or some variation of these titles.

In some school districts the learning disabilities teacher may do much of the required assessment, except for the determination of IQ, which must take place before actual placement may be accomplished. Who performs which function depends on many factors, but size of school district may be the major factor, with larger districts tending to have more highly specialized diagnostic/assessment personnel. In some districts, some of the assessment may be done by a private diagnostician on a contractual basis with the district. In others, some assessment may be done by a community agency. Again this is usually by contract.

The specialized teaching required by learning disabled students will be carried out by individuals who are primarily teachers, although they may be called specialists, consultants, resource teachers, or other simi-lar names. In a few instances, a teacher specializing in learning disabilities may have a self-contained class for students with severe learning disabilities. This may more often be the case when those students are also quite hyperactive. But for the most part, programs for children with learning disabilities are conducted through the use of resource rooms and by teachers who are most often called "resource room teachers."

The resource room method of service delivery appears to be the most common method of providing educational assistance to learning disabled students. A resource room is a school setting that is organized specifically as a place where students with unique learning needs can receive specialized instructional assistance. If properly organized, it contains materials and equipment that are appropriate for the students who come to this setting. Resource rooms may be organized for one or for several handicapping conditions. Usually the resource teacher works in the resource room. However, a wider concept of resource teacher is utilized in many schools. In this wider role, the resource teacher serves as a "resource person" for the regular classroom teacher regarding methods and materials, usually as such methods or materials relate to specific students in the regular classroom. The resource teacher may be called a consulting teacher, a learning disabilities consultant, a learning disabilities specialist, or other similar title. If this teacher moves about from building to building as a resource person, he may be called an itinerant teacher. In practice, we cannot assume that we know what a person actually does simply by virtue of their title. Similarly, we cannot assume that two persons who have quite different titles actually serve different functions. The fact is that most learning disabilitiy teachers (whatever they may be called) work in a number of different ways to serve the learning disabled student, and in so doing, must do all possible to assist the regular classroom teacher.

The preceding discussion of the varying roles of special education personnel who serve the learning disabled reflects in a very generalized way what special educators do to facilitate learning by learning disabled students. To provide more concrete visualization of an effective program, we have included a description the way a learning lab which was in Pitt County, North Carolina, operated just a few years ago. The program has been modified since then.

One type of resource room—the learning lab. The learning lab is a diagnostic prescriptive center designed to meet the individual needs of each student. Assets, deficits, and long-range prescriptions are recorded in individual folders. These assets and deficits have been determined by qualified assessment personnel, and the long-range plans were developed by teachers, assessment personnel, and parents.

As the student enters the learning lab each day, he picks up his "tote tray," which contains his *daily task folder* and other materials. The prescription centers (reading and language, writing, math, auditory perception, visual perception, and kinesthetic tactile) are identified by pictures of Walt Disney characters. The student goes to each center according to the arrangement of the Walt Disney cards in his task folder. Once he is in the assigned center, the teacher or aide assists him in getting the appropriate materials, understanding the instructions, and beginning the assigned task. The teacher then leaves the student to work independently and goes to other students in the same manner. "Help, please" signs are available at each center for the student who requires help in a task or who is ready to have his work checked.

Students may work in two or three centers each day. Constant monitoring and individual assistance are paramount considerations in the individualized approach. Incomplete tasks or unfinished center activities are ordinarily assigned for the next class period sequentially throughout the week. At the close of each

From Reinert, H. R.: Children in conflict: educational strategies, St. Louis, 1975, The C. V. Mosby Co.

Eric W. Blackhurst

day, individual daily prescriptions are written for the following day.

The center activities and tasks consist of commercial programmed materials, teacher-made games, laminated task cards, record players, cassette tape players, books, puppets, and assorted activity folders. Although most of the tasks are individually oriented, there is planned opportunity for social development through games, peer teaching, puppetry, and other group activities.

Approximately twenty students are served in the learning lab on a daily basis by the resource teacher and one aide. The resource teacher also serves as a consulting teacher for a limited number of students who do not come to the resource room. Five or six students at a time are served at any one time for a period of one to one and a half hours each day (Monday through Thursday). Friday is designated as a day for individual evaluations and testing, teacher and parent conferences, classroom observations, and follow-up activities in the regular classroom.

Learning disabled students are provided an opportunity to improve their self-concept through success-oriented tasks. Since each student works at his own level, at his own rate, and with materials designed to remediate his specific problems, the program is truly individualized. Teaching the student to work independently in the resource room and to continue to do so in his regular classroom is of prime concern. The ultimate goal is to enable each individual to function well within the regular classroom, thereby phasing the student out of the resource room as soon as the necessary remediation has been completed.

The learning lab just described provides a model that is particularly effective with elementary students when motivational props such as the Walt Disney characters (or some similar, elementary age–appropriate pictures) are used. With only minor modifications (eliminating the pictures, the signs, and the puppetry), the learning lab

concept can be applied at the secondary level. Cassette tapes, programmed materials, assignments based on assessment of assets and deficits, and many other aspects of this self-paced program will work well at almost any level. This type of programming for the learning disabled student is carried out by the special education staff. The role of the regular classroom teacher will be explored in the following section.

SUGGESTIONS FOR THE REGULAR CLASSROOM TEACHER

In most instances, the regular classroom teacher will proceed in one of two ways with the learning disabled student. The first is modifying the student's program in the manner suggested by the learning disabilities specialist. This will often relate to just one or two subject or skill areas, and the learning disabilities specialist should provide concrete examples of what may be done, including materials to be used. *However, the regular classroom teacher remains responsible for the program in her class and will apply suggestions, ideas, and materials as possible and practical.* The role of the learning disabilities specialist is to suggest and assist, not to dictate to the regular classroom teacher. This principle is important and will be supported by administrative staff in most, if not all, schools. This places the responsibility for management of the classroom squarely where it belongs—with the teacher in charge of that class.

The suggestions of the specialist will be of value most of the time, but since the specialist is not present as the school day progresses and as individual situations arise, it will take a number of modifications to make them work from hour to hour and day to day, even if the suggestions are unquestionably sound. In such situations, the regular classroom teacher must have some basis for further decision-making. She must also have a basis for program planning in areas of the curriculum where the specialist has not provided specific guidance. This leads to the second major way the regular classroom teacher may proceed in program planning, which involves principles and guidelines to follow as explained in the next section.

Principles for program planning for the learning disabled

Certain guidelines and principles have evolved through practice that are valuable when providing assistance to learning disabled students. These guidelines may be applied in the regular classroom or may be used by the learning disabilities teacher. This type of foundation for program planning is made necessary by the variety of conditions included in the definition of learning disabilities and the highly heterogeneous group of students enrolled in most learning disabilities programs.

The following set of principles are not techniques. It would be much easier if the teacher could use a "cookbook" approach to learning disabilities, for the teacher could then just follow the recipe, and learning would occur. Such an approach would be particularly undesirable for the learning disabled student, because the past use of cookbook approaches is often part of the problem. If teachers had tried more individualized approaches from the beginning, some (although not all) learning disabled students would never have required learning disabilities programming. The principles that follow should form the basis for decision making and should be sufficiently adaptable to fit a number of different basic teaching styles.

PRINCIPLE 1 • There is no single "right" method to use with learning disabled students

Students are referred for assistance in learning disability programs because they are *not* learning effectively through the ap-

proach used in the classroom with the general population of students.

Of course, a teacher who knew he was working with a deaf student would not use an approach that was primarily auditory in teaching word attack skills, but many regular classroom teachers continue to use methods that rely heavily on hearing sounds accurately with students who do not have the ability to discriminate between the sounds the teacher is using. A student may *hear sound* as well as others but be unable to discriminate between different phonemes that sound somewhat similar. An analogous situation may exist with a student who has good visual acuity but who cannot accurately discriminate between certain letters and thus does not do well with approaches based primarily on visual recognition. Acknowledgement of individual problems is essential, and forms a basis for trying a number of alternate approaches. It is a major step in understanding that there is no "right" method for dealing with learning disabilities. The idea that there is one right method that works for all children with learning disabilities violates common sense and is an outgrowth of a lack of understanding. We cannot always tell through present assessment techniques exactly how to approach every student with learning disabilities, but we can avoid the error of believing in a single approach and must realize that we may need to try a number of methods in certain difficult cases.

PRINCIPLE 2 • All other factors being equal, the "newest" possible method should be used*

When gathering data about educational history and background, the teacher should make every attempt to determine which approaches and materials have been used with each student. These may not be significant data in all cases but they will be in many.

---

*"Newest" means not previously used by the student.

Analysis of this information can have several applications. If certain approaches have been used with little or no success, this may indicate the inappropriateness of such approaches. This will not always be true, for such approaches may have been poorly implemented or the student may not have had certain requisite abilities at an earlier date and may possess them now; however, this does provide a starting point for further investigation.

An equally important point, and one too often overlooked, is that many students tend to develop a failure syndrome after trying to accomplish a task only to meet repeated failure. In the case of learning to read, the teacher will likely feel it necessary to continue to attempt to assist the student to learn to read, or to read more effectively, but *the teacher should make a deliberate attempt to use a method that "looks" and "feels" different to the child.* The more severe the learning problem and the longer it has been recognized and felt, the greater the need for this procedure. This principle dictates that when a variety of approaches are possible and all other factors are approximately equal, the approach that is most different from earlier methods is likely to be the most effective. The importance of checking on previous remedial attempts may be seen in cases in which earlier, poorly implemented remedial efforts have tended to cancel out the effectiveness of a later approach that is similar. This may happen even though all other clues and evaluative results indicate the probable effectiveness of such an approach. Sometimes the effect of such unsuccessful efforts can be overcome, but knowledge of their existence is essential for this.

PRINCIPLE 3 • Some type of positive reconditioning should be implemented

Pioneers in the learning disabilities field such as Fernald and Gillingham (see Gearheart, 1977, pp. 93-109) recognized the value of this principle, a value that remains today. The "newest possible method" (principle 2) is a part of this positive reconditioning effort, and additional attempts should be directed toward convincing the student that his inability to develop adequate reading (or arithmetic or language) skills is not his fault. Rather, it is caused by the failure of the school and teachers to recognize that he needed to learn by methods different from those used for other children. The obvious point of this effort is to convince the child that he is "O,K.," to boost his self-concept to the point that he will approach the learning task with increased confidence, and thus maximize his chances of success. A considerable amount has been written about the "self-fulfilling prophecy" effect on teachers when they are told that a given student is handicapped and therefore will not likely learn as well as or as much as a normal child. Think how devastating this effect must be when *you* as an individual become convinced, through painful experience, that you cannot learn. Unfortunately, most schools are organized in such a way that students with learning difficulties are reminded daily, sometimes hourly, that they are failures. There is a scarcity of research on the effects of planned positive reconditioning, but the experience of a number of learning disability teachers with whom we have worked, the historical testimony of Fernald and Gillingham, and simple logic indicate that *success must be planned.*

PRINCIPLE 4 • High motivation is a prerequisite to success; deliberate consideration of the affective domain is essential

Because this is such an obvious principle, it may not be properly emphasized. Attempts to maximize motivation are difficult to measure or monitor and may seem unglamorous, except as related to some unusual type of behavior modification system. Principles 2 and

3 are a part of the overall attempt to maximize motivation, but deliberate efforts beyond these two principles must be planned. In the case of older students who may have developed the basic learning abilities necessary for academic success, but developed them several years late, a program to promote higher motivation may be about the only workable procedure. The fact that various behavior modification techniques are in common use, many with apparent success, attests to the validity of this principle.

This principle also dictates some sort of planned investigation of the affective domain—a look at how the student feels about himself, both in general (in the world outside the academic boundaries) and with respect to his specific feelings as he attempts to achieve within the school setting. Some learning disabled students have such obvious emotional problems that they can scarcely be overlooked. In this case the best approach is to plan and initiate attempts to counteract, remediate, or in some manner attend to these problems. Many of the other principles have the effect of attending to the problems of low self-esteem, and if academic achievement improves, it automatically has a positive effect. But beyond these positive vectors, it is imperative that the affective components be deliberately considered to maximize the potential of other remedial efforts and to prevent the growth of negative emotional components. This investigation of the affective domain, even when there are no overt behavior problems, must be a part of the evaluation and planning program for learning disabled students.

PRINCIPLE 5 • The existence of nonspecific or difficult-to-define disabilities, particularly with older students, must be recognized

A serious educational problem in reading or arithmetic can be defined, but if, for example, a secondary student experienced significant visual perceptual problems at an early age and did not have the visual perceptual skills necessary for success in reading at 8 years of age but developed them later, it may be almost impossible to pinpoint the specific disability. What may exist is significant educational retardation and, in many cases, a negative attitude toward school. There may be a need to develop second- or third-grade reading skills in a 15-year-old student who has learned many ways to circumvent his reading problem. Some authorities, who want to describe learning disabilities only in terms of specific disabilities that may be neatly defined, might say that this is not a learning disability. Our point of view is that this is a learning disability and that it requires very careful consideration and planning.

One caution should be noted regarding this principle. In recognizing the possibility of these nonspecific disabilities, we must be careful not to use them as an "out," a convenient reason to not fully investigate and carefully consider each individual case in an attempt to determine specific guidelines for remediation and skill development.

PRINCIPLE 6 • It is critically important to be concerned and involved with both process and task-oriented assistance and remediation

It is of the utmost importance that this principle be followed for the most effective use of time and effort. Many of the earliest efforts to assist learning disabled students centered on remediation of process skills, and little or no attention was paid to assisting the student to carry these skills over into the actual task of learning to read or understanding arithmetic. Experience has indicated that most students require help in applying newly developed process abilities in the academic setting. The regular classroom teacher must play an important part in this matter, whether it be in a planned, coordinated effort with the learning disabilities specialist or in a situation in which the regular classroom teacher must provide the total program for the student. If a student cannot discriminate visually between *ab* and *ad*, he must learn to do so, but he also needs planned practice in using this newly developed ability in a variety of settings. In a similar manner, if a student cannot tell the difference aurally between the *b* sound and the *d* sound, he must learn to do so and must exercise this newly developed auditory discrimination. If the teacher is aware of this need and is alert for opportunities to provide this practice or exercise, it is of great value. Many specific activities may be suggested by resource personnel.

• • •

The preceding principles provide general guidelines within which planning for learning disabled students should take place. If the student is also being taught by a learning disabilities teacher, efforts must be jointly planned to ensure a coordinated program with fully complementary activities and efforts. If the regular classroom teacher must plan for the student without outside help, these principles will provide a starting point from which to consider various alternative methods and approaches. A number of method books containing specific detailed suggestions are listed at the close of this chapter.

On the following pages we review a number of specific suggestions and ideas that we believe may be of considerable value to regular classroom teachers. These ideas are presented in five major sections: (1) tactile and kinesthetic approaches to learning, (2) a simultaneous visual-auditory-kinesthetic-tactile (VAKT) approach, (3) ideas for dealing with hyperactive or distractible students, (4) ideas for use in teaching reading and/or language development, and (5) ideas for use in teaching arithmetic.

The first section includes a consideration of a number of techniques whereby the tactile and kinesthetic senses may be used to support the visual and the auditory senses. These ideas are primarily the result of practical experience in the classroom.

The second section is a description of an approach often called the VAKT or Fernald approach. This approach, which utilizes some of the ideas provided in section one, is a reading system that may be used as a total approach for periods ranging from several months to perhaps a year or more.

The third section includes a collection of ideas that may be of value in dealing with students who have been called hyperactive, hyperkinetic, or simply distractible. Ideas included in this section may be of use in conjunction with methods given in other subsections or with normal class procedures.

The fourth and fifth sections include an assortment of ideas for reading, language, and arithmetic development ideas, arranged approximately in order from those for elementary grades to those of value in secondary grades.

Ideas presented in this section will be of maximum value only if they are applied consistent with the six principles outlined on pp. 170 to 173. They are included here to provide a starting place for the regular classroom teacher and will hopefully lead to the development of many additional ideas in actual practice. Ideas suggested in the arithmetic or reading and language development sections are most often used in these areas, but they may be of value in other areas as well. With the exception of the VAKT (Fernald approach), which can be used as a complete approach or system, other suggestions are supplementary and cannot replace regular classroom methods. Rather, they should be considered for use in efforts to make normal teaching methods or approaches more meaningful for learning disabled students.

Tactile and kinesthetic approaches to learning

Students learn through all the sensory modalities, but for most students a majority of school-based learning takes place through the visual and auditory learning channels. This has proved to be the most effective general procedure, and the questions that relate to sensory modalities in planning the teaching of reading usually concern the balance between the use of auditory and visual channels. Most educators agree that students *must* be able to discriminate between visual symbols (letters) to be able to learn to read. In a similar manner, the role of adequate auditory abilities in the development of effective language is well known to educators and is thought to be essential to the normal development of reading skills. The role of tactile, kinesthetic, gustatory, and olfactory modalities are for the most part ignored.

An exception may be seen in the education of the blind and visually impaired. For students who cannot see, the sense of touch, the ability to feel shapes and forms and configurations, provides an effective substitute for sight, as applied to developing the ability to read. Certainly braille is different from the letters of the Roman alphabet, but the process of reading is similar, except that the incoming signals come through the fingers rather than through the eyes.

This strength of the tactile and kinesthetic learning channels can be utilized to assist some learning disabled students to learn to read. It may be used in a number of different ways.

Activities in which the young child learns to differentiate between two similar but different solid objects without looking at them appear to assist in the development of better visual discrimination. This may be accom-

plished in a variety of ways, many of which are outlined in the wide range of learning activity books presently on the market (see References and Suggested Readings at the end of this chapter). Simple examples include the use of solid objects in a cloth bag, or the use of a blindfold so that objects placed in front of the student cannot be seen. Sandpaper letters or geometric configurations provide another variety of this same principle. With 5- and 6-year-olds these activities can be accomplished in a game format.

In each of the preceding examples, the major purpose of the activities is to provide tactile and kinesthetic support for the visual modality, either to assist in developing skills that have been slow in developing or to attempt to "straighten out" previously scrambled reception and interpretation of visual signals. In some cases it may be well to have children "feel" a letter or word while looking at it, thus providing simultaneous signal reception through the visual and tactile senses. In other cases it may prove to be more effective to cut off the visual signal to be certain that the student is one hundred percent accurate in tactile sensing alone before adding the visual. In all of the preceding activities, *the important thing to understand is the principle of utilization of additional sensory modalities to assist in the development of other modalities.* The most common use of this principle is in the use of the tactile sense to support or assist the visual sense.

A somewhat different application of this same principle involves the teacher or a helping student tracing out letters, or sometimes words, on the arm or back of the student who needs help. This is significantly different in that the student receives no kinesthetic input, only the tactile. He may be looking at letter cards on his desk, attempting to find one matching the letter he feels traced out on his back, or he may have his eyes closed, concentrating on feeling the letter or word. In any event, a whole variety of games or activities may be developed using this type of assistance *when the evidence indicates that this is in fact a need of the student.* This type activity can be misused or overdone if not carefully monitored.

The preceding activities and approaches are most appropriate with primary age children who give evidence of developmental or remedial needs in the visual-perceptual abilities required for reading.

A simultaneous visual-auditory-kinesthetic-tactile approach

During the early 1920s, Grace Fernald began the development of a simultaneous visual-auditory-kinesthetic-tactile (VAKT) approach designed to assist students with severe reading disabilities. The account of her methodology (Fernald, G., 1943) is detailed in a full-length text, which has been used—with various adaptations—to this day. Reports of her work indicate a high degree of effectiveness, particularly with students of normal or above mental ability who have been in school at least two or three years.

Her approach has variously been called multisensory, a tracing approach, or a kinesthetic method. The terms "tracing" and "kinesthetic" have been applied because those are unique features of the approach, but the most accurately descriptive title is "simultaneous VAKT," which indicates the manner in which her methods are different from most others that have been called multisensory or VAKT.

Prior to actually starting a remedial program, the Fernald procedure requires "positive reconditioning." This is based on the assumption that almost all students who have experienced school failure have developed a low self-concept, particularly in relation to anything connected with school or with formal education. Four conditions are viewed

as ones to be carefully avoided in initiating and carrying through the remedial program:

1. *Avoid calling attention to emotionally loaded situations.* Attempts, either by teachers or parents, to urge the student to do better generally have negative effects. Reminding the student of the future importance of academic success or telling him how important it is to his family should be avoided. If the student is already a failure and knows it, these admonitions or urgings are at best useless and sometimes result in a nearly complete emotional block.

2. *Avoid using methods that previous experience suggests are likely to be ineffective.* This is important during remediation and during the time of reentry to the regular classroom. If the student is experiencing success in a temporary, out-of-class remedial setting (after school or for a set time period each day) and then must return to class and to methods by which he was previously unable to learn, the remedial program may be negated. Or, if after a period in which he has been out of class on a full-day basis and has found success in a new method, he must make an immediate return to the former methods with no planned transition, he may return to his old inability to learn.

3. *Avoid conditions that may cause embarrassment.* Sometimes a new method used in the new setting is effective and satisfactory, whereas in the old setting, unless some special provisions are made, it may seem childish or silly. For example, the tracing involved in the Fernald approach may seem so unusual in the regular classroom that the student may feel out of place there. The reward, that is, the learning, may not

be worth the feelings of conspicuousness and embarrassment.

4. *Avoid directing attention to what the student cannot do.* This is just a special kind of problem that might be included as a part of the first condition.

Regardless of what is required, attempting to bring about positive reconditioning and avoiding emotional reversal after the reconditioning has taken place are of prime importance.

Fernald VAKT approach. The first step in each remedial case in the actual classroom or clinic procedure is to explain to the student that there is a new way of learning words that really works. The student is told that others have had the same problem he is having and have learned easily through this new method.

The second step is to ask the student to select any word he wants to learn, regardless of length, and then to teach him to write and recognize (read) it, using the following method:

1. The word chosen by the student is written for him, usually with a crayon in plain, blackboard-size cursive writing. In most cases, regardless of age, cursive writing is used rather than manuscript. This is because the student will then tend to see and "feel" the word as a single entity, rather than a group of separate letters.

2. The student traces the word with his fingers in contact with the paper, saying the word as he traces it. This is repeated as many times as necessary until he can write the word without looking at the copy.

3. He writes the word on scrap paper, demonstrating to himself that it is now "his" word. Several words are taught in this manner, and as much time as necessary is taken to completely master them.

4. When the student has internalized the fact that he can write and recognize words, he is encouraged to start writing stories. His stories are whatever he wishes them to be at first, and the instructor gives him any words (in addition to those he has mastered) he needs to complete the story.

5. After the story is written, it is typed for him, and he reads it in typed form while it is still fresh in his mind. It is important that this be done immediately.

6. After the story is completed and the new word has been used in a meaningful way, the new word is written by the child on a card that he files alphabetically in his own individual word file. This word file is used as a meaningful way to teach the alphabet without undue emphasis on rote memory.

This procedure is often called the Fernald tracing method because the tracing is an added feature in contrast to the usual methods of teaching reading or word recognition. However, it should be noted that the student is simultaneously *feeling, seeing, saying,* and *hearing* the word. Thus this is truly a multisensory approach.

There are several points to be carefully observed and followed for maximum success:

1. *The word should be selected by the student.* If it is, motivation is maximized, and the likelihood that the student will be interested in using the word in a story is greater than with a teacher-selected word. In Fernald's case studies and in cases that we have known personally, students are able to master long, complicated words, and in fact may be able to do so with more ease than with short words.

2. *Finger contact is essential*, using either one or two fingers.

3. *The student should write the word, af-*

ter tracing it several times, without looking at the copy. Looking back and forth tends to break the word into small and sometimes meaningless units. He must learn to see, think, and feel the word as a total unit.

4. Because the word must be seen as a unit, *in case of error or interruption in writing, the word should be crossed out and a new start made.* If necessary, the student should go back to the tracing stage, but correcting the word through erasures is not permitted.

5. *Words should be used in context.* If the word the student wants to use is unfamiliar, a different one should be encouraged, or at least he should learn the meaning of the word before going through this procedure. He must learn that the group of alphabetical symbols called a word really means something.

6. *The student must always say the word aloud or to himself as he traces it and as he writes it.*

Although many additional details could be given, these points outline the essence of the Fernald approach. The addition of the tactile and kinesthetic avenues, or channels, to the visual and auditory channels may best explain the success this method has had when compared to more traditional approaches. After a period of tracing (stage one), which may vary in time from a few weeks to a few months, the student will be able to enter what Fernald calls stage two. In stage two, tracing is no longer required. The student simply looks at the new word in cursive writing, says it to himself as he looks at it, and then writes it without looking at the copy. He proceeds in the same manner as in stage one, except that he does not trace. In theory, the student is now "tracing" the word mentally.

If, during stage two, the student encounters difficulty with any particular word, he should go back to actual tracing until he masters that word. As soon as tracing is no longer necessary (except rarely), the large box used as a word file for the large, cursive words is exchanged for a smaller one for typed words.

In stage three, the student is able to study new words directly from a book or other printed copy. He should now be able to pronounce words to himself and write them from memory. Books consistent with his developing ability and interests are provided. He is told words that he cannot decode by himself, and these are recorded, reviewed, and written from memory after he finishes each section of the book. He no longer keeps a file on each new word.

Stage four involves decoding new words from their resemblance to words previously learned. He is not now "told" words but is helped to learn to figure them out through a sequence of structural analysis skills. If he is about to read difficult material, particularly material in which he will encounter technical terms (such as in science), he is encouraged to look over each paragraph in advance to find new words. These should be mastered ahead of time to permit greater comprehension.

This approach has been used with various students having a variety of problems, including those with problems in the auditory channel. However, it is probably most beneficial for students with visual channel problems, particularly problems of visual sequential memory or visual imagery.

There are a number of methods and materials on the commercial market that are advertised as multisensory. Technically speaking, they may be multisensory, but few are as total, as balanced, and as simultaneously multisensory as the Fernald approach. Some approaches are initially visual and become multisensory in later stages. Others are initially phonetic and evolve into multisensory approaches in succeeding stages. These approaches may be more or less effective than the Fernald **VAKT** approach, but the alert practitioner will do well to look carefully into what takes place in a given method, and the order in which it takes place, when analyzing it for possible use.

The simultaneous **VAKT** approach is likely to be most effective with children who have spent at least two years in school and thus have been rather thoroughly exposed to reading. It is one of only a few approaches that, in our experience, has been effective with secondary school students. Because much of its effectiveness depends on the ability to receive kinesthetic and tactile signals accurately, it will obviously have greatly reduced effectiveness with students in whom these channels are poorly developed. One other caution: *it is believed by some that certain types of neurological dysfunction may lead to a tendency for the receptive mechanisms of the brain to "short-circuit" if there are too many signals arriving simultaneously.* This is not an established fact, but the possibility of this type reaction to multiple stimuli should be kept in mind, particularly when dealing with hyperactive students.

Ideas for dealing with distractible or hyperactive students

The distractible or hyperactive student may exhibit the characteristics of hyperactivity for any of a variety of reasons, but one factor common to most of these students is that these symptoms are intensified by outside auditory or visual stimulation. As these students receive certain types of additional visual or auditory input, they overreact as compared to other students. We must realize that for some distractible or hyperactive students, the internal mechanisms that cause the problem are of such nature that simple changes in the classroom environment will have little or no effect on their behavior. However, the following suggestions do work

for many students. The basic idea behind each of these suggestions is the control of the classroom environment so that extraneous sensory stimulation is at a minimum; the suggestions are related to five basic types of distractibility or hyperactivity. These types do *not* fit any recognized system of classification and might be called "practical, teacher observation–based categories or classifications."

1. Students who appear to overreact to visual stimulation that involves movement, such as other students moving in their seats, someone going to the teacher's desk, wastepaper basket, or pencil sharpener; in other words, normal classroom movement.

2. Students who appear to overreact to visual stimulation that involves stationary objects at their desks or materials and equipment that may be a part of normal classroom procedures; these include bright pictures in books, brightly colored pencils, crayons, or other manipulable objects.

3. Students who appear to overreact to stimulating displays or materials in the classroom; these include science centers, the class aquarium, bright bulletin boards, and other similar interest centers.

4. Students who appear to overreact to normal auditory stimulation, such as questions other students ask the teacher (at the teacher's desk) during study periods, the normal request to borrow a pencil involving two students on the far side of the room, or the quiet opening of a door.

5. General hyperactivity or distractibility that cannot be related to any one type of stimulus.

The brief management suggestions that follow will be keyed to the five preceding statements by use of the numbers 1 to 5.

1, 2, 3, 4, 5 Change seating assignment according to assumed source(s) of distraction, *or*, if this does not provide enough environmental control, assign student to a study carrel. (Note that for younger students, this may be called an "office" and at times may be temporarily constructed out of large packing boxes.)

1, 2, 3, 4, 5 When differentiated assignments are possible, assign activities that involve fewer potential distractions; be careful in assignment of group activities for student; consider size of group, other students in group, and similar factors.

1, 4, 5 Move student to another classroom. This will probably be more necessary if the classroom is an open setting and another, less distracting setting is available.

2 Limit the amount and type of materials at the desk through use of a tote tray or by a storage and checkout procedure controlled by the teacher.

4 Use some sort of device (such as a headset) to cover the ears (used only at selected times).

The preceding suggestions are very general, and if the teacher can focus on the concept of environmental control and try many possible management ideas, hyperactivity and distractibility may be greatly reduced. When trying such ideas as a study carrel or headsets (to muffle sound), it is important that the student and the parent be informed of the reason for the tactic, so that they not interpret the situation as punishment. In practice, it is common that once such an option is tried and success is experienced, the student may request it in other classrooms or in subsequent school years.

Ideas for reading and/or language development

1. Have the student trace letters with templates and stencils.
2. Use dry gelatin powder, shaving cream, or finger paint for a base and have the student copy letters or words he usually reverses or write letters or words as you dictate them.
3. Have the student cut out letters or

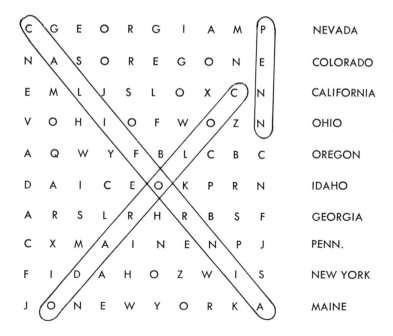

shapes. This helps in discrimination of letters and can provide practice in coordination.

4. Present partially completed letters and have the student complete them.

5. Suggest a mnemonic device for the student who reverses; for example, for a right-handed student, "the ball part of the b always points to the hand you write with. If it does not, then you know the letter is d."

6. Provide the student with pictures that have missing parts and ask him to draw them in.

7. Provide the student with a grid of letters that form spelling words, words from classroom subject areas, etc. Have him circle the words. If this is too difficult, indicate words he is to find (p. 179).

8. When learning the names of states, capitals, industry, or products, have the student trace first then have him draw from memory and compare results. The comparison is especially effective if the drawing paper is transparent and is laid over the original or if both are held up against the window.

9. Tape the student's favorite record (with vocal and instrumental background). Have the student listen to the tape and transcribe the lyric. Earphones prevent distraction of (and/or from) other students and a tape recording allows the student to stop when necessary and have time to write.

10. Provide the student with one or two paragraphs that have all the nouns, adjectives, or verbs omitted. The student can then fill in the missing words. For an alternate activity have the student fill in the missing words to make the paragraph humorous.

11. On field trips point out objects and simultaneously name them. Using simple sentences, explain the functions of objects or relationships. Have the student repeat important words and functions or relationships. This helps focus his attention.

12. After the field trip show pictures of objects and have the student name them and tell about their function. Have him describe similarities or differences between the picture and the object.

13. Put each step for a recipe on individual cards. Directions for building a model, playing a well-known game, or any other step-by-step directions can be used. Have the student put them in the proper sequence. If he has difficulty with this, ask him to "talk through" the procedure or, if possible, allow the student to attempt to determine the error.

14. Using newspaper clippings, list questions that are answered in either the article or in captions. To provide practice in skimming, time the student. For practice in critical thinking have the student locate possible bias or opinion; for practice in synthesizing have the student read the article and either tape or write a one-paragraph summary.

15. Cut comic strips and/or books apart and cover the captions (use simple ones if the student finds this difficult). Have the student write his own caption. Sometimes he can compare his captions with the original.

16. Establish a list of the student's assignments. Use a timer and provide the student with a time limit during which he is to complete each assignment. If the student completes the work during the specified time, provide him with a reward (five minutes to listen to a record, three minutes to watch a filmstrip, etc.).

17. Teach common punctuation marks such as the comma, question mark, quotation marks, and exclamation mark. Explain that they constitute a symbol system that

appears only in print. For example, have a student demonstrate what he would say if he saw a building on fire or saw someone fall off a bridge, and how he would write these exclamations ("Fire!" "Help!", etc.). Arrange other hypothetical situations. Provide the student with many opportunities to observe how these punctuation marks translate into our daily speech.

18. Prepare tapes of stories or selections. Have students read with the tape. Good readers can prepare the tapes.

Ideas related to arithmetic skills

1. Provide the student with many experiences of putting together and taking apart concrete objects to familiarize him with the concepts of addition and subtraction before introducing him to the symbols for plus and minus. Teach the words "plus" and "minus" as part of a separate mathematical language.

2. Teach multiplication as a faster, more efficient way of adding. Provide the student with opportunities to add, time him, and then demonstrate how multiplication shortens the time required to solve the problem. This will have to be repeated many times with some learning disabled students.

3. Encourage students to use objects and/ or materials when completing computation assignments. Usually when students are ready to proceed without manipulative materials, they will stop using them.

4. Using a piece of masking tape, make a number line by marking even spaces and numbering (much like a ruler with only inch marks) and place it on the student's desk for referral while he completes computation tasks.

5. Allow students, who find it helpful, to verbalize what they are writing as they complete arithmetic assignments. Often

hearing themselves assists them in understanding the task.

6. When a student has made errors in computation, especially when the concept is relatively new, ask him to explain what he did. This will often provide added insight in regard to errors made.

7. Use ordinary playing cards to match numbers or to practice addition and subtraction. The jack, queen, and king, can be zero or wild (student can decide each time what numerical value they will have).

8. To reinforce the association between numbers and sets, have the student put clothespins on a hanger as he counts. Or, have the student close his eyes and count the taps on a drum or piano. More able students can work with those having difficulty.

9. Have students compile daily time lines of the day's activities. These can be displayed on an overhead projector and compared for overlapping and for events that run concurrently. Reference can be made to the time line throughout the day, which assists the student in learning time concepts. These can be lengthened to include weekly or monthly activities.

10. On a tiled floor, use each block as a unit of measure (for example, one block equals one foot, one mile, or one city block). Then construct a room, building, town, etc. For students with unusual difficulty it is helpful to begin with the replication of a room so that they can refer to the room as a model for larger scale projects.

11. Provide the student with scaled diagrams of the school, campus, etc. Have him follow the map to get to specific locations. After the student can do this efficiently, provide him with directions without the diagram and ask him to tell

you where he will be located if he follows them.

12. Arrange hopscotch, climbing ladders, crossing rivers on rocks, or other similar games on the floor. The student can complete the game by adding, multiplying, dividing, or subtracting.

13. Prepare ditto sheets of multiplication tables. Encourage all students to use them when the task is a concept involving multiplication. In this way the student who is having difficulty memorizing the multiplication tables will not be penalized in learning other concepts.

14. Prepare charts that visually represent the relationship of fractions to the whole. Allow students to use these (as legal "cheat sheets") until they no longer need them.

15. Utilize a large manipulable clock and provide the students with individual clocks by which to plan the activities of the day. Change the time as activities change. Call attention to the time that has elapsed since the last activity; for ex-

ample, "It is now 9:40 or twenty minutes until 10. When we began the reading lesson, it was 9 o'clock. Forty minutes have gone by." This assists students in their conceptualization of short time periods and associates the concept with the clock.

16. Have students bring television schedules to school. Have them look up their favorite programs and arrange the hands of their individual clocks to show the times these programs are on. Bus, plane, or train schedules can be used in the same manner.

17. Provide real money or the closest possible replications and set up a store, amusement park, or other "business" and have the students buy items and receive change. Older students can "shop" from advertisements in the newspaper. They can prepare budgets, plan meals, "purchase" foods, and "buy" clothes. They can also compute the savings from advertisements for "30% off" or "half-price" sales.

From Marsh, G. E., Gearheart, C. K., and Gearheart, B. R.: The learning disabled adolescent, St. Louis, 1978, The C. V. Mosby Co.

Secondary-level programs for the learning disabled

As was mentioned with respect to secondary-level programs for EMR students, secondary programs for learning disabled students tend to take a different shape and form than elementary programs. Elementary programs are more likely to be remedially oriented, and in many instances this remedial effort is sufficiently effective that by the secondary level, no additional special programming is necessary. For these formerly learning disabled students, the only remaining effect may be that they find it valuable to use some of the special learning techniques that they used at lower academic levels. Unless they show a definite need for special assistance, they should be considered just like all other secondary students.

Another group of students in the secondary schools *will* need special assistance; these are students with obvious learning disabilities and those who have serious "leftover" effects from having been learning disabled for a long period of time. For these students there are a number of alternatives, including some that the regular classroom teacher will need to implement. The programs in which the regular classroom teacher will play the most prominent role are those that may be best described as involving *accommodation* and *compensatory* teaching. The following description of accommodation and compensatory teaching, as compared to remedial teaching, may help to clarify the change in focus required when planning secondary school efforts for the learning disabled.

Accommodation and compensatory teaching refer to a process whereby the learning environment of the student, either some of the elements or the total environment, is modified to promote learning. The focus is on changing the learning environment or the academic requirements so that the student may learn in spite of a fundamental weakness or deficiency. This may involve the use of modified instructional techniques, more flexible administrative practices, modified academic requirements, or any compensatory activity that emphasizes the use of stronger, more intact capabilities or that provides modified or alternative educational processes and/or goals.

Remediation or remedial teaching refers to those activities, techniques, and practices that are directed primarily at strengthening or eliminating the basic source(s) of a weakness or deficiency that interferes with learning. The focus is on changing the learner in some way so that he or she may more effectively relate to the educational program as it is provided and administered for all students. The presumption is made that there is something wrong with the learner that can be identified and corrected. (Marsh, Gearheart, and Gearheart, 1978, p. 85)

In either of these approaches, the goal is improved academic performance, but the older the student becomes, the more we must emphasize the learning of content through intact and/or developed learning abilities, as opposed to an emphasis on remediation. At the secondary level, accommodation and adaptation may mean any of a wide variety of modifications of course content: how the course is presented to the student, how the student is expected to respond (that is, by written papers, written

tests, outside reading), and others. The following list of types of accommodation includes the kinds of efforts that appear to be of the greatest value.

Examples of accommodation and adaptation

1. For students who can express themselves orally but are unable to prepare orderly, well-conceived written reports, a carefully taped response to an assignment might be permitted. Such a response would then be evaluated for content, thus avoiding a situation in which inability to express oneself in writing masks information and knowledge.

2. If taped reports cannot be accepted, the teacher could agree to address the content of reports without regard to mechanics. Some sort of grading or evaluation system may be devised that, in effect, does not lead to failure due to mechanics, but is based on understanding of subject content. Students and their parents must understand and agree to such an arrangement and be told—preferably in writing—that the skills that the student does *not* have (i.e., writing skills) are deliberately not being evaluated. This should ensure against the possibility of later claims by the student or parent that the student was not provided an effective education.

3. Peer tutors may be used in many ways and in a wide variety of subject areas.

4. Study-skill classes or sessions may be organized to help the student explore alternate ways to identify, analyze, categorize, and recall information. Since some students have been exposed to only one major method of learning, and since the learning disabled student is likely to require different learning styles and techniques, this may pay big dividends. Although in some instances this is best accomplished through special class sessions

taught by the learning disabilities specialist, in other cases regular classroom teachers have found time to assist students in their classes to learn to develop alternate study skills. This regular classroom effort may have positive effects on other students.

5. Although by the secondary level it may be too late to spend much time on teaching new basic reading skills (word attack skills and the like), it is not too late to teach students the need for different reading rates for different types of materials. This is another skill that is potentially valuable to other, nonhandicapped students.

6. Other skills, such as how to prepare for tests, how to take notes, and how to outline may be emphasized. In some instances, the teacher may agree to provide a student with an outline of material to be learned in advance as a framework within which to organize study.

7. The teacher can provide the student and the resource room teacher with lists of critical new vocabulary words in advance, so the student may study them before presentation in class.

8. The teacher can notify the learning disabilities resource teacher of areas in which the student is falling behind, particularly those that will be essential in future learning (sequential or cumulative skill and information areas).

In addition to these types of special assistance provided by the regular classroom teacher, the learning disabilities resource teacher or specialist must assist by attempting to assign the student to class sections that involve less abstract content and to teachers who have demonstrated an ability to adapt materials and teaching style. Although the regular classroom teacher will play an important role in adaptation and accommodation, it should be obvious that without help and guidance from a learning disabilities teacher, the program may not work. The matter of teamwork is particularly important in the secondary setting, where the student must meet and adapt to so many different teachers with different personalities, teaching styles, and academic expectations.

The preceding adaptive and accommodative approach is effective for many learning disabled students, and is particularly important for those who may try to go on to college. However, there seems to be a growing tendency to utilize some type of work-study program similar to that mentioned in Chapter 7 for learning disabled students. Learning disabled students can successfully manage job assignments that require higher level general mental ability, but often have just as much need to learn to work with others, to follow directions, to adjust to different job requirements, and to utilize all their positive attributes and abilities as EMR students. They need to learn which of their disabilities or academic deficits will cause problems and how to circumvent these problems. If problems and failure can be experienced in a supervised setting without dire consequences, these students may learn from these problems. This is much better than being fired from a job without an opportunity to benefit from the experience.

Learning disabilities programs at the elementary-school level are relatively new, and much remains to be learned about successful approaches for these students. Learning disabilities programs at the secondary level are even newer, but the preceding description reflects the trends of current programming. If the regular educator–special educator partnership can be more firmly established and fully utilized, perhaps more effective approaches will be developed. Events of the next decade will be critical in the development of programs for learning disabilities programs in the secondary school.

SUMMARY

Although it is the newest of the recognized handicapping conditions, learning disabled students will be the largest group the regular classroom teacher will deal with in most school districts. It is a widely varied group in terms of the educational modifications required for appropriate educational programming, and with the exception of disruptive or emotionally disturbed students, it is the only group of handicapped students for whom remediation is the usual goal.

Learning disabilities may be defined in a variety of ways, but in general, we think of the learning disabled student as one who has average or above-average mental ability but is not achieving academically in proportion to this ability. Causes of learning disabilities are often associated with perceptual dysfunctioning, but this is only one possible causation. The idea of minimal brain dysfunction is also commonly associated with learning disabilities, but this concept has little practical application for the regular classroom teacher. The definition of learning disabilities is often called an umbrella definition, indicating that it is a very general term designed to include a number of different disabilities.

Learning disabled students usually exhibit highly varied performance, with much higher academic success in some areas than others. Some learning disabled students may learn as rapidly as the average student in their class when learning through class discussions, audiovisual approaches, or other avenues that are not dependent on reading. Their reading ability may be very low. Others may do grade-level work in reading but have significant disabilities in mathematics; however, reading is the usual target of learning disabilities programming.

A number of guidelines for learning disabilities programming were presented in this chapter, along with certain approaches and specific teaching ideas that have been of value with learning disabled students. These included (1) ideas for use in teaching reading or language development, (2) ideas for use in teaching arithmetic, (3) tactile and kinesthetic approaches to learning, (4) the simultaneous VAKT approach, and (5) ideas for dealing with hyperactive or distractable students. The reader is again reminded, however, that there is no method that is always effective for all children with learning disabilities.

Learning disabled students may be served through the resource room or itinerant service, in addition to their placement in the regular classroom. An example of one type of such service, a learning disabilities learning lab, was provided in this chapter. It was also noted that secondary-level learning disabled students may benefit from a work-study program that is not much different from that provided for EMR students, or they may be served through adaptations and accommodations provided primarily through the regular classroom teacher.

Programs for the learning disabled can have positive ramifications for the entire student population. Because of its newness as an organized subarea of special education, there are likely to be a number of modifications and improvements in teaching approaches for the learning disabled in the next several years. Undoubtedly, some presently accepted procedures will be discarded. Teachers should therefore remain alert for new ideas and maintain an open mind about present approaches. One of the more exciting aspects of learning disabilities is the tremendous potential of certain techniques for carry-over to the teaching of other students. This is because the primary focus is on how to help students learn more effectively, an emphasis that will obviously be of benefit to all students, not just those students we presently call learning disabled.

REFERENCES AND SUGGESTED READINGS

Ayres, J. *Sensory integration and learning disorders.* Los Angeles: Western Psychological Services, 1973.

Bryan, T., & Bryan, J. *Understanding learning disabilities,* New York: Alfred Publishing Co., Inc., 1975.

Cruickshank, W. M. Myths and realities in learning disabilities. *Journal of Learning Disabilities,* 1977, *10* 51-58.

Feingold, B. *Why your child is hyperactive,* New York: Random House, 1975.

Fernald, G. *Remedial techniques in basic school subjects.* New York: McGraw-Hill Book Co., 1943.

Gearheart, B. *Teaching the learning disabled: a combined task-process approach,* St. Louis: The C. V. Mosby Co., 1976.

Gearheart, B. *Learning disabilities: educational strategies* (2nd ed.). St. Louis: The C. V. Mosby Company, 1977.

Hammill, D. D., & Bartel, N. R. (Eds.). *Teaching children with learning and behavior disorders,* Boston: Allyn & Bacon, Inc., 1978.

Johnson, O., Blalock, J., & Nesbitt, J. Adolescents with learning disabilities: perspectives from an educational clinic. *Learning Disability Quarterly,* Fall 1978, *1*(4), 24-36.

Johnson, D., & Myklebust, H. *Learning disabilities: educational principles and practices,* New York: Grune & Stratton, Inc., 1967.

Keogh, B. Hyperactivity and learning disorders; review and speculation. *Exceptional Children,* 1971, *38,* 101-109.

Lerner, J. W. *Children with learning disabilities,* Boston: Houghton Mifflin Co., 1976.

Marsh, G., Gearheart, C., & Gearheart, B. *The learning disabled adolescent: program alternatives in the secondary school,* St. Louis: The C. V. Mosby Co., 1978.

Myklebust, H. *Progress in learning disabilities* (Vol. 3). New York: Grune & Stratton, Inc., 1975.

Widerholt, J. Historical perspectives on the education of the learning disabled. In L. Mann & D. Sabatino (Eds.), *The second review of special education,* Philadelphia: Journal of Special Education Press, 1974.

Wiig, E., & Semel, E. *Language disabilities in children and adolescents,* Columbus, Ohio: Charles E. Merrill Publishing Co., 1976.

9

STRATEGIES FOR WORKING WITH TROUBLED STUDENTS

Barbara Colorosa

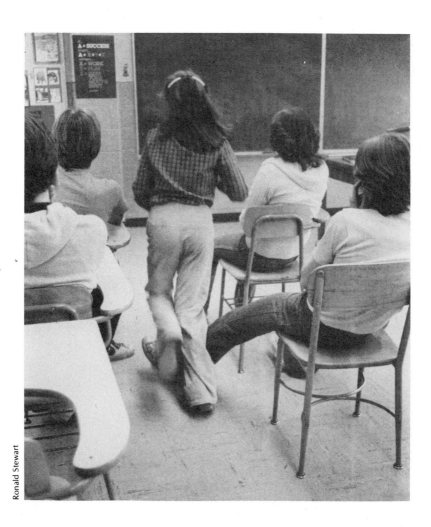

Ronald Stewart

Dear Teacher,

Management of troubled, disturbed, or acting-out students remains one of the most perplexing problems many classroom teachers must face. For the first edition of this text we asked Barbara Coloroso, a teacher educator who formerly taught such students, to share some of the insights and ideas we have heard her share with teachers in workshops and in-service meetings. We noted then that her efforts had been an inspiration to other teachers, and that her ideas had proved to be of practical value in a variety of settings.

Response to Barbara's chapter in our first edition verified our feelings. We have had continued positive response from students and professors alike. Although no specific set of ideas are the final answer in dealing with disturbed or acting out students, the strategies suggested in this chapter at least provide a starting point.

Much of this chapter is essentially the same as it was in the 1976 edition. However, a number of revisions and additions have provided additional ideas that are appropriate at the secondary level. Three additional sections, dealing with in-school suspension procedures, the use of "help notes," and performance contracts for secondary-level students, may be of particular interest.

We have asked Barbara to speak directly to you, the teacher, much as she does in in-service efforts. Therefore, the personal pronoun "you" will be found quite often in this chapter. We trust that this deviation from a more formal style of writing will be acceptable and perhaps more effective in conveying meaning in this critically important consideration of the troubled child.

BILL GEARHEART and MEL WEISHAHN

Troubled students—we know them, have them in class, hear them in the halls, see them on the playground, in parking lots, and on street corners. Of all the students who walk through the school doors, the troubled ones offer the most frustrating problems and the most potentially rewarding challenge to teachers.

Their behaviors range from extreme withdrawal to intense hostile aggression. They may cry easily or often or may refuse to cry at all. They may consistently fold under emotional stress and become depressed, hostile, or withdrawn, or they may resort to daydreaming to combat the stress. They may be battered and abused sexually, emotionally, or physically. Most of these troubled youth are in the regular classroom. They are often labeled emotionally disturbed, socially maladjusted, or delinquent, labels that do little to help the regular classroom teacher work effectively with them. The term *troubled* will be used throughout this chapter to describe the youth who exhibits behaviors that are deviant or have a damaging effect on his positive self-development and his relationship with others. Troubled does not connote an illness or disease as does "emotional disturbance," nor does it connote a severe character disorder. It does not assume that the problem is only within the student; it implies that the difficulty may be the result of the youth's interaction with the environment or significant others in his life. Troubled defies static definition and is not a damning or lasting label.

In this chapter we will briefly discuss (1) the nature of deviant behavior, (2) common behaviors of troubled students, (3) identification, (4) referral procedures, (5) overview of major approaches, (6) the responsibility-oriented classroom, (7) the role and responsibility of special education resource personnel, and (8) supportive services in the community.

NATURE OF DEVIANT BEHAVIOR

A student's deviant behavior can result from forces within the student or within the student's environment, including his interaction with "significant others" in his life.

Forces within the student may be viewed as (1) physiological factors and (2) psychological factors. Physiological factors include brain injury and physiological anomalies. An example of a physiological factor follows:

A student who was seemingly daydreaming, losing his place during reading, and accused of not listening was in fact experiencing petit mal seizures. He would "black out" for a few seconds, just long enough to miss important instruction for class. Once aware of the seizures, the teacher would repeat instructions for the class, enabling the student to reorient himself in the learning setting.

Although this example is relatively uncommon, it does occur and should be given consideration as a possible cause.

Irritability caused by glandular disturbances may appear as anger or hostility. Close observation by the regular classroom teacher, however, might disclose that these episodes occur every day just before lunch when the student's body is reacting to a basically physiological disorder. Teachers must be aware of the possible physiological reasons for deviant behavior and should make every effort to have them controlled or corrected through medical procedures.

Psychological factors may be the result of a discrepancy between the troubled student's capacity to relate realistically and the requirements of his environment. He may suffer from a marked lack of "coping skills." If a child is forced to attempt an assignment that he feels he cannot perform he may run from the task either physically or mentally. He may become excited or tense and may respond in anger to his textbook, the other students, or the teacher. He may resort to hostile behavior or withdraw when teased.

Environmental factors include variables such as extreme poverty, racial discrimination, school pressures, and deteriorating family units. The following are examples of environmental factors:

A poor student with large holes in his dirty socks reacted violently to being told to take off his shoes in physical education class and chose to be removed from class rather than be humiliated by classmates.

A teenager ditched school rather than face his classmates and teachers after the local paper carried a front-page story on an accident involving his drunk father.

A student who has experienced considerable failure in oral reading may demonstrate extremes of behavior when asked to read orally before his class.

A student who is identified as troubled because of his persistent withdrawal into fantasy or his frightful striking out at those around him may be an essentially normal student defending himself against damaging environmental pressures. Fritz Redl (1959a) indicates the following three causes of such behavior:

1. Inconsistent and sometimes borderline psychopathic behaviors by adults in the student's life—a battering parent or a sadistic teacher.
2. An environmental setting other than the normal home and school life every child needs.

3. Conflicts or challenges beyond those with which the student can cope, for example, a move from a stable rural setting to a large industrial city.

School can play a big part in pushing children into deviant behaviors. Exaggerated emphasis on grades or rate of progress contributes to acting-out or withdrawn behaviors. Rigid rules encourage rebellion. A teacher's comments can seriously damage a student's self-concept: "Why can't you be like your older brother? He was such a good student." "You are the slowest in the class, always the last to get anything done." "Your papers are so sloppy; can't you do anything right?"

Teacher conversations in the lounge or on final grade reports may leave little hope for a troubled student to rise above his past behaviors. "Oh, you have Johnny—he's a little thief. Watch out or he'll steal you blind." "Jill is such a cry baby." "Joey is so slow—he'll never learn to read."

Academic requirements may be unrealistic for the student in relation to his present level of readiness or to his abilities. A student may hit his peers or make loud noises during oral reading to draw attention away from the fact that he cannot read. In such a situation he may also be trying to get some kind of acknowledgement that he exists; he cannot get the acknowledgement by reading, so he will try a less appropriate form of behavior to get attention. Everyone needs to be acknowledged by significant others. We usually try appropriate behaviors first. If we are unsuccessful in this attempt, we may resort to more deviant forms of behavior to reach the same or similar ends. Students try to succeed and try to be the best at something, but many recognize that they cannot be the best in reading or math or the best runner so they become the "best-worst." These students become the "best-worst" troublemakers. We cannot deny, however, that they are "the best" even though their behavior is socially unacceptable. A student may try to please his parents by cleaning his room. If he doesn't receive praise or acknowledgement from his parents or if they yell at him for not making the bed perfectly, he will cease trying to gain recognition through appropriate behaviors and attempt to gain their acknowledgement through deviant behaviors.

COMMON BEHAVIORS OF TROUBLED STUDENTS

The following behaviors or characteristics are commonly seen in troubled students. These same behaviors may be seen in all students during stressful situations in their lives. It is the frequency, persistence, and intensity of these behaviors that would indicate a need for real concern by the regular classroom teacher. Reinert (1976) has described troubled youth as being "too precise, too worried, too angry, too happy; too easily disappointed and [they] manipulate others too much." Common behaviors include the following:

Hostile aggressiveness. Perhaps the most obvious sign or indication of a troubled student is hostile aggression toward teachers, peers, and parents. Kicking, hitting, biting, and fighting are means of expressing fears and anxieties.

Withdrawal into fantasy. The isolate in the class, the one who shuns involvement with peers or teachers, is sometimes far more troubled and in greater need of assistance than the aggressive student. However, the shy or withdrawn student is often overlooked by teachers. This student does not express antagonism toward authority and therefore may be ignored as the teacher exerts every effort toward finding help for the aggressive child.

Perfectionism. Fearing failure and criticism, this student is likely to destroy his assignment or artwork or "quit and take his ball home" if he makes a mistake or if things do not go his way.

Regression. A student may regress to forms of behavior that worked in previous situations (whining, thumbsucking, and infantile speech, for example)

Depression. The student is generally unhappy or depressed, even in situations that nearly all other students enjoy.

Unrealistic fears and phobias. This student attempts to avoid his real anxieties by developing unrealistic fears.

Bellyaches and headaches. This student complains of pains at the most opportune times, before math exams or during physical education, for example. He is constantly worrying about his health; a few drops of blood means bleeding to death and a rash must be an exotic disease with no known cure.

Accident proneness. This student falls out of chairs, trips down or up stairs, and collapses on level ground. He seems to thrive on the attention given to his wounds.

Overly dependent. This student is overly dependent on peers and teachers. He does not attempt a new task until he has received assurance from his peers or the teacher.

The "smelly" kid. Although this student may not be troubled because of his body odor or obesity, the resultant peer interaction (or lack of it) may cause the student to become a loner or isolate.

Although some of the preceding behaviors or characteristics are at opposite ends of a continuum, others overlap and appear in combination. Examples might include students who manifest a combination of some form of withdrawal and regression and infantile behavior, or perfectionism and some degree of hostile aggressiveness. As indicated at the outset, some degree of these behaviors may be expected in nearly all students; it is, however, the unusual frequency or intensity that is a signal that the student needs help. These behaviors are exhibited "in the wrong places, at the wrong time, in the presence of the wrong people, and to an inappropriate degree" (Reinert, 1976).

IDENTIFICATION OF THE TROUBLED STUDENT

The regular classroom teacher is often the first to identify troubled or troublesome students. She may be unable to clinically label the problem, but she knows one exists. She can be instrumental in screening or referring students who require a more careful diagnosis by special education personnel and possible mental health intervention beyond the school setting. A teacher can gather enough pertinent information about a troubled student during daily contacts with the student to make fairly accurate professional predictions about that student's future success or failure in school.

Checklists and rating scales for regular classroom teachers are not intended for clinical diagnosis. Knowing the clinical description for a student's deviant behavior—for example, psychotic, neurotic, sadistic—does not tell a teacher how a student learns and how he may respond to the many pressures and problems in the classroom. Therefore, screening instruments used by a regular classroom teacher should focus on behaviors relevant to the educational process, not to clinical diagnosis. The scales should be easy to administer and should help the teacher objectify behavioral judgments about pupils.

Care must be taken to select a screening device that meets the needs of a specific situation. Bower (1969) listed a number of specific criteria for evaluating screening tests. These include the following:

1. The screening procedure should include only that information a teacher can obtain without professional assistance.
2. The instrument should be easy to administer and score.
3. The results should be tentative; their purpose should be to identify troubled

Eric W. Blackhurst

students who could benefit most from a more thorough diagnosis.

4. The procedure should actively discourage the teacher from diagnosing emotional problems, drawing conclusions about causes, or labeling the student being tested.
5. Privacy of the individual student should not be invaded, nor should the questions be in poor taste.
6. The procedure should not be a threat to the student.
7. The screening test should be inexpensive.

The following list indicates the type and variety of screening instruments used for students from kindergarten through twelfth grade. Reference texts on assessment and evaluation will provide the names of additional checklists that are appropriate for regular classroom teachers.

Devereux Elementary School Behavior Rating Scale (Grades K-6)

The Devereux Elementary School Behavior Rating Scale (DESB) measures behaviors that indicate the student's overall adaptation to the classroom setting and his subsequent academic achievement in the classroom. The scale consists of forty-seven items that define the following eleven behavioral factors:

1. Classroom disturbance
2. Impatience
3. Disrespect/defiance
4. External blame
5. Achievement anxiety
6. External reliance
7. Comprehension
8. Inattentive and withdrawn
9. Irrelevant/responsiveness
10. Creative/initiative
11. Closeness to teachers

The Devereux Scale is based on the teacher's subjective norm of how the average student of the same sex and age behaves in the classroom. This instrument is easy to administer, taking about eight minutes to complete, and provides a profile of behaviors that interfere with classroom performance.

BY: Spivack and Swift
PUBLISHER: Devereux Foundation Press

Hahnemann High School Behavior Rating Scale (Grades 7-12)

The Hahnemann High School Behavior Rating Scale (HHSB), a forty-five–item rating scale, measures overt classroom behaviors related to a student's adjustment to the demands of a regular classroom at the junior and senior high school level. There are thirteen factors in the scale. Five of the factors relate positively to academic success:

1. Reasoning ability
2. Verbal interaction
3. Originality
4. Rapport with the teacher
5. Anxious producer (inner pressure to master a task)

The remaining factors relate negatively to academic success. These factors, with respect to an entire behavior profile, suggest negative feelings and behaviors:

1. General anxiety
2. Quiet/withdrawn
3. Poor work habits
4. Lack of intellectual independence
5. Dogmatic/inflexible
6. Verbal negativism
7. Disturbance/restless
8. Expressed inability

The HHSB provides norms and a method of charting the behavior profile. It is a valid instrument and is easy to use. The forty-five items are similar to those found in the DESB, with rating and scoring methods essentially the same.

BY: Swift and Spivack
PUBLISHER: Hahnemann Medical College

Pupil Behavior Inventory (Grades 7-12)

The Pupil Behavior Inventory measures "behavioral and attitudinal factors which affect the degree of success a pupil will have in accomplishing his educational objectives" (Vinter et al., 1966, p. 1). This one-page inventory lists behavioral items a teacher can readily observe. The items are rated on a five-point scale from "very frequently" to "very infrequently." The dimensions covered include the following:

1. Classroom conduct
2. Academic motivation and performance
3. Socioemotional state
4. Teacher dependence
5. Personal behavior

It is a very usable scale with explicit, easy-to-follow directions and is easy to score. Norms are available for junior and senior high.

BY: Vinter, Sarri, Vorwaller, and Schafer
PUBLISHER: Campus Publishers, Ann Arbor, Michigan

Walker Problem Behavior Identification Checklist (Grades 4-6)

The Walker Problem Behavior Identification Checklist (WPBIC) is a tool "the elementary teacher can rely upon in the difficult task of selecting children with behavior problems who should be referred for further psychological evaluation, referral and treatment" (Walker, 1967, p. 1). The checklist consists of fifty observable symptomatic behaviors that might limit a student's adjustment in school. The following are sample items from this checklist:

"Will destroy or take apart something he has made rather than show it or ask to have it displayed

"Disturbs other children: teasing, provoking fights, and interrupting others

"Refers to himself as dumb, stupid, or incapable

"Openly strikes back with angry behavior to teasing of other children

"Easily distracted away from the task at hand by ordinary classroom stimuli, minor movements of others and noises, for example."*

The factors scored include the following:

1. Acting out (disruptive and aggressive behavior)
2. Withdrawing (socially passive and avoidant behaviors)
3. Distractability (poor attentiveness and restlessness)
4. Disturbed peer relations
5. Immaturity

This is an initial screening device, not intended as an educational planning tool. It is easy to use and takes eight to ten minutes to complete.

BY: Hill M. Walker
PUBLISHER: Western Psychological Services

---

*Reprinted with permission. © 1970 by Western Psychological Services.

Behavior Problem Checklist (Grades K-8)

The Behavior Problem Checklist consists of sixty-nine items that are limited to the most frequently occurring behaviors of children referred to a psychiatric clinic. The items are rated on a three-point scale: (1) does not constitute a problem, (2) is a mild problem, and (3) is a severe problem. In the factoring process, the following four personality types are identified:

1. Conduct problem
2. Personality—neurotic
3. Inadequacy, immaturity
4. Socialized delinquency

The following are sample items from this checklist:

"1. Does not know how to have fun; behaves like a little adult
"2. Fighting
"3. Anxiety, chronic general fearfulness
"4. Depression, chronic sadness
"5. Often has physical complaints, e.g. headaches, stomach aches."

It is easily administered and scored. A unique aspect of this checklist is that Quay has developed educational programs that he feels are appropriate for the different personality types identified.

BY: Quay and Peterson
PUBLISHER: Children's Research Center, Champaign, Ill.

Bower-Lambert Scales For In-School Screening of Emotionally Handicapped Children

The screening procedure developed by Bower and Lambert consists of three rating scales used in combination with each other for one total evaluation of each pupil:

Teacher-rating scale
Peer-rating scale
Self-rating scale

It is the most extensive of the screening devices described in this chapter.

Teacher rating of pupils (all grades)

The teacher, using a normal distribution, indicates the relative position of each student on eight scales.

Peer rating

Class pictures (grades K-3)

Class play (grades 3-7)
Student survey (grades 7-12)

These three activities are designed for use at the different grade levels to analyze how children are perceived by their peers.

Self rating

Picture game (grades K-3). This activity is designed to give a measure of a student's perception of himself.

Thinking about yourself (grades 3-7). This activity is designed to show the degree of discrepancy between a student's perception of himself as he is and as he would like to be.

A self-test (grades 7-12). This test is designed to obtain a measure of the difference between self and ideal self.

Information from the three sources—teacher, peers, and self—are collated and weighted to arrive at behavioral evaluation of the child.

BY: Bower and Lambert
PUBLISHER: Education Testing Service

Many behavioral checklists are part of a total pupil rating scale that attempts to give a total educational profile of the student. One such checklist is part IV of the Pupil Behavior Rating Scale, a scale used for diagnosis in learning disabilities (see Appendix E).

It would be impractical to list all of the checklists or screening instruments used in the screening of behavioral deviances across the United States. Published checklists are continually being revised, adapted, and combined with other instruments by various school districts to fit the needs of the district and available services.

They do have the potential, however, to assist regular classroom teachers in identifying more objectively the students in their classrooms who may be in need of further assistance from special education personnel or from professionals outside of the school district.

REFERRAL PROCEDURES

Screening checklists and rating scales should not be substituted for concrete assistance or intervention. Once a teacher has identified a troubled child as being in need of assistance beyond what she can provide in a regular classroom setting, she should refer the child to the resource person or school psychologist for an in-depth evaluation.

When making the referral, the classroom teacher should be ready to describe the *specific behaviors* the student is exhibiting that lead her to believe that the student needs special assistance. This is the situation in which screening checklists and rating scales help. Also helpful are brief anecdotal notes a teacher might keep, similar to an abbreviated diary, noting events of each day. This requires very little time if completed at the close of every day. It can become a regular part of the daily routine, and it must be done *daily* if notes are to be of maximum accuracy and objectivity.

In many school systems the student is staffed by a team composed of the principal, the regular classroom teacher, the resource teacher, the school psychologist, the school social worker, the director of special education, a member of the medical profession and the student's parents.

The staffing team reviews and discusses all pertinent information and makes recommendations concerning educational placement and programming. The educational recommendations often include professional help and a modified educational program. The professional help can range from support provided to the regular classroom teacher by a resource person to psychiatric therapy in a mental health setting. The modified educational program can be as simple as establishing a behavior contract with the student or as involved as moving the child into a therapeutic detention home or residential facility.

One critical question is whether the student can function in the regular classroom with certain behavioral and educational adaptations. Should he be placed in a special class, or is his behavior so deviant that even special classes will be ineffective? The regular classroom teacher's input is invaluable at this time. Because of her interactions with the student, her perception of his behavior may be closer to the true operational reality of the student's difficulty than the information obtained from complete diagnostic studies, test results, or clinical interviews. She is the one who has experienced the student's anger or frustration in the educational setting.

There are many advantages in keeping the troubled student in the regular classroom, provided the classroom is responsibility- and reality-oriented. The following are just a few advantages offered by regular classroom placement:

1. The student has an opportunity to observe appropriate behavior of his peers and is able to interact with and receive support from them.
2. The student has an opportunity to "dispel the delusion of uniqueness," to reinforce the feeling that he is more like other students than different from them.
3. The student has the opportunity to function responsibly and realistically in a safe milieu in which creative abilities can be channeled into academic pursuits.
4. The student can see and experience appropriate responsible expressions of emotions.

There are several steps a regular classroom teacher can take before and during the referral process to make the classroom situation more tolerable and, perhaps, more creative and constructive for the teacher and the troubled student. These steps are also applicable if the troubled student, after screening, is to remain in the regular classroom with supportive services from a resource person or mental health personnel.

Step 1: What is it that the student is doing or not doing that upsets you? Write it down! How often does he do it, and when does he do it? If there is more than one behavior, and there usually is, list them according to the priority of your concern. What do you do when he exhibits the behaviors you recorded? If he is still throwing books, your approach is not affecting his behavior positively.

Step 2: Share your notes with the student— level with him. Determine what he is doing and what you are doing that is not working; then ask for his help in coming up with new "cue cards"! Alschuler and Shea (1974) have developed this step into a technique called "social literacy training," in which discipline problems are recognized as games with rules that can be renegotiated to change negative discipline cycles into the discipline of learning. You are not threatening or punishing the student— just acknowledging your awareness of the problem and your desire to work constructively with the student. Too often, everyone in the teacher's lounge knows about your awareness of Johnny's problem, but Johnny isn't aware that you know. Confronting the troubled student in a nonthreatening way and exploring with him alternatives to his deviant behavior is sometimes enough of a catalyst for a positive change. *It is important that your meeting with the student be nonthreatening and as positive as possible.*

Step 3: Greet the troubled student at the front door if necessary. Give him a positive stroke everyday—a compliment, a smile, or a touch on the shoulder *before* he has a chance to behave irresponsibly. Look for things he does well and share your observations with him. Often, when a student is experiencing difficulty, all the teacher thinks about are the negative things. It is generally an easy task to establish an extensive listing of things the student does not do well; why not attend to what he does well? *Every student has many desirable behaviors and characteristics;* you may have to observe carefully for a short period of time, but the desirable behaviors are present. Watch for them, and let the student know that you are aware of them. It may be a beautiful smile or a great laugh. Sometimes we can reverse the pattern of undesirable behavior simply by attending to the positive aspects and by letting the student know that he is seen as a positive, worthwhile, and valued individual. Acknowledge his presence in a positive way before he forces you to acknowledge him in a negative way. Then, when he has behaved in a positive, responsible way, acknowledge his behavior in writing.

Glad notes and glad phone calls

Glad notes, note cards with positive comments about a student, can be used to encourage and compliment the troubled student. They are effective positive reinforcers. Have a drawer full of different types of glad notes. When the student has worked extra hard to overcome some social or academic difficulty, fill out a glad note with a positive, personal message and give it to the student. You will find younger students taking these notes home to share with their parents; older students may stick the notes in their book to reread on a "down day." Glad notes may also be mailed home to the student's parents.

After the troubled student has had a good day in school, a *glad phone call* to his parents to share the good news can help establish positive communication and cooperation between parents, student, and school. Too often, most of the correspondence between the parents of a troubled student and the school is on a negative note: "What did he do wrong this time?" Parents need to hear

about the beautiful side of their children. Parent cooperation can be increased through your recognition and acknowledgement of their child's assets. They are already well aware of his liabilities. The use of glad notes or glad phone calls is effective with all students, not just those who are troubled. The following are examples of glad notes that have been used with young students. Consider making your own, appropriate for the age and interests of the students with whom you work.

Help notes

If a troubled student is being served by a resource person and several regular classroom teachers, or has one teacher appointed as an advocate to help him function adequately in various classes, it is important that a *simple* system be devised and accepted by all parties to alert the resource person or ad-

vocate to a problem before it becomes a major crisis.

A system that has been found to be simple, quick, and effective involves the use of small cartoon note cards that a teacher fills out with the necessary information when a problem arises that needs attention by the advocate or resource teacher. The note card is placed in the advocate's or resource teacher's mailbox. She should then contact the regular classroom teacher within a day and try to work out a reasonable solution to the problem. Samples of three different notes are provided here, but most teachers will want to work out their own personalized variations.

MAJOR APPROACHES USED IN WORKING WITH TROUBLED STUDENTS

There is no one "correct" way of working with troubled students. A teacher must be

IT WAS ONE OF THOSE DAYS!

_____
(Student)
NEEDS HELP IN

_____
(Subject)
PLEASE SEE ME
SOON!
_____
(Teacher)
_____
(Date)

S.O.S.

_____ IS IN TROUBLE IN
(Student)
_____
(Subject)
PLEASE SEE ME SOON! THANKS!
_____
(Teacher)

_____
(Student)
IS SINKING FAST
IN
_____
(Subject)
PLEASE SEE ME
SOON!
_____
(Teacher)
THANKS!   _____
(Date)

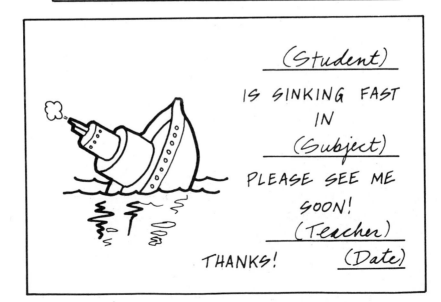

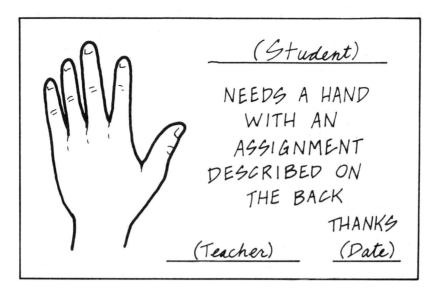

aware of various approaches that may be used realistically and effectively in the class-room. The following reference to authorities and contributors in this field will acquaint the reader with various approaches that may be investigated further.

Psychoanalytic approach

Bruno Bettelheim (1949), who was among the first to develop a specific school program for troubled students, used an orthodox psychoanalytic approach. The role of the teacher using this approach is to provide ways in which students can bring into consciousness their unconscious repressions.

The program is extremely permissive, with all program cueing coming from the student. The program developed by Bettelheim is carried out in a residential school, the Sonia Shankman Orthogenic School, and is not adaptable to a public school setting.

Fritz Redl (1959) and Ruth Newman (1967) have also taken a psychoanalytic approach in dealing with troubled youth. They stress the importance of bringing unconscious repressions into consciousness and of developing the ego. They differ philosoph-

ically from Bettelheim in that their approaches involve much more external structure.

Fritz Redl is known for his work with delinquent boys in residential treatment programs. He believes in a structure that allows for a wide range of choice in behavioral responses. Life space interviewing, a technique developed by Redl, exploits a life event at the time of the event or soon after. It is a way of offering "ego support on the spot" to achieve a developmental gain. This technique has been used successfully by regular classroom teachers and is suited to a teacher's responsibility in group management, social learning, and social adjustment.

Ruth Newman suggests that an essential part of the educational programming for the troubled student is allowing the student to act out. Her techniques involve the initial acceptance of undesirable symptoms, followed by tolerance but not acceptance, and finally setting a limit to the behavior.

Other psychoanalytically inclined authors include Pearson (1954), Slavson (1954), and Hirshberg (1953).

Humanistic approach

The humanistic approach in working with troubled students involves the acceptance of a student's behavior and the reflection of the behavior back to the student. It is through this reflection process that the individual grows in his capacity to develop insight and modify his own behavior. This approach, with its direct and uncomplicated framework, encourages the student to learn, to express, and to better understand his feelings in a caring, reflective environment.

Clark Moustakas (1953) considers the regular classroom teacher as having the potential to be a genuinely effective therapist by establishing an atmosphere of acceptance and warmth in the classroom.

Another humanistic psychologist, Carl Rogers (1951), advocates a permissive relationship, within defined limits, for a student's self-expression. Rogers feels that schools are too punitive for nondirective therapy and has made suggestions for adjusting teaching techniques to work in conjunction with treatment agencies.

Thomas Gordon (1974), utilizes Rogers' philosophy and basic attitudes about persons and elaborates on active and passive listening, both part of the humanistic approach, in his book, *T.E.T. Teacher Effectiveness Training*. Passive listening is defined by Gordon as a nonverbal message that shows acceptance by not intervening in the student's activities. Through active listening, a teacher verbally communicates acceptance by recognizing the student's feelings and reflecting them back. Also part of Gordon's approach to helping troubled children is group-centered problem solving, in which the students and teacher work cooperatively to make the educational experience a responsible and profitable one.

Virginia Axline (1947) is known for her work in play therapy. She feels that by providing understanding, acceptance, and recognition and clarification of feelings, a teacher can help a student grow in his understanding and acceptance of himself.

The humanistic system is a viable approach in dealing with troubled students in the public school setting if the attitudes of acceptance, trust, and empathic understanding are present.

Behavior modification

Behavior modification techniques offer the tools and systematic procedures that teachers may implement to change or modify behavior that is unacceptable or deviant and to encourage more acceptable and appropriate behaviors. The fundamental concept of behavior modification is that behavior, abnormal as well as normal, is learned. Environmental consequences may accelerate and/or increase the behavioral response or decelerate/decrease the frequency or rate of behavior.

The application of behavior modification principles with students in the regular classroom is a systematic and complex process. The dispensing of candy or gold stars cannot be properly called behavior modification. Behavior modification requires systematic and planned effort to be used effectively.

Behavior modification theorists are not primarily concerned with the causes of deviant behavior. Rather, they are concerned with overt behavior. The behavior is observed, measured, and analyzed quantitatively. Appropriate behavior modification techniques are applied in relation to the observable measurements.

Some of the individuals who have systematically applied behavior modification techniques in the classroom or have developed behavior modification techniques that can be used in the classroom include Homme (1970), Hewett (1968), Walker (1970), Lindsley (1971), Haring and Phillips (1962), and Patterson and Gullion (1968).

Other conceptual frameworks

Two other persons who have developed specific techniques for use in the regular classroom are Rudolph Dreikurs and William Glasser.

Rudolph Dreikurs, his philosophy rooted in Adlerian theory, suggests that schools must become truly democratic, with students playing an active role in the process of their education. Advocating the "art of encouragement" as a crucial tool in improving the adjustment a troubled student must make, he recommends that teachers give up punitive retaliation and begin sharing responsibility with the students, encouraging them to participate in decision making. Dreikurs believes that a teacher must understand the roles and the importance of the peer group as it relates to classroom conduct (Dreikurs, Grunwald, and Pepper, 1971).

William Glasser (1969) suggests that teachers, grading, and imposed curricula contribute to students' failure. According to Glasser (1969):

The schools assume built-in motivation, but when it does not occur, they attempt to motivate children with methods analogous to using a gun. Although guns have never worked, the schools, struggling to solve their problems, resort to using bigger and bigger guns—more restrictions and rules, more threats and punishments.

He has developed techniques for classroom meetings that give students more freedom to talk and think, to be responsible for their own behavior and academic success. Responsibility is the key element in his philosophy. A student must develop the ability to recognize and fulfill his or her needs and do so in a way that does not deprive others of the opportunity to fulfill their needs. By doing what is realistic and responsible, the student can maintain a satisfactory standard of behavior.

Other individuals could be mentioned, but such a review is not the purpose of this text. Those who wish to read further in these areas may find additional material provided in the references and suggested readings at the end of this chapter.

RESPONSIBILITY-ORIENTED CLASSROOM

This discussion will review techniques that reflect a combination of approaches that have been effectively used by teachers working with troubled students in the regular classroom.* This approach takes into consideration the *beauty of each student, provides an opportunity for each student to take an active part in his academic planning, and does not involve elaborate techniques.* It also allows for an exercise of the unique skills and competencies of each teacher.

You, as a regular classroom teacher, have the opportunity to provide a "safe" place for the troubled student and alternatives and choices to help the student change his attitudes and behaviors. Whether it be for the whole day, half a day, or one period, your class can be a place where the student can feel O.K.—needed, valued, and responsible.

In such a classroom, the student is responsible for his own behavior, academic success, and failures. He *owns* his actions. He cannot blame his environment, parents, or peers for his own behavior. He has the ability to choose.

You, as the teacher, have the responsibility to be yourself, establish structure that is realistic, program academic materials to fit the needs and abilities of your students, and encourage academic and social responsibility.

---

*I have worked with troubled students as a teacher in self-contained classrooms, as a resource teacher, and as a teacher educator in preservice and in-service programs. This discussion reflects a composite of ideas, concepts, and methods that I have found to be of maximum value.

You cannot *make* a student behave responsibly or realistically. You can coerce, threaten, or physically restrain a student, but then both you and the student lose. You and a student may set up destructive game rules in which neither of you can be a winner. A responsibility-oriented class involves the use of natural, logical, and realistic consequences, a simple structure, reasonable rules, the labeling and acceptance of feelings, group meetings, and the use of contracts. The students play a highly important role in their own educational planning in the responsibility-oriented class setting.

Rather than threaten, you can establish logical, realistic, and natural consequences and make it (hopefully) more comfortable for the student to choose the more responsible activity. The choice is still the student's to make. The idea is to make him aware of the negative and positive consequences of his choice. If the student does not know what to expect if he completes his assignment or what to expect if he does not get his assignment done, he does not really make a choice. The goal is to help a student see himself as responsible for and in control of what happens to him.

There is no one positive consequence or negative consequence that will work with all students. For example, staying in from recess may be positively reinforcing for one student, whereas another may feel that it is punitive. The consequences need to fit the situation and be such that the teacher and the student can follow through with them. If you say to a student, "I'll break your arm if I catch you stealing again!" what are your choices if he does steal again?

One way to find realistic and meaningful consequences is to ask your students to help you decide on the consequences. What the students consider positive or negative consequences may not have even occurred to you as being reinforcing.

The following are positive consequences that can be used in the regular classroom setting.

Positive consequences for elementary children

Go to the free corner
Help a slower classmate
Be a teacher-helper
Stay after school
Have free time with the teacher
Plan a media project
Present a project to the class
Be first in line
Draw
Paint
Work with clay
Take a five-minute break to play a game with a friend in the quiet corner
Listen to a record or radio with earphones
Use the overhead projector or tape recorder
Go the the classroom or school store
Operate the filmstrip projector for the class
Help the secretary, janitor, or principal
Be class messenger for the day
Use class camera and film
Use a typewriter
Read a motorcycle magazine

Positive consequences for secondary-age students

Work as a tutor for elementary students
Work with the janitor, secretary, or principal
Work in the guidance office
Plan own assignment schedule for the week
Read magazines of their choice
Plant a garden
Create a film or slide presentation
Take apart and reassemble electrical or mechanical equipment
Use a calculator or typewriter
Extra time in the class to work on homework assignments

Snack break
Free day
Card games
Plan, film, and show a videotape sequence
Listen to records or radio with earphones
Design and build playground equipment
    for young children
Refinish desks
Time off to volunteer at social service and
    other community agencies
Shoot baskets
Build a terrarium
Macrame
Leatherwork
Swim break

These are not the only positive consequences available to teachers. Be creative and encourage students to assist in determining positive consequences.

Structure and rules

You probably know which rules are most appropriate for your class to maintain some semblance of order, to keep the room intact, and to see that valuable learning takes place. Rather than post rules and dictate them, ask your students to help you come up with realistic guidelines for the class. Your role becomes that of guiding the discussion and offering suggestions. It is important that the rules help create a structure that serves as a backbone for learning, not as a brick wall that blocks it. The rules should be simple and consistently administered. Too little structure can result in chaos; too much structure, in defiance and rebellion. The structure should provide opportunity for the student to grow and time for him to think. The environment should be positive, acceptable, and nonthreatening. *A responsibility-oriented classroom is neither a teacher-dominated nor student-controlled room. Rather, it is a joint effort to learn, relate, and experience.*

Labeling and accepting feelings

The following was presented by Freed (1974):

> Remember, feelings are just as real
> as noses and toeses.
> So, let your feelings come out.
> You'll feel better, be happier and
> so will everybody else.

There are only two things to remember: (1) find someone who cares to listen to your feelings; and (2) don't dump your feelings on little people.

Another way to get rid of your angry feelings is to hit pillows. You can have neat temper tantrums in your room and not hurt anyone. You could pound clay, hammer your peg board, throw bean bags . . . or if you can find a safe place, throw clods of mud that won't hurt anybody. You can throw them at a tree, makes a nice thud.

Students need to know that it is all right to be angry, to be unhappy, and to be afraid and that there are responsible ways to express these feelings. A child who, in anger or frustration, throws a math book across the room may not be aware of other ways to express his anger. He may have witnessed his parents throwing plates across the room in anger. The child who beats up his peers may himself be brutally beaten by his parents for making a mistake or for just being in the way. The child who throws himself on the floor kicking and screaming when he does not get his own way has learned that this technique works on his parents and teachers. In all three of these situations the actions of the students are learned behaviors. Students, therefore, can learn to replace these irresponsible actions with more appropriate expressions of their feelings.

You as a teacher will not have to contrive situations to express feelings of anger or hurt in the classroom. The situations will be there. Labeling your feelings and encouraging a student to label his are the two essential components of the first step toward helping a troubled child accept and deal with his frustrations and anger.

The second step, discussing appropriate and realistic ways to express feelings, can be accomplished through the discussion of incidents in the class, group meetings (refer to an explanation of the Magic Circle on p. 208), and role-playing.

The third step is to actively encourage the appropriate expression of feelings in the classroom. When students express their feelings irresponsibly, you can talk through their anger, hurt, or fright and help them arrive at alternative behaviors with which they can feel comfortable.

More than structure, rules, and academia, you must convey to your students your trust and belief in them—all of them. They each have something unique and beautiful to bring to your class. You must believe in the troubled student to help him believe in himself. In developing a positive relationship it is important that you recognize and accept small efforts by the troubled student and freely express your real appreciation for that student's good behavior. The student needs to find out that joy, delight, and enthusiasm can be a part of his learning experience.

Group meetings

An integral part of a responsibility-oriented classroom is the group meeting. It fosters student involvement and initiative in learning. Teachers are teaching students to teach themselves.

Formats for these meetings have been described in detail by Glasser (1969), Dreikurs, Grunwald, and Pepper (1971), and others in the field of education. Group meetings are like kids—they come in all shapes and sizes. They can be five minutes or fifty minutes long and can involve two or thirty people.

There are three types of meetings, with many different labels, that seem to fit most of the situations arising in most classes.

These are:

1. Academic planning meetings
2. Problem-solving meetings
3. Crisis meetings

Academic planning meetings. In this type of meeting, the teacher and the students plan the academic program. This includes a discussion of the students' present academic status, where they are going, and the steps they will need to accomplish to reach their goal. Students, then, assume a responsible role in their own educational planning.

Students usually have a good idea of their level of progress in reading—especially if they are behind their classmates. Try as we might to disguise levels of reading groups, the "Buzzards" know that they are the bottom level if they are the poorest readers. Being straight with a student helps him to accept his level. What you are saying is that you know he is behind, he is okay, his present level is okay for now, you know he can learn more, and you have a plan to help him get ahead. The slow or underachieving student will then no longer feel hopelessly behind. He now has a goal and a realistic means to achieve that goal. You and the student become coplanners in the learning experience.

Openly discussing different levels of achievement takes the bite out of the malicious or hurtful talk of classmates that can destroy a student's self-esteem: "John's so dumb, he can't even read yet." "Ha, Ha, look at all the math problems Jill missed." Because you accept each one of them, you can help students accept themselves and one another for what they are, where they are, and where they are going.

At the beginning of each quarter you should discuss the learning objectives so that the students can get an idea of the total learning picture for the next nine weeks. Each week you should present the objectives for the individual week in relation to the whole term. At this time, students can discuss what they have already mastered and how they are going to accomplish their goals for the week. Keeping the learning experience on a positive note and in perspective with larger goals will not only help students learn to organize their time, but will enable them to see themselves progress. You will find that your teaching will be more organized and realistic.

The time spent in this type of meeting does take away from the reading or math periods, but you will find the time worthwhile as students go about the business of learning with a feeling that they are in control.

At the secondary level it is especially helpful for the troubled student to have a *written plan* covering the requirements for successful completion of his three- or four-year program. The courses, goals, and objectives for each term should be clearly stated and viewed as integral parts of the student's total educational and vocational preparation plan. This plan can be reviewed and updated as often as necessary by the student and his teacher or counselor so that the student retains a clear picture of his present status and where he is going with respect to his vocational and educational goals.

Problem-solving meetings. The problem-solving meeting is perhaps the most interesting and challenging of the three types of group meetings. Students learn to examine situations, propose solutions, and evaluate the results. The problem is stated simply and clearly; then the problem is clarified. The students select options and discuss the feasibility of their choices. Solutions are proposed and a plan of action is agreed on and carried out if possible. Students present their own ideas, listen to one another's reasoning, and work cooperatively to arrive at a solution.

The students begin to see, through these interactions, that there are not always definite rights and wrongs. Group choices involve give and take and much cooperation on the part of all concerned.

From this exercise, you and the students can move on to problem situations in the classroom, for example, where to go on a field trip when there is a gas shortage and a fifty-mile radius limit, how to get more equipment for the playground, or how to rearrange schedules.

Crisis meetings. The crisis meeting differs from the other two in that it is rarely planned; it is conducted whenever necessary. It can be held by two individuals, three individuals, or a group on the playground, in the classroom, or in the lunchroom. The rules for this meeting include the following:

1. All parties concerned must speak in soft tones—no shouting is permitted. A cooling-off time may be necessary before the parties can begin discussing the situation. Lowering your voice helps to quiet the students.

2. The first student expresses his feelings and states the problem situation *as he sees it.*

3. The other student (or students) is asked to repeat what he heard the first student say. This is an important step. Repeating what the other student said helps to take the edge off of any remaining anger.

4. Student number two then gives his side of the story and the first student repeats what he heard.

5. Now the situation is discussed at length. Could this situation have been avoided? How? What alternative behaviors might the students use in the future to avoid a similar situation? What should the consequences be for the students' irresponsible behavior? It is often quite effective to have the students determine the consequences. They are

usually very fair (and sometimes very hard on themselves).

These instant meetings can help a student realistically face his emotions and help him see more appropriate options and alternatives to the irresponsible ways in which he expressed his anger or hurt.

Magic Circle. Complete systems have been devised to help students develop self-esteem and the skills necessary for living a creative, responsible life.

One such system is the *Magic Circle*, developed by the Human Development Training Institute in La Mesa, California. It is a preventative program that can be used to help troubled students dispel the delusion of uniqueness—the delusion that they are very different from those around them. By talking and listening, students learn from one another that they have much in common. The program consists of specifically and developmentally programmed *topics* introduced by the teacher in daily twenty-minute sessions. During these sessions, students deal with negative and positive feelings and practice resolutions of conflict in an atmosphere of trust and acceptance. In planned stages, children learn how to express themselves meaningfully, to become confident in their abilities and to interact creatively and constructively with one another.

Through the Magic Circle you can foster an atmosphere of warmth and honesty in which each student contributes a part of himself and listens respectfully to his peers.

The program is based on the following three areas of human experience:

awareness knowing who he is, his own thoughts, feelings and actions. To own his own behavior, and his hurt and happy feelings.

mastery knowing his abilities and liabilities and how to utilize his abilities constructively and creatively.

social interaction knowing other people, how to be a friend, how to care for others.

The three work together to decrease a student's fear of facing everyday frustrations and give him confidence in dealing creatively with everyday situations. The program is developed through the ninth grade, complete with manuals and suggested supplementary activities that relate to the affective domain.

One note of caution with group meetings that deal with feelings and self-expression: keep the discussion from becoming a "show and tell all about family secrets" meeting. If a student blurts out in the group that his parents had a big fight last night or his dad came home drunk and beat up his mom, quietly express your concern and let him know you will talk about it with him at break or free time, as soon as possible. Care about the hurt the child is feeling and be supportive, not probing. Be certain to provide time that day for the student to talk with you alone.

THE USE OF CONTRACTS AND CONTRACTING

Contracts are a joint agreement between a student and teacher to accomplish a specific objective. The student and teacher may contract for a specific academic task or a desired behavior. Contracts may be drawn up to include most phases of school and home life. They involve a student and a teacher in a commitment to one another to relate realistically and responsibly. Contracts can be directed at a specific behavior or be more general in nature, that is, directed at improving a total relationship between a student and all school personnel in contact with him. Most importantly, the student must state that the behavior established in the contract is one that *he* feels the need to change and that the goal is one that *he* wants to achieve. One important factor if the contract is to be most effective is to be certain that the student is involved in deciding how it is going to work, that he feels it is fair, and that he makes a commitment to change his behavior.

Guidelines

Time. Contracts may be made for short periods of time (fifteen-minute segments), a class period, a school day, or an entire week. For the student who has difficulty disciplining himself, organizing his time and structuring his own activities, it would not be realistic or profitable to agree to a contract that was for an entire quarter. Smaller segments of time work best because the students may see success in a relatively short time.

Responsibility. The student is responsible for his contract, his behavior, and his acceptance of the consequences of that behavior. He cannot blame anyone else for his irresponsibility or accuse anyone of punishing him. He can take credit for his own positive behavior. The student is making the choice to complete or not complete an assignment, to behave responsibly or irresponsibly, and to accept the consequences of his choices, be they positive or negative.

Consequences. Consequences should be realistic and relevant to the situation. A student needs to know what to expect if he completes a task and what to expect if he chooses not to complete a task.

Types of contracts

The types of contracts to be considered here include the minicontract, the academic contract, the systematic suspension contract, and the in-school suspension contract. The minicontract is a short-term agreement directed at a specific behavior. The academic contract is a daily, weekly, or quarterly agreement for completion of specific academic assignments. The systematic suspension contract is an agreement between a student, his parents, and all school personnel directly involved with the student. It is aimed at changing a total relationship pattern. The in-school suspension contract is a similar agreement, except that the student is removed from the class situation as opposed to being removed from school entirely.

Minicontract. The minicontract is a short-term agreement drawn up by a student and teacher for the purpose of changing a specific behavior that both parties agree should be

MINICONTRACT

SHOP

_____FIND SEAT QUICKLY—*NO RUNNING AROUND*

_____LISTEN AND FOLLOW DIRECTIONS

_____HANDS OFF MATERIALS THAT ARE NOT FOR YOUR USE

_____STAY THE WHOLE PERIOD

STUDENT: _____

INSTRUCTOR: _____

MINICONTRACT

P. E.

_____LISTEN AND FOLLOW DIRECTIONS

_____PARTICIPATE IN ACTIVITIES

_____STAY THE WHOLE PERIOD

STUDENT: _____

INSTRUCTOR: _____

changed. Examples of such behaviors might include swearing, tardiness, incomplete assignments, kicking, or daydreaming. This type of contract is most effective if the student himself records his appropriate behaviors. You let him know you believe he is a responsible person capable of managing this contract with your support.

Academic contract. The academic contract may be drawn up for an individual student or for an entire class. If it is done for an individual student, the student and teacher should discuss the student's academic level in a specific academic area, his goal for the quarter (or semester), his goal for the week, and his daily goal. Weekly, the student and teacher should review what the student has accomplished that week in relation to his goal for the quarter.

The purpose of determining goals for all three time intervals is to permit the student to see realistically where he is in a given subject area, where he is going, and how he can, step-by-step, reach his goal. This is most important for a student who is behind in school. If he is three years behind in math at the be-

ginning of the semester and two and a half years behind at the end of the semester, without the step-by-step goals he might not be able to see any improvement. Without the short-term goals, he is just "still behind." With the goals, he is moving ahead.

Directions for use of weekly academic contracts. The teacher and student plan the activities in math (or any other subject) for the week. The specific assignments are written in the assignment column. There are several variations that could be used in this column.

1. *Green circles.* Write down the number of the problems a student is expected to complete. If a student chooses to do more problems, write the additional numbers down and circle these numbers in green. A student will often try to do more than what is expected of him, especially if the material is geared to his abilities. The problems circled in green serve as a message to the student's parents that the student did more than was assigned.

2. *Free day.* Write free day in one square. The student may use any math ma-

NO SWEARING CARD					
8:45-9:00	☺	☺	☺	☺	☺	
9:00-9:15		☺		☺	☺	
9:15-9:30	☺		☺	☺	☺	
9:30-9:45	☺	☺	☺		☺	
9:45-10:00	☺		☺	☺		
10:00-10:15		☺			☺	
10:15-10:30	☺	☺	☺	☺		
10:30-10:45				☺	☺	
10:45-11:00			☺	☺	☺	
11:00-11:15	☺	☺			☺	
	M	T	W	TH	F	

terials (or reading or language arts) that are available in the room or that he can bring from home. The only rule is that the student spend the entire period on the assignment of his choice.

3. *Listening day.* Some class activities do not require a written assignment. The student needs to learn to listen in an active, responsible manner. Discuss with the student the general rules for acceptable listening behavior during the class session. Write listening day in the appropriate assignment column.

The comments column is perhaps the most important and profitable part of the contract. It is a space for *positive* evaluation of a student's work habits and attitude, *not* his grades. At the end of each class, you should assess with the student his performance for that class period. Place a *smile face* or positive comment in this column.

If a student did not do well that day, *no* comment is placed in the column. If a negative comment is written, a student may become frustrated, tear the contract up, or refuse to continue with the plan. Accent the positive and put it in writing. Remember, this is not a grade report. It reflects work habits and attitudes. The slow learner and the underachieving student have a chance to be successful. Inform parents that they too can accent the positive and assume that a blank space indicates the student had a problem that day and that the problem was handled adequately at school. It need not be further elaborated at home.

The contract also contains space for writing

WEEKLY ACADEMIC CONTRACT

Contract

	DATE	ASSIGNMENT	COMMENTS
MATH	MONDAY		
	TUESDAY		
	WEDNESDAY		
	THURSDAY		
	FRIDAY		

CONSEQUENCES: _____

_____

_____

_____

_____

STUDENT: _____

TEACHER: _____

DATES: _____

ADDITIONAL COMMENTS:

consequences. These consequences should be stated positively if at all possible. This should be a joint effort by the student and teacher, in determining relevant consequences.

The student and teacher sign the contract on the indicated lines. The signing respects the integrity of the student and teacher and establishes a written commitment on the part of both parties.

Once the contract is signed, the two parties agree to be responsible for it. This can often be more difficult for the teacher than the student. For example:

Johnny draws during math period. You remind him of the contract (do not nag—just remind and offer him your help). You and he agreed to the consequences beforehand. Math class is over and his math is not completed. It is a beautiful day, and his friends are getting up a basketball game. He comes up to you with crocodile tears and begs, "Please let me go out today, I promise to do my math tomorrow." If you let him go out, you are doing the student an injustice. An appropriate response would be, "We agreed to the contract, and I want to help you be responsible. Today you chose not to complete your math during the class period, and the consequence of your choice is to stay in and complete your math during break." Then, walk away; do not argue with him. It was his choice. You are not punishing him. You offered your help; you reminded him of the contract; and now you must let him accept the consequences of his own behavior.

If you really care and the student knows this, he will respect you for your resistance to his pleading or arguments. He will also move one step toward being a more responsible individual.

If you give in to the tears today, the student may indeed get his work done tomorrow. However, the next time he feels like not working, he will again pull his tear game, hoping you will give in to him and allow him to be irresponsible. He does not grow. At best, he refines his game, enabling him to more easily manipulate and control you.

You can also "dress up" the contract with cartoons or write legal terms in it. Examples of such contracts are shown on pp. 214 to 218.

Systematic suspension. The systematic suspension contract is a plan to send a troubled student home on any day that he is not able to conform to a set of standards previously agreed on by the teacher, pupil, and parents (Chapman, 1962). The student is suspended immediately on violation of any term of the contract but may return to class the next day and remain as long as he controls his behavior. It requires full cooperation by parents, teachers, principal, and counselor to be an effective behavior management tool. If the parents are reluctant, systematic suspension may be presented to them as a possible solution along with permanent exclusion and residential placement.

Systematic suspension is used as a last resort, after the usual methods of behavior management have failed. It is not a substitute for these methods but is used when the usual approach has not been successful. It is a therapeutic tool to help with discipline and control.

Chapman (1962) has provided specific procedures to be used in systematic suspension.

The contract on pp. 219 to 220 illustrates the procedures to be followed in systematic suspension.

In-school suspension. Some school systems, confronted with tougher regulations with regard to suspension and exclusion, and recognizing the need for a step before implementation of either of the two, have instituted in-school suspension. For violations formerly resulting in, for example, three-day suspension, students are sent to the suspension room (often referred to as the "think tank" or "slammer") to spend the entire day in isolation. Regulations vary from elemen-

Text continued on p. 221.

Contract

Subject	MONDAY	TUESDAY	WEDNESDAY	THURSDAY	FRIDAY
MATH					
READING					
SPELLING					
P. E.					

IF ALL ASSIGNMENTS ARE COMPLETED EACH DAY I MAY

_____

IF ALL ASSIGNMENTS FOR THE WEEK ARE COMPLETED I MAY

_____

IF I DO NOT COMPLETE AN ASSIGNMENT DURING THE ALLOTTED TIME I WILL

_____

STUDENT: _____

TEACHER: _____

DATE: _____

COMPLETED ASSIGNMENTS:

Reading baseball

SCORE BY COMPLETING THE FOLLOWING TASKS:

2nd
base _____

3rd
base _____

1st
base _____

Home
run! _____

AS A VICTORY CELEBRATION I WILL _____

_____

_____

_____

_____

_____

BATTER: _____   PITCHER: _____

DATE: _____

Math football

TO REACH YOUR GOAL COMPLETE THE FOLLOWING TASKS:

50 Yd. _____ 50 Yd.

40 Yd. _____ 40 Yd.

30 Yd. _____ 30 Yd.

20 Yd. _____ 20 Yd.

10 Yd. _____ 10 Yd.

GOAL _____ GOAL

TOUCHDOWN!

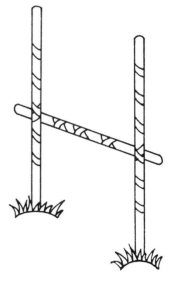

AFTER EACH 10 YARD GAIN I WILL _____

_____

AS A VICTORY CELEBRATION I WILL _____

_____

FAILURE ON MY PART TO COMPLETE ANY OF THE YARDS GAINED WILL RESULT IN

_____

DATE: _____ PLAYER: _____

COACH: _____

Responsibility contract

The undersigned _____ hereby agrees to undertake the following *responsibility:*

_____

_____

_____

_____

for which he shall receive upon successful completion of his responsibility certain *privileges,* stated below:

1. _____

_____

_____

_____

2. _____

_____

_____

_____

3. _____

_____

_____

_____

Failure to comply with said contract shall result in the revocation of said privileges.

This contract shall be binding for the week of _____

DATE SIGNED: _____ STUDENT: _____

RENEGOTIATION DATE: _____ TEACHER: _____

Performance contract

STUDENT _____ TEACHER _____

CLASS _____ PERIOD _____ CREDITS _____

BASIC OBJECTIVES FOR THE COURSE:

    1. _____

    2. _____

    3. _____

    4. _____

ASSIGNMENTS TO BE SUCCESSFULLY COMPLETED IN ORDER TO RECEIVE CREDIT
FOR THE COURSE: (OR FOR THE WEEK, MONTH, ETC.)

    1. _____

    2. _____

    3. _____

    4. _____

    5. _____

BEHAVIORAL OBJECTIVES (LIST SPECIFIC BEHAVIORS NECESSARY FOR SUCCESSFUL
COMPLETION OF THE COURSE):

    1. Attend class _____

    2. Bring materials _____

    3. Other behaviors unique to a student's situation _____

STUDENT CONTRACT FOR A GRADE (IF APPLICABLE):

    I understand the requirements for the course and plan to meet
    the requirements necessary to receive a _____for_____
                      (grade)   (credits)

_____   _____

        Date   Signature of student

Systematic suspension contract

PARTICIPANTS

1. _____ (student)

2. _____ (principal)

3. _____ (counselor)

4. _____ (teacher)

5. _____ (parent)

6. _____ (parent)

7. _____ (teacher)

8. _____ (teacher)

GENERAL RULE

On violation of any stated limit STUDENT will be sent from the classroom to the counseling office. His parents will be called and STUDENT will be sent home for the remainder of the day.

LIMITS

1. Not being in attendance at every class to which STUDENT is assigned is a violation.

2. Kicking, hitting, biting, pinching, poking, shoving, jabbing, or tripping any other person is a violation.

3. Add additional limits as needed: _____

_____

RESPONSIBILITIES

1. Student: STUDENT agrees that he is fully responsible for himself and that everything he does or does not do is done or not done by his own choice. He agrees to take credit for his failure, as well as his success, regardless of how people treat him.

2. Teacher: On detection of a violation the teacher will send STUDENT to the counseling

Continued.

SYSTEMATIC SUSPENSION CONTRACT—cont'd

RESPONSIBILITIES—cont'd

office. The teacher will on no occasion try to influence him to do or not do anything (no urging, reminding, coaxing, encouraging, or scolding). The teacher agrees to respect the pupil's right to fail or succeed on his own and to acknowledge that he is not responsible for the success or failure of this pupil.

3. Counselor: On notification of any violation, the counseling office will receive STUDENT and call his parents. The counselor agrees not to discuss with STUDENT in any way his behavior (there will be no persuasion, encouragement, reminders, or scolding).

4. Parents: On being called by the counseling office, Mr. and Mrs. PARENT agree to pick up STUDENT and remove him from the school for the remainder of the day. The parents agree not to discuss with STUDENT in any way his behavior (there will be no scolding, persuasion, encouragement, reminders, or urging). The parents agree to keep the counseling office informed as to where they can be reached at all times during the school day. STUDENT must stay at home during the time school is in session but after school is over, can do whatever he usually does after school.

5. Principal: The principal agrees to the content of this contract and will enforce it in all regards.

PROMISE OF THE SCHOOL

1. To allow STUDENT freedom to choose to be a responsible student.
2. To issue to STUDENT a weekly pass that allows him to come to the counseling office on request by him.
3. To allow STUDENT to choose which activity he will pursue during his daily independent-study period.
4. To encourage the other students to facilitate STUDENT in fulfilling the requirements of this contract by supporting his responsible actions.

In witness whereof, this agreement is signed and sealed by the following:

STUDENT: _____   PARENT: _____

PRINCIPAL: _____   PARENT: _____

COUNSELOR: _____   TEACHER: _____

TEACHER: _____   TEACHER: _____

DATE: _____

tary school to high school, district to district, but the results appear to be the same—a reduction in repeaters and irresponsible behavior. The key, again, is that the student knows in advance that by behaving irresponsibly, he is choosing a day in the "think tank".

In-school suspension must be approved by the school board, and some sort of arrangement must be established whereby parents or guardians indicate in writing that they accept this procedure as a substitute for out-of-school (regular) suspension. A contract similar in many ways to that for systematic suspension may be drawn up. After such legal and administrative arrangements are formalized, the practice seems to hold much promise as an alternative to traditional suspension.

GENERAL GUIDELINES AND SUGGESTIONS

When working with a troubled child in the classroom, it is your attitude that counts most; whatever you do for or with the child reflects your attitude. Do not let an opportunity to care and to show your concern for him go by. If you do not do it, it may never be done.

Be friendly, smile, notice him in a positive way

Point out his successes

Point out his good points to him and to his peers

Encourage him

Call on him

Teach him a skill he can be proud to share with others

Plan activities in which he can succeed

The following are some basic techniques that can help in managing misbehavior in the regular classroom. This not meant to imply that they will be the "answer" to your problem. They are techniques I have found to be helpful in the classroom.

1. Stop misbehavior in time. Do not wait until the situation is totally out of hand before stopping it. Stop the act before you become angry and lose control or before the whole class gets into the act.

2. Program for a variety of changes. Activities with a great deal of manual emphasis are more likely to succeed than heavy doses of desk work.

3. Make tasks clear and orderly and give the student time to complete one task before beginning another. A troubled student needs to know what is expected of him in an activity. He needs closure on one activity before he can freely and without frustration move onto a new task. Insist that the student complete an activity. Be sure that the task is on the student's ability level and that he understands the directions.

4. Comment positively when the student is attending appropriately to a task. Let him know you know he is working constructively. Praise him. Smile.

5. Establish limits and maintain consistent, clear ground rules. This structure gives the student the necessary backbone to function successfully in the class. He needs to know what is appropriate or inappropriate. He needs to know what the consequences of his behavior will be. Be consistent in following through with legitimate consequences. Threats and bribes will not work.

6. Manage transitional times with quieting-down periods between two activities. Take the time to allow a student to slow down from one activity, such as physical education, to be ready for another activity, such as reading.

7. Set up filler corners, activity centers a student can go to when he has com-

pleted required activities. These can be media corners or game corners.

8. Set up a quiet corner where a student can go to be alone, to cry, or to calm down. The corner should not be used for punishment; rather it should be a place to gain control. If a student needs to be sent to the quiet corner, send him calmly and quickly. He is to stay in the corner until *he* feels able to return and behave responsibly. Do not set a time limit. Let the student decide when *he* is in control of feelings and behavior.

9. Plan for anger breaks; give a distraught, anxious, or angry student a chance to swim laps in a pool, run laps around a track, beat pillows, hit a punching bag, throw bean bags at a wall, pedal an exercise bike, jump rope, or pound clay. Follow this anger break by providing activities that trigger a heavy dose of laughter; then, arrange for a quiet period.

10. Provide success; be sure the material is relevant, interesting, and appropriate for the student.

Steps that are *inappropriate* for helping a troubled student include the following:

1. Using brute force: "You hit me, I'll hit you back!"
2. Accusing the student of misbehaving. You are, in a sense, forcing the student to lie to save face.
3. Comparing the student's behavior with that of his peers.
4. Arguing—you cannot win an argument with a student. Usually, you both lose.
5. Embarrassing the student in front of his peers.
6. Removing the student from activities he does well and enjoys doing.
7. Ridiculing the student for his mistakes or misbehavior.

Most of the preceding suggestions and guidelines are simple, applied common sense. All teachers might do better in dealing with troubled students were it not for the fact that teachers are human too and can become angry and lose their perspective. With thirty or more students in a class, with emphasis on academic standards, and with societal pressure to "remain in control of the schools," it is easy and natural to say and do what is precisely the wrong thing. Thinking through problems and alternatives in advance, as suggested here, may help to save the day for the teacher and for the troubled child.

As you consider and implement various plans or systems, you must recognize that students can continue to say no to being responsible—the choice is theirs. The teacher can not *make* them behave responsibly. If all of the resources of a school or school district have been tried and none of them have been effective or adequate, you must recognize that certain troubled students need help beyond that which can be provided in a public school setting.

In a responsibility-oriented classroom the structure and rules are simple, reasonable, and defined; consequences for appropriate and inappropriate behaviors are realistic, logical, and natural. Students learn to label, accept, and express feelings appropriately. The students themselves also play an important role in their own educational programming.

A responsibility-oriented classroom is neither a teacher-dominated nor student-controlled room. Rather, it is a joint effort to learn, relate, and experience.

ROLE OF THE SPECIAL EDUCATION/RESOURCE PERSONNEL

Owing to the scarcity of treatment facilities and adequate programs, most of the seriously troubled students in the United States remain in regular classrooms. School administrators and resource personnel are becoming more aware that to help this growing number of students effectively, they must, for the most part, change their emphasis from helping individual students to helping regular classroom teachers work with these students in their classrooms. The role and responsibility of the resource personnel will vary greatly, depending on the age or grade level of the troubled students served, number of teachers or buildings served by the resource person, and the local school district policy concerning specific responsibilities.

One variety of resource service sometimes provided is the *crisis* or *helping teacher*. The crisis or helping teacher provides temporary support and control to troubled students when the students are unable or unwilling to cope with the demands of the regular classroom. The type of service the crisis teacher provides requires that she be available at the time of the crisis. Working closely with the regular classroom teachers, she provides support, reassurance, and behavioral management strategies. Troubled students come and go on either a regular or an episodic basis, depending on the needs of the individual student. When the resource teacher is not dealing with a crisis, she can be helping less troubled students academically and behaviorally. She can make referrals to supportive services, provide the needed intensive assistance for the more severely troubled students, and follow up on specific recommendations. She becomes an active partner with the teacher, mental health personnel, and parents in helping this student.

Cooperation

The key to a successful learning program for the troubled student is the cooperative working arrangement between regular classroom teachers, resource persons, and support services. The regular classroom teacher should feel free to ask for help and not feel that she has failed because she has been unable to deal effectively with a troubled student. Often, the resource person can observe situations in the classroom objectively and help the classroom teacher see "games" or unhealthy transactions occurring between the teacher and student. The resource person and the teacher can jointly plan behavioral strategies and modify educational materials to fit the unique needs and abilities of the student.

Orientation/in-service education

Resource teachers play an important role in the in-service education (formal and informal) of regular classroom teachers. In-service education can range from an overview of student growth and motivation to more specific behavior management techniques. Resource teachers may offer workshops on contracting, group meetings, behavior management, and parent education.

It is important that the resource teacher make herself visible to the regular classroom teachers with whom she works and readily available to help and support them.

Demonstration teaching

The resource teacher can help set up group meetings in a classroom, lead the initial meeting, and help the regular classroom teacher plan follow-up meetings. She can also take small groups of students from the class and work with them on self-concept development through the use of games, dialogues, and role-playing. Working in the regular classroom, she can organize her groups to include children with various behavioral abilities and liabilities. By nature of her training, the resource teacher may demonstrate new materials or those that are unfamiliar to the regular teacher.

Modify, adapt, and procure materials

The resource teacher can help the regular classroom teacher develop contracts, glad notes, and relevant consequences for the troubled child. She can also work closely with several teachers who may be teaching the same child to ensure that the contracts and consequences will be consistent throughout the day.

Assignments often need to be restructured and defined clearly for the troubled student. The resource teacher can present academic materials to the student in a nonthreatening way, offering him a successful learning experience that can be carried over into the regular class. A student needs to learn that he can learn—that school can be a positive experience.

Serve as a liaison between mental health personnel, parents, administrators, community agencies, and the regular classroom teacher

The resource teacher generally has a good understanding of behavioral deviance, delinquency, and therapeutic techniques for the troubled student. She can serve as a communication link between the psychologist or mental health therapist, the regular classroom teacher, and the parents. In addition, she could serve as a liaison between social services agencies, juvenile authorities, and the public school. She can translate the recommendations from these agencies into workable educational strategies. She will be responsible for following up and evaluating the implementation of these strategies.

Counseling

The resource teacher may assist the regular classroom teachers in counseling the troubled student and his family. She can also attempt to help parents and the troubled student to relate more effectively with one another.

SUMMARY

Troubled students offer a frustrating but potentially rewarding challenge to teachers.

Their behaviors are extreme; they cry too easily, are too worried, and are too angry. It is the unusual frequency or intensity of these behaviors that signal the need for help. A troubled student's deviant behavior can result from forces within himself or from forces in his environment, including his interaction with "significant others" in his life. Forces within the student can be either physiological or psychological. Environmental factors include extreme poverty, racial discrimination, deteriorating family units, and school pressures, such as unrealistic academic requirements, rigid rules, unreasonable teacher expectations, and exaggerated emphasis on grades. A student who is identified as troubled because of his deviant behaviors may simply be defending himself against damaging environmental pressures.

Once a student is identified as being in need of assistance beyond that which can be provided in the regular classroom, he should be referred to the resource person or school psychologist for an in-depth evaluation. Following the evaluation, a staffing team should review the pertinent information available and make recommendations concerning educational programming and placement. There are a number of positive steps the teacher can take to make the situation creative and constructive for both the troubled student and teacher. Many of these can be effectively implemented within a responsibility-oriented classroom.

A responsibility-oriented classroom is a setting in which students and teacher work cooperatively, sharing educational responsibilities. The student is responsible for his own behavior, academic success, and failures. Realistic consequences are established and carried out. Feelings are labeled, appropriate ways of expressing them are explored and actively encouraged. More than structure, rules, and academia must be conveyed by the regular classroom teacher; she must convey trust and belief in each student. An integral part of the responsibility-oriented class is the group meeting. It fosters student involvement and initiative in learning. Three types of meetings, the academic planning meeting, the problem-solving meeting, and the crisis meeting, have demonstrated merit in practice.

The use of contracts is also an important part of the responsibility-oriented classroom. They involve the student and the teacher in a commitment to one another to relate realistically and responsibly.

Owing to the scarcity of treatment facilities and adequate programs, most troubled students remain in the regular classroom. It is the role of the resource person to provide support, reassurance, and behavioral management strategies to help the regular classroom teacher effectively work with the troubled student.

The troubled student needs a safe place where he can be himself, learn to know himself, and take important, frightening steps toward an *OK* life position. A *safe* classroom atmosphere in which, with peer and teacher support, the troubled student can relate more realistically, responsibly, and constructively to his environment should be the goal of education.

REFERENCES AND SUGGESTED READINGS

Alschuler, A., and Shea, J. The discipline game: playing without losers. *Learning*, 1974, 3(1), 80-90.

Axline, V. *Play therapy*. Boston: Houghton Mifflin Co., 1947.

Axline, V. *Dibs: in search of self*. Boston: Houghton-Mifflin Company, 1964.

Bettleheim, B. *Love is not enough*. New York: The Free Press, 1949.

Blanco, R. *Prescriptions for children with learning and adjustive problems*. Springfield, Ill.: Charles C Thomas, Publisher, 1972.

Bower, E. M. The emotionally handicapped child and the school: an analysis of programs and trends. *Exceptional Children*, 1959, 26, 182-188.

Bower, E. M. *Early identification of emotionally handicapped children in school*. Springfield, Ill.: Charles C Thomas, Publisher, 1969.

Bower, E. M., & Lambert, N. M. *Teachers manual for in-school screening of emotionally handicapped children*. Princeton, N.J.: Educational Testing Service, 1961.

Chapman, A. H. *The games children play*. New York: Berkley Medallion Books, 1971.

Chapman, R. W. School suspension as therapy, *Personnel and Guidance Journal*, 1962, 40, 731-732.

Clark, D., & Lesser, G. *Emotional disturbance and school learning: a book of readings*. Chicago: Science Research Associates, Inc., 1965.

Cleaver, E. *Soul on Ice*. New York: McGraw-Hill Book Co., 1968.

Dee, V. Contingency management in a crisis class. *Exceptional Children*, 1972, 38, 631-634.

Dispert, L. *The emotionally disturbed child: an inquiry into family patterns*. Garden City, N.Y.: Anchor Books, 1965.

Dreikurs, R., Grunwald, B., & Pepper, F. *Maintaining sanity in the classroom: illustrated teaching techniques*. New York: Harper & Row, Publishers, 1971.

Ellis, D., & Miller, L. Teachers' attitudes and child behavior problems. *Journal of Educational Psychology*, 1936, 27, 501-511.

Farber, J. *The student as nigger* (2nd ed.). New York: Pocket Books, 1970.

Fargo, G., Behrns, C., & Nolen, R. *Behavior modification in the classroom*. Belmont, Calif.: Wadsworth Publishing Co., Inc., 1970.

Feder, B. Resolving classroom tensions: a group approach. *Psychology in the School*, 1967, 4, 36-39.

Freed, A. *T.A. for tots*. Los Angeles, Calif.: Price/Stern/Sloan Publishers, Inc., 1974.

Gearheart, B. *Learning Disabilities: Educational Strategies* (2nd ed.). St. Louis: The C. V. Mosby Co., 1977.

Glasser, W. *Reality therapy*. New York: Harper & Row, Publishers, Inc., 1965.

Glasser, W. *Schools without failure*. New York: Harper & Row, Publishers, 1969.

Glavin, J., Quay, H., Annesley, F., & Werry, J. An experimental resource room for behavior problem children. *Exceptional Children*, 1971, 38, 131-137.

Glidewell, J. *Parental attitudes and child behavior*. Springfield, Ill.: Charles C Thomas, Publisher, 1961.

Gordon, T., & Burch, N. *T.E.T. Teacher Effectiveness Training*. New York: Peter H. Wyden/Publisher, 1974.

Gullotta, T. Teacher attitudes toward the moderately disturbed child. *Exceptional Children*, 1974, 41, 49-50.

Haring, N., & Phillips, E. *Educating emotionally dis-*

turbed children. New York: McGraw-Hill Book Co., 1962.

Harshman, H. (Ed.). *Educating the emotionally disturbed: a book of readings.* New York: Thomas Y. Crowell Company, Inc., 1969.

Hentoff, N. *Our children are dying.* New York: The Viking Press, Inc., 1966.

Hewett, F. *The emotionally disturbed child in the classroom.* Boston: Allyn & Bacon, Inc., 1968.

Hirshberg, J. C. The role of education in the treatment of emotionally disturbed children through planned ego development. *American Journal of Orthopsychiatry,* 1953, *23*, 684-690.

Homme, L. *How to use contingency contracting in the classroom.* Champaign Ill.: Research Press, 1970.

Johnson, O. G. The teacher and the withdrawn child. *Mental Hygiene,* 1956, *40*, 529-534.

Kirk, S., & Weiner, B. (Eds.). *Behavioral research on exceptional children.* Washington, D.C.: Council For Exceptional Children, 1963.

Kounin, J., Friesen, W., & Norton, A. Managing emotionally disturbed children in regular classrooms. *Journal of Educational Psychology,* 1966, 57(1), 1-13.

Krasner, L., & Ullman, L. P. *Research in behavior modification.* New York: Holt, Rinehart and Winston, Inc., 1965.

Lindsley, O. Precision teaching in perspective: an interview with Ogden R. Lindsley. *Teaching Exceptional Children,* Spring, 1971, 3(3), 111-119.

Long, N., Morse, W., & Newman, R. (Eds.). *Conflict in the classroom.* Belmont, Calif.: Wadsworth Publishing Co., Inc., 1971.

Lovin, G., and Simmons, J. Response to praise by emotionally disturbed boys. *Psychological Reports,* 1962, *11*, 10.

MacMillan, D. *Behavior modification in education.* New York: Macmillan, Inc., 1973.

Madsen, C., Becker, W., & Thomas, D. Rules, praise and ignoring: elements of elementary school control. *Journal of Applied Behavior Analysis,* 1968, *1*, 139-150.

Maes, W. The identification of emotionally disturbed children. *Exceptional Children,* 1966, *32*, 607-613.

Morse, W. C. The crisis teacher: public school provisions for the disturbed pupil. University of Michigan, *School of Education Bulletin,* 1962, 37, 101-104.

Moustakas, C. E. *Children in play therapy.* New York: McGraw-Hill Book Co., 1953.

Moustakas, C. E. *The teacher and the child.* New York: McGraw-Hill Book Company, 1956.

Nelson, C. Techniques for screening conduct disturbed children. *Exceptional Children,* 1971, 37, 501-507.

Newman, R. G., & Keith, M. M. *The schoolcentered life space interview.* Washington, D.C.: School Research Program, Washington School of Psychiatry, 1967.

Patterson, G. R., & Gullion, M. *Living with children: new methods for parents and teachers.* Champaign, Ill.: Research Press, 1968.

Pearson, G. H. J. *Emotional disorders of children.* New York: W. W. Norton & Co., Inc., 1954.

Peter L. *Prescriptive teaching.* New York: McGraw-Hill Book Co., 1965.

Powers, H. Dietary measures to improve behavior and achievement. *Academic Therapy,* 1973-1974, *9,* 203-214.

Quay, H. C., & Peterson, D. R. *Manual for the behavior problem checklist.* Champaign, Ill.: Children's Research Center, University of Illinois, 1967.

Redl, F. The concept of a therapeutic milieu. *American Journal of Orthopsychiatry,* 1959a, *29,* 721-734.

Redl, F. The life space interview. *American Journal of Orthopsychiatry,* January 1959b, *29,* 1-18.

Reinert, H. R. *Children in conflict: educational strategies.* St. Louis: The C. V. Mosby Co., 1976.

Rogers, C. R. *Client-centered therapy.* Boston: Houghton Mifflin Co., 1951.

Slavson, S. *Re-educating the delinquent through group and community participation.* New York: Harper & Row, Publishers, 1954.

Spivack, G., & Swift, M. *Devereux elementary school behavior rating scale manual.* Devon, Pa.: Devereux Foundation, 1967.

Spivack, G., & Swift, M. The classroom behavior of children: a critical review of teacher-administered rating scales. *Journal of Special Education,* 1973, *7,* 55-89.

Swift, M., & Spivack, G. *Hahnemann high school behavior rating manual.* Philadelphia: Departmental Health Sciences, Hahnemann Medical College and Hospital, 1972.

Szasz, T. *The myth of mental illness: foundation of a theory of personal conduct.* New York: Harper & Row, Publishers, 1961.

Tallman, I., & Leving, S. The emotionally disturbed child in the classroom situation. *Exceptional Children,* 1960, *27,* 114-126.

Vinter, R., Saari, R., Vorwaller, D., & Schafer, W. *Pupil behavior inventory.* Ann Arbor, Mich.: Campus Publishers, 1966.

Walker, H. *Walker problem behavior checklist manual.* Los Angeles: Western Psychological Services, 1970.

Walker, H., & Buckley, N. *Modifying classroom behavior: a manual of procedures for classroom teachers.* Champaign, Ill.: Research Press, 1970.

Whelan, R., & Haring, N. "Modification and maintenance of behavior through systematic application of consequences. *Exceptional Children*, 1966, 32, 281-289.

Woody, R. *Behavior problem children in the schools.* New York: Appleton-Century-Crofts, 1969.

Zax, M., & Cowen, E. Early identification and prevention of emotional disturbance in a public school. In Cowen, E., Gardner, E., & Zax, M. (Eds.). *Emergent approaches to mental health problems.* New York: Appleton-Century-Crofts, 1967.

10 THE IMPORTANCE OF GOOD PERSONAL INTERACTION (OR WHAT IT'S REALLY ALL ABOUT)

From Marsh, G. B., Gearheart, C. K., and Gearheart, B. R.: The learning disabled adolescent, St. Louis, 1978, The C. V. Mosby Co.

September, 19 (whatever)
Public Schoolsville, U.S.A.

Dear Teacher,

We want to tell you about several teachers in your school who have come to our attention. We would like to ask your help in changing some of these professionals who work just down the hall from you. We know you are busy, but the actions of these teachers have such devastating effects on students we are sure you will want to help. Please read through the following vignettes and anecdotes and see if you recognize members of your professional staff. If you do, please help them, for their own sake and for the sake of the children in your school.

Our sincere appreciation,
BILL GEARHEART and MEL WEISHAHN

PAIN IN SCHOOL IS having an indifferent teacher*

My unhappy experience was when I was—well—just last year. I worked on a project for about two weeks 'cause my parents didn't think I was doing enough extra projects for school. So, they wanted me to do one. So I did it. Then, when I brought it to school (these were the last few days) my teacher told me that—well—she didn't really tell me—but she didn't pay very much attention to my project. I made a map. And it just sat in the back of the room for a few days and I finally brought it home. I never got a grade on it, or anything.

PAIN IN SCHOOL IS learning to feel embarrassed*

While in the second grade a question was asked and I raised my hand with much anticipation because I knew the answer and I was the only one who had any idea of the correct answer.

I was wrong and the teacher proceeded to tell me how dumb I was to think that I could do better than her more well-versed students. This tirade went on for about ten minutes while she told me to go to the head of the class and talk about why I had made such a "stupid" answer. At the end of this she told me my zipper was down which gave me much more embarrassment.

PAIN IN SCHOOL IS traveling a lonely road with a hurt that takes many years to heal*

"I am sure you will be better off in the service. The service can teach you a trade. Maybe you can finish high school while in the service."

Seventeen years old and my world had just completely collapsed around me. I had just been told by my counselor that I would be better off in the service than in school.

He was polite, very sympathetic but he was still saying "Sorry, boy, you are too dumb for school!" Even today I would like to tell him to stick his advice in his ear! My work in school had not been good, but I felt much of that was due to the fact that I did more playing than studying.

When I left school that day I wondered what I would tell my parents. What could I tell myself? How could I fight a gnawing, cancerous emo-

*From Schultz, E., Heuchert, C., and Stampf, S. *Pain & Joy in School*. Champaign, Ill.: Research Press, 1973. Used with permission.

*From Schultz, E., Heuchert, C., and Stampf, S. *Pain & Joy in School*. Champaign, Ill.: Research Press, 1973. Used with permission.

tion of worthlessness? I wondered how I could face my buddies. I remember having an overwhelming urge to run, to hide, to get away. But, where does a seventeen-year-old boy hide? The only hiding place I could find was the service. That day, I enlisted in the Navy before I went home. There was only one paper to be signed before I left for the service, that was a parental permission paper for men under eighteen years of age —they signed!

The hurt I felt that day almost twelve years ago has actually helped me today. When I am working with a boy who is called stupid, can't read, maybe he feels like he isn't worth much. I can go a little further than just sympathizing with him, I can feel what he feels. . .

Some refer to such feeling as sensitivity. Call it what you will, but I can simply tell my students to "move over, brother, you have company. I've been down this road before once by myself. It's a lonely road, let me travel with you."

I TAUGHT THEM ALL*
Naomi J. White

I have taught in high school for ten years. During that time I have given assignments, among others, to a murderer, an evangelist, a pugilist, a thief, and an imbecile.

The murderer was a quiet little boy who sat on the front seat and regarded me with pale blue eyes; the evangelist, easily the most popular boy in school, had the lead in the junior play; the pugilist lounged by the window and let loose at intervals a raucous laugh that startled even the geraniums; the thief was a gay-hearted Lothario with a song on his lips; and the imbecile, a soft-eyed little animal seeking the shadows.

The murderer awaits death in the state penitentiary; the evangelist has lain a year now in the village churchyard; the pugilist lost an eye in a brawl in Hong Kong; the thief, by standing on tiptoe, can see the windows of my room from the county jail; and the once gentle-eyed little moron beats his head against a padded wall in the state asylum.

All of these pupils once sat in my room, sat and

*From *The Clearing House*, November 1937. Used with permission.

looked at me gravely across worn brown desks. I must have been a great help to these pupils—I taught them the rhyming scheme of the Elizabethan sonnet and how to diagram a complex sentence.

ABOUT SCHOOL

This poem was handed to a high school English teacher the day before the writer committed suicide. Original source unknown.

He always wanted to explain things,
  but no one cared.
So he drew.

Sometimes he would just draw
  and it wasn't anything.
He wanted to carve it in stone
  or write it in the sky
  and the things inside him that needed saying.

And it was after that that he drew the picture.
It was a beautiful picture.
He kept it under his pillow
  and would let no one see it.
And he would look at it every night
  and think about it.
And it was all of him and he loved it.

When he started school he brought it with him.
Not to show anyone, but just to have it with him
  like a friend.

It was funny about school.
He sat in a square brown desk
  like all the other square brown desks
  and he thought it would be red.
And his room was a square brown room
  like all the other rooms.
And it was tight and close. And stiff.

He hated to hold the pencil and chalk,
  with his arm stiff and his feet flat on the floor, stiff,
  with the teacher watching and watching.

The teacher came and spoke to him.
She told him to wear a tie like all the other boys.
He said he didn't like them
  and she said it didn't matter.
After that he drew. And he drew all yellow
  and it was the way he felt about morning.
And it was beautiful.

The teacher came and smiled at him.
"What's this?" she said.
"Why don't you draw something
    like Ken's drawing?
Isn't it beautiful?"
After that his mother bought him a tie
    and he always drew airplanes and rockets
    like everyone else.

And he threw the old picture away.
And when he lay out alone looking at the sky,
    it was big and blue, and all of everything,
    but he wasn't anymore.
He was square and brown inside
    and his hands were stiff.
And he was like everyone else.
All the things inside him that needed saying
    didn't need it anymore.

It had stopped pushing. It was crushed.
Stiff.
Like everything else.

THE POOR SCHOLAR'S SOLILOQUY*

No, I'm not very good in school. This is my
second year in the seventh grade and I'm bigger
and taller than the other kids. They like me alright
though even if I don't say much in the classroom
because outside I can tell them how to do a lot of
things. They tag me around and that sort of makes
up for what goes on in school.

I don't know why the teachers don't like me.
They never have very much. Seems like they
don't think you know anything unless you can
name the book it comes out of. I've got a lot of
books in my room at home—books like *Popular
Science Mechanical Encyclopedia*, and the Sears'
and Ward's catalogues—but I don't very often just
sit down and read them through like they make
us do in school. I use my books when I want to
find something out, like whenever Mom buys anything secondhand I look it up in Sears' or Ward's
first and tell her if she's getting stung or not. I can
use the index in a hurry.

In school though we've got to learn whatever is
in the book and I just can't memorize the stuff.
Last year I stayed after school every night for two

weeks trying to learn the names of the Presidents.
Of course, I knew some of them like Washington and Jefferson and Lincoln, but there must
have been thirty altogether, and I never did get
them straight.

I'm not too sorry though because the kids who
learned the Presidents had to turn right around
and learn all the Vice Presidents. I am taking the
seventh grade over but our teacher this year isn't
so interested in the names of the Presidents. She
has us trying to learn the names of all the great
American inventors.

I guess I just can't remember names in history.
Anyway, this year I've been trying to learn about
trucks because my uncle owns three and he says I
can drive one when I'm sixteen. I already know
the horsepower and number of forward and back-
ward speeds of 26 American trucks, some of them
Diesels and I can spot each make a long way off.
It's funny how that Diesel works. I started to tell
my teacher all about it last Wednesday in science
class when the pump we were using to make a
vacuum in a bell jar got hot but she said she didn't
see what a Diesel engine had to do with our experiment on air pressure so I just kept still. The
kids seemed interested though. I took four of
them around to my uncle's garage after school and
we saw the mechanic, Gus, tear a big truck Diesel
down. Boy, does he know his stuff!

I'm not very good in geography either. They
call it economic geography this year. We've been
studying the imports and exports of Chile all
week, but I couldn't tell you what they are. Maybe
the reason is I had to miss school yesterday because my uncle took me and his big trailer truck
down state about 200 miles and we brought almost 10 tons of stock to the Chicago market.

He had told me where we were going, and I
had to figure out the highways to take and also the
mileage. He didn't do anything but drive and turn
where I told him to. Was that fun! I sat with a
map in my lap and told him to turn south, or
south-east or some other direction. We made 7
stops, and drove over 500 miles round trip. I'm
figuring now what his oil cost and also the wear
and tear on the truck—he calls it depreciation—
so we'll know how much we made.

I even write out all the bills and send letters to
the farmers about what their pigs and beef cattle

---

*From *Childhood Education*, January 1944. Used with
permission.

brought at the stockyards. I only made three mistakes in 17 letters last time, my aunt said, all commas. She's been through high school and reads them over. I wish I could write school themes that way. The last one I had to write was on "What a Daffodil Thinks of Spring," and I just couldn't get going.

I don't do very well in school arithmetic either. Seems I just can't keep my mind on the problems. We had one the other day like this:

"If a 57 ft. telephone pole falls across a cement highway so that 17 3/5 feet extend from one side and 14 9/17 feet from the other, how wide is the highway?"

That seemed to me like an awfully silly way to get the width of a highway. I didn't even try to answer it because it didn't say whether the pole had fallen straight across or not.

Even in shop I don't get very good grades. All of us kids made a broom holder and a bookend this term and mine were sloppy. I just couldn't get interested. Mom doesn't use a broom anymore with her new vacuum cleaner, and all our books are in a bookcase with glass doors in the parlor. Anyway I wanted to make an end gate for my uncle's trailer, but the shop teacher said that meant using metal and wood both, and I'd have to learn how to work with wood first. I didn't see why, but I kept still, and made a tie rack at school and the tail gate after school at my uncle's garage. He said I saved him ten dollars.

Civics is hard for me, too. I've been staying after school trying to learn the "Articles of Confederation" for almost a week, because the teacher said we couldn't be good citizens unless we did. I really tried because I want to be a good citizen. I did hate to stay after school, because a bunch of us boys from the south end of town have been cleaning up the old lot across from Taylor's Machine Shop to make a playground out of it for the little kids from the Methodist home. I made the jungle gym from old pipe, and the guys made me Grand Mogul to keep the playground going. We raised enough money collecting scrap this month to build a wire fence clear around the lot.

Dad says I can quit school when I am fifteen and I am sort of anxious to because there are a lot of things I want to learn how to do, and as my uncle says, I'm not getting any younger.

THE GERANIUM ON THE WINDOW SILL JUST DIED BUT TEACHER YOU WENT RIGHT ON*
Albert Cullum

You're so proud of your shiny new car.
You're so proud of your new color hair,
    your vacation tan,
    and your nice clean blackboards.
I sit in the third row, last seat.
Teacher, are you ever proud of me?

• • •

I'm so quiet sitting in the first row,
    first seat.
I feel you like me.
I mind, and I am never late.
Do you like me?
I always do all of my homework,
    and I gave you the biggest valentine
    of all.
Do you like me?
Sometimes I'm scared of you though.
The way you look, the way you smile.
But that's when you like me best of all—
    when I'm scared.

• • •

I want you to come to my house,
    and yet I don't.
You're so important,
    but our screen door has a hole in it.
And my mother has no fancy cake to serve.
I want you to come to my house, teacher,
    and yet I don't.
My brother chews with his mouth wide open
    and sometimes my dad burps.
I wish I could trust you enough, teacher,
    to invite you to my house.

• • •

You talk funny when you talk to the
    principal.
Or when the teacher next door borrows
    some paper.
And when my mother comes to see you,
    you talk funny.
Why don't you talk to them like you
    talk to us?

*From the Harlin Quist Book by Albert Cullum.

CIPHER IN THE SNOW*
Jean E. Mitzer

It started with tragedy on a biting cold February morning. I was driving behind the Milford Corners bus as I did most snowy mornings on my way to school. It veered and stopped short at the hotel, which it had no business doing, and I was annoyed as I had to come to an unexpected stop. A boy lurched out of the bus, reeled, stumbled, and collapsed on the snowbank at the curb. The bus driver and I reached him at the same moment. His thin, hollow face was white even against the snow.

"He's dead," the driver whispered.

It didn't register for a minute. I glanced quickly at the scared young faces staring down at us from the school bus. "A doctor! Quick! I'll phone from the hotel . . ."

"No use. I tell you he's dead." The driver looked down at the boy's still form. "He never even said he felt bad," he muttered, "just tapped me on the shoulder and said, real quiet, 'I'm sorry. I have to get off at the hotel.' That's all. Polite and apologizing like."

At school, the giggling, shuffling morning noise quieted as the news went down the halls. I passed a huddle of girls. "Who was it? Who dropped dead on the way to school?" I heard one of them half-whisper.

"Don't know his name; some kid from Milford Corners," was the reply.

It was like that in the faculty room and the principal's office. "I'd appreciate your going to tell the parents," the principal told me. "They haven't a phone and, anyway, somebody from school should go there in person. I'll cover your classes."

"Why me?" I asked. "Wouldn't it be better if you did it?"

"I didn't know the boy," the principal admitted levely. "And in last year's sophomore personalities column I note that you were listed as his favorite teacher."

I drove through the snow and cold down the bad canyon road to the Evans place and thought about the boy, Cliff Evans. His favorite teacher! I thought. He hasn't spoken two words to me in two years! I could see him in my mind's eye all

right, sitting back there in the last seat in my afternoon literature class. "Cliff Evans," I muttered to myself, "a boy who never talked." I thought a minute. "A boy who never smiled. I never saw him smile once."

The big ranch kitchen was clean and warm. I blurted out my news somehow. Mrs. Evans reached blindly toward a chair. "He never said anything about bein' ailing."

His stepfather snorted. "He ain't said nothing about anything since I moved in here."

Mrs. Evans pushed a pan back off the stove and began to untie her apron. "Now hold on," her husband snapped. "I got to have breakfast before I go to town. Nothing' we can do now anyway. If Cliff hadn't been so dumb, he'd have told us he didn't feel good."

After school I sat in the office and stared bleakly at the records spread out before me. I was to close the file and write the obituary for the school paper. The almost bare sheets mocked the effort. Cliff Evans, white, never legally adopted by stepfather, five young half-brothers and sisters. These meager strands of information and the list of D grades were all the records had to offer.

Cliff Evans had silently come in the school door in the mornings and gone out of the school door in the evenings, and that was all. He had never belonged to a club. He had never played on a team. He had never held an office. As far as I could tell, he had never done one happy, noisy kid thing. He had never been anybody at all.

How do you go about making a boy into a zero? The grade-school records showed me. The first and second grade teachers' annotations read "sweet, shy child"; "timid but eager." Then the third grade note had opened the attack. Some teacher had written in a good, firm hand, "Cliff won't talk. Uncooperative, Slow learner." The other academic sheep had followed with: "dull", "slow-witted"; "low (IQ)." They became correct. The boy's IQ score in the ninth grade had been listed at 83. But his IQ in the third grade had been 106. The score didn't go under 100 until the seventh grade. Even shy, timid, sweet children have resilience. It takes time to break them.

I stomped to the typewriter and wrote a savage report, pointing out what education had done to Cliff Evans. I slapped a copy on the principal's

---

*From the *N.E.A. Journal*, November 1964. Used with permission.

desk and another in the sad, dog-eared file. I banged the typewriter and slammed the file and crashed the door shut, but I didn't feel much better. A little boy kept walking after me, a little boy with a peaked, pale face; a skinny body in faded jeans, and big eyes that had looked and searched for a long time and then had become veiled.

I could guess how many times he'd been chosen last to play sides in a game, how many whispered child conversations had excluded him, how many times he hadn't been asked. I could see and hear the faces and voices that said over and over, "You're a nothing, Cliff Evans."

A child is a believing creature. Cliff undoubtedly believed them. Suddenly it seemed clear to me: when finally there was nothing left at all for Cliff Evans, he collapsed on a snowbank and went away. The doctor might list "heart failure" as the cause of death, but that wouldn't change my mind.

We couldn't find ten students in the school who had known Cliff well enough to attend the funeral as his friends. So the student body officers and a committee from the junior class went as a group to the church, being politely sad. I attended the services with them, and sat through it with a lump of cold lead in my chest and a big resolve growing through me.

I've never forgotten Cliff Evans nor that resolve. He has been my challenge year after year, class after class. I look up and down for veiled eyes and bodies slumped into a seat in an alien world. "Look, kids," I say silently, "I may not do anything else for you this year, but not one of you is going to come out of here a nobody. I'll work or fight to the bitter end doing battle with society and the school board, but I don't want to have one of you coming out of here thinking himself a zero."

Most of the time—not always, but most of the time—I've succeeded.

• • •

Many teachers forget or tend to minimize the influence they have on their students. Teachers must recognize that each student needs to be acknowledged as an individual in his own right and know that significant others in his life care about what he does and how he feels. It is easy to become trapped in a learning atmosphere that is primarily mechanical, which emphasizes achievement, test scores, and rules and regulations. We fully appreciate the tremendous demands placed on today's teachers, but a perspective that recognizes the worth of every individual is essential to the achievement of our basic educational goals. Throughout this book it has been emphasized that the teacher is the single most important factor in the successful integration of handicapped students. There is little question that teachers have a *profound influence* on student behavior and achievement. We want to encourage every teacher to be aware of this influence and to make certain that it is *positive* in nature.

We will further emphasize the importance of the interaction between teachers and students by reviewing several studies that have demonstrated the influence of teacher expectations on student behavior, achievement, and feelings of self-worth. We will also consider ways in which these interactions may be assessed through formal and informal instruments. Student interactions will be reviewed, and techniques and materials will be described that may enhance positive interactions. At the conclusion of this chapter, vignettes and anecdotes reflecting the importance of positive interactions will be presented. We will admit in advance that we are deliberately attempting a "hard sell" of the importance of positive interactions between teachers and students. We believe that in this one instance this is the only tenable position to take. We further believe that those who "buy" this idea will be better teachers and happier persons for having made this decision.

THE BASIS OF A HANDICAP

We accept the fact that handicapped students have certain limitations imposed as a result of their handicap. By the very nature of the condition, we can predict the need for certain modifications or adaptations of curriculum, materials, teaching strategies, or a combination of these factors. A student with impaired vision, for example, must have modified materials to participate fully in regular classrooms. Hearing impaired students need adapted approaches and the specialized services of support personnel, and students with crippling or other health impairments may need to have architectural barriers removed and some special equipment provided if they are to be educated in regular classrooms. When considering the limitations imposed by handicapping conditions, it is quite clear that the condition itself necessitates modifications or adaptations. There are, however, a relatively large number of students for whom we cannot clearly establish the reason for school difficulties. For these students it may not be educationally sound to assume that there is some internal factor contributing to their failure. In these instances, there may be external factors contributing to his failure, or the student's failure may be the result of a number of interacting factors.

If a student is having difficulty in reading or math, for example, or is withdrawn or acting out in class, we must consider a number of variables that may have an influence on his poor achievement or unusual behavior. Among the variables that should be considered are (1) the student, (2) the teacher or teachers, (3) the materials being used, and (4) the environment. The influence of these variables is depicted in the following diagram.

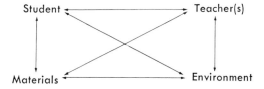

It is possible that the primary nature of the student's problem may rest with any one of these variables, but more commonly it is the interaction of one or more of these factors that influence the student's behavior. To assess the difficulty, we must analyze the interaction between these factors.

Student-environment interaction

A student who is being reinforced by his classmates for being the classroom clown provides an example of poor student-environment interaction. In other situations, the influence of poor student-environment interaction may be demonstrated by a student who is highly distracted by a noisy classroom (environment) or by a classroom that is visually distracting. As a result, this student may not be able to attend to the task or assignment. Most students can "filter out" these distractions, but there are some who cannot. An example that illustrates this problem might be the last time you studied for an examination. Did you seek out an area that was free of auditory distractions (such as a quiet corner of the library) or were you able to listen to hard rock music and sit at a table with your friends who were laughing and having a good time? Some individuals have little or no difficulty studying with considerable distractions present, whereas others prefer a relatively quiet atmosphere. If you are one who prefers an environment that is free of distractions but were unable to get away from them and as a result did poorly on the examination, who or what should be blamed? In this instance your reply might be, "I just couldn't concentrate because there were so many distractions; as a result I did very poorly on my exam." This situation is very similar to the student who is distracted by extraneous visual or auditory signals in the classroom environment. In such cases is it safe to assume that the problem is within the student? In all likelihood it is not;

the difficulty undoubtedly relates to the interaction between the student and environmental factors.

Student-materials interaction

The appropriateness of educational materials may also influence a student's achievement or behavior. This may seem obvious, but we believe that not enough time and effort are directed toward observation, planning, and evaluation of educational materials. Often the reading materials required for a particular subject may not be appropriate to the actual reading level of the student. The student may be "required" to read a text or some other material that is far beyond his skill level. Teachers should administer an informal reading inventory (IRI) to determine if the student has sufficient skills to successfully read the assigned material. The readability level of material being used may also be assessed. Studies have indicated that intermediate texts (grades 3 to 6) may have a readability level from second to tenth grades. When the readability level of a particular textbook is far beyond the instructional reading level it is not safe to assume that the problem is exclusively with the student. There is also some evidence that students have preferred learning styles—auditory, visual, tactual, and kinesthetic—and that if assessment is made of the preferred learning channel or style, and if materials are matched to this preferred channel, we can increase the student's learning rate and improve his achievement.

The four-point interaction matrix (p. 235) should be given serious consideration when efforts are initiated to analyze the needs of any given student. It is not safe to assume that the failure of a student is primarily the fault of the student. Rather, it may relate to inadequacies in the environment, educational materials, instructional techniques, or interactional patterns in the classroom. This may be particularly true with a student who is exhibiting only mild problems and for whom there is no known reason for the difficulty. Teachers should attempt to objectively consider which factors are contributing to a particular student's difficulty and make the necessary adjustments to correct the situation.

The preceding discussion has related to interaction between the student and his educational environment and between the student and his educational materials. Two highly important areas of concern, teacher-student and student-student interaction, will be the central focus of the remainder of this chapter.

TEACHER-STUDENT INTERACTION

There is little question that the teacher has a profound influence on student behavior, achievement, and feelings of self-worth; the way in which the teacher relates can either seriously impede or greatly facilitate a student's success in school. This interaction is an important factor to consider with all students but has even more implications for the student who is not achieving, apathetic, nonconforming, acting out in the classroom, or identified as "handicapped."

The nature and quality of the interaction between teacher and student may be strongly influenced by the teacher's expectations. Such expectations may be too low, that is, expecting only minimal achievement or little acceptable behavior, or too high, which may cause the teacher to pressure the student to achieve beyond his capabilities, resulting in discouragement, behavior problems, or failure. Expectations are not in and of themselves bad if teachers are willing to modify an initial expectation as a result of additional information and experience. It must be emphasized that although to some extent, we all form expectations on the basis of preconceived information or as a result of initial interactions, we must maintain a *flexible attitude* concerning these expectations and be willing to change them. In some cases, expectations might be better labeled "biases."

The teacher's expectations for a particular student or group of students may become a self-fulfilling prophecy. If we expect a particular type of behavior from a student, we may only observe and react to those behaviors that were initially expected. The following anecdote illustrates this principle:

A discussion among teachers in the teachers' lounge centered around the unacceptable, disruptive behavior of a number of children from the same family. Teachers who had previously taught members of the Jones family indicated that they *all* were troublemakers and, in general, were the most disruptive members of their classes. As a result of this discussion, Mr. Carlson, the sixth grade teacher, had a preconceived notion about the behavior of Jimmy Jones, a new arrival in his sixth grade classroom. Mr. Carlson was ready and waiting for disruptive behavior from Jimmy. Whenever Jimmy was the least bit disruptive (even though his behavior was not significantly different from other class members), Mr. Carlson was able to fulfill his prophecy, "I knew Jimmy was going to be a problem, and I'm going to stop it before it gets started." In this instance, Mr. Carlson was so certain that he would observe disruptive behavior, he interpreted only minor problems as disruptive.

The preceding illustration was initiated by conversation in the teachers' lounge, but expectations concerning a particular student may also be influenced by information contained in a student's cumulative folder, taken from related nonschool experience with the family, or acquired in many other ways. However, special mention is made of faculty lounges, since it is often here that information is shared in an unguarded and sometimes unprofessional manner. Whereas we acknowledge that in the majority of teachers' lounges the topics of discussion are professional and in the best interests of students, there are times when discussion of a particular student can be demeaning and damaging. Frequently the discussion concerns poorly achieving students or extreme behavior problems. We recognize that teachers must vent their feelings, and that often the teachers' lounge is the most logical place to do this, but teachers should consider the influence such discussions may have on other teachers and the ultimate effect on the students being discussed.

In a teachers' lounge where this had become a serious problem, the faculty decided to post a readily observable sign stating: IF IT'S NOT GOOD DON'T BOTHER! When asked what the sign meant they were quick to say, "If you don't have something positive to say about students (or any other matter) don't say it. If it is necessary to discuss a particular student, attempt to do so outside of the teachers' lounge." This concern may seem like a trivial matter when compared with other problems that occur in schools, but we feel that very often teachers' attitudes and interactions with students are influenced by teachers' lounge talk.

Expectations, student behavior, and achievement. In the following paragraphs, we will briefly review research studies that have demonstrated a relationship between teacher expectations, student behavior, and achievement and discuss the implications of these studies.

The most commonly quoted research study related to this topic was conducted by Rosenthal and Jacobson (1968). Although this study has been seriously questioned because of reported methodological weaknesses, it has served as the catalyst for other studies that have reported essentially the same findings and have more concisely delineated the variables that underlie the effect of the self-fulfilling prophecy.

The main purpose of the Rosenthal-Jacobson study was to determine if teachers' favorable expectations could be responsible for significant IQ gains of students. A group-administered test (with which the students were unfamiliar) was given to all students who would be returning to one elementary school the next fall. The test, the Harvard Test of Inflected Acquisition, was interpreted as being a test that would predict with near absolute certainty the students who would show "academic spurt"—to designate "late blooming." The test in actuality was Flannigan's Test of General Ability (1960) and yielded scores in verbal ability, reasoning, and a total IQ score. Upon completion of the testing, twenty percent of the students were selected to participate in the study, were randomly assigned to an experimental group, and labeled as "bloomers." Teachers were given a list of the children in their classrooms who might exhibit marked intellectual growth. From this information the teachers erroneously assumed that the other children (those who were not identified) did not have the potential for marked intellectual growth.

The findings of this study indicated a significant expectancy advantage in favor of the students who were identified as "late bloomers." In other words, the students who were identified as most likely to show "academic spurt" did spurt as evidenced by mean gains in total IQ.

As mentioned previously, this study has been the subject of considerable debate and is not unanimously accepted by professionals. There have been, however, numerous other studies that have examined the influence of teacher-student interaction, and they have established that teacher expectation does have the potential to seriously impede or facilitate student achievement and behavior (Beez, 1972; Rubin and Balow, 1971; Keogh and Becker, 1973; Adelman, 1970; Rothbart, Dalfen, and Barnett, 1971).

An interesting experience concerning the effects of intelligence test data on achievement was recently shared with us. Although this experience cannot be scientifically documented, it provides an interesting dramatization of the effect of the self-fulfilling prophecy.

The setting was a large urban junior high school. In an attempt to establish a sense of community and to increase the interaction of students to a level that might be expected in a smaller school, several "pods" were established. Approximately one hundred students were assigned to a pod, with roughly four homerooms in each pod. By design, the pod was established to serve as a school within the larger school.

Several weeks after school began, teachers received a random listing of students assigned to their pod. Preceding each students' name was an assigned number, with numbers ranging from 50 to 150. It was assumed by some teachers that the numbers were the results of group intelligence tests, and accordingly, many teachers established groups on the basis of the number.

After several weeks it was learned that the numbers were not IQ test results but locker numbers. The ironic side effect was that the students with high locker numbers tended to be doing very well in their classes and teachers highly valued their interactions; students with relatively low locker numbers were not doing as well.

This may seem an extreme example of the influence of student data wherever or however it may be obtained, but it does further illustrate our concern. In all fairness, however, we must indicate that further investigation of this real-life situation revealed that a number of teachers were quick to question the "IQs" on the student listing. Our concern is the potentially damaging effects of those teachers who could not objectively observe and evaluate their students even after several weeks.

Thus far, we have been primarily concerned with the general nature of the effects of teacher expectations on student performance. Certain administrative procedures have been developed that may, in some cases, have similar effects. "Tracking" may have such an effect in many instances.

Tracking. Grouping on the basis of ability, or tracking, may impose serious limitations on some students. Although this practice has been challenged in the courts, it is still widely practiced in many schools. This system is seen as an advantage for high-track students who are in a group of the same ability, but it may impose serious limitations on the student who is placed in a low track. Teachers generally use ability groups to provide more homogeneity in achievement level for instructional purposes. Although this practice may be a viable and necessary approach to providing instruction at the students' level, caution must be exercised in its use. The tracking of students into ability groups *must be flexible* and *based on the instructional level of the particular subject being studied*. A given student may be placed in the low reading group but in another subject may be most appropriately instructed in a high group. A general problem relating to tracking is a type of "spread phenomenon." The student is placed in either a high track for all activities regardless of the achievement level in that subject or the student is placed in all low tracks on the basis of achievement in one particular subject area. Teachers must make every effort to maintain considerable flexibility when tracking students for instructional purposes.

In a study by Hargreaves (1972), it was found that seventy-three percent of the students in the low track felt that their relationships with teachers were poor, whereas only ten percent of the students in the upper track felt this way. Hargreaves also found that upper-track students were much more oriented to their teachers' values than were lower-track students. The frustration felt by students in lower tracks is demonstrated in the following quotation: "I don't like the work here. In the first year we was doing addition and all that and we're still doing that now. . . . It's not worth it, is it? We should have learnt more in third year, but we

didn't" (Hargreaves, 1972). Tracking may maximize the achievement of students placed in higher tracks but is likely to minimize the achievement of students in lower tracks.

"Handicapped" students. Considerable debate has occurred concerning the disadvantages of labeling and categorizing students. Although it is necessary to use some system of identification and classification for such purposes as eligibility for programs, funding, and evaluation, there are many problems related to the labeling process.

Students identified and labeled "handicapped" may be stereotyped on the basis of some preconceived attitude or experience with handicapped individuals. Although the stereotype may reflect either positive or negative behavior and expectations, it generally reflects a negative attitude about a population as a whole. Once the student has been labeled, there seems to be a generalized influence on teachers' views of the student. The label "mentally handicapped," for example, often carries a very negative connotation and may result in a significantly lower level of expectation. The results of the label may not only lower the level of expectation but may also reinforce the regular classroom teacher's feeling that "I (the teacher) don't know enough about teaching mentally handicapped children; the student should be in a special classroom."

The influence of the label on the student is obvious; the student may play the role of "a person who fails." Just as success breeds more success, failure and negative thinking are powerful forces for continued failure. The following situation serves as an example of how a label may become a self-fulfilling prophecy for a student.

One of the authors recently observed a classroom for emotionally disturbed students from the ages of 8 to 13 years. The teacher was having considerable difficulty with one student that morning. When asked to line up outside the classroom, the student blatantly refused. After several requests the teacher asked the observer to assist, thinking that perhaps a different person might have a positive effect. The observer simply asked the student to line up and said that his teacher had some very exciting activities planned and that the sooner he lined up the sooner he would be allowed to participate in these activities. The student looked up at the observer and replied, "Sir, I can't be expected to line up." When asked why, the student replied, "Sir, I can't be expected to line up because *I am emotionally disturbed.*"

As indicated previously, a student may play the role of someone who is "slow" if he is expected to fail. Likewise, if a student is expected to act strangely or in a disturbing way he may play the role of someone who is disturbed. In this instance the label was used by the student to justify unusual behavior; the label becomes a self-fulfilling prophecy.

Another effect of labeling is that it is often difficult to remove a label. An analogy often used to illustrate this point is the difficulty experienced when attempting to remove a paper label from a jar. Removing the label may be a difficult and tedious job, and often part of the label remains. The same is true when attempting to remove a label from a student; it is very difficult and some of the label often stays with the student.

Achievement test results. There is considerable evidence that achievement test scores may negatively influence teacher expectations. In a study conducted by Beez (1972), it was found that teachers who expected high performance from students tried to teach more, and teachers expecting low performance tended to teach less. He demonstrated this by randomly assigning a group of students to high and low achievement groups by using falsified achievement scores. At the end of the term teachers were asked to rate the students using a five-point scale, with five being high and one being low in the following areas: social competency, achievement, and intellectual ability. Table 6 reflects the teacher ratings.

Table 6. Teacher ratings

	Social competency	Achievement	Intellectual ability
Students identified as high achieving	3.33	3.50	3.43
Students identified as low achieving	2.57	1.90	1.93

Good (1970) indicated that teachers interact more often with high achieving than with low achieving students and that their interactions with high achievers are more facilitative and positive than with low achievers. Other studies have indicated that students of different achievement levels are exposed to different verbal interactions. Students in lower groups receive less praise and more negative comments or criticisms than their classmates in higher groups (Beez, 1968; Morrison and McIntyre, 1969).

Membership in racial or ethnic minority groups. Membership in racial and ethnic minority groups also appears to contribute to lowered teacher expectations and different patterns of interaction when compared with those for other students. For example, there is an indication that white students are held in higher esteem than black students by white teachers (Leacock, 1969). Large differences in the extent to which teachers praise Anglo students compared with the amount of praise given Mexican-American students have also been reported. The quantity and quality of verbal interaction also seems to be influenced in a negative direction by minority group membership (Jackson and Cosca, 1974).

Other student characteristics. There are a number of other student characteristics that lead to negative attitudes, lower expectations, and less desirable interactions. Among the more common are *sex* (Palardy, 1969; Arnold, 1968; Helton and Oakland, 1977), *speech and language characteristics* (Williams, Whitehead, and Miller, 1972), *physical attractiveness* (Dion, Bersheid, and Walster, 1972; Fleming and Anttonen, 1971; Ross and Salvia, 1975; Clifford and Walster, 1973; Salvia and Algozzine, 1977), and *personality* (Schmuck, 1963, Feshback, 1969).

The crucial factor to consider is whether the teacher firmly believes that students who possess a particular characteristic are, in fact, less able to complete assigned tasks. Often these expectations stem from preconceived notions or misinformation rather than from actual experience. For instance, if the teacher firmly believes that girls tend to be higher achievers than boys in language arts and are more capable in general than boys, boys will most likely receive greater teacher criticism, be given less praise, and experience greater rates of failure.

The first step in attempting to avoid this type of situation is for the teacher to recognize that her preconceived attitudes and expectations can significantly influence a student's behavior, achievement, and feelings of self-worth. As mentioned previously, expectations in and of themselves are natural and are neither good or bad. We all form opinions of individuals with whom we interact. The expectation may not be of any significant consequence unless it becomes a self-fulfilling prophecy. In this instance expectations become the cause of student behavior. Some school faculties have addressed this concern by conducting in-service meetings and/or open discussions concerning student characteristics that may negatively influence teacher expectations. In this way, teachers recognize that their feelings are not unique and that their colleagues share similar feelings. Often a student characteristic identified by a colleague will seem to be quite trivial or humorous, although it is very real to the teacher identifying it. By sharing their feelings teachers may come to realize how absurd some feelings about student characteristics can be. Teachers may then share ways

in which they have overcome such feelings.

One other type of interaction between teachers and students must be considered— the interaction between teachers and physically impaired students (visually impaired, hearing impaired, crippled, and other health impaired) who are being educated in regular classrooms. The interaction with these students may be the opposite of what we have reviewed in the preceding paragraphs. Rather than rejective interactions, the teachers may demonstrate a very sympathetic, pitying, or oversolicitous attitude toward the student. This type of attitude is demonstrated by such comments as, "Isn't it wonderful that a blind student can do so well!" or "I think, because she is in a wheelchair, that she deserves a letter grade of B." Although it may be difficult to criticize this type of comment, teachers must be made aware of the inherent dangers of such an attitude. This type of attitude and interaction may defeat the very purpose of regular classroom placement. To set the student up as someone so special that he becomes the "classroom pet" may do a serious disservice to that student. Teachers must be aware of the influence of their attitudes, be they negative, sympathetic, pitying, or positive.

We have only briefly reviewed the nature of teacher expectations and the specific student characteristics that appear to influence the interaction between teachers and students. It is imperative that teachers recognize the *profound influence* they have on student behavior and achievement and that they also recognize the factors that contribute to negative interactions.

Brophy and Good (1974) identified several variables that may communicate low expectations. They are as follows:

1. Waiting less time for lows (low achieving students) to answer
2. Staying with lows in failure situations (persisting in such a manner as to call attention to failure)

3. Rewarding inappropriate behavior of lows (praising marginal or inaccurate responses)
4. Criticizing lows more frequently than highs
5. Praising lows less frequently than highs
6. Not giving feedback to public responses of lows
7. Paying less attention to lows
8. Calling on lows less often
9. Differing interaction patterns to highs and lows
10. Seating lows farther from the teacher
11. Demanding less from lows

By recognizing these variables, teachers may begin to understand the basis of their perceptions and consider modifying their interactions (if such modification is needed) by maintaining a flexible and open attitude about all students.

MONITORING AND EVALUATION TECHNIQUES

Students depend very heavily on their interaction with teachers for clues to their success; therefore it is crucial that teachers attempt to analyze their interactions with their students. There are a number of ways that teachers may assess their interactions; some are informal and do not require specific instruments or a great deal of training in their use. Others are the product of research studies and provide very specific information concerning interactions. We will consider both types of analysis.

Informal techniques*

The number and variety of available informal techniques are limited only by individual ingenuity, but certain types of approaches appear to be in fairly common use. We will

---

*Our thanks to Clifford Baker, who provided a number of informal techniques presented in this discussion.

relate these techniques, but teachers are encouraged to modify these informal procedures to fit individual need. Such modification is not acceptable with standardized or formal techniques.

Time analysis. The time analysis technique may provide information concerning the teacher's interaction with students. The following checklist and set of directions provides an example of this technique.

I	II	III
Students: most time	How is time spent?	Pleasurable or nonpleasurable
1. 2. 3. 4. 5.		
Students: least time		
1. 2. 3. 4. 5.		

Column I. List the five students in the class with whom the most time is spent. List five with whom the least time is spent.

Column II. Identify what is done with the student during that time—how is the time spent?

Sample key
XH = Extra help, academic
BM = Behavior management
L = Listening to the student
T = Talking to the student
PL = Playing with the student

Column III. Write a "P" if the time spent is pleasurable and "NP" if it was nonpleasurable.

Analyze the results. The following questions should be answered:

1. At what kinds of activities do you spend most of your time?
2. Is most of your time spent with these ten students pleasurable?
3. What is different about the students with whom you spend the most time?

4. Do the students with whom you spend more time need you more?
5. What is the difference between the students with whom the time is pleasurable and the students with whom the time is nonpleasurable?

The teacher may add any number of questions to analyze the findings, depending on the specific purpose of the analysis.

The time analysis technique is simple to administer and interpret and can provide considerable information concerning how the teacher spends her time and the nature of her interactions.

Peer (teacher)—observer. A trusted colleague can come in and observe the teacher in action. The colleague should keep a series of running notes on the teacher's interactions during a period of several days. Often it is very helpful if the observing teacher has a checklist or an indication of specific behaviors to be recorded; otherwise at the end of the period only very general comments may be shared. The teachers may later change roles if this is agreeable to both.

Videotape. The teacher may arrange to have her teaching videotaped. She should view the videotape alone, noticing how she interacts with different students. Next, if desired, the teacher can view and discuss the videotape with a colleague. It may be necessary to tape several sessions so that typical patterns of behavior and interaction will be recorded, not just "showmanship" on the part of teachers or students. It may be helpful to arrange for a series of taping sessions, for example, once every two or three months. Nearly every school district has videotaping equipment and local instructional media personnel may be able to assist with the taping.

Role-playing. Another procedure that is particularly appropriate with elementary-level students is role-playing. Young children are very honest and open and are quick to role-play typical classroom situations. To

be most effective, it is advisable for the regular teacher to switch classes with another teacher so that the students are not inhibited by their own teacher's presence. The students may be asked to act out the role of a good teacher and a poor teacher, for example. Other roles might be:

1. How does your teacher act when he is happy or sad?
2. How does your teacher look and what does he say when you interrupt him?
3. How does your teacher look and what does he say when you ask him to repeat the directions for an assignment?
4. How does your teacher look and what does he say when you make a mistake?
5. How does your teacher look and what does he say when you misbehave?
6. How does your teacher look and what does he say when you do something well?

Teachers may add other situations about which they are most interested in obtaining feedback. The role-playing may be taped on a video or audio recorder so that a firsthand evaluation is received. Again, it may be helpful for the teacher to exchange classes with a colleague so that the students will not be inhibited by their own teacher's presence. Although the initiation of such role-playing may require different introduction and presentation at the elementary level than at the secondary level, it will work at both levels with just a little innovation by the teacher.

Teacher-made checklists. The teacher may develop a checklist that will fit almost any situation. The items on the checklist can relate to the teacher's interaction through verbal or nonverbal behavior or general classroom procedures. Such checklists seem to be very popular with teachers, and so we have provided two examples. One is for elementary students, and the other is more appropriate in a secondary classroom. The items are merely examples, and teachers are encouraged to modify the lists or add statements that are of particular interest or concern to them.

Students should not be asked to sign their names, since this may inhibit their openness and sincerity. Analyze the results by averaging the responses and plotting the averages so that it is possible to get a picture of teacher interactions. Checklists may be administered several times during the year to measure changes that have occurred. For ad-

ditional discussion of the use of pupil-reaction inventories, see Medley and Klein, 1957.

Formal techniques

Formal procedures offer concrete indications of a teacher's instructional strategies and various interactions with students. By design, these techniques for measuring teacher-student interaction may facilitate the decision-making process concerning teaching

	Al- ways 3	Sel- dom 2	Never 1
1. I can get extra help from the teacher when I need it.	—	—	—
2. The teacher praises me when I do well.	—	—	—
3. The teacher smiles when I do something well.	—	—	—
4. The teacher listens attentively.	—	—	—
5. The teacher accepts me as an individual.	—	—	—
6. The teacher encourages me to try something new.	—	—	—
7. The teacher respects the feelings of others.	—	—	—
8. My work is usually good enough.	—	—	—
9. I am called on when I raise my hand.	—	—	—
10. The same students always get praised by the teacher.	—	—	—
11. The teacher grades fairly.	—	—	—
12. The teacher smiles and enjoys teaching.	—	—	—
13. I have learned to do things from this teacher.	—	—	—
14. When something is too hard, my teacher makes it easier for me.	—	—	—
15. My teacher is polite and courteous.	—	—	—
16. I like my teacher.	—	—	—

style and interactions with students. These interaction analysis systems are generally quite reliable, offer a descriptive picture rather than a subjective judgmental impression, and emphasize the interaction process rather than the end product. Some are quite time-consuming and require specific training to obtain reliable results, whereas others do not require a great deal of intensive preparation. Some instruments analyze interactions by examining verbal behavior of teachers and students, some are concerned primarily with the verbal behavior of teachers, whereas other instruments measure nonverbal behavior (teacher movements or actions). Although each has its unique emphasis, all have the potential of providing teachers with a record of instructional strategies and interactions that may serve as a basis for change. Often teachers who have used informal techniques and see the advantages of measuring their interactions, after gaining experience, will

The teacher:	Al-ways 5	Some-times 4	Often 3	Sel-dom 2	Never 1
1. Is genuinely interested in me.	—	—	—	—	—
2. Respects the feelings of others.	—	—	—	—	—
3. Grades fairly.	—	—	—	—	—
4. Identifies what he/she considers important.	—	—	—	—	—
5. Is enthusiastic about teaching.	—	—	—	—	—
6. Smiles often and enjoys teaching.	—	—	—	—	—
7. Helps me develop skills in understanding myself.	—	—	—	—	—
8. Is honest and fair.	—	—	—	—	—
9. Helps me develop skills in communicating.	—	—	—	—	—
10. Encourages and provides time for individual help.	—	—	—	—	—
11. Is pleasant and has a sense of humor.	—	—	—	—	—
12. Has pets and spends most time with them.	—	—	—	—	—
13. Encourages and provides time for questions and discussion.	—	—	—	—	—
14. Respects my ideas and concerns.	—	—	—	—	—
15. Helps me develop skills in making decisions.	—	—	—	—	—
16. Helps me develop skills in using time wisely.	—	—	—	—	—

use some of the formal procedures because they want more specific information.

On the following pages we will review a few of the more commonly used interaction analysis instruments. To effectively use any of these systems, it would be necessary to initiate a more detailed study of that specific system.

Flanders' classroom interaction analysis. The Flanders procedure is one of the most widely used systems. In fact, the name Flanders has become synonymous with interaction analysis, and these terms often are used interchangeably to describe this procedure (Flanders, 1965). The system takes into consideration the verbal behavior of the teacher and the student. Interaction is analyzed on the basis of ten categories. Seven are used when the teacher is talking; two are used when the student is talking; and the last category is used to indicate silence, noise, or confusion. These categories are believed to exhaust all possibilities and include all kinds of communication.

The Flanders is concerned with two kinds of events, response and initiation. To initiate means to make the first move (to lead, to introduce an idea or concept for the first time). To respond means to take action after an initiation (to expand, to counter, to react to ideas already expressed). The ten major categories take into account these two factors.

An observer in the classroom records the communication patterns by placing a tally in the category that is best represented. Observation continues at a rate of twenty to twenty-five tallies per minute—approximately one tally every three seconds. Tape recording and video recording may be used to assist with this task.

Specific systems are described that assist in determining any imbalance between initiation and response. These specific systems also assist in determining ways to decode, procedures for displaying data, and more

complicated or flexible category systems. As mentioned previously, this is a precise system requiring study, understanding, and practice to be used effectively. It has the potential to assist in making decisions about desired changes in teacher-student interaction.

Flanders' categories		
Teacher talk	Response	1. Accepts feelings 2. Praises or encourages 3. Accepts or uses ideas of pupils
		4. Asks questions
	Initiation	5. Lectures 6. Gives directions 7. Criticizes or justifies authority
Pupil talk		8. Response
		9. Initiation
No communication		10. Silence, noise, or confusion

Galloway's nonverbal system. Galloway (1968) developed a system to measure the nonverbal behavior of the teacher. It is based on the premise that teacher nonverbal behavior either encourages or restricts communication and interaction. This system contains a procedure for recording nonverbal cues associated with six of the seven teacher behaviors of the Flanders system.

Four teacher activities are noted by Galloway that are more likely to set the tone in the classroom than verbal interaction.

1. Use of space—such as the physical set-

up of desks, chairs, and the teacher's desk

2. Teacher travel—movement of the teacher to the blackboard, remaining at desk, and away from or near students
3. Use of time—the amount of time the teacher spends on a topic or topics
4. Control maneuvers—nonverbal cues, such as hands on hips, smiling, and fingers at lips

It is suggested that these acts may play a more significant role than many of verbal cues.

The following system places teacher nonverbal communication into a model with six dimensions, each on a continuum ranging from encouraging to restricting.

Teacher move analysis. *Teacher Move Analysis* (Arnold, Glaser, and Ernst, 1971) goes beyond verbal interaction between teacher and student by placing teaching behavior into eight categories, called teacher moves.

The eight teacher moves are classified on the basis of the following three general areas: (1) noninstructional, (2) input moves (moves that cause student passivity), and (3) output moves (moves that call for student activity).

The classroom observer records teacher moves on an 8½ × 11-inch grid approximately every five seconds or whenever there is a change from one type of move to another by using the preceding numerical values. Upon completion of a particular observation, it is necessary to obtain percentages for respective move categories. The analysis may relate to the relative amount of input/output moves or to any of the eight specific moves. In addition, a framework is provided enabling the individual to record and analyze teacher moves in light of the stated purposes of a lesson. Teacher-move analysis is described in a well-written, but brief, programmed instructional manual. The procedure requires very little time on the part of

Teacher move analysis	
1. Class management move	Noninstructional move
2. Exposition move 3. Illustration move 4. Demonstration move	Input moves
5. Discussion—closed move 6. Discussion—open move 7. Exploration—regulate move 8. Exploration—free move	Output moves

the teacher to complete, is easy to use, and allows teachers to quickly "get on with" measurement of their interactions.

Other formal observational systems that also may be of interest have been reported by Medley and Mitzel (1958), Hughes (1959), Perkins (1964), Medley (1963), Fink and Semmel (1971), and Soar, Soar, and Ragosta (1971).

Summary of interaction analysis

We have reviewed only a few of the formal teacher-student observational systems available. Individuals interested in obtaining information or competency in the use of these instruments should refer to the references and suggested readings at the end of this chapter to obtain more information about a specific system.

A prerequisite to the use of any of these systems is an interest and desire to change or enhance interactions with students. This requires time, but teachers who are sincerely motivated to change their interactive style will find these systems to be valuable aids. Self-examination is one of the most effective ways to grow, both personally and professionally.

STUDENT-STUDENT INTERACTIONS

The mere physical placement of a handicapped student in a regular classroom does not ensure that the nature of the interaction

Ronald Stewart

with peers and teachers will be positive. In fact, there are some indications that unless specific efforts are made to enhance student interaction the handicapped student may be rejected by nonhandicapped students and teachers.

Johnson and Johnson (1978), in reviewing the general definition of least restrictive environment, add a thought-provoking aspect: "Mainstreaming is defined as providing an appropriate educational opportunity for all handicapped students in the least restrictive alternative, based on individualized educa-

tional programming and aimed at providing handicapped students with *access to and constructive interaction with nonhandicapped peers.*" They extend their definition by stating: "It is when handicapped students are liked, accepted, and chosen as friends that mainstreaming becomes a positive influence on the lives of both handicapped and normal progress students."

The extent to which a handicapped student is accepted by other students as a contributing and valuable member of a class is dependent on the following four factors:

1. *The extent to which the teacher accepts the student as an individual.* The effects of modeling, students using the teacher as a model for their behavior and interaction with handicapped students, is well established (Bandura, 1965).
2. *The interactions between students and modeling of peers* (Peterson et al., 1977; Bricker and Bricker, 1976).
3. *The attitudes and value systems of nonhandicapped students* (Bricker and Bricker, 1976; Wolfensberger, 1972).
4. *The extent to which systematic efforts provide nonhandicapped students with specific information, experience, and the opportunity to discuss experiences involving handicapping conditions.* This involves structuring programs to make group interaction an integral part of classroom instruction (Chennault, 1967; Lilly, 1971; Rucker and Vincenzo, 1970).

These four factors must be given serious consideration when planning and programming for handicapped students in regular classrooms. The following sections will review ways that teachers may assess the interactions between handicapped and nonhandicapped students and provide specific suggestions on how to increase their interactions.

Teacher influence in student-student interactions

In previous sections of this chapter it was emphasized that teachers must recognize the influence they have on a student's progress and consider specific techniques to measure their interactions. In addition, teachers must recognize that they serve as a model and that their interactions may influence how students perceive each other. The manner in which the teacher interacts with a particular student may determine how other students interact with that student.

If the teacher rejects a particular student (regardless of whether this student is labeled "handicapped"), it is very likely that other students will model this attitude and type of interaction. Conversely, if the teacher accepts each student as a unique and valued individual, this positive attitude may be modeled by nearly all students. A specific attitude is often observed when a physically disabled student (hearing impaired, visually impaired, or crippled) is being educated in a regular classroom situation. Although this attitude may be acceptable to the inexperienced, it is potentially very harmful to the physically disabled student. It has been observed by the authors on a number of occasions that the handicapped student has been treated very differently from the other students (by the teacher), and as a direct result of this teacher-student interaction, the nonhandicapped students have modeled this attitude.

Measuring handicapped students' status

There are a number of ways teachers may examine the interaction of students in their classroom. One such technique is to administer a sociometric scale to determine the degree of acceptance or rejection. There are many ways in which sociometric data may be obtained, but we would suggest the teacher develop a preference form similar to the following:

Name: _____

In working on a project I would like to work with:

1. _____

2. _____

3. _____

During breaks I would like to be with:

1. _____

2. _____

3. _____

I would like to sit next to:

1. _____

2. _____

3. _____

I would not like to work with:

1. _____

2. _____

3. _____

The directions for administration are:

1. Today I am going to ask you to indicate on your paper the name of a classmate with whom you would like to share certain activities. We all work better when we have the opportunity to work with someone we get along with well. I am gathering this information to find out who in this class would work well together. I hope you will be completely honest. No other student will know whom you have chosen.
2. Hand out preference forms with questions similar to those we have indicated.
3. At the top of this form, write the names of three classmates you would like to work with in school if you had a free choice.
4. Write in the middle of your paper the names of three classmates that you would like to be with during breaks. You may write down any or all of the three names used previously.
5. Next write the names of three classmates you would like to sit near in school if you had a free choice. You may write any or all of the names previously used.
6. At the bottom of this form write the names of classmates with whom you would not like to work.

After the students have made their choices, the teacher can tabulate the results. Any reasonable status categories may be used to determine the sociometric status of any specific student, for example:

Star: One who was chosen fourteen or more times by his classmates.
Above average: One who received from nine to thirteen choices.

Below average: One who was chosen between three and eight times.
Neglected: One who was chosen less than three times.
These numbers are based on an average classroom enrollment of between twenty-eight and thirty-five and may be changed proportionately depending on the size of the class.

The use of sociometric information should not stop with the tabulation of choices and an assignment of sociometric status. Several meaningful extensions can be made. For example, it may be helpful to determine the number of mutual choices (two students who chose each other). It may also be of interest to determine whether the handicapped student was chosen in academic or social areas. The teacher should devise her own method of analysis that is unique to her situation. The use of sociometric data may provide considerable insight into a student's status academically or socially. It may provide direction for procedures to facilitate interaction.

The use of sociometric data is not the only way to analyze classroom interaction; most teachers are keenly aware of social interactions in their classroom. Naturally, they should be aware of their role as a model and of how they are interacting with "different" students. There may be times, however, when even though the teacher's interactions with handicapped students are very positive, nonhandicapped students do not reflect an accepting, empathic, and objective attitude toward handicapped students. In this instance a conscious effort on behalf of the teacher to structure cooperative learning experiences and systematic efforts to provide experiences and open discussion must be planned.

What if the handicapped student's status is low? What can be done to improve his status?

Buddy system. Buddy systems are discussed in some detail on pp. 50 and 80, and will only briefly be mentioned here. The most important factor to consider when selecting a buddy is the compatibility of the two students. This situation must be handled very carefully, and the teacher must observe closely to be certain the handicapped student is gaining independence. The wrong buddy could lead to increased dependence. The buddy's responsibilities will usually depend on the particular type of handicap—auditory, visual, crippling, intellectual, or emotional. The buddy or helper may be rotated every few weeks so that one student is not burdened with the responsibility.

A logical extension of the buddy system is to establish a cooperative learning atmosphere. The work of Johnson and Johnson (1975, 1978) provides considerable insight regarding the benefits of serving handicapped students in regular classrooms and the social interdependence factors that increase interaction between handicapped and nonhandicapped students. They have found that the heterogenous-cooperative grouping of students, rather than the traditional competitive structure, considerably enhances the interaction of all students. In structuring the classroom Johnson and Johnson recommend small, cooperative heterogenous groups in which students help each other, share among themselves, and encourage and tutor each other. The use of this approach will probably increase acceptance and appreciation of differences among students.

Rap sessions. Rap sessions may be held to bring students together to discuss such things as the nature of a handicap, the degree of a handicap, how a handicap affects learning, levels of realistic expectation, prognosis, and cause of the handicap. The type of handicap and how comfortable the teacher and handicapped student feel about the topic should be considered when determining who is included in the rap session. For some reason, society (people and students, for example) usually associate more negative con-

notations with intellectual handicaps as compared to physical handicaps. Generally, it is a good idea to include the student with a physical impairment (hearing, vision, or crippling condition) in the rap session, but occasionally it may be best to discuss the problems in an open manner without the handicapped student present. These sessions may be handled by the special education resource teacher or the regular classroom teacher, or both.

If the rap session is handled properly, it can do a great deal to increase the nonhandicapped students' understanding of the handicapped student and often greatly enhances interaction between students. This of course depends on the type of handicap, age of the students, and whether the teacher has developed a classroom climate that allows open and honest discussion of problems (for a discussion of group meetings see Chapter 9). It may be a good idea to consult with the handicapped student and his parents prior to the rap session. Rap sessions may do more harm than good if not handled properly. Informal rap sessions may be helpful but should not take the place of planned, systematic efforts to provide specific information, as described on pp. 253 to 254.

Mini–in-service sessions. Mini–in-service sessions are most appropriate for students with physical disabilities. If the handicapped student uses special equipment (braille typewriter, hearing aid, or wheelchair, for example), the other students may not understand its use and purpose. In a mini–in-service session the student can explain the use of and actually demonstrate how the various equipment operates. Often the other students' curiosity and lack of understanding about the special equipment may distract them from their own work. Once the special equipment is demonstrated and its use explained, this distraction usually is alleviated.

An example of this type of session might be the visually impaired student demonstrating magnification devices and explaining their value and use. He may also explain the rationale for using a regular typewriter or the use of braille or large-type materials. Other types of aids and appliances, such as tape recorders, tape players, talking book machines, arithmetic aids, and embossed or enlarged maps, may also be demonstrated. Units of study on the eye or ear may be presented by the regular classroom teacher or special education resource teacher in cooperation with the visually or hearing impaired student.

The age of the handicapped student and his willingness to participate are factors the teacher should consider when planning the mini–in-service session. If the student is unwilling, perhaps the special education teacher (vision specialist or hearing specialist) will conduct the in-service session. Regardless of who participates, the session must be handled very carefully so the student is not made too "special." If the presentation implies that the handicapped student is someone "super" or someone to feel sorry for, the very purpose of the session may be defeated.

Reading books about handicapped persons. There are many films and trade books available that relate to handicapped persons (see Appendix F for an annotated listing of books). Some are stories about animals that are handicapped, whereas others relate to the adjustment of handicapped children and adults. Films may be shown in class, and the reading materials may be placed on a reading shelf or in the library; students may be encouraged to read these materials. Generally, these materials provide a great deal of insight into the problems of the disabled and the feelings handicapped persons have about themselves. The viewing of a film or a report on one of the books could serve as a starting point for the previously mentioned rap sessions or mini–in-service sessions.

Values education and clarification

Another suggestion that is worthy of consideration is the use of values clarification materials. Values clarification activities and materials have been used with increasing frequency and may be of considerable assistance in facilitating more positive interaction between handicapped and nonhandicapped students.

Although these materials (books, journal articles, and commercially developed materials) are to assist individuals to reexamine and clarify their beliefs, feelings, attitudes, and values, it appears that they may also be appropriate in facilitating a more positive interaction between students. By design these activities relate to values such as cooperation, trust, acceptance, respect for individual differences, and understanding. These values are an important prerequisite to positive interactions, and through the use of these activities and materials, it is probable that the individual will direct his attention to self-actualization. An assumption underlying the use of value clarification activities and materials is that if an individual is concerned with self-actualization and is provided the opportunity to reexamine his values, he will, as a result, become more self-actualizing. He thus may be more accepting of differences in other individuals—differences that are found in every classroom.

These activities and materials have three major goals or components:

1. To encourage the individual to think about his values and to share his thoughts with others through group discussion, role-playing, games, and simulation activities
2. To learn to discuss the thoughts, beliefs, ideas, and feelings of others in a nonjudgmental way and to encourage each individual to accept, without criticism, the other person's feelings
3. To stimulate additional thinking, so an individual can become more accepting, and to move toward a more comprehensive way of valuing.

An annotated listing of specific values-education materials available from commercial sources is provided in Appendix G. By reading these brief descriptions the teacher may better understand the nature of values-education materials, how they might be used, and their potential for use in the classroom.

SPECIAL MATERIALS

Special materials have recently been developed to assist nonhandicapped students to better understand and accept the differences and similarities of their handicapped classmates. These materials are similar to values education and clarification approaches, but have been designed specifically to provide information about handicapped individuals and to promote positive attitudinal changes.

It appears that attitudes of the general public toward the handicapped are slowly changing in a positive direction. Whereas some mass media efforts such as telethons and other fund-raising projects continue to emphasize the significant differences of the handicapped, many others have brought to public attention the fact that handicapped persons are first of all individuals; human differences are acknowledged while the inherent similarities in the general needs of all people are recognized.

As an increasing number of handicapped students are served in regular classrooms it becomes essential that efforts be initiated to provide specific information about handicapping conditions, not only to enhance the interaction between handicapped and nonhandicapped students in their classrooms, but also to help prepare students for an adult world of which more and more handicapped persons are a part. Helping students learn about the world around them and how to deal with it is an important part of their education. Obviously this theme includes respect for human differences and recognition of inherent similarities. Placement of handicapped students in the least restrictive setting does not ensure respect for human dif-

ferences. The placement of handicapped students in regular classrooms does not guarantee that nonhandicapped students will interact positively with them or reflect desirable attitudes and behaviors.

Since our attitudes, beliefs, and behaviors toward differences are based on values learned from important others such as family members or from meaningful experiences, it seems imperative that the school curriculum provide such information and experience. Nonhandicapped students should have the opportunity to participate in simulations of handicapping conditions, discussions, interviews, and presentations by handicapped adults and students, and to preview films, filmstrips, and other media about handicapped persons.

One program designed to provide this information is called *BUDY—Better Understanding Disabled Youth* (Weishahn and Baker, 1980) has been found to be very successful in providing specific information and changing attitudes of nonhandicapped students. A description of this program follows:

BUDY is a series of five multimedia units designed to provide specific information about disabled individuals. Although BUDY is designed for students from kindergarten through the sixth grade it may be modified and used with older students. The five units are:
1. The visually impaired
2. The hearing impaired
3. Crippled and other health impaired
4. Learning handicaps
5. Behavioral handicaps

Each unit contains introductory activities, simulations, children's stories, filmstrips and accompanying audio tapes, books and media, table games and puzzles, bulletin board ideas, and follow-up activities such as suggestions on the use of community resource personnel. Specific knowledge tests and attitudinal surveys that may be used on a pre- and posttest basis are also included.

Efforts should be initiated to provide specific information concerning "differences"

May, 19 (whatever)
Public Schoolsville, U.S.A.

Dear Teacher,

We truly value your help in assisting other teachers to develop more sensitivity in their relationships with children. Their change in attitude has improved the emotional climate of your school and has resulted in increased academic performance on the part of many children. We hope it has made it a more pleasant place for you to work, in addition to the positive benefits to children.

We have decided we should share some additional anecdotes with you. These are about really *good* teachers. They, too, are in your building. Are you one of them?

Thanks again for your assistance,
BILL GEARHEART and MEL WEISHAHN

and this content should be an integral part of every student's education. It is apparent that we must provide the conditions that will enable students to work toward satisfying their basic needs. One such basic need is an interaction or socializing experience that begins with carefully designed instruction to assist students in relating to others in their environment.

SUMMARY

Throughout this chapter and the entire text we have emphasized that the teacher is the single most important factor in the success or failure of handicapped students being educated in the least restrictive environment. In addition to the methods and behavior of the teacher, the materials being used in the class and the classroom environment itself should be given serious consideration when there is a problem. It must be recognized that there are times when a problem situation in a classroom can clearly be identified as coming from within the student, but more frequently such problems are the result of the interaction between the teacher, the materials, the classroom environment, and the student.

There are many methods and techniques that are of value in promoting the positive feelings and reactions that are so important to both handicapped and nonhandicapped students. We have tried to suggest some of these methods and techniques in this chapter, but these are only a starting point. The motivation for positive relationships must come from *within* the teacher. When it does, the feeling will spread throughout the class and sometimes even to adjoining classrooms.

We started this chapter with a "Dear Teacher" letter in which we noted some of the poor attitudes we have seen in the educational universe in which we live. We want to close this chapter and this text in a much more upbeat mood, and we have chosen to do this with the letter above. Please read and accept it in the sincere manner in which it was written.

JOY IN SCHOOL IS having a contagious teacher*

My first taste of geography came in the fourth grade, and I didn't think much of it. I approached fifth grade geography with a fairly negative attitude, but the first few classes brought with them a pleasant surprise.

My teacher was really interested in the subject material. She knew what she was talking about and she was enthusiastic about introducing us to the subject.

I think it was as much my teacher as her methods of instruction that made fifth grade geography so enjoyable. She had a genuine concern for us as individuals as well as an interest in our academic growth, and she let us know it.

JOY IN SCHOOL IS mutual respect*

My senior homeroom teacher and I had very different, if not opposite, approaches to almost everything. I respected and feared her to a degree and yet I challenged some of her opinions. Throughout the year, she had always given the impression of being angered by my statements and I used to wonder whether I should just shut up and leave her alone. Graduation night, she made a special effort to find me and she said, "I enjoyed having you in my class. I think we've both learned a lot from each other."

JOY IN SCHOOL IS having a sensitive teacher*

The happiest thing that ever happened to me was when I was first coming into school. All the kids made fun of me and the teacher took me in and was kind to me.

---

*From Schultz, E., Heuchert, C., and Stampt, S. *Pain & Joy in School*. Champaign, Ill.: Research Press, 1973. Used with permission.

TEACHERS WHO BELIEVE PEOPLE ARE DEPENDABLE*
Arthur Combs

Let me use this example also to show you why you cannot tell the difference between the good ones and the poor ones on the basis of the methods which they use. Take two teachers, each of whom believes children are "able." Now one of these teachers, because she believes the children are able, makes them work real hard because she knows they can and the message that gets through is, She thinks I can. She is tough. Here is another teacher who also believes the children are able, but she says to them, "You know that is an interesting idea, why don't you take the rest of the afternoon to work on it by yourself?" She is a softy. Now here are two widely different methods, both of them used by good teachers. The important question is not what they are doing but the message that is conveyed by what they are doing, and the message comes from their beliefs, not what they did. In each case the same message gets through, "She thinks I can, she has confidence in me. She believes I am able." The important question we have to look at is the message that is conveyed by what people do rather than the things which they say.

There is an old Indian saying, "What you do speaks so loudly, I can't hear what you say." And that is true; the beliefs you have betray you in spite of yourself. Not long ago I was listening to a psychiatrist who was talking about the difficulties he had with some kinds of patients who came to his office. "I don't seem to be getting the kind of results that you people are getting," he said. "I believe in the same kind of therapy that you do. I believe in the dignity and integrity of my clients and I believe that the client ought to be helped to find his own answers," and so on. Then, when he was through with all this, he said, "I have great difficulty in making my patients understand." His real belief shows in spite of the fact that he knows

---

*From Arthur W. Combs. "The Human Aspect of Administration." *Educational Leadership*, November 1970, 28(2), 197-205. Reprinted with permission of the Association for Supervision and Curriculum Development and Arthur W. Combs. Copyright © 1970 by the Association for Supervision and Curriculum Development.

the right words to say. His behavior is a function of the belief system which he has.

In research after research the good helpers all turn out to believe people are able and dependable and friendly and worthy and dignified and persons of integrity and value. The poor come out on the other side of that picture. You might ask yourself, do I really believe that people are really dependable?

RANDY—GRADE OF A
Jacqueline Murphy

Randy is a bright-eyed, enthusiastic, not very quick, but not easily frustrated eleven-year-old boy. He works carefully, slowly, methodically. He tries very hard. He seems to accept his slower mind philosophically. He said to me once, "You don't have to be smart to be good at everything. I'm great at baseball!" But there is in him a strong, clear desire to do better—to star. The things he does to his satisfaction delight him—he beams.

One time I gave him an A in history. His work was very ordinary, perhaps 'worth' a C, but he did the best he could. Carefully. And when I was making out those report cards and thought of how happy it would make him to get an A in something —probably the only A he would ever get in his school life—when I imagined his face brightening, the excitement and joy and pride, the decision made itself.

I watched him out of the corner of my eye as I was handing out the report cards, anticipating his reaction. His hand shot up excitedly after he glanced over his card. "Miss Murphy!" "Yes, Randy?" "Miss Murphy, but how'd I get to be so smart?"

He looked both genuinely puzzled and delighted. I felt warm and good. I don't know who was more delighted, he or I. And I was again reminded of how Randy viewed himself as intellectually inferior.

"You worked hard, Randy. You deserved that A." He looked down at his report card, beaming.

I will never forget that look.

TEACHER WHO RECOGNIZED YOUNG LOST STUDENT*
Arthur Combs

In one of the schools in the outskirts of Atlanta a very lovely girl was teaching the first grade. This young woman had beautiful long hair which she was accustomed to wearing in a pony tail down to the middle of her back. She wore her hair this way the first three days of the school year. Then, on Thursday, she decided to do it differently. She did it up in a bun on top of her head, and went to teach her first grade. Well, one of her little boys came, looked in her room, and did not recognize his teacher. That sometimes happens when a woman changes her hairdo. So the little boy was lost, all by himself out in the hall.

Soon, along came a supervisor who said, "What's the trouble?" He said, "I can't find my teacher." The supervisor then asked "What's your teacher's name?" Well, he did not know, so she said, "What room are you in?" but he did not know that either. He had looked in there and it was not the right place. So she said, "Well, come on. Let's see if we can find her," and they started down the hall together, the little boy and the supervisor, hand in hand. She opened the doors of several rooms without much luck. Finally, they came to the room where this young woman was teaching. As they opened the door the young teacher turned, saw the supervisor with the little boy standing in the doorway and said, "Why, Joey, it's so good to see you, son. We were wondering where you were. Do come in. We've missed you so." The little boy pulled out of the supervisor's hand and threw himself into the teacher's arms. She gave him a hug, a pat on the fanny, and he trotted to his seat.

While the supervisor was telling me this story, she and I were riding along in a car. She said to me, "Art, I said a prayer for that teacher, she knew what was important. She thought little boys were important!" We got to kicking this around; suppose she had not thought little boys were im-

---

*From Arthur W. Combs. "The Human Aspect of Administration." *Educational Leadership*, November 1970, 28(2), 197-205. Reprinted with permission of the Association for Supervision and Curriculum Development and Arthur W. Combs. Copyright © 1970 by the Association for Supervision and Curriculum Development.

portant, suppose she thought supervisors were important? In that case she would have said, "Why, good morning, Miss K., we've been hoping you would come and see us, haven't we, boys and girls?" And the little boy would have been ignored. Or she might have thought that the lesson was important. In that case she would have said, "Well, Joey, for heaven's sakes, where have you been? Come in here and get to work." Or she might have thought that the discipline was important. In that case she would have said, "Joey, you know very well when you are late you must go to the office and get a permit. Now run right down there and get it." But she didn't. She behaved in terms of what she believed was important, and so it is for each of us.

REFERENCES AND SUGGESTED READINGS

Adelman, H. An interactional view of causality. *Academic Therapy*, 1970, 6, 43-52.

Arnold, R. The achievements of boys and girls taught by men and women teachers. *Elementary School Journal*, 1968, 68, 367-371.

Arnold, W., Glaser, N., & Ernst, L. *Teacher move analysis*. Dubuque, Iowa: Kendall/Hunt Publishing Co., 1971.

Bandura, A., & Rosenthal, T. Vicarious classical conditioning as a function of arousal level. *Journal of Personality and Social Psychology*, 1965, 3, 54-62.

Barr, R. *Values and youth*. Washington, D.C.: National Council for the Social Studies, 1971.

Beez, W. V. Influence of biased psychological reports on teacher behavior and pupil performance. In Morrison, A. & McIntyre, D. (Eds.) *The Social psychology of Teaching*. Baltimore, Md.: Penguin Books, Inc., 1972.

Bricker W., & Bricker, D. The infant, toddler, and preschool intervention project. In P. D. Tjossem (Ed.), Intervention strategies for high-risk infants and young children, Baltimore, University Park Press, 1976.

Brophy, J., & Good, T. *Teacher-student relationships— causes and consequences*. New York: Holt, Rinehart & Winston, Inc., 1974.

Chennault, M. Improving the social acceptance of unpopular educable mentally retarded pupils in special classes. *American Journal of Mental Deficiency*, 1967, 72, 455-458.

Clifford, M., & Walster, E., The effect of physical attractiveness on teachers expectations. *Sociology of Education*, 1973, 46, 248-258.

Combs, A. The human aspect of administration. *Educational Leadership*, November, 1970, 28, 197-205.

Cullum, A. The geranium on the window sill just died but teacher you went right on. New York: Harlin Quist Books, 1973.

Dion, D., Berscheid, E., & Walster, E. What is beautiful is good. *Journal of Personality and Social Psychology*. 1972, 24, 285-290.

Feshback, N. Student teacher preferences of elementary school pupils varying in personality characteristics. *Journal of Educational Psychology*, 1969, 60, 126-132.

Fink, A., & Semmel, M. *Indiana behavior management system II*. Bloomington, Ind.: Center for Innovation in Teaching the Handicapped, 1971.

Flanagan, J. *Test of general ability: technical report*. Chicago: Science Research Associates, Inc., 1960.

Flanders, N. *Teacher influences, pupil attitudes, and achievement*. Washington, D. C.: U.S. Department of Health, Education, and Welfare, Office of Education, 1965.

Flanders, N. *Analyzing teaching behavior*. Boston: Addison-Wesley Publishing Co., Inc., 1970.

Fleming, E., & Anttonen, R. Teacher expectancy or my fair lady. *American Educational Research Journal*, 1971, 8, 241-252.

Galloway, C. Teacher nonverbal communication. *Educational Leadership*, October, 1966, 24, 55-63.

Galloway, C. Nonverbal communication. *Theory Into Practice*, December 1968, 7, 172-175.

Galloway, C. Body language. *Today's Education*, December 1972, 61, 45-46, 62.

Good, T. Which pupils do teachers call on? *Elementary School Journal*, 1970, 70, 190-198.

Hall, B. *Values clarification as learning process*. San Diego: Pennant Educational Materials, 1973.

Handy, R. *Value theory and the behavioral sciences*. Springfield, Ill.: Charles C Thomas, Publisher, 1969.

Hargreaves, D. Teacher-pupil relations in a streamed secondary school. In Morrison, A., and McIntyre, D. (Eds). *The social psychology of teaching*. Baltimore, Md.: Penguin Books Inc., 1972.

Harmin, M. *Clarifying values through subject matter*. Minneapolis: Winston Press, 1973.

Hawley, R. *Human values in the classroom: teaching for personal and social growth*. Amherst, Mass.: Education Research Associates, 1973.

Hawley, R., & Hawley, I. *Human values in the classroom: a handbook for teachers*. New York: Hart Publishing Co., Inc., 1975.

Helton, J., and Oakland, T. Teachers attitudinal responses to differing characteristics of elementary school students. *Journal of Educational Psychology*, 1977, 69(3), 261-265.

Hughes, M. Development of the means for the assessment of the quality of teaching in elementary schools. *Cooperative Research Project No. 353, U.S. Office of Education.* Salt Lake City: University of Utah Press, 1959.

Jackson, G., & Cosca, G. The inequality of educational opportunity in the southwest: an observational study of ethnically mixed classrooms. *American Educational Research Journal,* 1974, *11,* 219-229.

Johnson, D. W., & Johnson, R. T. *Learning together and alone: cooperation, competitive, or individualization.* Englewood Cliffs, N.J.: Prentice-Hall, 1975.

Johnson, D. W., & Johnson, R. T. Mainstreaming: will handicapped students be liked, rejected, or ignored? *Instructor,* February 1978, *87,* 152-154.

Keogh, B., & Becker, L. Early detections of learning problems: questions, cautions, and guidelines. *Exceptional Children,* 1973, *40,* 5-11.

Leacock, E. *Teaching and learning in city schools.* New York: Basic Books, Inc., Publishers, 1969.

Lilly, S. Improving social acceptance of low sociometric status, low achieving students. *Exceptional Children,* 1971, *37,* 341-347.

Medley, C. Experiences with the OSCAR technique. *Journal of Teacher Education,* 1963, *14,* 267-273.

Medley, D., & Klein, A. Measuring classroom behavior with a pupil-reaction inventory. *Elementary School Journal,* 1957, *57*(6), 315-319.

Medley, D., & Mitzel, H. A technique for measuring classroom behavior. *Journal of Educational Psychology,* 1958, *49,* 86-92.

Mitzer, J. Cipher in the snow. *N.E.A. Journal,* November 1964, *53,* 8-10.

Morrison, A., & McIntyre, D. *Teachers and Teaching.* Baltimore: Penguin Books, Inc., 1969.

Palardy, J. What teachers believe—what children achieve. *Elementary School Journal,* 1969, *69,* 370-374.

Perkins, H. A procedure for assessing the classroom behavior of students and teachers. *American Education Research Journal,* 1964, *1,* 249-260.

Peterson, C., Peterson, J., & Scriven, G. Peer imitation by nonhandicapped and handicapped preschoolers. *Exceptional Children,* 1977, *43*(4), 223-224.

The Poor Scholar's Soliloquy. *Childhood Education,* January 1944, *20,* 219-22.

Raths, L. *Values and teaching.* Columbus, Ohio: Charles E. Merrill Publishing Co., 1966.

Rosenthal, R., & Jacobson, L. *Pygmalion in the classroom.* New York: Holt, Rinehart & Winston, Inc., 1968.

Ross, M., & Salvia, J. Attractiveness as a biasing factor in teacher judgments. *American Journal of Mental Deficiency,* 1975, *80*(1) 96-98.

Rothbart, M., Dalfen, S. S., & Barnett, R. Effects of a teacher's expectancy on student-teacher interaction. *Journal of Educational Psychology,* 1971, *62*(1), 49-54.

Rubin, R., & Balow, B. Learning and behavior disorders: a longitudinal study. *Exceptional Children,* 1971, *38,* 293-298.

Rucker, W. *Human values in education.* Dubuque, Iowa: Kendall/Hunt Publishing Co., 1969.

Rucker, C., & Vincenzo, F. Maintaining social acceptance gains made by mentally retarded children. *Exceptional Children,* 1970, *36,* 679-680.

Salvia, J., Algozzine, R., & Sheare, J., Attractiveness and school achievement. *Journal of School Psychology,* 1977, *15*(1), 60-67.

Schmuck, R. Some relationships of peer liking patterns in the classroom to pupil attitudes and achievement. *School Review,* 1963, *71,* 337-359.

Schultz, E., Heuchert, C., & Stampf, S. *Pain and joy in school.* Champaign, Ill.: Research Press, 1973.

Simon, S., & Clark, J. *More values clarification: strategies for the classroom.* San Diego: Pennant Educational Materials, 1974.

Simon, S., Howe, L., & Kirschenbaum, H. *Values clarification: handbook of practical strategies for teachers and students.* New York: Hart Publishing Company, Inc., 1972.

Simpson, B. *Becoming aware of values.* San Diego: Pennant Educational Materials, 1973.

Soar, R., Soar, R., & Ragosta, M. *The Florida climate and control system,* Gainesville, Fla.: Institute for Development of Human Resources, College of Education, University of Florida, 1971.

Theory into practice, October 1971, *10.* Columbus, Ohio: Ohio State University. (Entire issue is devoted to nonverbal communication.)

Weishahn, M. & Baker, C. *BUDY: Better understanding disabled youth,* Oak Lawn, Ill.: Ideal School Supply, 1979.

White, N. J. I taught them all. *The Clearing House,* November 1937, *12,* 151, 192.

Williams, F., Whitehead, J., & Miller, L. Relations between language, attitudes, and teacher expectancy. *American Educational Research Journal,* 1972, *9,* 263-277.

Wolfensberger, W. Normalization: the principles of normalization in human services. Toronto: National Institute on Mental Retardation, A72.

GLOSSARY

academic planning meeting Group meeting in which the students and the teacher plan the academic program.

acuity Acuteness or keenness, as of hearing or vision.

adaptive behavior Individual's ability to meet standards set by society for his/her cultural group. The American Association on Mental Deficiency considers three areas of performance in assessing adaptive behavior: maturation, learning, and social adjustment.

adaptive physical education Physical education programs designed to meet the specific needs of handicapped students.

Adlerian theory Theory suggesting that schools must become truly democratic, with students playing an active role in the process of their education. One advocate is Rudolph Dreikurs.

ambulation Art of walking without assistance from others. It may include the use of crutches, a cane, or other mechanical aids.

aphasia Loss or impairment of the ability to use oral language.

articulation problems Most common types of speech problem. Include: additions, "buhrown" for brown, "cuhow" for cow; distortion, "shled" for sled; omission, "pay" for play, "cool" for school, "ift" for lift; substitution "dat" for that, "wabbit" for rabbit, or "thum" for some.

audiogram Graph on which results of audiometric evaluation are charted. Provides an indication of the person's ability to hear each tone at each of the presented frequencies.

audiologist Hearing specialist who administers an audiometric examination.

audiometer Produces sounds at varying intensities (loudness) and varying frequencies (pitch).

audiometric evaluation Presents a series of carefully calibrated tones that vary in loudness and pitch. This assists in determining the extent and type of hearing loss so that proper remedial or medical steps can be taken to overcome the hearing problem.

aura, epileptic Subjective sensation that precedes and marks the onset of an epileptic seizure.

autism Childhood disorder rendering the child noncommunicative and withdrawn.

behavior modification Techniques offering the tools and systematic procedures that teachers may implement to change or modify unacceptable or defiant behavior and encourage more acceptable and appropriate behavior.

Behavior problem checklist Checklist for grades K to 8 consisting of sixty-nine items that are limited to the most frequently occurring behaviors of children referred to a psychiatric clinic. Developed by Quay and Peterson.

Bureau of Education for the Handicapped (BEH) Major unit within the federal government responsible for administration of educational policies affecting handicapped children and youth.

cane technique Use of a cane as an aid to mobility.

CEC Abbreviation for the Council for Exceptional Children.

central nervous system (CNS) That part of the nervous system to which the sensory impulses are transmitted and from which motor impulses originate. In vertebrates the brain and spinal cord.

cerebral palsy A group of conditions that may seriously limit motor coordination. It is frequently present at birth, but may be acquired any time as the result of head injury or infectious disease. It is characterized by varying degrees of disturbance of voluntary movement.

class action suit Litigation or law suits instigated on behalf of a group of individuals in a common situation (i.e., students with similar handicapping conditions).

cleft lip or palate Congenital fissure of the palate or lip that can cause articulation errors and

259

problems with nasality. Normally corrected by surgery.

colostomy Surgical procedure in which an artificial anal opening is formed in the colon.

conductive hearing loss Hearing loss caused by interference with transmission of sound from the outer ear.

congenital To be present in an individual at birth.

continuum of alternative placements Full spectrum of services that may be tailored to the individual needs of each student at any given time during the student's educational career.

contracture Condition of muscle characterized by fixed high resistance to passive stretch and generally caused by prolonged immobilization.

control braces Braces to prevent or eliminate purposeless movement or to allow movement in only one or two directions.

cooperative plan Plan in which the student is enrolled in a special class, but attends a regular classroom for part of the school day. The student's homeroom is a special class.

corrective braces Braces for prevention and correction of deformity during a child's rapid growth years.

crisis or helping teacher Teacher who provides temporary support and control to troubled students when they are unable or unwilling to cope with the demands of the regular classroom.

cystic fibrosis Hereditary disease resulting from a generalized dysfunction of the pancreas.

decibel (dB) Unit of measurement used to express intensity of sound

defiant behavior Stubborn or aggressive behavior resulting from forces within the student or within his environment, including his interaction with significant others in his life.

delayed speech Condition wherein a child does not talk when normal developmental guidelines would indicate that he should be talking.

Devereux Elementary School Behavior Rating Scale Scale that measures behavior which indicates the student's overall adaptation to the classroom setting and his subsequent academic achievement in the classroom.

diabetes Metabolic disorder wherein the individual's body is unable to utilize and properly store sugar. It is the result of the inability of the pancreas to produce a sufficient amount of the hormone insulin.

diabetic coma Condition caused by too much sugar (too little insulin) resulting from failure to take insulin, illness, or neglect of proper diet.

diagnosogenic theory Theory that places the blame for stuttering on individuals in a child's early environment who labeled normal disfluencies as stuttering.

direction-taking Method employed by visually impaired individuals using an object or sound to establish a course of direction toward or away from an object.

disability Objective, measurable lack of function or form.

dog guide Dog used to guide visually impaired people.

Duchenne (childhood) muscular dystrophy Generally fatal disease characterized by slow deterioration of the voluntary muscles ending in a complete state of helplessness.

due process Procedures and policies established to ensure equal educational opportunities for all children. Public Law 94-142 contains due process procedures specific to handicapped students.

dyslexia Severe reading disability accompanied by visual perceptual problems and problems in writing, such as reversals and mirror writing.

educable mentally retarded/handicapped Term used to describe a youngster who displays the behavior of the mentally handicapped, who has an IQ of 50 to 70, and similarly retarded adaptive behavior. The concept of mild or educable mentally handicapped (EMR) implies that the student can be educated and that, with proper educational opportunity, he can be a self-supporting, participating member of society.

efficacy studies Research specifically established to determine the extent to which given educational practices or procedures achieve the desired effects.

electronic mobility devices Devices to enhance hearing efficiency, detect obstacles, enable an individual to walk in a straight line, or reveal specific location of obstacles in the environment.

environmental factors Variables such as poverty, racial discrimination, school pressures, and deteriorating family units considered when evaluating students.

epilepsy Not a disease in itself, but a sign or symptom of some underlying disorder in the nervous system. Convulsions or seizures are the main symptoms.

etiology The study of causes or origins of a disease or condition.

Flanders classroom interaction analysis Teacher evaluation tool that takes into consideration the verbal behavior of the teacher and the student. The interaction is analyzed on the basis of categories.

frustration theory Theory on the cause of stuttering based on the idea that a student may have an unusual need to be listened to, and in the drive to keep the listener's attention, normal disfluencies cause the speaker to become more and more frustrated.

Galloway nonverbal system Teacher evaluation system that contains a procedure for decoding nonverbal cues associated with six of the seven teacher behaviors of the Flanders category system.

glad notes Notes given to a student or a student's parents by the teacher for something the student has done to overcome social or academic difficulty.

Hahnemann high school behavior rating scale Scale that measures overt classroom behavior related to a student's adjustment to the demands of the regular classroom. Designed by Swift and Spivak.

handicap Subjective or environmental limitation associated with disability.

hearing loss Inability to perceive sounds. For definition of relative degrees of loss, see Chapter 3, pp. 45 to 46.

hemophilia Hereditary blood disorder resulting in insufficient clotting.

hertz (Hz) Unit of measurement used to express frequency of sound.

hospital and homebound Term used for students with chronic conditions that require long-term treatment in a hospital or students who are homebound and receive special instruction from homebound/itinerant special education personnel.

hostile aggressiveness Behavior characterized by violence toward teachers, peers, and parents, including, kicking, hitting, biting, and fighting.

humanistic approach Approach toward troubled students that involves the acceptance of a student's behavior and the reflection of that behavior back to the student. This direct and uncomplicated framework encourages the student to learn, to express, and to better understand his feelings in a caring, reflective environment.

hyperactivity Condition characterized by incessant motion or activity that interferes with learning.

hypoactivity Opposite of hyperactivity; condition characterized by lethargy and lack of activity that interferes with learning.

hypoglycemia Insulin reaction caused by an increase in metabolism resulting from too much exercise, too much insulin, too little food, or nervous tension.

incontinence Lack of bowel and bladder control.

Individualized educational program (IEP) Tool for management of the educational program to assure that each student is provided for individually.

insulin Protein hormone produced by the pancreas and secreted into the blood where it regulates carbohydrate (sugar) metabolism. Used in treatment and control of diabetes mellitus.

insulin reaction See *Hypoglycemia.*

integration To become a part of the mainstream. Implies joint effort on behalf of special and general educators.

intensity The volume of sound (loudness or softness), usually expressed in decibels

itinerant teacher Traveling teacher who works with a given student on a regularly scheduled basis depending on the student's needs at the particular time.

kinesthesis The sense by which movement, weight, position, etc. are perceived.

kyphosis Curvature of the spine; hunchback.

language nonfluency General lack of smoothness in language production.

learning disabled student Student who displays the following characteristics: (1) significant discrepancy between the individual's achievement and his apparent ability to achieve or perform; (2) normal or above-average intelligence; and (3) normal sensory acuity.

learning lab Diagnostic/prescriptive center designed to meet the individual needs of each student.

legally blind Category of visually impaired individuals having central visual acuity of 20/200 or less in the better eye after correction, or visual acuity of more than 20/200 if there is a field defect in which the widest diameter of the visual field subtends an angle distance no greater than 20 degrees.

listening helper/buddy Peer in the classroom who helps the hearing impaired student in such things as turning to the correct page, taking notes, or adjusting to a new class or school.

litigation The act of initiating and carrying on a suit in a court of law.

Magic Circle Technique used by elementary education teachers to help troubled students dispel the delusion that they are significantly different from those around them. The teacher attempts to foster an atmosphere of warmth and honesty in which each student contributes his thoughts and feelings and listens respectfully to his peers.

mainstreaming Maximum integration of handicapped students into the regular classroom, coupled with concrete assistance for nonspecial education teachers.

memory disorder Disability of the auditory or visual memory.

mental retardation Significantly subaverage general intellectual functioning existing concurrently with deficits in adaptive behavior and manifested during the developmental period.

mobility Individual's movement from one point in his environment to another.

muscular dystrophy A progressive condition in which the muscles are replaced by fatty tissue.

myelomeningocele Type of spina bifida in which a sac containing part of a malformed spinal cord protrudes from a hole in the spine.

near-point vision Ability to see at close range, such as in reading.

neurotic tendencies theory Theory that portrays stuttering as the outcome of such needs as satisfaction of anal and oral desires, infantile tendencies, and other Freudian-based regressions.

occupational therapy Therapy directed at upper extremities emphasizing activities of daily living such as tying shoes, eating, or other routine activities.

ophthalmologist Medical doctor specializing in the diagnosis and treatment of diseases of the eye. He is also licensed to prescribe glasses. Also called an *oculist*.

Optacon Device that converts printed material to either a tactual or auditory stimulus.

optician Craftsman who makes glasses and fills the prescriptions of ophthalmologists and optometrists.

optometrist One who specializes in eye problems but does not possess a medical degree. Licensed to measure visual function and prescribe and fit glasses.

orientation Blind individual's use of his remaining senses to establish his position and relationship to objects in his environment.

orthoptist A nonmedical technician who directs prescribed exercises or training to correct eye muscle inbalances and generally works under the direction of an ophthalmologist.

osteoarthritis Degenerative arthritis usually confined to one joint.

otologist Medical doctor specializing in diseases of the ear.

overattention Condition in which an individual focuses on one particular object and seems unable to break the focus.

paralysis Loss or impairment of function in a part of the body.

paraplegia Paralysis of the lower limbs or lower section of the body.

partially sighted Category of individuals whose visual acuity is better than 20/200.

perceptual disorders Disorders involving visual, auditory, tactual, or kinesthetic perception.

perfectionism Extreme fear of failure or criticism sometimes seen in troubled students.

perseveration Persistent repetition without apparent purpose.

petit mal seizures Epileptic seizures of short duration (5 to 20 seconds) that may occur as many as 100 times a day. The student may become pale and stare into space, his eyelids may twitch, and he may demonstrate jerky movements.

physical therapy Therapy directed at lower extremities emphasizing posture, gait, movements, and the prevention of contractures.

plus factors Additional instruction that visually impaired students might need in nonacademic areas, for example, braille, orientation and mobility, and typewriting.

poliomyelitis Acute viral disease characterized by involvement of the central nervous system. Sometimes results in paralysis.

pressure theory Theory that places emphasis for the cause of stuttering on developmental pressures that promote disfluency.

problem-solving meeting Group meeting in which students learn to examine situations, propose solutions, and evaluate the results.

prosthesis Artificial arm or leg to replace an amputated part of the body.

psychoanalytical approach Approach to troubled students in which the teacher provides ways for the students to bring into consciousness their unconscious repressions. All program cueing comes from the student. Used in residential schools and not adaptable to a public school setting.

psychomotor or temporal lobe seizures Complex seizures that affect motor systems and mental processes and are manifested by peculiar behavior such as licking or chewing of lips or purposeless activities. May last for a few minutes or several hours.

Public Law 93-380 Educational Amendments of 1974.

Public Law 94-142 Education for All Handicapped Children Act of 1975. See *Federal Register*, August 23, 1977, *42*(163) for details on the rules governing this act.

Pupil Behavior Inventory System used in grades 7 to 12 to measure behavioral and attitudinal factors that affect the degree of success a pupil will have in accomplishing his educational objectives. Designed by Vinter, Sarri, Vorwaller, and Schafer.

quadriplegia Paralysis affecting both arms and both legs.

readability level Indication of the difficulty of reading material in terms of the grade level at which it might be expected to be read successfully.

rehabilitation To restore to a former capacity. For example, a student may suffer damage to a limb and, through therapy, the limb may be restored to good condition and use. The term frequently is applied to a variety of services designed to assist individuals in overcoming handicaps, especially in preparation for employment. Such services are referred to as *vocational rehabilitation services.*

remediation Correction of a deficiency. Often used in referring to correction of academic deficits, for example, problems in reading.

residential or boarding school Schools established for visually or hearing impaired, emotionally disturbed, or mentally retarded because local school districts did not offer the needed services and which usually provide 24-hour care and treatment.

residual hearing Individual's remaining hearing after some hearing loss.

resource room teacher Teacher who provides supplemental or remedial instruction (usually daily) to a child enrolled in a regular classroom. The assistance is regularly scheduled in a room that has been specifically designated for that purpose.

responsibility-oriented classroom Classroom in which student is responsible for his own behavior, his academic success, and his failure. He cannot blame his environment, parents, or peers for his own behavior; he has the ability to choose. The classroom is neither a teacher dominated nor student controlled room, but rather is a joint effort to learn, relate, and experience. One advocate is William Glasser.

rheumatoid arthritis Systemic disease characterized by inflammation of the joints and a broad spectrum of other manifestations, involving destruction of the joints with resultant deformity.

rubella German measles.

scoliosis Abnormal lateral curvature of the spine (C-curve).

Section 504 Section 504 of the Rehabilitation Act of 1973, containing requirements designed to guarantee the civil rights of the handicapped (See *Federal Register*, May 4, 1977, *2*, [86]).

seizures Excessive electrical discharges released in some nerve cells of the brain resulting in loss of control over muscles, consciousness, senses, and thoughts.

sensorineural hearing loss Hearing loss associated with damage to the sensory end-organ or a dysfunction of the auditory nerve.

sighted guide technique Technique in which a visually impaired individual grasps a sighted person's arm just above the elbow, enabling him to "read" any movement of the guide's body.

Snellen chart Chart consisting of letters, numbers, or symbols of graduated sizes to be read at a distance of 20 feet to determine field visual acuity. A special Snellen chart to be read at a distance of 14 inches may be used to measure near vision.

spastic cerebral palsy A condition characterized by jerky or explosive motions when a child initiates a voluntary movement.

special education A subsystem of the total educational system for the provision of specialized or adapted programs and services or for assisting others to provide such services for exceptional youth and children.

special educator One who has had specialized training or preparation for teaching the handicapped and who may also work cooperatively with the regular classroom teacher by sharing unique skills and competencies.

speech handicap A disorder of speech that (1) interferes with communication, (2) causes the speaker to be maladjusted, or (3) calls undue attention to the speech as opposed to what is said.

spina bifida Serious birth defect in which the bones of the spine fail to close during the twelfth week of fetal development resulting in a cyst or sac in the lower back that is generally surgically treated during the child's first 24 to 48 hours of life. Varying degrees of paralysis in the lower extremities are generally observed.

tactile Pertaining to the sense of touch.

Teacher move analysis Tool that evaluates interaction between teacher and student by placing teacher behavior into eight categories, called teacher "moves."

Teacher's manual for in-school screening of emotionally handicapped children Screening device that consists of three rating scales used in combination with each other for one total evaluation of each pupil (teacher rating, peer rating, and self-rating). Designed by Bower and Lambert.

tinnitus Hearing noises within the head.

total communication Total language approach for the hearing impaired in which there is equal emphasis on speech, auditory training, and a system of visual communication.

trailing To follow lightly over a straight surface with back of fingertips to locate specific objects or to get a parallel line of direction.

visual acuity Measured ability to see.

Visual-auditory-kinesthetic-tactile (VAKT) approach Multisensory approach to teaching reading. Designed by Grace Fernald to assist children with severe reading disabilities.

visually impaired Inability to see. For definitions of relative sight loss, see Chapter 4, p. 68.

voice problems Disorders of pitch, intensity, quality, or flexibility of the voice.

Walker problem behavior identification checklist Checklist used by elementary education teachers to help select children with behavior problems who should be referred for further psychological evaluation, referral, and treatment.

A CAPTIONED FILMS FOR THE HEARING IMPAIRED

The following annotated listing of captioned films are representative of titles that are available. The collection of films numbers more than 600, and to include the entire list would take too much space; therefore, only representative titles have been included.*

They may be obtained through the school's resource/itinerant teacher of the hearing impaired, the state instructional materials center for the hearing impaired, or the state department of special education.

The following abbreviations are used in describing these films:

1. CFD number (for example, CFD 83)—this number should be used when ordering the film
2. B & W or Color—black and white or color
3. Min.—length of film in minutes
4. P—primary
   I—intermediate
   J—junior high
   S—senior high
   A—adult

Air Pollution

CFD 53C   Color   9½ min.   I—A
Presents the origins and effects of air pollution and explains the steps that are being taken to control it. The film stresses that all living things depend on clean air.

---

*Taken from *Catalog of Captioned Films for the Deaf*, Bureau of Education for the Handicapped, U.S. Office of Education, Division of Educational Services, Media Services and Captioned Films.

Aircraft Machinists

CFD 252   B & W   14 min.   J—S
Describes the vast amount of handwork necessary to build giant passenger jets: shows the labor involved from the first strut to the flight. Points out the growing area of employment in this industry.

Animals In Autumn

CFD 89   B & W   11 min.   P—I
Shows typical autumn activities of various animals, including deer, foxes, rabbits, ground squirrels, raccoons, cold-blooded animals, birds, and insects as they search for food, build homes, and prepare to migrate or hibernate in winter.

Artificial Respiration

CFD 465   Color   8 min.   A
Two methods of artificial respiration, mouth-to-mouth breathing and the Sylvester method, are explained in this film.

Banks and Credit

CFD 339   Color   11 min.   J—S
Shows the nature and activities of a commerical bank; defines credit, showing how it is created, transferred, and put to work by the bank to serve the community. Illustrates how deposits help supply funds.

Belgium and the Netherlands: Lands and Peoples

CFD 99   B & W   11 min.   I
A survey of the low countries showing how their culture and economy are affected by environmental factors such as easy access to the North Sea, dense population, and large coal resources.

Butterfly—Life Cycle of an Insect

CFD 107   B & W   8 min.   I
Uses environmental sounds and close-up photo-

graphs to follow the development of a monarch butterfly as it goes through the stages from egg to larva, to pupa, to adult.

The Country Mouse and City Mouse

CFD 4   B & W   8 min.   P

An animated film that tells the Aesop fable about the adventures of the country mouse who visits his city cousin, pointing to the age-old maxim that travel may be fun, but home is the best place.

Curious George Rides a Bike

CFD 116   Color   10 min.   P

The adventures of a little monkey who is given a bicycle by his friend, the man in the yellow hat. An iconographic film.

The Ears and Hearing

CFD 458   Color   22 min.   A

Shows the structure and functions of the human ear and demonstrates how the ear transmits sound waves to the brain. Describes how hearing aids and surgery may improve the hearing of some people.

Electricity: Principles of Safety

CFD 120   B & W   11 min.   J—S

Shows the hazards of electricity and their causes. Overloaded or short circuits can cause fires. Shows that a proper knowledge of electricity can prevent bodily harm.

Forces: Composition and Resolution

CFD 126   B & W   11 min.   S

Presents a simple example of forces acting in a straight line at a single point. Defines forces as vector quantities and illustrates how components and resultants may be determined graphically.

Gravity: How It Affects Us

CFD 13   B & W   14 min.   I—J

The film graphically depicts the importance of gravity by showing how it affects our daily activities, the earth in the universe, and its effects on an imaginary space traveler. Galileo's and Newton's experiments are shown.

Hitler: Anatomy of a Dictatorship

CFD 545   B & W   22 min.   S—A

To the German nation, torn by economic, political, and spiritual crises, Adolf Hitler promised strong leadership and a policy of revenge against supposed enemies. Through newsreel clips, the viewers will see Hitler's rapid rise to power and his eventual defeat by the Allies, after he produced an unmatched record of dictatorial brutality.

How To Change a Chemical Reaction

CFD 280   B & W   28 min.   I—J

A chemical reaction occurs when several solutions are combined and either a gas is diffused or the solutions change color. How to effect further chemical change through temperature or concentration is also described.

How Your Blood Circulates

CFD 274   B & W   28 min.   I—J

Examines the heart of a calf; uses a model of the human heart to explain how it functions. Demonstrates how to make a simple stethoscope.

Johnny Appleseed: a Legend of Frontier Life

CFD 150   B & W   15 min.   I—J

Depicts the life of Johnny Appleseed. Describes his work in spreading the word of God and encouraging the cultivation of apple trees throughout Pennsylvania and the Ohio territory.

Know Your Library

CFD 153   B & W   11 min.   J

A young girl discovers the value of the library, showing how to use the card catalog, to find books classified by the Dewey Decimal System, and to use reference materials such as an encyclopedia and the *Reader's Guide to Periodical Literature*.

Man Without a Country

CFD 63   B & W   25 min.   J—A

A dramatization of the book by the same title. The story is told by a judge to a group of new citizens to help them develop a sense of loyalty to their adopted country.

The Metric System

CFD 332   Color   13 min.   S
Defines the basic metric units of length, volume, and weight as a set of units with easy-to-remember interrelationships. Points out its advantages and shows how to convert from English to metric and vice versa.

The Midnight Ride of Paul Revere

CFD 23   B & W   11 min.   I—S
Tells the story of Paul Revere's ride by dramatizing the action and comparing the story with the one told in Longfellow's poem. Recreates episodes of April 18, discussing the significance of Paul Revere's ride.

Navajo Silversmith

CFD 302   Color   11 min.   I
Pictures of the Navajo Indian as a master of a very delicate craft, silversmithing. It bridges a span of years by showing how objects of another century were made. The film is set in the rugged land where the Navajos live.

People Are Different and Alike

CFD 410   B & W   11 min.   I
Illustrates that all people need friendship and love, food, and a place to live and that they want an education, fun, and happiness. Points out that people are more alike than different.

Reading Improvement: Vocabulary Skills

CFD 406   Color   11 min.   I
Suggests specific vocabulary-building skills and exercises that are helpful in increasing reading effectiveness. Designed to develop students' desire to increase their vocabulary.

Rocky Mountain Area: Backbone of the Nation

CFD 70   B & W   16 min.   I—J
Discusses ways in which the Rocky Mountains serve the nation, with resources for mining, grazing, irrigation farming, hydroelectric power, lumbering, and tourism and the need for using natural resources wisely.

Scandinavia—Norway, Sweden, Denmark

CFD 71   B & W   22 min.   I—J
Discusses the cultural ties and physical geography of the Scandinavian countries; describes the contrasts in regional patterns of living, natural resources, and types of industrial development.

The St. Lawrence Seaway

CFD 27   B & W   17 min.   S
Explains what the St. Lawrence Seaway is, what it looks like, how it was built, and how it works. Indicates some of the many changes the seaway has brought about in the world, pointing out how it has affected world trade.

Track And Field Events For Girls: Track Events, Part I

CFD 571   Color   22 min.   I—A
Covers the track events in girl's competition— sprints, middle-distance and distance runs, hurdles, and relays. It presents each event in overall performance and then breaks down each event to analyze specific techniques and forms.

The Ugly Duckling

CFD 35   B & W   10 min.   P
Follows the misfortunes of the unwanted ugly duckling who finally grows into a beautiful swan. Filmed in Europe from Hans Christian Andersen's famous fairy tale.

The War of 1812

CFD 187   B & W   15 min.   J—S
Covers the highlights of the military and naval action in the main theaters of The War of 1812 and discusses the conduct of the British and their impressment of American sailors as a cause of the war.

NATIONAL ORGANIZATIONS AND SERVICES FOR THE HEARING IMPAIRED

Acoustical Society of America
335 E. 45th St.
New York, New York 10017

American Foundation for the Blind, Inc.
Services for Deaf-Blind Persons
15 W. 16th St.
New York, New York 10011

American Speech and Hearing Assn.
10801 Rockville Pike
Rockville, Maryland 20852

Better Hearing Institute
1430 K St., N.W., #800
Washington, D.C. 20005

The Canadian Hearing Society
60 Bedford Rd.
Toronto, Ontario, Canada M5R 2K2

C.H.E.A.R., Inc.
P.O. Box 2000-871 McLean Ave.
Yonkers, New York 10704

Deafness Research Foundation
366 Madison Ave.
New York, New York 10017

Ear Research Institute
2130 W. 3rd St.
Los Angeles, California 90057

Easter Seal Research Foundation
National Easter Seal Society for Crippled
  Children and Adults
2023 W. Ogden Ave.
Chicago, Illinois 60612

National Assn. of Hearing & Speech Action
814 Thayer Ave.
Silver Springs, Maryland 20910

National Hearing Aid Society
20361 Middlebelt Rd.
Livonia, Michigan 48152

**American Academy of Ophthalmology
  and Otolaryngology**
15 2nd St., S.W.
Rochester, Minnesota 55901

American Board of Otolaryngology
220 Collingwood
Suite 130
Ann Arbor, Michigan 48103

**American College of Surgeons, Dept. of
  Otorhinolaryngology**
55 E. Erie St.
Chicago, Illinois 60611

American Laryngological Assn.
c/o William M. Trible, M.D.
Washington Hospital Center
Washington, D.C. 20010

**The American Laryngological, Rhinological &
  Otological Soc., Inc.**
c/o Ann R. Holm
2954 Dorman Rd.
Broomall, Pennsylvania 19008

**American Medical Assn. Section Council on
  Otorhinolaryngology**
Richard B. Carley, M.D., Secy.
Central Medical Bldg.
393 N. Dunlap
St. Paul, Minnesota 55104

American Otological Society
1000 E. High St.
Charlottesville, Virginia 22901

American Rhinologic Society
Penn Park Medical Center
2929 Baltimore, No. 105
Kansas City, Missouri 64111

Society of University Otolaryngologists
ENT Dept.
Univ. of Michigan School of Medicine
Ann Arbor, Michigan 48104

PROFESSIONAL ORGANIZATIONS AND CENTERS OF INFORMATION ON DEAFNESS

Alexander Graham Bell Assn. for the Deaf, Inc.
3417 Volta Pl., N.W.
Washington, D.C. 20007
  Oral Deaf Adults Section (ODAS)
  International Parents' Organization (IPO)
  American Organization for the Education of
    the Hearing Impaired

Conference of Executives of American Schools
  for the Deaf
Howard M. Quigley, Exec. Secy.
5034 Wisconsin Ave., N.W.
Washington, D.C. 20016

Council for Exceptional Children
1920 Association Drive
Reston, Virginia 22091
  State-Federal Information Clearinghouse for
    Exceptional Children (SFICEC)
  CEC Information Center on Exceptional
    Children

Educators of Professional Personnel for the
  Hearing Impaired (EPPHI)
Teachers College, Columbia University
Department of Special Education Box 223
New York, New York 10027

Executive Audial Rehabilitation Society (EARS)
Box 1820
Corpus Christi, Texas 78403

Gallaudet College Alumni Association
1021 Leo Way
Oakland, California 84611

Information Center for Hearing, Speech, and
  Disorders of Human Communication
Wood Basic Sci. Bldg.
The Johns Hopkins Medical Institutions
725 N. Wolfe St.
Baltimore, Maryland 21205

Mainstream
1200 15th Street, N.W.
Washington, D.C. 20005

National Association of the Deaf
814 Thayer Ave.
Silver Springs, Maryland 20910

National Association of State Directors of
  Special Education, Inc.
1201 16th St., N.W., Suite 610-E
Washington, D.C. 20036

National Catholic Educational Association
  Special Education Department
1 DuPont Circle, Suite 350
Washington, D.C. 20036

National Center on Educational Media &
  Materials for the Handicapped
c/o Linc Services, Inc.
829 Eastwind Drive
Westerville, Ohio 43801

National Education Association
Project to Improve Language Instruction to Deaf
  Children
1201 16th St., N.W.
Washington, D.C. 20036

Volta Speech Association for the Deaf
1537 35th Street N.W.
Washington, D.C. 20007

APPENDIX

C* SOURCES OF MATERIALS FOR THE VISUALLY IMPAIRED

As mentioned in Chapter 4, the resource/itinerant teacher of the visually impaired will have considerable information concerning the sources of materials that the teacher may need. If for some reason, however, such a resource person is not available to assist in acquiring materials, the following listing of sources of materials should be helpful.

The teacher's first attempt to obtain materials should be directed at the local school district's director of special education or to the individual serving the visually impaired. Another source of information would be the state education department—consultant for the visually impaired.

Many states have organized centers to coordinate resources and educational materials of public and private state and national agencies that have specialized materials for the visually impaired. Individual states that provide state-wide service for the coordination of special materials are listed below.

California Clearinghouse/Depository
721 Capitol Mall
Sacramento, California 95814

Colorado Instructional Materials Center for the Visually Handicapped (CIMC/VH)
State Library Bldg.
1362 Lincoln St.
Denver, Colorado 80203

---

*Adapted from Schrotberger, W. B. "Sources of Materials for the Visually Handicapped." In *Handbook for Teachers of the Visually Handicapped*, Louisville, Ky.: American Printing House for the Blind, 1974.

Connecticut Board of Education and Services for the Blind
170 Ridge Rd.
Wethersfield, Connecticut 06109

Florida Instructional Materials Center for the Visually Handicapped
204 Knott Bldg.
Tallahassee, Florida 32304

Hawaii Department of Education
Honolulu District Office
4967 Kilauea Avenue
Honolulu, Hawaii, 96816

Illinois Instructional Materials Services for the Visually Impaired
100 N. 1st St.
Springfield, Illinois 62777

Indiana Division of Special Education
120 West Market, Tenth floor
Indianapolis, Indiana 46204

Iowa Commission for the Blind
Fourth and Keosauqua
Des Moines, Iowa 50309

Kansas Department of Education
Division of Special Education
120 E. 10th St.
Topeka, Kansas 66612

Louisiana Learning Resources System
Vocational Education Center
18th St.
Lafayette, Louisiana 70501

Maine Department of Education and Cultural Services
State House
Augusta, Maine 04333

Massachusetts Department of Education
Library for the Visually Handicapped
271 Boylston St.
West Boylston, Massachusetts 01583

Michigan Department of Education
Box 30008
Lansing, Michigan 48909

Montana Office of the Superintendent of Public Instruction
Division of Special Education
State Capitol
Helena, Montana 59601

Nebraska Instructional Material Center for the Visually Handicapped
Nebraska School for the Blind
Nebraska City, Nebraska 68410

Nevada Department of Education
400 West King St.
Carson City, Nevada 89710

New Hampshire Materials Center for the Visually Handicapped
870 Hayward St.
Manchester, New Hampshire 03103

New Jersey Commission for the Blind and Visually Impaired
1100 Raymond Blvd.
Newark, New Jersey 07102

North Carolina State Department of Public Instruction
Division of Special Education
Raleigh, North Carolina 27611

Ohio Central Registry
Ohio School for the Blind
5220 N. High St.
Columbus, Ohio 43214

Oregon Board of Education
942 Lancaster Dr., N.E.
Salem, Oregon 97310

Pennsylvania Department of Education
Bureau of Special Education
Box 911
Harrisburg, Pennsylvania 17126

Texas Education Agency
201 E. 11th St.
Austin, Texas 78701

Virginia Commission for the Visually Handicapped
Education Services Department
3003 Parkwood Ave.
Richmond, Virginia 23221

Wisconsin Instructional Material Center for the Visually Handicapped
1700 W. State St.
Janesville, Wisconsin 53545

OTHER AGENCY SOURCES

The following listing of public and private agencies may be helpful in obtaining large type materials:

Albert Whitman Company
(Recreational large type)
560 W. Lake St.
Chicago, Illinois 60606

American Bible Society
(Bibles and religious literature)
1865 Broadway
New York, New York 10023

American Printing House for the Blind
(National organization for the production of literature and the manufacture of educational aids for visually handicapped)
1839 Frankfort Ave.
Louisville, Kentucky 40206

Bell and Howell Company
(Microfilm enlargement, catalog available)
Micro Photo Division
Duopage Department
1700 Shaw
Cleveland, Ohio 44112

Charles Scribner
(Recreational)
Large Type Editions
597 5th Ave.
New York, New York 10017

Children Press
(Children's books)
1224 W. Van Buren St.
Chicago, Illinois 60607

Children's Press, Inc.
(Type sizes ranging from 10 pt. to 30 pt.)
Jackson Blvd. and Racine Ave.
Chicago, Illinois 60607

Christian Record Braille Foundation, Inc.
(Publishes books and magazines for all age levels
in large print)
4444 S. 42nd St.
Lincoln, Nebraska 68506

Dakota Microfilm Co.
(Microfilm enlargement, catalog available)
501 N. Dale St.
St. Paul, Minnesota 55103

Dakota Microfilm Co.
(Textbook, catalog available)
345 N. Orange St.
Orlando, Florida 32801

Economy Blueprint & Supply Co.
(Microfilm enlargement, catalog available)
123 S. LaBrea Ave.
Los Angeles, California 90036

G. K. Hall
(Large type, recreational, textbooks)
70 Lincoln St.
Boston, Massachusetts 02111

Guide for Large Print Books, Inc.
(Recreational)
211 E. 43rd St.
New York, New York 10017

Harper & Row
(Harper Crest large type editions)
49 E. 33rd St.
New York, New York 10022

J. B. Lippincott Company
(Recreational; elementary and secondary)
E. Washington Square
Philadelphia, Pennsylvania 19105

Jewish Braille Institute of America, Inc.
(Maintains circulating large type library)
110 E. 13th St.
New York, New York 10016

Keith Jennison Books
(Recreational)
575 Lexington Ave.
New York, New York 10022

Lanewood Press
(Recreational and textbooks)
729 Boylston St.
Boston, Massachusetts 02116

Lutheran Braille Workers, Inc.
(Provides religious and educational materials in
large print in English and 16 other languages)
11735 Peach Tree Circle
Yucaipa, California 92399

Lutheran Library for the Blind
(Operates free lending library of materials in
large print)
3558 S. Jefferson Ave.
St. Louis, Missouri 63118

The Macmillan Co.
(Recreational reading)
866 3rd Ave.
New York, New York 10022

Microfilm Business Systems Co.
(Microfilm enlargement, catalog available)
5810 W. Adams Blvd.
Los Angeles, California 90016

Microfilm Company of California
(Microfilm enlargement, catalog available)
Library Reproduction Service
1977 S. Los Angeles St.
Los Angeles, California 90011

**National Association for the Visually
   Handicapped, Inc.**
(Produces and distributes large print, 18 pt.; read-
ing materials on request)
3201 Balboa St.
San Francisco, California 94121

National Braille Press, Inc.
(Provides, on request, large print materials)
88 St. Stephen St.
Boston, Massachusetts 02115

Random House, Inc.
(Recreational, secondary)
457 Madison Ave.
New York, New York 10022

Stanwix House
(Textbooks)
3020 Chartiers Ave.
Pittsburgh, Pennsylvania 15204

Ulverscoft Large Print Books
(Nearly 200 titles)
Oscar B. Stiskin
P.O. Box 3055
Stamford, Connecticut 06905

University Microfilms, Inc.
(Microfilm enlargement, catalog available)
Enlarge Editions Service
313 N. 1st St.
Ann Arbor, Michigan 48107

Viking Press, Inc.
(Recreational)
625 Madison Ave.
New York, New York 10022

Volunteer Services for the Blind, Inc.
919 Walnut St.
Philadelphia, Pennsylvania 19107

Volunteer Transcribing Services
(Microfilm enlargement, catalog available)
617 Oregon Ave.
San Mateo, California 94402

Walker and Company
(Recreational)
720 5th Ave.
New York, New York 10019

William Morrow
(Childrens books, good list with point type listed,
    recreational)
105 Madison Ave.
New York, New York 10016

Xavier Society for the Blind
(Maintains free lending library of hand-trans-
    cribed large type books of primarily, but not ex-
    clusively, religious materials)
154 E. 23rd St.
New York, New York 10010

Xerox Corporation
(Microfilm enlargement, catalog available)
Box 33
P.O. Box 33
Grand Central Station
New York, New York 10017

NATIONAL ORGANIZATIONS CONCERNING THE CRIPPLED AND OTHER HEALTH IMPAIRED

American Academy of Allergy
611 E. Wells St.
Milwaukee, Wisconsin 53202

American Academy for Cerebral Palsy
c/o James E. Bryan
1255 New Hampshire Ave. N.W.
Washington, D.C. 20036

American Academy of Pediatrics
1801 Hinman Ave.
Evanston, Illinois 60204

American Academy of Physical Medicine and Rehabilitation
30 N. Michigan Ave.
Chicago, Illinois 60602

American Association for Clinical Immunology and Allergy
P.O. Box 912 DTS
Omaha, Nebraska 68101

American Association for Rehabilitation Therapy
P.O. Box 93
North Little Rock, Arkansas 72116

American Association for Respiratory Therapy
1720 Regal Row
Dallas, Texas 75235

American Cancer Society
777 Third Ave.
New York, New York 10017

American Corrective Therapy Association
c/o Kirk Hodges
Rt. 2, Box 199
Jonesboro, Tennessee 37659

American Corrective Therapy Association, Inc.
811 St. Margaret's Rd.
Chillicothe, Ohio 45601

American Diabetes Association
600 Fifth Ave.
New York, New York 10020

American Epilepsy Society
Division of Neurosurgery
University of Texas Medical Branch
Galveston, Texas 77550

American Heart Association
7320 Greenville Ave.
Dallas, Texas 75231

American Lung Association
1740 Broadway
New York, New York 10019

American Medical Association
535 N. Dearborn St.
Chicago, Illinois 60610

American Nurses' Association
2420 Pershing Rd.
Kansas City, Missouri 64108

American Occupational Therapy
6000 Executive Blvd.
Rockville, Maryland 20852

American Orthopaedic Association
444 N. Michigan Ave.
Chicago, Illinois 60611

American Orthopsychiatric Association
1775 Broadway
New York, New York 10019

American Orthotic and Prosthetic Association
14444 N. St. N.W.
Washington, D.C. 20005

American Physical Therapy Association
1156 15th St., N.W.
Washington, D.C. 20005

American Public Health Association
1015 18th St., N.W.
Washington, D.C. 20036

American Rehabilitation Counseling Association
1607 New Hampshire Ave., N.W.
Washington, D.C. 20009

American Rheumatism Association
3400 Peachtree Rd., N.E.
Atlanta, Georgia 30326

American Speech and Hearing Association
10801 Rockville Pike
Rockville, Maryland 20852

Arthritis Foundation
3400 Peachtree Rd., N.E.
Atlanta, Georgia 30326

Association of Handicapped Artists
(Information and advice about handicapped
    artists)
503 Brisbane Building
Buffalo, New York 14203

Center for Independent Living, Inc.
2539 Telegraph Ave.
Berkeley, California 94704

Children's Asthma Research Institute and
    Hospital
AKA National Asthma Center
1999 Julian St.
Denver, Colorado 80204

Closer Look
1828 L. Street, N.W.
Washington, D.C. 20036

Conference of Lung Association
Staff
1740 Broadway
New York, New York 10019

Council for Exceptional Children
1920 Association Dr.
Reston, Virginia 22091

Cystic Fibrosis Foundation
3379 Peachtree Rd. N.E.
Atlanta, Georgia 30326

Directory for Exceptional Children
Porter Sargent, Publisher
11 Beacon St.
Boston, Massachusetts 02108

Disability Insurance Training Council
(Information about insurance for the handicapped)
145 North Ave.
Hartland, Wisconsin 53029

Epilepsy Foundation of America
1828 L St. N.W., Suite 406
Washington, D.C. 20036

Federal Association for Epilepsy
1729 F. St., N.W.
Washington, D.C. 20006

Foundation for Child Development
345 E. 46th St.
New York, New York 10017

Goodwill Industries of America, Inc.
9200 Wisconsin Ave.
Washington, D.C. 20014

Hemophilia Research, Inc.
60 East 42nd St.
New York, New York 10017

Rehabilitation International
432 Park Ave., South
New York, New York 10016

Juvenile Diabetes Foundation
23 E. 265th St.
New York, New York 10010

Leukemia Society, Inc.
211 E. 43rd St.
New York, New York 10017

Mainstream
1200 15th Street, N.W.
Washington, D.C. 20005

Muscular Dystrophy Association of America
810 7th Ave.
New York, New York 10019

Myasthenia Gravis Foundation
15 E. 26th St.
New York, New York 10010

National Amputee Foundation
12-45 150th St.
Whitestone, New York 11357

National Association for Retarded Citizens
2709 Avenue E, East
Arlington, Texas 76011

National Association of the Physically Handicapped
76 Elm St.
London, Ohio 43140

National Cancer Foundation
1 Park Ave.
New York, New York 10016

National Cystic Fibrosis Research Foundation
3379 Peachtree Rd., N.E.
Atlanta, Georgia 30326

National Easter Seal Society for Crippled Children and Adults
2023 W. Ogden Ave.
Chicago, Illinois 60612

National Epilepsy League
203 N. Wabash Ave.
Chicago, Illinois 60601

National Foundation — March of Dimes
1275 Mamaroneck Ave.
White Plains, New York 10605

National Genetics Foundation
250 W. 57th St.
New York, New York 10019

National Heart, Lung and Blood Institute
9600 Rockville Pike
Building 31, Room 5A52
Bethesda, Maryland 20014

National Hemophilia Foundation
25 W. 39th St.
New York, New York 10018

National Institute of Arthritis, Metabolism and Digestive Diseases
Bethesda, Maryland 20014

National Kidney Foundation
Two Park Avenue
New York, New York 10016

National Multiple Sclerosis Society
205 E. 42nd St.
New York, New York 10017

National Paraplegia Foundation
333 N. Michigan Ave.
Chicago, Illinois 60601

Parkinson's Disease Foundation
640 W. 168th St.
New York, New York 10032

Society for the Rehabilitation of the Facially Disfigured
550 1st Ave.
New York, New York 10016

United Cerebral Palsy Association
66 E. 34th St.
New York, New York 10016

E   PUPIL BEHAVIOR RATING SCALE

The Pupil Behavior Rating Scale reprinted here first appeared in *Learning Disabilities: Educational Strategies* (Gearheart, The C. V. Mosby Co., 1973). It is an adaptation of a scale developed under a U.S. Public Health Service research grant and used in the Aurora Public Schools, Aurora, Colorado. Since 1973, it has appeared in other publications and has demonstrated its value in continued use. It is similar to other rating scales in use in the elementary schools and is to be completed by the classroom teacher. Children are "rated" in five major areas of learning and behavior in comparison to their classmates; thus this scale is most effective after a teacher has worked with a group of children for several weeks, or preferably, several months.

Completion of this scale leads to an objectification of the classroom teacher's observations of children in her class, with the student-screening profile indicating relative performance in five major areas and twenty-four subareas. Low ratings on this scale *do not* indicate the presence of a learning disability. They do indicate that the pupil's performance should be further investigated and evaluated. The various possibilities that might be indicated by low ratings may be illustrated by considering an actual case in which a first grade child rated quite low in section I, auditory comprehension and listening, and section II, spoken language. This little girl appeared more capable in other areas of first grade work than in reading and, in contrast to the low ratings in sections I and II, had very high ratings in parts of section III, orientation, and all of section V,

motor. Her school performance was erratic; that is, she did very well in some tasks and was relatively low in others. In many ways she sounded like a learning disabled child—perhaps one with auditory perceptual problems. However, after completing the rating scale and noting the low areas, her teacher discovered that she had been absent during the week in which the audiologist had completed hearing screening with her class. Upon referral, it was learned that she had a borderline mild to moderate hearing loss, but because she was quite intelligent (a fact discovered after completing individual intelligence testing), she was able to compensate for her loss to a considerable extent, thus it had not been discovered. It was also discovered that her hearing loss was slowly becoming more severe, but medical intervention helped reduce the loss and stopped the deterioration.

In this case, the Pupil Behavior Rating Scale was a "failure" in discovering a learning disability, but was a real success in assisting in educational assessment and amelioration (in this instance, medical amelioration). The Pupil Behavior Rating Scale and other systems like it have been used most in screening for children with learning disabilities, but in the process has been highly valuable in providing a meaningful point of focus for further investigative efforts on behalf of children other than the learning disabled. Low scores on such scales indicate two things —they indicate we should look further (with certain children) and where the focus of our investigation should be.

PUPIL BEHAVIOR RATING SCALE*
Instruction manual

One of the most important techniques for diagnosis in learning disabilities is the Pupil Behavior Rating Scale. This scale is used to assess areas of behavior that cannot be measured by standardized group screening tests. Therefore your careful rating of individual pupils is necessary.

You are asked to rate each student on these five areas of learning and behavior:

I. Auditory comprehension and listening

In this section, you evaluate the pupil as to his ability to understand, follow, and comprehend spoken language in the classroom. Four aspects of comprehension of language activities are to be evaluated.

II. Spoken language

The student's oral speaking abilities are evaluated through the five aspects comprising this section. Use of language in the classroom and ability to use vocabulary and language in story form are basic to this ability.

III. Orientation

The student's awareness of himself in relation to his environment is considered in the four aspects of learning that make up this section. You are to rate the student on the extent to which he has attained time concepts, knowledge of direction, and concepts of relationships.

IV. Behavior

The eight aspects of behavior comprising this section relate to the student's manner of participation in the classroom. Self-discipline in relation to himself (that is, ability to attend) as well as in relation to others is critical to your rating in this section.

V. Motor

The final section pertains to the student's balance, general coordination, and use of hands in classroom activities. Three types of motor ability are to be rated: general coordination, balance, and manual dexterity. Rate each type independently because a student may have no motor difficulties, only one type of difficulty, or any combination of those listed.

*Adapted from a project developed under Research Grant, USPHS Contract 108-65-42, Bureau of Neurological and Sensory Diseases.

Name _____ No. _____ Sex _____ Date _____

School _____ Grade _____ Teacher _____

PUPIL BEHAVIOR RATING SCALE*

1	2	3	4	5

I. Auditory comprehension and listening
Ability to follow directions

1	2	3	4	5
Always confused; cannot or is unable to follow directions	Usually follows simple oral directions but often needs individual help	Follows directions that are familiar and/or not complex	Remembers and follows extended directions	Unusually skillful in remembering and following directions

Comprehension of class discussion

1	2	3	4	5
Always inattentive and/or unable to follow and understand discussions	Listens but rarely comprehends well; mind often wanders from discussion	Listens and follows discussions according to age and grade	Understands well and benefits from discussions	Becomes involved and shows unusual understanding of material discussed

Ability to retain orally given information

1	2	3	4	5
Almost total lack of recall; poor memory	Retains simple ideas and procedures if repeated often	Average retention of materials; adequate memory for age and grade	Remembers procedures and information from various sources; good immediate and delayed recall	Superior memory for both details and content

Comprehension of word meanings

1	2	3	4	5
Extremely immature level of understanding	Fails to grasp simple word meanings; misunderstands words at grade level	Good grasp of grade level vocabulary for age and grade	Understands all grade level vocabulary as well as higher level word meanings	Superior understanding of vocabulary; understands many abstract words

II. Spoken language
Ability to speak in complete sentences using accurate sentence structure

1	2	3	4	5
Always uses incomplete sentences with grammatical errors	Frequently uses incomplete sentences and/or numerous grammatical errors	Uses correct grammar; few errors of omission or incorrect use of prepositions, verb tense, pronouns	Above-average oral language; rarely makes grammatical errors	Always speaks in grammatically correct sentences

*Adapted from a project developed under Research Grant, USPHS Contract 108-65-42, Bureau of Neurological and Sensory Diseases.

Continued.

PUPIL BEHAVIOR RATING SCALE—cont'd

1	2	3	4	5

II. Spoken language—cont'd
Vocabulary ability

| Always uses immature or improper vocabulary | Limited vocabulary including primarily simple nouns; few precise, descriptive words | Adequate vocabulary for age and grade | Above-average vocabulary; uses numerous precise descriptive words | High level vocabulary; always uses precise words to convey message; uses abstraction |

Ability to recall words

| Unable to call forth the exact word | Often gropes for words to express himself | Occasionally searches for correct word but adequate for age and grade | Above-average ability; rarely hesitates on a word | Always speaks well; never hesitates or substitutes words |

Ability to formulate ideas from isolated facts

| Unable to relate isolated facts | Has difficulty relating isolated facts; ideas are incomplete and scattered | Usually relates facts into meaningful ideas; adequate for age and grade | Relates facts and ideas well | Outstanding ability in relating facts appropriately |

Ability to tell stories and relate experiences

| Unable to tell a comprehensible story | Has difficulty relating ideas in logical sequence | Average ability to tell stories | Above average; uses logical sequence | Exceptional ability to relate ideas in a logical meaningful manner |

III. Orientation
Promptness

| Lacks grasp of meaning of time; always late or confused | Poor time concept; tends to dawdle; often late | Average understanding of time for age and grade | Prompt; late only with good reason | Very skillful at handling schedules; plans and organizes well |

Spatial orientation

| Always confused; unable to navigate around classroom or school, playground or neighborhood | Frequently gets lost in relatively familiar surroundings | Can maneuver in familiar locations; average for age and grade | Above-average ability; rarely lost or confused | Never lost; adapts to new locations, situations, places |

Judgment of relationships: big, little; far, close; light, heavy

| Judgments of relationships very inadequate | Makes elementary judgments successfully | Average ability in relation to age and grade | Accurate judgments but does not generalize to new situations | Unusually precise judgments; generalizes them to new situations and experiences |

PUPIL BEHAVIOR RATING SCALE — cont'd

1	2	3	4	5
III. Orientation — cont'd				
Learning directions				
Highly confused; unable to distinguish directions as right, left, north, and south	Sometimes exhibits directional confusion	Average, uses right vs. left, north-south-east-west	Good sense of direction; seldom confused	Excellent sense of direction
IV. Behavior				
Cooperation				
Continually disrupts classroom; unable to inhibit responses	Frequently demands spotlight; often speaks out of turn	Waits his turn; average for age and grade	Cooperates well; above average	Cooperates without adult encouragement
Attention				
Never attentive; very distractible	Rarely listens; attention frequently wanders	Attends adequately for age and grade	Above average; almost always attends	Always attends to important aspects; long attention span
Ability to organize				
Highly disorganized; very slovenly	Often disorganized in manner of working; inexact, careless	Maintains average organization of work; careful	Above-average ability to organize and complete work; consistent	Always completes assignments in a highly organized and meticulous manner
Ability to cope with new situations: parties, trips, unanticipated changes in routine				
Becomes extremely excitable; totally lacking in self-control	Often overreacts; disturbed by new situations	Adapts adequately for age and grade	Adapts easily and quickly with self-confidence	Excellent adaptation, utilizing initiative and independence
Social acceptance				
Avoided by others	Tolerated by others	Liked by others; average for age and grade	Well liked by others	Sought by others
Acceptance of responsibility				
Rejects responsibility; never initiates activities	Avoids responsibility; limited acceptance of role for age	Accepts responsibility; adequate for age and grade	Enjoys responsibility; above average; frequently takes initiative or volunteers	Seeks responsibility; almost always takes initiative with enthusiasm
Completion of assignments				
Never finishes, even with guidance	Seldom finishes, even with guidance	Average ability to follow through on assignments	Above-average ability to complete assignments	Always completes assignments without supervision

Continued.

PUPIL BEHAVIOR RATING SCALE—cont'd

1	2	3	4	5
IV. Behavior—cont'd *Tactfulness*				
Always rude	Usually disregards other's feelings	Average tactfulness; occasionally socially inappropriate	Above-average tactfulness; rarely socially inappropriate	Always tactful; never socially inappropriate
V. Motor *General coordination: running, climbing, hopping, walking*				
Very poorly coordinated; clumsy	Below-average coordination; awkward	Average coordination for age	Above-average coordination; does well in these activities	Exceptional ability; excels in this area
Balance				
Very poor balance	Below-average falls frequently	Average balance for age; not outstanding but adequate equilibrium	Above-average; does well in activities requiring balance	Exceptional ability; excels in balancing
Ability to manipulate utensils and equipment; manual dexterity				
Very poor in manual manipulation	Awkward in manual dexterity	Adequate dexterity for age; manipulates well	Above-average manual dexterity	Almost perfect performance; readily manipulates new equipment

STUDENT SCREENING PROFILE

Date of birth _____

Name _____ Sex _____ Date _____

School _____ Grade or level _____ Teacher _____

I. Auditory comprehension and listing

  A. Ability to follow directions   A. _____
      1   2   3   4   5

  B. Comprehension of class discussion   B. _____
      1   2   3   4   5

  C. Ability to retain information   C. _____
      1   2   3   4   5

  D. Comprehension of word meanings   D. _____ Total I _____
      1   2   3   4   5

II. Spoken language

  A. Ability to speak in sentences   A. _____
      1   2   3   4   5

  B. Vocabulary ability   B. _____
      1   2   3   4   5

  C. Ability to recall words   C. _____
      1   2   3   4   5

  D. Ability to formulate ideas   D. _____
      1   2   3   4   5

  E. Ability to tell stories   E. _____ Total II _____
      1   2   3   4   5

III. Orientation

  A. Promptness   A. _____
      1   2   3   4   5

  B. Spatial orientation   B. _____
      1   2   3   4   5

  C. Judgment of relationships   C. _____
      1   2   3   4   5

  D. Learning directions   D. _____ Total III _____
      1   2   3   4   5

Continued.

STUDENT SCREENING PROFILE—cont'd

IV. Behavior

   A. Cooperation
       1   2   3   4   5
                        A. _____

   B. Attention
       1   2   3   4   5
                        B. _____

   C. Ability to organize
       1   2   3   4   5
                        C. _____

   D. Ability to cope with new situations
       1   2   3   4   5
                        D. _____

   E. Social acceptance
       1   2   3   4   5
                        E. _____

   F. Acceptance of responsibility
       1   2   3   4   5
                        F. _____

   G. Completion of assignments
       1   2   3   4   5
                        G. _____

   H. Tactfulness
       1   2   3   4   5
                        H. _____   Total IV _____

V. Motor

   A. General coordination
       1   2   3   4   5
                        A. _____

   B. Balance
       1   2   3   4   5
                        B. _____

   C. Manipulative skills
       1   2   3   4   5
                        C. _____   Total V _____

F ANNOTATED BIBLIOGRAPHY OF BOOKS ABOUT HANDICAPPED INDIVIDUALS

The following annotated listing of books written for children may be very helpful in providing information about handicapped individuals and their adjustment. It is arranged on the basis of the type of handicap, with the last section offering general titles that may be of interest. Some of the selections relate to adults, others are concerned with school-aged children, whereas others relate to animals. Age ranges are provided to assist in determining the approximate reading level.

CRIPPLING CONDITIONS
Mine for Keeps

Sally, crippled with cerebral palsy, has many fears about returning home after five years in a school for the handicapped. Understanding parents and teachers help her discover that other children have similar fears. Training a dog brings her new friendships and a chance to encourage other handicapped children. (Ages 9-11 years)

BY: Jean Little
PUBLISHER: Little, Brown and Company, 1962

The Door in the Wall

Robin, son of a great lord in medieval England, is crippled by an illness. The brothers in a monastery teach him to strengthen his hands and arms through wood carving and swimming so that he is able to serve his king courageously in ways other than riding into battle. (Ages 10-12 years)

BY: Marguerite DeAngile
PUBLISHER: Doubleday & Company, Inc., 1949

On the Move

After becoming involved with other handicapped youth, a formerly sheltered paraplegic girl realizes that she can also learn to lead an independent life. (Ages 8-13 years)

BY: Harriet May Savitz
PUBLISHER: The John Day Company, 1973

It's a Mile From Here to Glory

Early MacLaren is the school's star runner until a freak accident almost cripples him completely. Early's fight back toward health and toward the realization that being a person is more important than being a star is what this fast-moving sports book is really all about. (Ages 9-13 years)

BY: Robert C. Lee
PUBLISHER: Little, Brown and Company, 1972

Spring Begins in March

Meg is the youngest of the Copeland family. She is the family clown turned rebel. Meg shares a room with her handicapped sister who has learned to make the best of her physical disabilities. The story tells about Meg's problems in dealing with her family and school situation. (Ages 10-12 years)

BY: Jean Little
PUBLISHER: Little, Brown and Company, 1966

Screwball

Mike's polio-crippled arm makes him poor at baseball and earns him the unkind nickname of "Screwball." But his skill and sportsmanship in building a racer win him a respected place with his family and friends. (Ages 11-13 years)

BY: Alberta Armer
PUBLISHER: World Publishing Company, 1963

Wheels for Ginny's Chariot

After Ginny is paralyzed in an automobile accident, wise parents and teachers help her accept a wheelchair existence and find that she can be happy, useful, loved, and loving as she was before her accident. (Ages 11-13 years)

BY: Earline W. Luis and Barbara F. Millar
PUBLISHER: Dodd, Mead & Company, 1966

Let the Balloon Go

John has cerebral palsy and is spastic. This book tells of the day when he decides that grown-ups are not going to say "you can't do it" anymore. (Ages 9-16 years)

BY: Ivan Southall
PUBLISHER: St. Martin's Press, 1968

The F. D. R. Story

The life, career, struggles, and triumphs of the man who, after a crippling polio attack, became our thirty-second president. (Ages 11-14 years)

BY: Catherine Owens Peare
PUBLISHER: Thomas Y. Crowell Company, 1962

Tall and Proud

Gail is struck down by polio and her recovery is almost slowed to a halt until a horse brings back her desire to walk. Together, the girl and horse triumph over fear and pain. (Ages 12-16 years)

BY: Vian Smith
PUBLISHER: Doubleday & Company, Inc., 1966

Karen

This touching account by the mother of a child suffering from spastic cerebral palsy is to be recommended not only for its warm, realistic portrayal of the emotional trauma involved, but also for its factual explanation of this exceptionality and of what parents can do for such a child. (Ages 14 years and up)

BY: Maria Killilea
PUBLISHER: Prentice-Hall, Inc., 1962

LEARNING DISABILITIES AND AUTISM
Dibs

A classic work that relates to a young "autistic like" child named Dibs. Miss Axline records her weekly play therapy sessions with a gifted, rejected little boy. (Ages 14 years and up)

BY: Virginia Axline
PUBLISHER: Houghton Mifflin Company, 1964

Please Don't Say Hello

This book helps to explain the phenomenon of infantile autism to young people through the story of 9-year-old Eddie, the most unusual new arrival to the neightborhood. This deeply moving story makes a strong plea for acceptance of autistic and other exceptional children. (Ages 7-13 years)

BY: Phyllis Gold
PUBLISHER: Behavioral Publications, Inc., 1974

I Never Promised You a Rose Garden

The story of Deborah and her conflict in the world of reality that opposed her world. Every aspect of hospital life is shown through the experiences of a pretty, bright, autistic teenager. (Ages 14 years and up)

BY: Hannah Green
PUBLISHER: Holt, Rinehart and Winston, Inc., 1964

Sue Ellen

Sue Ellen has a learning disability and is surprised and happy with her new special class. A touching story of a child who is finally given the opportunity to learn. (Ages 9-14 years)

BY: Edith Hunter
PUBLISHER: Houghton Mifflin Company, 1969

One Little Girl

Because she is somewhat retarded, grown-ups call Laurie a "slow child." Laurie learns that she is only slow in doing some things. (Ages 7-13 years)

BY: Joan Fassler
PUBLISHER: Behavioral Publications, Inc., 1968

SPEECH
The Skating Rink

Tucker is silent most of the time because he is embarrassed by his stuttering. He is rescued from silence and ridicule by the owner of the new skating rink. (Ages 11 years and up)

BY: Mildred Lee
PUBLISHER: The Seabury Press, Inc., 1969

How You Talk

This book tells how we use different parts of our mouth to talk. It explains the speech process and discusses the fact that some children speak incorrectly but should not be laughed at. (Ages 5-9 years)

BY: Paul Showers
PUBLISHER: Thomas Y. Crowell Company, 1966

HEARING IMPAIRED
David in Silence

David, born deaf in a small town in England, is harassed by children of his own age. His efforts to make friends result in disaster. Eventually, he proves his competence and courage after a hair-raising trip through an abandoned tunnel and finds acceptance and friendship. (Ages 10-12 years)

BY: Veronica Robinson
PUBLISHER: J. B. Lippincott Company, 1966

Martin Rides the Moor

A boy who loses his hearing in a swimming accident learns to live with his disability after he reluctantly accepts the gift of a moor pony and later takes all the responsibility for its care and training. (Ages 9-11 years)

BY: Vian Smith
PUBLISHER: Doubleday & Company, Inc., 1965

Gallaudet, Friend of the Deaf

Biography of the man who was instrumental in the education of the deaf in America. (Ages 10-12 years)

BY: Etta DeGering
PUBLISHER: David McKay Co., Inc., 1964

Burnish Me Bright

A story of friendship between Auguste, a deaf-mute, and Monsieur Hilaire, a mime. Through mime, Auguste is accepted by the village and becomes very close to Monsieur Hilaire. (Ages 11-14 years)

BY: Julia Cunningham
PUBLISHER: Pantheon Books, Inc., 1970

Lisa and Her Soundless World

This unique children's book represents a new approach to teaching nondeaf children about their deaf peers, while at the same time teaching deaf children how they can successfully participate in the social environment. (Ages 8-13 years)

BY: Edna A. Levine
PUBLISHER: Behavioral Publications, Inc., 1974

MENTAL RETARDATION
Our Jimmy

A father talks with his two children about their younger brother who is retarded, explains his special needs and explains ways in which they can help him learn. A warm and loving book for parents and children. (Ages 5-8 years)

BY: Ruth K. Doorly and Kenneth Boudreau
PUBLISHER: Service Associates, 1967

The Blue Rose

Emotionally moving photographs of Jenny, a young retarded girl. The accompanying descriptive text probes the world of a retarded child.

BY: Gerda Klein; with photographs by Norma Holt
PUBLISHER: Lawrence Hill & Company, Pubs., Inc., 1974

Don't Take Teddy

Afraid that his retarded brother, Teddy, will be taken away because he accidently injured a boy, 13-year-old Mikkel runs away with him to a mountain cottage. The relief of safety becomes hysteria when Teddy becomes painfully ill. (Ages 11-13 years)

BY: Bobbie Friis Baastad
PUBLISHER: Charles Scribner's Sons, 1967

A Racehorse for Andy

This sensitive portrayal of a retarded boy's desire to be included in his friend's games is well drawn. (Ages 9-15 years)

BY: Patricia Wrightson
PUBLISHER: Harcourt, Brace and World, Inc., 1968

A Girl Like Tracy

Kathy feels responsible for her retarded older sister who has been overprotected by their parents. She helps her sister learn simple skills and self-respect in a sheltered workshop and, thereby, frees herself to live her own life. (Ages 12-13 years)

BY: Caroline Crane
PUBLISHER: David McKay Co., Inc., 1966

Long Shot for Paul

Story of a retarded boy whose brother teaches him to play basketball and encourages him to join a team. Paul works hard and is finally accepted by the team and wins a game for them. (Ages 8-13 years)

BY: Matt Christopher
PUBLISHER: Little, Brown and Company, 1966

Listen, Lissa!

Melissa is a candy-striper who becomes deeply involved with a neighbor child who is retarded. Through her concern for Artie, she becomes involved with other retarded children. The story also reveals the anguish a family goes through as they decide to institutionalize their retarded son. (Ages 13 years and up)

BY: Earlene W. Luis and Barbara F. Millar
PUBLISHER: Dodd, Mead & Company, 1968

Take Wing

When Laurel finally is relieved of taking care of her retarded brother, she finds a new world of friends and activities open to her. Her brother gets the help that he needs, and Laurel realizes that although she loves him, she can't protect her brother forever. (Ages 9-14 years)

BY: Jean Little
PUBLISHER: Little, Brown and Company, 1968

Flowers for Algernon

This book describes an experiment whereby Charlie Gordon's IQ is raised from 79 to 185 in about three months. However, the change will not be permanent and Charlie knows it. He describes day by day the burnout and the regression, and then finally he returns to his old job at Donner's bakery. (Ages 14 years and up)

BY: Daniel Keyes
PUBLISHER: Harcourt, Brace and World, Inc., 1959

The Wild Boy of Aveyron

This books tells the story of Victor. Victor was a wild boy who was found in the woods of southern France, was taken in by a doctor, and was supposedly civilized by him. (Ages 16 years and up)

BY: J. Itard and G. Gaspard
PUBLISHER: Appleton-Century-Crofts, 1962

VISUALLY IMPAIRED

Stevie's Other Eye

A blind boy learns about the outside world and teaches something to his sighted companions. He proves that he can do many of the things they can do and earns their respect and admiration. (Ages 7-10 years)

BY: Lois Eddy
PUBLISHER: McDoccell, 1962

About Glasses for Gladys

After getting glasses that are just right, Gladys no longer is teased by her classmates about her nearsighted way of reading. (Ages 7-9 years)

BY: Mark K. Ericsson
PUBLISHER: Melmont Publishers, 1962

Windows for Rosemary

Blind from birth, Rosemary enjoys all ordinary childhood activities because her parents' loving, unsentimental attitude towards her gives her a sense of security and independence. Her sighted brother is a good friend. (Ages 8-10 years)

BY: Marguerite Vance
PUBLISHER: E. P. Dutton & Co., Inc., 1956

Dead End Bluff

Despite his blindness, Quig wants to be as much like other boys as he can be, but an overprotective father prevents this. A summer job tests and proves his capabilities and also shows his father he can climb and swim like other boys. Both Quig and his family discover which obstacles he can surmount and which he cannot. (Ages 9-11 years)

BY: Elizabeth Wetheridge
PUBLISHER: Atheneum Publishers, 1966

Mary Low and Johnny: An Adventure in Seeing

When Mary Low befriends her young blind neighbor, he helps her with her problems and together they brighten life for each other and for their friends—a story that emphasizes the importance of not treating the handicapped with pity. (Ages 9-11 years)

BY: Mildred Hart and Noel McQueen
PUBLISHER: Franklin Watts, Inc., 1963

The Story of My Life

The story of Helen Keller and how she fought the great struggle that liberated her from a dark and soundless world. (Ages 11-16 years)
BY: Helen Keller
PUBLISHER: Doubleday & Company, Inc., 1954

Helen Keller's Teacher

The story of Anne Sullivan, the woman who finally broke through the silence and darkness that surrounded Helen Keller to discover an exciting, intelligent girl. (Ages 9-15 years)
BY: Mickie Davidson
PUBLISHER: Scholastic Book Services, 1966

Seeing Fingers, Louis Braille

This is the story of how a French inventor of a system of reading for the blind adjusted to his own disability. (Ages 9-12 years)
BY: Etta DeGering
PUBLISHER: David McKay Co., Inc., 1963

The Blind Connemara

The beautiful white pony is going blind. Rhonda knows that a sightless horse is dangerous to himself and his rider, but she cannot stand the thought that he might have to be put away. When "Pony" is given to her, she is overjoyed. With patience and devotion she begins to gain his trust and to teach him to move with confidence again. (Ages 11-13 years)
BY: C. W. Anderson
PUBLISHER: Macmillan, Inc., 1968

The Cay

This is the story of Philip, a boy who loses his sight from a blow to the head. He and Timothy find themselves cast on an island after the freighter on which they were traveling is torpedoed. It tells of their struggle for survival and of Philip's efforts to adjust to his blindness and overcome a learned prejudice of black people. (Ages 11-13 years)
BY: Theodore Taylor
PUBLISHER: Doubleday & Company, Inc., 1969

Finding My Way

An autobiography. A well-known author gives a gripping account of her day-to-day experiences, learning to live with total blindness, continuing her career, and leading a full life. (Ages 11-13 years)
BY: Borgheld Dahl
PUBLISHER: E. P. Dutton & Co., Inc., 1962

Triumph of the Seeing Eye

A blind man writes of the history and workings of the *seeing eye* and explains the great love between a seeing-eye dog and his master. (Ages 11 years and up)
BY: Peter Putnam
PUBLISHER: Harper & Row, Publishers, 1963

A Light in the Dark

The story of Samuel Gridley Howe, who directed the Perkins Institution for the Blind in 1831 and also helped found a school for education of deaf-mutes. (Ages 8-17 years)
BY: Milton Meltzer
PUBLISHER: Thomas Y. Crowell Company, 1964

Touch of Light

The story of Louis Braille and how he developed an alphabet for the blind. (Ages 8-13 years)
BY: Anne E. Neimark
PUBLISHER: Harcourt, Brace and World, Inc., 1970

To Catch an Angel

An autobiography written by a man who was blinded at the age of 5 years, yet proceeded to become a great scholar, fine wrestler, and finally an associate professor, all through his leonine determination. (Ages 14 years and up)
BY: Robert Russell
PUBLISHER: Vanguard Press, Inc., 1962

Light a Single Candle

A young girl finds she must face a very different way of living when she loses her sight at 14 years. The greatest challenges are the attitudes of other people rather than her physical handicap. (Ages 11-15 years)
BY: Beverly Butler
PUBLISHER: Dodd, Mead & Company, 1965

Louis Braille: Windows for the Blind

A biography of the famous man who developed an alphabet for the blind. (Ages 12 years and up)
BY: Alvin J. Kugelmass
PUBLISHER: Julian Messner, 1951

Young Louis Braille

Louis Braille in his childhood and some of the events that led to his life's work with the blind are described in this book. (Ages 12-17 years)
BY: Clare Abrahall
PUBLISHER: Roy Publishers, Inc., 1965

Teacher of the Blind: Samuel Gridley Howe

An exciting story of the achievement of a famous teacher of the blind. (Ages 12 years and up)
BY: Katherine E. Wilkie and Elizabeth R. Mosler
PUBLISHER: Julian Messner, 1965

Follow My Leader

Story of an 11-year-old boy who is blinded in an accident and how he overcomes his blindness with the use of a seeing-eye dog. (Ages 9-13 years)
BY: James B. Garfield
PUBLISHER: The Viking Press, Inc., 1967

Helen Keller

An excellent book that tells the courageous story of Helen Keller and her teacher, Anne Sullivan. (Ages 8-11)
BY: Margaret Davidson
PUBLISHER: Hastings House, Publishers, Inc., 1970

GENERAL
Child of the Silent Night

The story of Laura Bridgman who suffered an illness that left her blind and deaf. She is sent to the Perkins Institute where she is taught to see and hear. (Ages 8-13 years)
BY: Edith Fisher Hunter
PUBLISHER: Yearling Books, 1963

Challenged by Handicap: Adventures in Courage

A collection of stories about handicapped people and their courage in fighting against all obstacles as they try to lead fulfilling lives. (Ages 9-13 years)
BY: Richard Little
PUBLISHER: Reilly and Lee, 1971

Take Wing

The story emphasizes the problems of shyness and difficulty in making friends. (Ages 5-14 years)
BY: Jean Little
PUBLISHER: Little, Brown and Company, 1968

Home From Far

A deeply moving account of Jenny and her family facing the terrible loss of her twin brother, Michael, who has been killed in an automobile accident. Suddenly, Jenny was not "one of the MacGregor twins" any longer. Jenny's parents decided it was time to help, not just Jenny, but all of the family, with courage and understanding. (Ages 10-12 years)
BY: Jean Little
PUBLISHER: Little, Brown and Company, 1965

The Smallest Boy in the Class

A little boy, nicknamed "Tiny" by his classmates, proves to himself and to them that size is not a real measure of worth. An easy-to-read book. (Ages 6-8 years)
BY: Gerrold Beim
PUBLISHER: Marrow, 1949

Kate

Story about Emily, who wrote a character sketch of her best friend, Kate. It told everything about her except that she was Jewish. For Kate, it was a year of insight and discovery of learning as much about others as she does about herself. (Ages 10-12 years)
BY: Jean Little
PUBLISHER: Harper & Row, Publishers, 1971

Kristy's Courage

Kristy's scarred face and blurred speech, the result of an automobile accident, are difficult handicaps. She has to cope with schoolmates who tease her cruelly, but she keeps her troubles to herself. When her mother comes home with a new baby, Kristy finally turns to the hospital for help, but it is her own courage which eventually overcomes her difficulties. (Ages 10-12 years)

BY: Bobbie Friis Baastad

PUBLISHER: Harcourt Brace Jovanovich, Inc., 1965

One Little Boy

This is the story of 8-year-old Kenneth, who had an asthma problem and many problems with his mother and father. The book is narrated by the consulting psychologist who helped Kenneth understand his deep-rooted feelings, and it can help all of us better understand the minds of troubled children. (Ages 14 years and up)

BY: Dorothy Baruch

PUBLISHER: Julian Press, Inc., 1952

Jennifer Jean, the Cross-eyed Queen

Story of a cross-eyed girl and how she avoids ridicule even when her eyes are in the process of being straightened. She has to wear glasses and a patch. (Ages 5-13 years)

BY: Phyllis Naylor

PUBLISHER: Lerner Publications Company, 1967

Sounder

A black sharecropper, his family, and his dog transcend great affliction in this poignant story of cruelty and dignity, tragedy and courage. (Ages 11-13 years)

BY: William H. Armstrong

PUBLISHER: Harper & Row, Publishers, 1969

In a Mirror

Perceptive story of a college girl who hid her sensitive spirit under the burden of overweight. As she grows in maturity and reaches out to friendship, she finds satisfaction in her own world. (Ages 12-14 years)

BY: Mary Stolz

PUBLISHER: Harper & Row, Publishers, 1953

Don't Worry Dear

Jenny is a little girl who sucks her thumb, wets her bed, and stutters on some of her words. Surrounded by the warmth and acceptance of a loving family, she is given an opportunity to outgrow these habits at her own pace and gradually manages to overcome them all. (Ages 7-12 years)

BY: Joan Fassler

PUBLISHER: Behavioral Publication, Inc., 1971

The Littlest Rabbit

Story of the littlest rabbit and how prejudice is shown against him. He grows up and protects other little rabbits. (Ages 5-10 years)

BY: Robert Kraus

PUBLISHER: Harper & Row, Publishers, 1961

Tall Tina

Tina is not too self-conscious about being tall until she is teased by a new classmate. It tells of her different approaches to dealing with the problem and ends with a lesson on empathy and how some differences can have value (Ages 6-9 years)

BY: Muriel Stanek

PUBLISHER: Whitman Books, 1970

About Handicaps

An interesting story that explains "extraordinary ways that ordinary children between 3 and 8 years of age attempt to make sense of difficult events in their lives." The story is about a boy and his friend with cerebral palsy. It is well written, and the photographs are excellent. (Ages 11 years-adult)

BY: Sara Bonnett Stein

PUBLISHER: Walker and Co., 1974

G VALUES EDUCATION/CLARIFICATION MATERIALS

Focus on Self Development *(Grades K-6)*

This program is available in three different stages. Each stage contains materials that can be used throughout one school year. The materials have been compiled into separate units that can be used sequentially, in different topical arrangements, or whenever a classroom situation seems to point to a specific unit.

Stage One (K-2): Child's awareness of self, others, and environment

Stage Two (2-4): Encourages child's response to personal, social, emotional, and intellectual life

Stage Three (4-6): Encourages child to examine his involvement with self, others, and environment.

Includes: filmstrips, story records, photoboards, activity books, and teacher's materials.

> PUBLISHER: Science Research Associates (SRA)
> 155 N. Wacker Drive
> Chicago, Illinois 60606

Inside/Out *(Grades 3-6)*

This thirty-lesson series engages the minds and feelings of 8- to 10-year-old students through the presentation of situations common to their own lives. The programs deal compellingly with social, emotional, and physical problems that have traditionally been the concerns of health educators. However, the series takes an affective approach to the problems, showing that an open-minded understanding of human feelings is needed to balance knowledge of a more factual or cognitive kind.

Includes: teacher's materials and thirty, fifteen-minute color programs that serve as the stimulus for discussion.

> SOURCE: Agency for Instructional Television (formerly National Instructional Television)
> Box A
> Bloomington, Indiana 47401

Developing Understanding of Self and Others *(Grades K–Lower Primary and 4-8)*

There are two Developing Understanding of Self and Others (DUSO) kits, level I (K–lower primary) and level II (grades 4-8). Each kit contains materials and suggested activities designed to help students better understand social and emotional behavior. They are designed to help the student become more aware of interpersonal and intrapersonal relationships—relationships between himself and others and relationships within/between his own needs and goals.

The program is structured for use on a daily basis; however, selected activities may be used to fit specific needs. The eight units are interrelated and provide a variety of activities, for example, role playing, group discussion, and puppetry.

Includes: story books, records, cassettes, posters, discussion cards, puppetry and role-playing cards, puppets, and teacher's manual.

> BY: Dinkmeyer
> PUBLISHER: American Guidance Service, Inc.
> Circle Pines, Minnesota 55014

Search for Values *(Grades 9-12)*

A tool kit of strategies and techniques designed to help students direct their actions and sort out their feelings about the world within and around them. This can help the students see more clearly the directions their day-to-day choices are taking and can help the student come to grips with their personal value system.

Includes: teacher's guide and spirit masters.

> BY: Curwin, Curwin, Kramer, Simmons, and Walsh
> PUBLISHER: Pflaum/Standard Publishing
> 2285 Arbor Blvd.
> Dayton, Ohio 45439

Analysis of Public Issues Program *(Grades 9-12)*

This program consists of a set of concepts necessary for analyzing public issues plus the materials and strategies for teaching them. It relates to issues such as biases, stereotypes, value conflicts, and differing frames of reference.

Includes: multimedia materials, including cassettes, filmstrips, overhead visuals, student text, duplicating masters, instructor's manual, and problem books.

BY: Shaver and Larkins
PUBLISHER: Houghton Mifflin Company
1 Beacon Street
Boston, Massachusetts 02107

Becoming *(Junior High School)*

This multimedia program stimulates students to learn about themselves and their relationships with other people and to consider the kind of persons they would like to become. The three modules are: Relating, Interaction, and Individuality.

Includes: audio cassettes, games, picture cards, puzzles, personal workbook logs, and teachers manual.

BY: Cromwell, Ohs, Roark, and Sanford
PUBLISHER: J. B. Lippincott Co.
E. Washington Square
Philadelphia, Pennsylvania 19105

Toward Affective Development (TAD) *(Upper Elementary Grades)*

The central focus of TAD is directed at providing real-life experiences of students—their feelings, interests, aspirations, and conflicts. It is extension of the popular DUSO program.

Includes: filmstrips, cooperative games, illustrated career folders, tapes, posters, and activity sheets.

BY: Dupont, Gardner, and Brody
PUBLISHER: American Guidance Service, Inc.
Circle Pines, Minnesota 55014

Dimensions of Personality *(Grades 1-6)*

Group-centered activities presented through a variety of materials. Provides numerous classroom experiences and a systematic presentation of the principles of mental health. Search for Meaning and Search for Values are also available from Pflaum/Standard Publishing.

Includes: texts, workbooks, and activity sheets
BY: Limbacher
PUBLISHER: Pflaum/Standard Publishing
2285 Arbor Blvd.
Dayton, Ohio 45439

Developing Basic Values *(Grades 2-6)*

This kit presents stories and samples of class discussions that illustrate the following basic values: consideration for others, acceptance of differences, and recognition of responsibilities.

Includes: filmstrips, cassettes, script/guides, and teacher's materials.

BY: Singer Society for Visual Education, Inc.
1345 Diversey Parkway
Chicago, Illinois 60614

First Things: Values *(Grades 2-5)*

This series consists of six sound filmstrips designed to help elementary students reason about moral issues. The kits are entitled, The Trouble with Truth; That's No Fair!; You Promised!; But It Isn't Your . . .; What Do You Do About Rules?; and A Strategy for Teaching Values.

Includes: six audiovisual kits, each containing color filmstrips, record or cassette tape, and teacher's guide. Five kits are classroom materials; one is a teacher training kit.

BY: Kohlberg and Selman
PUBLISHER: Guidance Associates, Inc.
Pleasantville, New York 10570

First Things: Social Reasoning *(Grades 2-5)*

This series is based on research findings indicating that social reasoning is based largely on the ability to understand other people's perspectives. This perspective-taking ability develops through a logical sequence of levels. Development of perspective-taking skills helps children solve social problems, enrich personal relationships, communicate effectively, and make reasoned ethical or "fairness" judgments. First Things: Social Reasoning can help the teacher facilitate perspective-taking development in several ways.

Includes: filmstrips, cassettes, discussion guide.

BY: Kohlberg, Byrne, Selman, and Low
PUBLISHER: Guidance Associates, Inc.
Pleasantville, New York 10570

The Adventures of the Lollipop Dragon
(Preschool, Kindergarten, and Lower Primary)

This multimedia kit is illustrated in cartoon style. The stories use the Lollipop Dragon and the children of Tum-Tum to demonstrate the positive values and conduct stated in the following areas: sharing, working together, and taking turns, for example.

Includes: filmstrips, cassettes, script/guides, coloring book, and teacher's materials.

BY: Singer Society for Visual Education, Inc. in cooperation with Lollipop Dragon Productions, Inc. Copyright LPD, Inc.
1345 Diversey Parkway
Chicago, Illinois 60614

Making Value Judgments: Decisions for Today *(Grades 7-12)*

This book uses an inquiry-oriented approach to help students clarify their values to find their own identity and give purposeful direction to their lives. After exposing students to the nature of values and the steps in the decision-making process, it presents available facts and various viewpoints on vital problem areas. Students are then encouraged to make choices from alternatives, to consider the consequences, and to use the values they choose for themselves as a basis for action.

Each chapter involves students through special features and activities designed to promote analysis and decision-making. Profile—brief biographies of people who have made important decisions based on their own value judgments; Put Yourself in His/Her Place—case studies that involve students in open-ended, problem-solving situations; What Do You Think?—thought-provoking, open-ended discussion questions; How Can You Get Involved?—suggested activities; Value Response Statements—statements of commonly held value judgments for students to analyze.

BY: Elder
PUBLISHER: Charles E. Merrill Publishing Co.
1300 Alum Creek Drive
Columbus, Ohio 43216

Decision: A Values Approach to Decision Making
(Grades 7-12)

This multimedia program provides a semester course in which students can clarify values and analyze processes of decision making. Emphasis is on inductive thinking, primarily in group discussion format, with the teacher acting as a facilitator of activities. The student-oriented nature of the program encourages self-analysis of problems and values and personal response to hypothetical values–challenging situations.

Includes: activity cards, student data sheets, sound filmstrips, cassettes, and teacher's manual.

BY: Miguel, Elder, Raths, Harmin, and Simon
PUBLISHER: Charles E. Merrill Publishing Co.
1300 Alum Creek Drive
Columbus Ohio 43216

Searching for Values: A Film Anthology
(Grades 9-12)

A series of fifteen edited and adapted popular motion pictures (averaging sixteen minutes showing time) that may be used in the classroom are included in this package. The films depict conflicts and problem situations by the characters. After a showing, the students are asked to discuss the values, conflicts, and decisions of the characters, as well as broaden the themes and issues. Some motion pictures used are *Bridge on the River Kwai*, *Bless the Beasts and the Children*, *On the Waterfront*, and *To Sir, With Love*.

Includes: films and teacher's materials.

BY: Hanley and Thompson
PUBLISHER: Learning Corporation of America
711 Fifth Avenue
New York, New York 10022

Prejudice: The Invisible Wall *(Grades 7-12)*

This kit consists of stories, articles, plays, letters, cartoons, and pictures that relate to the theme of prejudice and to the interests of today's teenagers.

Includes: Student booklets, teacher's materials, posters, a logbook, and a record.

BY: Goody Koontz
PUBLISHER: Scholastic Book Services
904 Sylvan Avenue
Englewood Cliffs, New Jersey
07632

The Human Values Series *(Grades K-6)*

This is a supplementary reading program for K-6. Primary level materials include a set of ten mounted pictures and a comprehensive teacher's edition providing read-aloud stories correlated with the pictures and lesson plans for introducing value concepts to kindergarten and primary children. The prime objectives of the series are to provide opportunities for children (1) to formulate concepts about what human values are, (2) to communicate about human value relationships, (3) to develop strategies for self-concept enhancement and for contributing to the development of the self-concepts of others, and (4) to provide motivation for reading comprehension through having a different reason for reading.

BY: Arnspiger, Blanchette, Brill, and Rucker
PUBLISHER: Steck-Vaughn Company
807 Brazos, Box 2028
Austin, Texas 78767

Understanding Values *(Grades 5-12)*

Understanding Values is a filmstrip series that presents open-ended situations. The situations deal with difficult areas of values, such as Other's Values/Your Values, Who Cares/Staying Involved, Cheating, and Lies.

Includes: filmstrips, cassettes, and teacher's materials.

PUBLISHER: Eyegate
146 Archer Avenue
Jamaica, New York 11435

How Do You Feel? *(Primary-Intermediate)*

The recurring theme of these filmstrips is that everyone is different and has different feelings about other people and about daily events.

Children of various ages and backgrounds, from urban and rural environments, are seen reacting to everyday experiences. No value judgments are made, but by identifying with the positive and negative feelings presented in each filmstrip, children are led to realize that their own feelings are neither unique nor inherently "bad." Many questions are used to provoke thought and discussion, thereby helping children to achieve a better understanding of their own values and of themselves in relation to others.

Includes: captioned filmstrips and teacher's materials.

PUBLISHER: Learning Resources Company
P.O. Drawer 3709
202 Lake Miriam Drive
Lakeland, Florida 33803

What Do You Think? *(Primary-Intermediate)*

The universal childhood conflicts enacted in these filmstrips encourage children to think critically about their own values and behaviors. The open-ended questions the filmstrips pose cannot be answered by an easy yes or no. Instead, they stimulate children to express their feelings about the people portrayed and to discuss why these people act as they do.

This set of filmstrips can be used across a wide range of grade levels because the student's responses will vary according to their maturity and personal experiences.

Includes: captioned filmstrips and teacher's materials.

PUBLISHER: Learning Resources Company
P.O. Drawer 3709
202 Lake Miriam Drive
Lakeland, Florida 33803

Two Sides To Every Story
(Primary-Intermediate)

The purpose of this set is to present different points of view from which children can see themselves in relation to other people. Familiar problems and conflicts are examined candidly—misunderstanding, hurt feelings, a child's role in family relationships, and individual needs.

Each filmstrip motivates students to consider the origin and possible resolution of these problems. By encouraging self-awareness, this set enables children to appreciate the feelings of other people. It also prepares them to discuss values and standards of behavior within the family, peer groups, and the community at large.

Includes: captioned filmstrips and teacher's materials.

PUBLISHER: Learning Resources Company
P.O. Drawer 3709
202 Lake Miriam Drive
Lakeland, Florida 33803

Open-ended Stories *(Primary–Lower Intermediate)*

As each story unfolds, a realistic conflict situation arises, presenting serious consequences to the children involved. The stories end unresolved but with several alternatives apparent. The viewers are asked to discuss the possible solutions.

This set can be used to involve children in examining and strengthening positive values. It does not preach. Instead, by presenting true-life adventures, it allows children to talk about their own feelings and examine what they feel is right and good and important. Thus the set aims at an affective level of learning. The values involved are integrity, responsibility, courage, friendship, and respect for the property of others.

Includes: filmstrips, records or cassettes, study guide, and teacher's materials.

PUBLISHER: Learning Resources Company
P.O. Drawer 3709
202 Lake Miriam Drive
Lakeland, Florida 33803

They Need Me *(Primary-Intermediate)*

This set was designed to make children aware of emotional and social interdependence between themselves and their family, friends, and community.

The format of this set is somewhat unusual. A need situation is shown by a filmstrip with a question that calls for a solution. The following frame offers a resolution pictorially but with no caption. This structure is repeated throughout the set as each filmstrip presents a number of situations, requiring the class to discuss the responsible part that children can play in everyday relationships.

A child can emerge from these experiences with a greater feeling of worth and a clearer picture of the role he plays in his community. Although designed for use at the primary level, this set also can be used effectively with older children in special education classes.

Includes: captioned filmstrips and teacher's materials.

PUBLISHER: Learning Resources Company
P.O. Drawer 3709
202 Lake Miriam Drive
Lakeland, Florida, 33803

INDEX